Ethnic Revival and Religious Turmoil

Ethnic Revival and Religious Turmoil

Identities and Representations in the Himalayas

Edited by

MARIE LECOMTE-TILOUINE
PASCALE DOLLFUS

OXFORD
UNIVERSITY PRESS

OXFORD
UNIVERSITY PRESS

YMCA Library Building, Jai Singh Road, New Delhi 110 001

Oxford University Press is a department of the University of Oxford. It furthers the University's objective of excellence in research, scholarship, and education by publishing worldwide in

Oxford New York

Auckland Bangkok Buenos Aires Cape Town Chennai
Dar es Salaam Delhi Hong Kong Istanbul Karachi Kolkata
Kuala Lumpur Madrid Melbourne Mexico City Mumbai Nairobi
São Paulo Shanghai Taipei Tokyo Toronto

Oxford is a registered trade mark of Oxford University Press
in the UK and in certain other countries

Published in India
By Oxford University Press, New Delhi

First published 2003

ISBN 0 19 565592 3

Typeset by Comprint, New Delhi 110029
Printed by Maha Laxmi Printers, Delhi 110 020
Published by Manzar Khan, Oxford University Press
YMCA Library Building, Jai Singh Road, New Delhi 110 001

Contents

Contributors

EBERHARD BERG is a Research Fellow at the Lumbini International Research Institute, Bhairahawa, Nepal.

VERONIQUE BOUILLIER is a Researcher at the Centre for the Study of India and South Asia, EHESS-CNRS, Paris, France.

STEVE BROWN is Lecturer in English at Ecole Centrale de Paris, France.

BEN CAMPBELL is Lecturer in Social Anthropology, University of Manchester, United Kingdom.

GIL DARYN is a Post Doctoral Fellow at the British Academy, United Kingdom.

ANNA DE SALES is a Researcher at the Centre National de la Recherche Scientifique, (CNRS), Paris, France.

WILLIAM B. DOUGLAS (Will Tuladhar-Douglas) is a Consultant with the Clay Sanskrit Series.

PASCALE DOLLFUS is a Researcher in the Environment, Society and Culture in the Himalayas team at the Centre National de la Recherche Scientifique (CNRS), Paris, France.

MARC GABORIEAU is Director of Research and Director of the Centre for the Study of India and South Asia, EHESS-CNRS, Paris, France.

MARTIN GAENSZLE is a Researcher at the South Asia Institute, University of Heidelberg, Germany.

DAVID N. GELLNER is Lecturer in the Anthropology of South Asia at Oxford University, United Kingdom.

ANDRAS HÖFER is former Professor of Anthropology at the South Asia Institute, University of Heidelberg, Germany.

MICHAEL HUTT is Reader in the Department of Languages and Cultures of South Asia, School of Oriental and African Studies (SOAS), London, United Kingdom.

KARL-HEINZ KRÄMER is a political scientist at the South Asia Institute, University of Heidelberg, Germany.

MARIE LECOMTE-TILOUINE, is a Researcher in the Environment, Society and Culture in the Himalayas team at the Centre National de la Recherche Sceientifique (CNRS), Paris, France.

ANTJE LINKENBACH is a Researcher in Social Anthropology at the South Asia Institute, University of Heidelberg, Germany

JOANNE MOLLER is a Researcher in Anthropology at the University of Manchester, United Kingdom.

JOANNA PFAFF-CZARNECKA is Professor of Social Anthropology at Bielefeld University, Germany.

PHILIPPE RAMIREZ is a Researcher at the Centre National de la Recherche Scientifique, Villejuif, France.

NICOLAS SIHLÉ is Assistant Professor of Anthropology, University of Virginia, United States of America.

MARTIN SÖKEFELD is Assistant Professor in Anthropology at the University of Hamburg, Germany.

GÉRARD TOFFIN is Director of Research at the Centre National de la Recherche Scientifique (CNRS), Meudon, France.

MARTIJN VAN BEEK is Lecturer in Social Anthropology, University of Aarhus, Denmark.

Introduction

MARIE LECOMTE-TILOUINE, PASCALE DOLLFUS

The multi-ethnic and multi-caste communites of the Himalayan countries constitute the theatre of a deep revival of ethnic and religious identity. Although group taxonomy is an old exercise in this area, it has found new modes of expression, particularly among the so-called 'tribal groups'. The theme is extremely broad and is of primordial importance because of its potential and indeed actual political ramifications.

This volume gathers the communications and discussions of a workshop held in Meudon, France in 1998 and entitled: *Representation of the Self, Representation of the Other in the Himalayas: Space, History, Culture*. All the participants chose to treat this question from the inside, that is the relations between different Himalayan groups. As a prelude to this corpus, we would like to bring a complement dealing with the external aspect of this relation where the scholar is the *Self* and his object of study, the *Other*. This apparently decentred complement lies in fact at the very heart of this volume. It is made of contributions of western scholars, most of them anthropologists, presenting the way a specific group, articulates, constructs and instrumentalizes its relation with its Others. The legitimacy of this approach has been extensively discussed since the last few decades.

One of the major criticisms addressed at social anthropology concerns the nature of the analytical procedure that a foreigner, a westerner to be more precise, applies to social facts which are by nature foreign to him and which would thus be translated into categories that are specific to his culture. Thus the notion of ethnic group is a western construction which has no exact equivalent in the Himalayan region, where people refer to their groupings as castes, tribes, and so on. This criticism goes against the Kantian theory of the universality of understanding categories and the universality of man developed by the philosophers of the Enlightenment—a theory which was specifically applied to social anthropology by Claude Lévi-Strauss as a condition rendering its existence possible. Lévi-Strauss' response to his critics admits that a residual meaning is certainly left aside as a result of the anthropological analysis. For him however, '. . . those who pretend that the experience of the Other—individual or collective—is by essence incommunicable' take shelter behind 'a new obscurantism' (1977, p. 10). He shows that this argument, taken to its logical conclusion, implies the impossibility of understanding the Other, and even of dialogue, since any dialogue implies a minimum of identity (1977, p. 330)[1].

More recently, another criticism directed at anthropology, and especially at its western tenants, has been formulated by Edward Said, in his *Orientalism*[2]. The argument, in brief, is that any discourse on the Other is a form of domination/subjection and is made possible by this domination. If the author's book itself is an obvious counter-example to the second part of the argumentation, even the first part is open to objection although it certainly contains an important truth. If considered true, this assertion should be generally applicable to all discourses on the Other, be they internal or external to a named/given group, especially in the case of such a vague regrouping as 'Oriental'. One arrives at the famous paradox of the Cretan liar who says he is a Cretan (the Oriental *scholar* who says he is Oriental). In no way could the discourse of an Oriental about his group be an exception to this general rule. And it may well even be that it implies and leads to a much more pregnant relationship of domination, because internal alienation is more difficult to escape, almost always being more legitimate and closer to the subjects. As the first criticism examined, this would lead to the end of any production which is not introspection. Even this egoistic form of knowledge could be considered as a domination of a particular kind of thought on others (the non-published thoughts) or could be viewed ultimately as constructed on a relation of domination, that characterizes the building of the Ego.

If these criticisms constitute important warnings about the possible drifts which may occur in the social sciences in general and in social anthropology in particular, their argumentation leads rapidly to a contradiction; they may be viewed as an ideological expression of the Other's illegitimacy of studying and speaking for the Self. They thus constitute signs of 'the end of Man', as announced by Michel Foucault in his book *Les mots et les choses*, 'Man is an invention which the archaeology of our thought easily shows to be of recent date. And may be near the end'[3]. Commenting on this assertion, Edmund Leach seems to misunderstand its meaning when he tries to develop it from a biological and sociological point of view. He reaches the conclusion that biologically, humans constitute one unique species but that social institutions distinguish the similar and dissimilar within humanity. He curiously proposes to accept diversity without aiming at social equality as a conclusion[4]. On the other hand, Foucault's theory is that social sciences could emerge only at the point when Man became an end in itself for men, having declared with Nietzche that God is dead. For the author, this first murder can only be followed by the killing of the murderer.

Although Foucault's statement might seem intuitive, recent developments in the social sciences seem somehow to turn him into a prophet. Invariably the aim and legitimacy of social sciences, social anthropology in particular, is questioned. Ethnicity is by nature a process which emphasizes particularisms. It anchors identity in a self-constructed and overall particular model in which universality has no place: it is thus that one human group is ascribed one distinctive language, territory, or general style of life and any cultural trait shared with another group is seen as emerging from a common origin. Of course the relationships which are thus established between communities are selected and invented—notably by the dominant members of the group—on the basis of choices which can easily be read as political. To take a Himalayan example, the Tharus who speak an Indian language are thus assimilated into the 'Mongol tribes' on the basis of their physical type, despite their language. They represent more than one million individuals and obviously bring a greater weight to the Mongol organization. But their assimilation follows equally the logic of the Mongol ideology which views the Hindus and the Indians (that they call the Aryas) as dominating groups which cannot therefore encompass dominated groups like the Tharus or the Dalits, lest it complicates the scheme.

Nor has social anthropology been left aside from this general phenomenon as the development of communalism within it shows. In the United States, black studies or women's studies are mostly done by blacks or women, and in France, regional studies appear to follow the same rule. Parallel to the increasing epistemological difficulty of accepting identity, which alone allows the study of Others, the interest in the Others is now waning.

Our discipline developed out of the encounter with foreign cultures, a phenomenon accelerated by the European discovery of the New World, but with almost certainly known antecedents, such as the travelogues of the Chinese pilgrims in India and the Himalayas, Alberuni's description of India or Julius Caesar's invaluable observations on Gaul, to cite a few examples.

Distantiation is peculiar to anthropology. As Lévi-Strauss clearly states in *Structural Anthropology* (1967: 360)[5], 'While sociology seeks to advance the social science of the observer, anthropology seeks to advance that of what is observed—either by endeavouring to reproduce, in its description of strange and remote societies, the standpoint of the native themselves, or by broadening its subject so as to cover the observer's society but at the same time to evolve a frame of reference based on ethnographical experience, and independent both of the observer and of what he is observing.' Indeed if distantiation does not erase a stereotyped vision of one specific culture, resulting from the culture of origin of the observer, it surely aims at a greater degree of objectivity in its approach. Freud even recommended that analysts should not treat a patient whose personal interests were close to their own, for fear of being caught inside their discourse and losing their analytical faculties.

However, distance is not necessarily geographical (or historical). While anthropology is no longer limited to the analysis of 'strange and remote societies', but tends to take an ever greater interest in the interpretation of the observer's own society, distantiation remains a guiding principle. The scholar, whatever his origin, should, according to Emile Durkheim's famous recommendation, 'treat social facts like things' ('traiter les faits sociaux comme des choses'), he should '(. . .) embark upon the study of them by adopting the principle that one is entirely ignorant of what they are, that their characteristic properties, like the unknown causes upon which they depend, cannot be discovered by even the most careful form of introspection'. Durkheim further specifies that, '(. . .) the representation that we have been able to make of them in the course of our lives, since they have been made without method and uncritically, lack any scientific value and must be discarded'[6].

Indeed, objectivation of one own's group and values seems to be a difficult exercise as impassioned reactions are quite impossible to prevent, '(. . .) the transition is difficult to operate between the objectivity for which we strive when we look at communities from outside, and the situation in which we are placed, willingly or not, inside our own community'[7]. Beyond the difficulty conferred by the internal position of the scholar to the objectivation during the observation part, the necessary involvement of the subject in his object of study adds another obstacle to the difficult imperative of dissociation between the scholar and the politician advocated by Max Weber in the presentation of results and teaching[8]. Without distanciation, the master may well become a chief rather than a professor. Ultimately, it seems that it is adhesion which leads from science to politics. In our post-modern period, one would certainly have to modify the definition of the object of social anthropology given by Lévi-Strauss, in his introduction to the work of Marcel Mauss (p. XXIX)—'Any society different from our own is an object, any group of our own society other than our group is an object, any use of this group to which we do not adhere, is an object'[9]. Any adhesion to a group or to a use prevent the possibility of its objectivation by any subject. Engagement can be reified and raised as an object of study but as a personal disposition, it is certainly an obstacle to the analytical faculties of the observer.

As for the aim of our discipline, the new focus on the Self seems to advocate two paths, which are indeed fashionable but of little help to build new understandings of the functioning of social facts: deconstructivism and fiction[10].

Besides these trends which are noticeable in theoretical and general approaches, regional anthropology is still constructivist and less affected by the crisis. The Himalayan region studied in this volume embraces two distinct sets: the kingdom of Nepal and the Indian Himalayas (to which northern areas of Paksitan are added). Nepalese society, which is the focus of this book, seems recently to have witnessed a counter process to that which was imposed on local communities. From a period of integration, which was certainly also a subordination, it seems that the country has entered into a process of disintegration. This morphological dislocation is undoubtedly due to political factors—the loss of a legitimate central, unique and ultimate power with the 1990 revolution—and more generally, the result of the crisis of caste ideology. The process of Hinduization under which political power had placed the country since the Middle Ages is now perceived as alienation among the tribal groups. At the same time the high castes themselves are tending to break their traditional links with their artisanal low castes, contributing to the global imbalance. Politically inexpressible because the Nepalese law forbids parties based on ethnic or religious basis[11], ethnic feelings find a means of expression in different political parties, hence masking the real problems. Simultaneously, caste groups tend to organize themselves on the same model, developing a kind of ethnic consciousness.

The concept of ethnic group and its derived forms has been greatly discussed. Here we shall use it to designate a group of people who recognize and share the same ethnonym (generally in the case of Himalayas, an endogamous group which has the idea of a common origin). The Nepalese territory was closed to foreigners until 1951. It has never been colonized by westerners, but, according to most ethnic thinkers, the colonization has come from Indian caste groups. Since the revolution of 1990, ethnic minorities mobilized themselves to fight what they call *bahunvad*, or brahmanocracy. Their aim is to form scholars issued from their ranks to fight the Brahmans on their own ground: history, speculation, politics.

Hazardous as it may be, the ethnic revival movement can also be viewed as a kind of Renaissance. Books, leaflets and journals have flourished. Debates are organized daily. Dance and song performances form part of the meetings. Young intellectuals wander through villages in search of their traditions. If these symptoms are often judged critically by westerners as 'the beginning of the end', that is folklorization, we are forced to admit that this is also a fascinating post-colonialist period, where people are starting to consider themselves as active, thinking agents. The danger, of course, is also great, because the group's thinkers have a double legitimacy, being both scholars and members of the group they study. Their discourse is endowed with a truth that cannot or should not be discussed. As part of the group, they know better than any foreigner and as scholars, the other members of the group lack the conceptual tools to engage in a real debate with them. Furthermore, their discourse responds to a certain demand. If we could generalize this last assertion to all writings, it is clear in this case that the enterprise is praised by the group, that it responds to a crucial need, as can be understood, for instance, by the letters of thanks to the Magar historians published in ethnic journals of this group. The enthusiasm generated by their works among their 'group' raises several questions: will these works be less partial then what was produced by the Brahmanocracy? What will the relations between this new type of scholar and the western scholars be? People understand intuitively that the latter do not work for them, that their writings will be inaccessible to them—written in a foreign language and aiming to fuel a discipline in which the object of studies are depersonalized. Indeed, the depersonalization is clearly perceptible in the way that some western scholars tend to erase or falsify toponyms and even peoples' names, as something indecent[12], whereas local scholars mention them precisely, thereby attaching an importance to the subjects. In the same way, Himalayan scholars render a constant homage to village culture as expressed in songs and poems, a subjective material much neglected by westerners, in contrast to ritual recitations and myths for which the opposite is true. Through their focus, these indigenous works are extremely useful as they put in perspective an approach often thought of as universal and unquestionable, as well as our own taboos—such as the question of the origin of groups. But to give them a higher status[13] denotes the same post-colonialist attitude as ignoring or despising them because of their perspective, of their evident instrumentalization or the way the argumentation is organized.

The ethnic movements thus question the role of western scholars and the utilization of their texts by ethnic thinkers, an appellation which includes also those westerners who speak *for* the group studied and not *about* them. A dual attitude emerges.

The western scholar is used as an expert, a counsellor, and rejected as someone whose work is not 'useful'—'what is the use of your writings for us?'. In contrast, in Nepal, the attitude towards the most ancient western writings is quite different, being often the only sources about local groups and history, or the only sources which have not been written by the dominant local groups. Thus in Nepal, the first scholars are quoted without any questioning on the conditions of their production and their ideological purposes. It is certainly so because their writings serve the cause of tribal groups and fit well in the present context. Indeed, an obvious anti-Brahmin stance is apparent in the major book of Francis Buchanan Hamilton, *An Account of the Kingdom of Nepal*, as well as a suspicion about the Rajput origin of the Nepalese royal dynasties. The situation is more contrasted in Ladakh. In fact, the earliest accounts of the region offered by British administrators and scientists, which reflect 'Tibeto-centricity' describing Ladakh as a Buddhist Land ('a Little Tibet') and ignoring or dismissing the Muslims as foreigners, not to say impostors, have been the object of much debate.

For obvious reasons, this view largely shared by scholars until recently is appreciated by the Buddhist activists who rely on it, but is criticized by Muslim Ladakhis to whom Ladakhi identity is denied. Siddiq Wahid[14] goes as far as to claim that these earliest western writings, reinforced by a concentration of academic studies on Buddhists and Buddhist religion in Ladakh, are responsible for the conflict which opposes Buddhists, Muslims and Christians in Ladakh and led to the recent anti-Muslim boycott in 1989. He asserts that the Ladakhis have been 'corrupted' by those westerners who have confused ethinicity with religion and accuses 'intellectual colonialism—and its tenants who victimised the Ladakhis, particularly the Muslims, for having succeeded in planting the idea into their heads that 'being Ladakhi is to be Buddhist' or in other words that 'the idea of a Ladakhi Muslim was inadmissible'.

Ultimately, previous writings may be fully corrected by ethnic scholars. The most striking example of such an exercise is the recent

English translation of Bernard Pignède's book about the Gurungs of Nepal[15] . In its new form, the text has been augmented with new comparative data resulting from an inquiry made some 25 years later, which is a good and valid initiative. It is puzzling to know that the principal informant of the late anthropologist has been asked by the editors to add his own comments to the text, in the form of notes. These are extremely controversial, both in form and in content, as their purpose is not to engage in a post modern discussion but obviously to re-establish the truth about the tribe. It goes still further with the surprising initiative taken by the editors to simply delete from the text passages displeasing for the Gurung's, for instance, people's names, passages which, to be honest, the Gurungs should evaluate themselves. This edition is a good example of what can happen to a text when written *for* a specific group and underlines the crucial role of (mental) distantiation in the free exercise of research. Ethnic 'dictatorship' gives rise to a new type of scholar, whose task is not to understand reality but to judge it, as part of ethnic tradition or not, as authentic or not, as good or not[16]. This kind of literature flourishes in the Himalayas. Western scholars may have some responsibility for it, as studying the most remote ('pure'?) ethnic groups has certainly been initiated by them.

In such a context, can or should the anthropologist remain neutral? Should he/she remain an external observer, refuse to act as a consultant or as a policy-maker? Should he/she accept or not to attend ethnic or nationalist meetings, to speak there or to write in their publications? Should he/she engage him or herself in the cause of the group? If any clear-cut answer is problematic, it is obvious that burying one's head in sand cannot be preferred to an engaged attitude. Analysis requires and causes distance. Once the analytical tools have been built up, a reciprocal debate is not only mandatory because of the post-colonialist period, but necessary if there is to be progress in our field. All this is only possible within a democratic context. In a country like Bhutan, where the authorization to do research is given under royal approbation, the scholar's freedom of speech and objectivity are thus restricted to the politically correct. It is therefore difficult or impossible to criticize the policy adopted for the southern minorties or the governmental action to preserve Bhutanese 'culture', in the last Buddhist kingdom. . .

In the Indian Western Himalayas, group identity has followed a different history. There, the absence of ethnonyms and of the idea, prevailing among the Nepalese ethnic groups, of a common origin has given rise to communalism. In Ladakh for example, specific myths of origin or of village foundation are almost absent. The term Ladakhi or Ladakh-pa only means 'people of Ladakh'. To this vague definition corresponds a no less vague territory, whose borders are not even clear for the local activists. As M. van Beek[17] (2000: 173) clearly shows 'the proclamation of tribes and other "racial", "ethnic" or "community" classifications failed to find a shared identity that could capture the identifications of people in Ladakh'. In such a context, religious identity has become prevalent, being widely used as the effective principle of classification, a heritage from British preoccupations and reflecting the British perception of the essence of Indian society: caste and religious community. In such a view, commonly shared by scholars until recently, 'real' Ladakhis are properly Buddhists, while Baltis, Purigpas or Bedas are treated as Muslims.

But Ladakh, being a part of India, has also known a phenomenon specific to this country which established a special status for the Scheduled Tribes and Castes and reservation policy. In 1989, eight Scheduled Tribes were thus officially recognized among the population: some of the names referred to regional identifications (e.g. Balti from Baltistan, Changpa from Changthang, or Purigpa from Purig), others to social or occupational criteria (Mon, Beda), or religious affiliation (Bot/Boto). To benefit from this ST Certificate was a temptation for it brought numerous advantages in terms of education, government employment, loans and economic assistance. All those who were excluded considered the measure to be discriminatory. It is thus that the Arghon Sunni Muslims of Ladakh, the offsprings of a Ladakhi mothers converted to Islam and a Muslim fathers from outside, felt very disappointed to be denied this status under the pretext that they had Kashmiri or Punjabi ancestors. Moreover, this status was given to Dogra Arghons (of mixed Ladakhi and Dogra parentage) and Nepali Arghons (of mixed Nepali and Ladakhi parentage).

This collective volume aims to present research in the making and the plurality of approaches to identity phenomena. Through the comments that follow each contribution, we have chosen to preserve as much as possible, the interactive form and dynamics of the gathering which led to this book[18]. We tried to encourage contributions covering a wide geographical range, from eastern Nepal to Gilgit, in northern Pakistan, and treating the subject from different perspectives: anthropology, history, geography and literature.

A similar recent publication focussing on Nepal[19] has been much criticized by a local scholar and ethnic activist[20]. Besides the numerous aggressive remarks directed towards the high Hindu castes (embodied in the person of one Nepalese contributor), his arguments may well apply to this volume as well and may be summarized as thus: most of the authors are Europeans; the groups included in the study do not adequately represent the diverse features and aspirations of Nepalese society; the book should be made accessible to the indigenous people, by translating it into Nepali and even into the different mother tongues spoken in Nepal. This author offers in this review his personal idea of the anthropologist's task: '. . . all theory, fact should come from the participant and [the] observer should reflect them because they cannot represent them'.

Although we do not deny that a specific focus on a group may have important consequences because it will benefit from this publicity via tourism, foreign aid, and more generally via the interest it will raise, these are side-effects of the social sciences which are not directly under the control of individuals.

A collective book dealing with a specific geographical area does not aim to represent equally (according to their statistical importance, or to their ideological importance) all the groups inhabiting it. Such an ambition would be totally utopian—as would be the translation of the volume in all the languages spoken in Nepal[21]. As any science, anthropology can develop at one time a dynamic of questioning about one specific group or phenomena, which acts as a 'object à penser' (a thing to think of) susceptible to highlight other groups or phenomena which are not the immediate subject of enquiry. Furthermore, collective works are always dependent on circumstances and this volume does not contradict this general rule[22]. As for the task of the anthropologist, as defined by K.B. Bhattachan and taken here as a widely spread new conception of our discipline, it is obviously a utilitarian and subordinating point of view, turning the scholar into a spokesman, a mouthpiece. The main difficulty for such an anthropologist would be to treat equally all theories and facts gathered about one specific group. This is quite an ambitious task; even if we imagine that this could be done on a small scale, the result would not help the reader much, since he would be left alone to analyze materials himself. Here again, reacting to this point of view does not mean that analysis should mask the data of facts and local theories, and that our task is to reduce cultural production and social facts to a disembodied result such as an equation or empty theory. The suggestion of Krishna B. Bhattachan reminds us that field data as well as interpretation and theoretical abstraction should be offered to the reader because they form material which others may interpret differently[23].

Identity and ethnicity being increasingly more being studied by social anthropologists in parallel to the increasing uses of ethnicity in the political debates in several countries. In a recent publication, Luc de Heusch analyses the modern critics of the concept of ethnic group. He shows how Frederik Barth[24], when rejecting the idea that ethnic groups are definable by some total inventory of cultural traits that their members share, neglected the heritage of a socio-cultural system, which, changing and fluctuating as it may be, should nevertheless be named. In contrast to those who think that ethnic groups were only produced by colonial administration, he argues that it is the result of a classificatory thought, which is much older than bureaucracy[25]. In Nepal, ethnicity has been absorbed into a Hindu model of caste system, crystallized in the legal code of 1854 where each group was named and ranked in a linear order. But this ancient and constraining superstructure never erased the specificity of the ethnic groups incorporated in it as this volume will show.

The rejection of the Other's construction of the Self finds a striking example in the first contribution by Michael Hutt. In the novel *Sumnima*, written by B.P. Koirala, a famous Brahman political leader, the Brahman hero revalues the values of his own culture while staying in the wildness of a Kirant tribe. In this perception of the Other, the Kirant is a noble savage who incarnates opposite values. The most obvious example of this phenomenon lies in the fact that the Kirants are described in the novel as a matrilineal group, a purely imaginative feature. As noted by Martin Gaenszle in his discussion of the paper: 'the Other is not taken as different in its own right, but rather it is seen as an inversion of the Self'. The Other's reaction to the novel was no less radical, since the book was publicly burnt by the Kirants who rejected the image imposed on them without commenting much on the reasons of their act. One of them may be that B.P. Koirala found his inspiration partly in the corpus of oral tradition of the Kirants. This corpus, called the Mundhun, has been recently written down and is held in great sanctity by the Kirants, who commonly claim that they follow 'the Mundhun religion'. B.P. Koirala's brahmanic Mundhun was probably seen as a sacrilege, as can be understood by the comparison made between his novel and the *Satanic verses.*

The relation with the Other was carried to the other extreme by the Khasa rulers of the Middle Ages. Indeed the repetitive worship of Matsyendranath, the protector of the Kathmandu Valley, by the sovereigns of western Nepal, suggests a strong identification with the Other, despite the geographical distance and the absence of known links between the two royalties. William Douglas attributes this identity to the fact that the Khasa rulers of western Nepal were Buddhists during the Middle Ages and used to identify themselves with Lokesvara. Now the Kathmandu Matsyendranath is also known as Lokesvara. Thus, we could argue that a process of identification and unification between distant societies could be realized through religious geography and identification between gods and kings, forming a network of identities overwhelming the realms. But Véronique Bouillier's comments show that if this relation existed, it was not the only motivation for the long journeys the kings of western Nepal undertook on several occasions upto the Kathmandu valley. Besides praying to Matsyendranath, they also paid homage to Hindu gods. This observation does not invalidate the general remark made by W. Douglas: '. . . it is clear that the Khasa observances were not a claim to sovereignty in the valley of Nepal, but part of their own dynastic ritual . . .'. It only complicates the model, which is attractive, but should be explored further as for its origins and implications. The Khasa empire collapsed at the end of the 14th century and is documented by few documents only, but similar instances taken from neighbouring and/ or more recent kingdoms could certainly bring a deeper understanding of what it meant to worship your neighbour's god.

After these interesting incursions into literature and history, the following contributions come from social anthropologists. This series begins with an important article by David. N. Gellner who examines how global egalitarianism and the multiculturalism it implies faces specific difficulties when applied to the Newar group, which is quite multiform according to the points of view taken into consideration: at a national level, it is one of the 69 or 61 groups (castes and ethnic groups) which are said to form the Nepalese nation, at the local level, it is a community made up of several distinct castes and finally at the caste level, it is again subdivided. Gellner notes: '. . . the multiculturist ideal is taken up as far as the largest cultural unit that can support it'. As a result of this complex structure, ethnic activists debate about what the Newars are: a nation, a group or ethnic group (*jāti*), a tribe, nationality or ethnic group (*janajāti*), or a community? They deplore the numerous caste organizations with developed inside their group using the very same words as the nationalists when speaking about ethnic associations. In the former case, it is said to weaken ethnic solidarity, in the latter, the national unity. The double approach to the identity phenomena undertaken by Gellner, which allies field observation and an examination of the written production of the members of the group allows him to distinguish two levels: the views and choices of the activists and the lay majority. This leads him to an important criticism of Taylor's book and a general fundamental remark: 'By ignoring the distinction it allows the activists' definitions to be imposed on the others, denying the latter the choice the activists themselves had'. To this first level of objection, Gérard Toffin in his discussion remarks that gender should be added, since ethnic activism is male dominated.

Johanna Pfaff-Czarnecka focuses on the shift of meanings of established symbols and the construction of ethnic markers which is described as a reactive process based on power relationships between groups. The shifting of meaning would follow the shifting of power: 'The very fact that specific symbols have been associated with the former power arrangements can induce social actors to challenge them publicly, once the power shifts'. The shifts are often radical: previous symbols of unity turn rapidly into symbols of oppression. Such is the case of the Dasai, the national festival of

Nepal which is now read as celebrating the victory of the Aryas over the Mongols (i.e. the high caste Hindus over the tribes). The discussion shows that the shifting of meanings as part of political action (in the exemplary case of Dasai) is conditioned by the position of the different tribal groups to the central power—although all the tribal groups share the same discourse. The boycott of Dasai by the Tamang leaders is not really revolutionary since this group has never had in the past a central role in this huge state ritual. When the Magar leaders adopt the same attitude or discourse, this is a real shift of meaning, so radical indeed that it is not yet accepted by the great majority of the group. Here again, discourse of the leaders and exemplary practices should be distinguished from the praxis of the group.

This very use of 'group'. to designate the Nepalese Hill Brahmans, is criticized by Gil Daryn who claims that Bahuns do not see themselves as a group but are seen as a group by outsiders on the basis of the common type of relation they have with them. His approach, deeply influenced by Barth and Eriksen, led him to define the Bahuns as a category with a dormant identity which may well evolve, under external pressure, into an ethnic group, transforming 'the category into a politically active group'. In his discussion, Phillippe Ramirez shows that the kinship structure of the Bahuns determines their identity, an identity which is dissociated from culture. These two views may be discussed. First, Daryn's Barthian conception of the Bahuns raises several problems, notably the assumption that they do not form a *group* but a *category*. Now a category is a class of elements sharing the same nature. In fact this last definition applies well to the Bahuns who would very commonly define themselves on the basis of their particular nature within humanity, describing themselves as 'human gods' or 'gods on earth'. On the other hand it does not fit with the Barthian definition of the Bahuns as unlinked elements defined by their relations to the Others. Indeed, if the Bahuns are conceived as linked between themselves, as we indeed think, they then form a group or a category depending on their link: a substantial one results into a category and an organizational one into a group. A set of relations may form a collectivating relation creating an *ensemble* but certainly not a category. Now it should be assumed that any Bahun would have the same kind of relation with a given Other though we may notice in passing that relations too may be fluctuating. Even if we stick to this hypothesis, how will a Bahun behave as a superior creature, even in his urban, open and liberal form, towards the groups he considers at his service—the low castes—and as an equal with another Bahun (we should note here that equality is foreign to the Hindu society where many factors, and especially kinship, may induce differences of status even within the same caste)? On what basis will one element of the ensemble adapt his relation when encountering a foreign element? This cannot be answered through understanding relations only. These relations are indeed so old and organized in such a systematic way that they now form a classificatory thought which is shared by the Bahuns and by those with whom they are in relation.

Ben Campbell examines this notion of identity from a different point of view: he proposes to consider the relation with the environment as being a major element through which identity is constructed. Tamang representations of relationship to natural diversity is examined through narratives presenting matrimonial alliances as a negotiation with difference. For the Tamangs, alliance is the coming together of difference and is examined in extreme cases where the exchanging group consists of animals or vegetables. The narratives of nature would imply a direct continuous engagement of the Tamangs with their environment, which has been altered recently by the creation of a park. András Höfer's comments reinforce some of Campell's statements, such as the non-existence of a separation between nature and culture, leading however to a less abrupt conclusion. If there is no clear separation between cultivated zones and non-cultivated zones, there are small spaces belonging to the gods which are strictly protected. Thus '. . . the demarcation between the realms of nature and Man is *focal*, rather than *zonal'*. The author shows the limitation of the attempt to understand structures of identity through direct relation with the environment and even the way the Tamangs exploit the natural resources. He underlines the autonomy of the 'cultural stuff'. One of the major issues in the debate about identity appears in this set of communication as well: a relation (here with environment) is set up as a starting point to understand a local identity, which is defined as polymorphic at some point but generally treated as 'Tamang' whereas this refers only to a language in the studied context. If we do not deny that locality is a fundamental aspect of identity in the area and that identity can be studied through relation with the local environment, the question is whether this relation is globalizing or incorporated in and organized by other(s), more sociological dimensions: in the case presented here, by kinship.

Eberhard Berg argues that religion (Tibetan Buddhism) is the most important idiom through which the Sherpas define themselves in their dealings with Others. He examines how Sherpa identity is shaped through the performance of religious festivals and points out the key-role of ritual patronage in this process. But, according to Nicolas Silhé, in doing so Berg confuses two notions quite distinct, even though related. He mistakes the community membership with identity, which as a construction 'becomes apparent mainly through discourse'. It should be noted that social institutions are also constructions and are prone to modifications, especially the patronage of rituals. Several examples in the Himalayan region show that the financing of rituals forms a strong link between a group, a god—or ensemble of gods—and a territory—or a sacred place which appears as a power point within a territory. These components are central to the way in which identity is constructed. The financing of rituals appears as a fluctuating social institution which lies at the heart of the image the groups try to present of themselves or the position other groups try to confer on them.

To end with the Nepalese group of papers, Karl-Heinz Krämer presents the main ethnic arguments and claims while adopting their views. In her comments, Anne De Sales warns against an approach based on the militant discourse and suggests that 'alienation may be more a feature of the janajati leaders' discourse than of ordinary villager's representation of the situation'.

Discourse is also the base on which Joanne Moller, dealing with community and identity in Kumaon, builds her argumentation. Her paper, as the ones that follow deal with the Ladakh and Gilgit cases and how ethnicity has become particularly salient in social relations when the politics of everyday life accentuate the significance of certain cultural differences. She especially analyses the impact of reservation policy on the construction of identity.

Referring to the anti-reservation protest and pro-autonomy campaign in the Himalayan region of Uttar Pradesh, Joanne Moller suggests that these recent events must be understood both in terms of political economy and discourses of identity. She points out how Kumaoni high caste villagers organize their social world, on every level of identification, on a binary principle articulated by an opposition between the 'insiders' (i.e. themselves) and 'outsiders' (plains people and low castes), in which the latter are seen 'to eat' at the expense of the former. This 'rhetoric of hunger'—she argues—is rooted in the history of Kumaon, a region which has for centuries been characterized by geographical, political and cultural isolation, and then was given a lowly place in the new politico-economic order, leading to a deep resentment among the population against external powers. Additionally, this discourse of deprivation is also relevant in the relations between householders and affines, or even between humans and supernatural agents. In her comments, Antje Linkenbach refuses to explain the struggle for autonomy in the U.P. Hills through ethnicistic arguments and argues that construction of Self and Other cannot be reduced to a single pattern. Along with Martijn van Beek and Martin Sökefeld, she emphasizes the ambiguity, multiplicity and fluidity of identity/ties, showing how people identify with different social groups, which may be based on age, gender, language, habitat or even on 'degree of exposure to modern discourses', and shift identities frequently and repeatedly. On the other hand, Martijn van Beek follows the construction of Ladakhi identity in its fluidity, analysing thoroughly how in the contestation between scientists, bureaucrats and local activists over the 'true'characteristics of Ladakh 'identity' in the context of the granting of regional autonomy, representations appearing as 'identities' are produced. Yet these identities are necessary fictions. In her comments, Pascale Dollfus agrees with the statement according to which Ladakhi-ness is a fluid and unbounded entity varying according to a given context, but regrets that the data taken into consideration are only drawn from official reports, academic accounts and discourses or leaflets written by local activists. As a matter of fact, the 'non-published thoughts' are left aside. And one would have welcomed some supportive ethnographic elaboration about the different sets of identities built upon the difference(s) one chooses to emphasize. The last contribution by Martin Sökefeld gives an in-depth understanding of the multiplicity of identities in Gilgit, in the northern areas of Pakistan, a region which accomodates at least five 'dimensions of difference': sectarian affiliation, *qôm* (i.e. roughly speaking ethnic groups), clan, locality and language. Keeping in mind the local complexities of his subject matter, Sökefeld suggests that one should analyse the intersectionality between multiple identities rather than work out a particular difference at the expense of others': an innovative methodology which proves very operative to account for the complexity of this area. Dealing with the claim for autonomy which, like the call for holy war in Islam supersedes all differences, Gaborieau in his comments remarks that 'nationalism in modern times is invested with the same conceptual and emotional content as religion was in mediaeval times'. To conclude Sökefeld proposes a new approach to the study of identities and ethnicity which requires the dissolution of the unequivocal and unequal dichotomy of the anthropologist as Self versus his/her objects of study as Other 'into a plurality of relations between the anthropologist (as a subject) and the *subjects* he or she studies that can signify both difference and identity'.

We cannot but agree with this proposal and would like to conclude this short presentation by a general remark which emerges from this volume as it does from social anthropology more generally: the tendency to build identity against others prevails strikingly in our domain and this creates an enduring difficulty in reconciling theories which were constructed in opposition to the previous ones but which are not in fact so exclusive.

Notes

1. '. . .ceux qui prétendent que 1' expérience de 1' autre- individuel ou collectif-est par essence incommunicable (. . .)' prennent refuge dans 'un nouvel obscurantisme'. (p. 10). *L'identité,* séminaire dirigé par Claude Lévi-Strauss, Paris: PUF, 1977.
2. Edward W. Said, *Orientalism,* New York: Random House, 1979.

3. 'L'Homme est une invention dont l'archéologie de notre pensée montre aisément la date récente. Et peut-être la fin prochaine'. Michel Foucault, *Les mots et les choses,* Paris: Gallimard, 1966. p. 398. Our translation (*The Order of Things: An Archaeology of the Human Sciences,* New York: Pantheon, 1970).
4. 'The Unity of Man: The History of an Idea', unpublished communication given in Columbia University in 1976. Translated in French and published in Edmund Leach, *L'unité de l'homme et autres essais,* Paris: Gallimard, 1980, pp. 363–89.
5. C. Lévi-Strauss, *Structural Anthropology* (*Anthropologie structurale,* Paris: 1958) translated from the French by C. Jacobson and Brooke Grundfest Schoeff, New York: Anchor Books, 1967.
6. '(. . .) en aborder l'étude en prenant pour principe qu'on ignore absolument ce qu'ils sont, et que leurs propriétés caractéristiques, comme les causes inconnues dont elles dépendent, ne peuvent être découvertes par l'introspection, même la plus attentive'. '. . . les représentations qu'on a pu s'en faire au cours de la vie, ayant été faites sans méthode et sans critique, sont dénuées de valeur scientifique et dovient être tenues à l'écart'. Emile Durkheim, *Les règles de la méthode sociologique,* Paris: PUF 1981, 1st ed. 1937. P. XIII. (Translated by W.D. Halls, edited by S. Lukes as *The Rules of Sociological Method,* London: Macmillan Press, 1982, p. 36).
7. '. . . le passage est très difficile à faire, entre cette objectivité àquoi on s'efforce, quand on regarde les société' C. Lévi-Strauss in G. Charbonnier, *Entretiens avec Claude Lévi-Strauss,* Paris, Plon Juillard, 1961, p. 16. Our translation. (Published in English as: *Conversations with Claude Lévi-Strauss,* London: Cape, 1969).
8. *Two Conferences: Wissenschaft als Beruf, 1919 and Politik als Beruf,* 1919 published together in French with an introduction by Raymond Aron as: *Le savant et le politique* Paris: Plon, 1959.
9. Claude Lévi-Strauss: 'Introduction à l'oeuvre de Marcel Mauss', pp. IX–LII in Marcel Mauss, *Sociologie et anthropologie,* Paris: PUF, 1950. p. XXIX: 'Toute société différente de la nôtre est objet, tout groupe de notre propre société, autre que celui dont nous relevons, est objet, tout usage de ce groupe même, auquel nous n'adhérons pas, est objet'. Our translation. (Published in English as: *Introduction to the Work of Marcel Mauss,* London: Routledge, 1987).
10. To quote one example of a widespread position: 'Fiction. . . may offer accounts which are more authentic than our documentary studies, precisely because, to be convincing, it has to present the reader with the self conscious individual'. p. 192 in Anthony P. Cohen, *Self Consciousness, and Alternative Anthropology of Identity,* London and New York: Routledge, 1994.

11. Indeed, it is forbidden by the Nepalese law to create a political party on a communal basis, such as ethnic group, caste, religion. This point is rather paradoxical since the nation is Hindu as declared by the constitution—and thus perceived as communalistic. This has been noticed by K.H. Krämer in this volume.
12. The reasons for this attitude are usually to preserve the anonymity of the informants who generally have not asked for it, from their government, tourists or their neighbours. In fact, this procedure prevents comparison and the questioning of data, creating a very comfortable position for anthropologists, whose writings are thus unverifiable.
13. See for instance Mary Des Chene, 'Ethnography of the Janajati Yug' in *Studies in the Nepalese History and Society*, vol. 1, 1, 1996, p. 105–6, who writes: 'While I have read much more about Nepal in foreign languages than I have yet read in indigenous ones, the ratio of learning has been quite reverse and if I had to give up one or the other, the choice would be clear in favor of the languages of Nepal'.
14. Siddiq Wahid, 'Riots in Ladakh and the Genesis of a Tragedy', *Himal*, Sept-Oct. 1989, pp. 24–5.
15. Bernard Pignède, *The Gurungs,* English ed. by S. Harrison and A. Macfarlane, Kathmandu: Ratna Pustak Bhandar, 1993 (French edition 1966).
16. This exercise recalls the Greek etymology of the *Ethnos*, a concept associated with *Ethos*, custom, the ethnic group as 'a group of people who share the same customs', hence the importance of knowing the specific customs of the group.
17. M. van Beek, 'Dissimulations: Representating Ladakhi Identity', in H. Driessen and T. Otto (eds.), *Perplexities of Identification: Anthropological Studies in Cultural Differentiation and the Use of Resources*, Aarhus: Aarhus University Press. 2000, pp. 164–88.
18. A workshop organized by us in 1998 at Meudon (France), and aiming to gather the subscribers of the *European Bulletin of Himalayan Research*. The workshop was financed by the Centre National de la Recherche Scientifique. We deliberately asked the authors not to change their text with regards to the remarks of the discussants.
19. *Nationalism and Ethnicity in a Hindu Kingdom: The Politics of Culture in Contemporary Nepal*, David N. Gellner, Joanna Pfaff-Czarnecka and John Whelpton (eds.), Amsterdam: Harwood Academic Publishers, 1997.
20. Krishna B. Bhattachan: 'Making no Heads or Tails of the Ethnic "Conundrum" by Scholars with European Head and Nepalese Tail', *Contributions to Nepalese Studies*, vol. 25, 1, 1998, p. 111–30.
21. Especially if we consider all the dialectal forms and the fact that many Himalayan languages are oral.

22. We regret, for instance, that we could not invite Himalayan scholars to open the discussion with them at this occasion.
23. For instance it is rather difficult to utilize many 19th century western books on India because the names of the gods are directly translated into their presumed Greek or Latin corresponding names without any mention of the local name.
24. Frederik Barth, Introduction to *Ethnic Groups and Boundaries*, London: George Allen and Unwin, 1969, pp. 9–38.
25. Luc de Heusch: 'L'ethnie: Les vicissitudes d'un concept', *Archives Européennes de Sociologie*, Tome XLII, 2001, no. 1, pp. 79–100.

Reading *Sumnimā*

Michael Hutt

This is a discussion of a Nepali novel entitled *Sumnimā: Kirāt Deśko Eutā Kathā* (*Sumnimā: A Story of the Kirāta Country*) by Bishweshwar Prasad (B.P.) Koirala. It was written in Sundarijal jail near Kathmandu over a period of eight days (21–28 June 1964) during the fourth year of Koirala's imprisonment by King Mahendra after his dismissal of the elected Congress government in 1960. *Sumnimā* was BP's third novel, and was first published in Varanasi, India, in BS 2027 (1970/71).

B.P. Koirala was the most important figure on Nepal's political stage between the anti-Rana revolution of 1950–1 and his death in 1982, although he spent many years of the last two decades of his life either in prison, in exile in India, or underground. Several biographies have appeared in English (e.g. Chatterji 1990, S.P. Misra 1985, K. Mishra 1994), and their primary focus has been BP's political career. The three standard histories of the Nepali novel (Pradhan 2043, Rai 2050, Subedi 2053) discuss and analyse BP's writings at some length, and the publication in 1997 of BP's *Jail Journal* (*Jel Jarnal*), covering the period from February 1961 to December 1964, provided further insights into the ways in which BP's private ruminations on matters such as spiritualism, materialism, sexuality, compromise, and reconciliation found public expression in his novel and stories.

This essay begins by summarizing the plot of *Sumnimā*, and then goes on to discuss the various readings of the novel suggested by the *Jail Journal* and the existing critical literature, and also by the flames that consumed the novel in a public demonstration just four or five years ago. Despite the considerable interest it generated, and its availability in print for close to three decades, the novel has not been translated into any language other than Hindi. Despite the long-standing world-wide scholarly interest in Nepal, there can be few literatures that have been more resolutely ignored by foreign researchers than Nepali literature. The following translations of extracts from the novel, of comments on the novel, and of extracts from the *Jail Journal*, are therefore my own.

The Novel

Sumnimā is set in the ancient past, and it imagines a primeval encounter between orthodox Brahmanical culture and the culture of the peoples the author calls 'Kirata', who may be identified with the Rai and Limbu communities of eastern Nepal's Himalayan foothills[1]. A family of Brahmans arrives in a forested region and chooses a spot upon which to found an ashram and commence the *araṇyavāsa* stage of the orthodox life. The son and only child is named Somadatta.

Somadatta takes the family's cow to graze every day on the bank of the river Koshi. There he meets the Kirata girl Sumnimā, 'with a body as yellow as a kernel of corn and naked in every limb' (p. 6) and the relationship between them that is the book's core narrative is established:

'Oh, golden-bodied girl! Who are you?'

The girl answered firmly, 'I am a Kirati daughter, Sumnimā. And who are you, thin boy?'

'I am Somadatta, son of the Aryavanshi Brahman Suryadatta' said Somadatta (p. 6)

The differences between the boy and the girl are quickly identified:

As soon as they met [on the second day] Sumnimā asked, 'Oh Somadatta, why did you call your mother *mātā* yesterday?'

Calmly, Somadatta replied, 'This is the language of the gods (*deva-bhāṣā*)'.

'So, since you are a human, why don't you talk in human speech? If you're human, you shouldn't behave like a god. When you're a human you should behave like a human, Somadatta!'

'Sumnimā! Oh innocent girl! We are Brahmans, we can acquire godliness (*devata*) through the power of penance (*tapa*). Our sacrifices, rituals, rules and observances, these are all an effort to obtain deliverance from humanity. Do you understand?' (p. 7)

A prince arrives in the region, accompanied by his army. Declaring to Somadatta's father, Suryadatta, that a Kshatriya's duty is to serve the Brahmans, he summons all the leaders of the local 'Kirata' and 'Bhill' tribes to the ashram to announce that cow-and pig-slaughter will henceforth be forbidden in the area, which is now a *tapobhūmi*. Sumnimā's father is Bijuwā[2] and he ordains that this order will have to be obeyed, but as a Bijuwā he is entitled to appoint a new location where such sacrifices can continue to take place. When they meet the next day, both Somadatta and Sumnimā are happy, Somadatta because righteousness has been established:

'Sumnimā, today is an auspicious day like no other. I am extremely happy. In heaven the gods and goddesses will be supremely satisfied too. Today *dharma* has triumphed over *adharma*, the Aryan flag has been established on this land of asceticism (*tapobhūmi*)'. (p. 15)

Sumnimā is happy because the Bhill faction that favoured armed opposition has not won the argument in her village:

'I am really happy too. That's why I hurried here to tell you the happy news. It's a wonderful day for us. No harm will come to you, and nothing will happen to any of us'. (p. 15)[3]

Sumnimā and Somadatta discuss and argue about their various conceptions of life on numerous occasions. Somadatta grows into a young man, and is required to follow the path of Brahmacharya, resisting all sensual attractions. But the only young woman he has ever known, apart from his mother, is Sumnimā, because when he left the village of his birth he was still very young. He begins to wonder whether Sumnimā might not be 'an illustration sent to test him by some jealous god' (p. 21) and later, driven to distraction by her beauty, he declares, 'Your body obstructs the development of my soul!' (p. 25). This leads the two characters into an argument about the relative value of the body and the soul. Somdatta argues that because the soul is everlasting and the body ephemeral, it is the soul whose well-being must take precedence, while Sumnimā argues that for precisely the same reasons the opposite should be the case. Somadatta is at his wits' end and eventually he says, 'Sumnimā, I am telling you, this body of yours is sin, it is poison, it is filth. Take this hell out of my sight' (p. 27). Sumnimā tells him that the hell is within him, and they agree to part and never meet again.

Having decided that his austerities have not freed him from sensual desire, Somadatta renounces the ashram and sets out to wander through the hot deserts and snowy wastes of the world. At each juncture of his journey he looks within himself to see whether any remnant of Sumnimā's memory remains. Eventually he finds that she has vanished, and he returns to the ashram at last, reduced to skin and bone but claiming total victory over the senses.

His parents are delighted by his yogic attainments, but after some time has passed they begin to urge him to marry, reminding him that procreation is a sacred duty that is expected of him by their ancestors. Soon, a young Brahman woman, Puloma, is brought by her parents to the ashram, and she and Somadatta are married. Puloma is just as prone as Somadatta is to making profound pronouncements on the need to renounce the pleasures of the senses, and it seems they are ideally suited. Once Somadatta and Puloma have married, the four parents announce that they are taking the road to the north and entering the final stage of their lives.

Puloma and Somadatta go about the task of producing a son with elaborate vedic rituals that exhaust them both, and the author's extremely detailed description of the first of the day-long performances is surely intended to be ironic if not frankly satirical. Despite the couple's meticulous efforts to produce a son, Puloma does not conceive and the marital relationship begins to deteriorate. Puloma, for instance, begins to take issue with Somadatta's interpretations of certain highly esoteric points in the upanishads, and the monthly exertions become for both of them an immense physical and spiritual trial in which neither places any hope of success.

Eventually, Somadatta begins to wonder whether their lack of success is due in some measure to the fact that they dwell in Kirāta country and, 'like a drowning man clutching at a straw' (p. 47) he sets out to find Sumnimā's father, who he recalls is a 'Dharmaguru' for the Kirātas. The Bijuwā asks him why he wants a son, and Somadatta explains that it is his duty to his ancestors:

Then the Bijuwā said very gravely, 'Brahman, your Manuvā is angry, because you tried to kill it with your *tapasyā*. You must bathe in Manuvā-Daha.' (p. 49)[4]

The Bijuwā assigns to his daughter Sumnimā (by now a married mother) the task of taking Somadatta to the sacred pool of Manuvā-Daha:

'Somadatta, you need not be afraid. Father has told me to bathe you in Manuvā-Daha and then decorate you in front of the goddess of river, to change your appearance so that you are unrecognizable.' (p. 52)

Manuvā-Daha is located in the forests high above the Kirata village, and when they reach the highest point of the climb Sumnimā urges Somadatta to look back and identify the distant ashram that is his home. She points it out to him several times, but he is unable to discern it among the trees. They move on to the sacred pool, and here the tone of the narrative changes. Until this point the novel has been a dialogue between two archetypes, whom the author uses to articulate the conflicts and contradictions within himself. Their debates and arguments are of course staged and artificial, and they do not strike the reader as conversations that would authentically take place between the characters the author has created or in the context within which they are set. However, when Sumnimā and Somadatta arrive at Manuvā-Daha the narrative begins to resonate a little, to provide the reader with some tangible sense of the misery to which Somadatta has subjected himself in his life of self-denial. Exhausted, he yields to Sumnimā's invitation to indulge his senses for the first time in his life, by bathing in the pool, by eating honey and yoghurt (Sumnimā takes pains to ensure that his Brahmanhood is respected at every stage), by submitting to a massage with oil, and finally by being dressed in the costume of a Bhill. He is reluctant to leave the pool, but Sumnimā urges him homeward, saying that the deity of the pool is powerful and easily angered. When they reach the riverbank near Somadatta's ashram, the place of their childhood encounters, Sumnimā grants him one kiss as her farewell gift, and they part.

The narrative then turns to Somadatta's wife, Puloma, who has spent the day alone at the ashram remembering the friendship that developed between herself and a Bhill youth in the village where she was born—a relationship that was eventually proscribed by her parents, who were soon to bring her to Somadatta. At night, Somadatta returns, aroused by Sumnimā's kiss and still dressed in the plumes and feathers of the Bhill. He and Puloma engage in spontaneous sexual intercourse—but all the while Puloma firmly believes that he is the Bhill youth of her pre-marital years, while, although Somadatta knows that she is Puloma, he imagines that she is Sumnimā.

After this, the relationship between them gradually becomes one of mutual hatred. At first, Puloma is weighed down by guilt at what she supposes has been her infidelity, but Somadatta knows the truth and takes some pity upon her. When Puloma announces that she is pregnant, Somadatta at last reveals to her that the Bhill youth was in fact himself. But she refuses to believe him, and treats his claim as a sign of jealousy, and an attempt to appropriate from her the only experience of sensual pleasure she has ever had. Thus, 'even the thin social thread of the relationship of a husband and wife broke that day' (p. 90).

Near the end of this 101-page novel, we meet Somadatta's son and Sumnimā's daughter many years later, playing together beside the river just as Sumnimā and Somadatta once did. They begin to address one another as *yāvā*, 'friend'. When Somadatta and Puloma both die, Sumnima takes the boy into her own village, and eventually he and Sumnimā's daughter marry. Sumnimā tells her daughter:

'Daughter, the one that you have chosen as your husband is the son of a Brahman. His blood is different. His mind is in all kinds of things. They are creatures of the wind, their wish is to fly through the air. They are not content with the completeness of this life, they are attracted by its emptiness. So they go about performing all kinds of *tapasyā* searching for that emptiness. They do not hesitate to renounce sensual pleasures and even their own body itself. . . . And your blood is different. You are the daughter of a Kirati. We are creatures of the Kirati soil, our love is for the soil. We are deep in the pleasures and enjoyments of life, we do not see what it lacks. For us, our body is the dearest thing. The Brahmans seem to us like kites broken loose from their strings. And we must seem to them like the earthworms of the soil'. (p. 100)

Finally, Sumnimā addresses Somadatta's son:

'Son, your father was a greatly ascetic man. He used to say that the contemplation of the soul was the most important thing. You are his offspring. Today you have made a Kirati girl your wife. Her Kirati nature is fickle. She knows nothing except her own body. I don't know how far she will be able to go with you when you fly. But if you understand her ethnic tradition (*jāti-paramparā*) and if you see the path she is walking, you will be able to understand my daughter well. My daughter must also be prepared to understand you and to leave her own path a little. So you too must try to compromise, and be prepared to leave your own path a little. May you be well. May your children be able to find the path of compromise'. (p. 100)[5]

The narrator concludes the novel thus:

Nature reclaimed the place where a Brahman had tried to scratch out a place of his own. They say that the same condition had been Vishvamitra's too in the Treta Yug. A Brahman had mixed his blood into the Kiratis' ethnic bloodstream. In that ocean of ethnic blood, one drop could not retain an existence. The unobstructed flow of the Koshi river flowed on just as ever, cutting through the peace of nature. In the silence of forest and sky, Somadatta's ashram disappeared. (p. 101)

Readings

Nepali critics have identified at least three different conflicts or tensions within this novel. The first is a conflict between materialism and spiritualism. The second is a conflict between the *id* and the super ego: between what a person actually is, and what s/he aspires to be (Pradhan 2043: 179). The third is the tension between the Aryan/Brahmanical view of life and the non-Aryan view of life, and this third condition eventually subsumes, at least in symbolic terms, the other two, as opposites are reconciled at the end of the novel.

Koirala creates two archetypal characters. Somadatta, the Brahman archetype and in Pradhan's formulation the super ego, represents spiritualism (*adhyātmāvād*) viewed through the lens of the author's own sceptical agnosticism. He is helpless and emotionally blocked, a prisoner of rules and a victim of self-inflicted punishments. He regards his own group as superior and segregates himself from humanity, nature, and emotional and sexual spontaneity. Although Sumnimā is his only hope of salvation, Somadatta's orthodox way and self-denial ultimately destroy him. Somadatta and Puloma's attempts to produce an issue involve a suppression of the *id*, their own true instinctive nature, which none the less bursts out in an unexpected manner.

Sumnimā represents materialism (*bhautiktāvād*) and physicality (*dehavād*). She is free and eventually dominant, and she symbolizes the natural, the warm and beautiful. The author's perspective on her is that she is a means of deliverance for Somadatta from his self-inflicted suffering. Ethnic and gender stereotyping may be said to combine in one woman: her ethnicity is perhaps more central to her identity than her gender, but it might also be argued that the novel would be saying very different things if the gender of the two main protagonists were reversed (Rayamajhi 1997). The society she belongs to is apparently a matriarchal one: even after she has married, Sumnimā appears to continue to live in her father's home, and Somadatta's son moves to Sumnima's village when he marries her daughter. Sumnimā underlines this in an argument with Somadatta:

> 'There, despite what you say, since it is mother who gave birth to us you had to know who she is first. So we Kiratis know [our] mother first, and [our] father is the man she shows to us'. (p. 13)

The novel brings the two characters close together in order to show that the denial of self on the part of the Brahman is a path to misery and failure, and that healing can take place and harmony can be established only through a compromise between the two protagonists' very different ways of life.

The Material versus the Spiritual

B.P. Koirala's *Jail Journal* contains many ruminations about spiritualism, and generally their tone is sceptical. BP admits that within him there does exist some religious instinct: 'I am perhaps of a spiritual tendency, although my thinking is materialist' (p. 113), but the *Journal* contains many critical, even caustic evaluations of several books on spiritualism he reads during his imprisonment. In several places he reaches conclusions such as

> But in truth, no, the Upanishads are uninterested in the problems and questions of life. They contain no answers to questions, no solutions to problems. They are completely irrelevant to life. (p. 106)

Broadly, I have reached the conclusion that the thing that is ordinarily called spiritualism is the sign of an indifference to life. (p. 121)

These opinions, developed in numerous philosophical discussions between BP and his fellow political prisoners, particularly Ram Narayan Mishra and Divan Singh Rai, quite clearly inform his characterizations of Somadatta and Sumnimā. In particular, it is his view that the suppression of sexual instincts and desires is inherently unhealthy:

To what extent can these original/basic (*maulik*) needs of man be neglected? Does such neglect not take murderous revenge in its own manner? In my opinion, the natural fulfilment of these original/basic needs is essential for peace of mind. (p. 63)

Because it is possible to control the tangible manifestation of sexual desire, most people believe that total victory can be achieved over sexual instincts. This is a great and terrible delusion, on which many of our society's rules, prohibitions and values depend. If sexual desire is not stilled by the sexual act, Nature takes great revenge. (p. 63)

Somadatta's self-denial and ultimate self-destruction may be discerned in these ideas, which quickly lead on to some hint of Sumnimā's role and identity in the yet-to-be-written novel. Here BP begins to talk in terms of levels of social sophistication, of 'civilized' and 'uncivilized':

In this connection, it is worth considering the discord that arises from the construction between social rules and man's instinctive nature. Particular social rules and systems are fashioned with that society's ideals in mind; whatever ideal the society establishes, it establishes its rules and ordinances in accordance with that ideal. There is no need for the objectives and arrangements of that society to be in accordance with the basic/original instincts of human nature. In reality, most social rules are not founded in opposition to human instincts, and [but?] one finds that the more complex a society's arrangement becomes the more its rules and ordinances neglect natural human instinct and establish themselves in opposition to it. The further up the stairway of civilization a society rises, the more difficult the fulfilment of its members' human needs through simple natural means becomes, and as a result they have to pay the price of numerous mental disorders and instabilities out of respect for civilization. Uncivilized races have greater mental peace as compared with those races that are called civilized. (pp. 63–4; entry dated 31 October 1962; emphasis added)

These arguments are articulated several times by the two

archetypal characters in the early pages of the novel. On one occasion a dove flies towards the tree beneath which they are sitting. Just as it is about to settle on a branch of the tree, a hawk swoops down to attack it but Somadatta's cry of alarm frightens it away. The dove falls stunned to the ground, and the incident provides the context for a full-blown philosophical debate. Sumnimā admires the dove's beauty, and Somadatta declares 'Ah, its life has been saved!' But Sumnima retorts, 'But shame!' The hawk's has not!' (p. 17) and she argues against his belief in non-violence (*ahiṃsā*):

'I don't know anything about dharma and adharma. You are the Pandit, you can understand that. But trying to break down the character of Nature is the same as corrupting yourself.'

'So don't you find any difference between violence and non-violence?'

'The hawk doesn't do violence, our killing a cow isn't violence either. But when your princes go hunting, that is truly violence; the Mahābhārata that your books and Puranas think is fine is truly violence too. Your dharma has disturbed the character of nature, that's why violence has become possible in the world.' (p. 18)

Another disagreement ensues when Sumnimā express pleasure in her own appearance:

'Mother said I'm very pretty. She says my body's shapely, my stomach is neat, my breasts are well-formed. Isn't that so, Somadatta?

'You shouldn't say such things, Sumnimā!' said Somadatta, 'These are words of sin!'

Sumnimā was startled. She moved nearer to Somadatta and asked, 'Sin?'

'The body is a pit of sin, and that is what you are praising, Sumnimā' said Somadatta.

Sumnimā sighed. 'You see nothing but sin in everything—in violence, in cow meat, in not bathing in the morning, in not praying, in having a nice body. . . What torture it must be for you to live surrounded by sin!' (p. 19)

Narahari Acharya (2053: 170) argues that Koirala did not set out to establish that Somadatta's austere and orthodox lifestyle was completely without meaning, but to suggest that it was unbalanced or incomplete. This view is borne out by various comments in the *Jail Journal*, such as the following evaluation of Gurudatta's Hindi novel *Shastrabahū*, dated 16 October 1962:

This novel is written on the theme of the conflict between Science and Religion. From materialism and spiritualism the author has chosen his side as spiritualism. Even though one has to accept that spiritualism is to some extent necessary in life, when one sees an attempt to link it with conservative beliefs one feels a certain aversion to it. While the ultimate condition of materialism is selfishness, sensual pleasure and the expression (*hāhākār*) of discontent, the ultimate condition of spiritualism is conventional beliefs and behaviour and intellectual blindness. When the writer takes the side of spiritualism one finds that he becomes partial to superstition and obscurantism. A balanced position—whether it be materialism or spiritualism—is worth taking, but both extreme positions are at fault; because it is biased an extreme position can prove damaging in life. (p. 57)

Sumnimā as Ethnic Parable

Although the above concerns never disappear from the narrative and dialogue of this short novel, in its later pages it begins to assume the character of a parable about the relationship between what one might crudely term the Parbatiya and Janajati communities, and about the origins of Nepal's modern population. If the two protagonists are to be taken as representatives of two sectors of Nepal's ethnic mix, they are, as suggested above, extreme archetypes: an austere, life-denying male Brahman whose world view depends on a narrow interpretation of the Vedas, who encounters a sensual, life-affirming, naked female Kirata. The two characters are perhaps representations of elements of the author's own inner conflict rather more than they are realizable individuals.

Rajendra Subedi addresses the novel at both levels of interpretation, and suggests that this fable of an ancient reconciliation and union between Brahman and 'Kirata'

raises a question mark over the dogmatic insistence that the historic influences (*saṃskār*), notions of ancestry, ethnic origins, lineage, religion, ethics, conduct, and family deity that are rooted deep in the mentality of today's Nepali person are in any way unique or authentic. (Subedi 2053: 238)

A union between Sumnimā and Somadatta is unthinkable despite their attraction to one another at a sub-conscious level, and despite the fact that both Somadatta and Puloma are sexually attracted to a 'non-Aryan'. Indeed, Puloma cannot conceive a child until she believes that she is having intercourse with a 'Bhill'. However, their offspring can throw off their parents' prejudices and can marry, with the result that a Brahman then mixes 'his blood into the Kiratis' ethnic bloodstream' (p. 106). Yagyanidhi (2053:181) asserts that in an eastern hill district that B.P. Koirala once visited there are still 'Kiratas' who wear the sacred thread and worship Shiva, who claim that they are the offspring of Sumnimā and descendants of Vishvamitra, and whose *iṣṭa deva* is Parohang.[6] This claim leads Yagyanidhi to the conclusion that 'Sumnimā is Mother Nepal' (*ibid.*: 184).

The Influence of Politics

It is commonly asserted that B.P. Koirala's literary and political persona should be analysed separately, and indeed the former aspect of his life and work is generally neglected in English-language sources. However, given the circumstances in which several of his novels were written, it is difficult to imagine that his condition and the establishment during his imprisonment of the Panchayat system had no bearing upon what he wrote: In the *Jail Journal* he records:

> It is a dilemma for me—what to write about the politics of Nepal? We do not know the circumstances in which we will come out [of jail]. Because of this difficulty my attention has gone towards the purely literary side, I've a tendency to write poems, stories and novels. I don't want to write about political subjects. I can write autobiography, and the history of Nepal, which I have begun to write as well. Ganeshmanji [Ganesh Man Singh] says that I should write a book about contemporary politics too. But he doesn't understand my difficulty. (*Jel Jarnal*, p. 195, entry dated 18 June 1964)

BP's composition of *Sumnimā* commenced three days later, and although there is no mention of the novel in the *Jail Journal* the next entry is dated 16 October 1964.

Sumnimā's final words about the need for compromise between her Kirata daughter and her new Brahman son-in-law are commonly read as a call for harmony among Nepal's variegated ethnic groups. However, they may also reflect BP's concern for national reconciliation in political terms, (Bhattarai 2053:209) for compromise between the monarchy and the political parties, and for unity within the fractious Congress Party. They may also be a reaction to the king's claim that the new panchayat system grew from Nepal's soil (see *Jail Journal* entry dated 15 December 1962, pp. 81–2). One must pay due heed to Koirala's own declaration that 'I am one person in politics and in literature I am quite another, it seems to me that inside me there are two beings doing two different things' (quoted in Acharya 2053: 173) but one must also allow for a degree of disingenuousness and wishful thinking in the writer's description of himself.

The Burning of *Sumnimā*

Sometime during the Bikram Samvat year 2051 (1994–5), a number of individuals staged a public burning of *Sumnimā* in Biratnagar. The Royal Nepal Academy passed a motion of regret, and many literary associations condemned the action. The reasons for burning the novel were apparently not stated with any clarity, and remain a matter for conjecture (Bhattarai 2053: 207). It is generally assumed that those responsible for the book-burning were objecting to what they considered a negative portrayal by a Brahman author of the culture of the Rai and/or Limbu communities of eastern Nepal. Although I have so far failed to obtain any contemporary reports of the incident, I have been informed that Rai activists took offence at this book because of its depiction by a Brahman author of a young Kirata girl named after the consort of the culture-hero Parohang who went naked and espoused the opposite of much that might be considered moral or civilized behaviour by more conservative modern Nepalis.

Bhattarai's is the only discussion I have located so far of the issues surrounding the burning of this book. Bhattarai argues that if *Sumnimā* was burnt because it was felt to devalue a particular culture or way of life, then there are equal grounds in the book for it to be burned by 'Brahman and Kirata', or Arya and Anarya' (2053: 207). He suggests that a Brahman might have the following reasons for burning the book:

1. Somadatta's miserable failure of a life makes a mockery of the Aryan tradition;
2. The failure of the many rituals performed for the production of offspring suggests a questioning of Vedic texts;
3. Showing that an Aryan could not have a son without soliciting help from a non-Aryan is an insult to Aryan tradition;

4. The union of an Aryan son with a non-Aryan daughter is a subversion of social ideals;
5. By not performing funeral rites [for Puloma and Somadatta], Brahmanhood is slandered;
6. Since Somadatta cannot win over Sumnimā in their arguments, this is a mockery of the bases of his arguments: the Vedas, Upanishads, etc. (Bhattarai 2053: 208)

In the Post-People's Movement atmosphere of heightened minority ethnic assertiveness, and possibly influenced by the debates that took place over *Bāhunvād* during the early 1990s, *Sumnimā* appears to have been identified by certain individuals as a text created by a member of the politically dominant Bahuns to slander the culture of a marginal Janajati community. These individuals therefore took it upon themselves to stage a public burning of the book, which for them symbolized the political marginalization of their community and the denigration of its culture.

The 'true meaning' of a text must always remain open to question, because it derives not only from the arrangement of words on pages but from interactions between a text and its readers, which will produce different reactions from different readers at different times. With regard to *Sumnimā*, the *Jail Journal* enables us to ascertain with some measure of certainty what was on its author's mind at the time that the text was created, or at least the thoughts that its author felt impelled to commit to writing during the weeks and months of his confinement leading up to June 1964. It would be useful to compare the burning of *Sumnimā* to book-burning elsewhere and at other times. For instance, one wonders whether the Biratnagar activists were motivated by an anger that was in some way similar to that of the British Muslims who burned copies of Salman Rushdie's *The Satanic Verses* in the streets of Bradford and other towns during the mid-1980s. At this stage that is a matter for further inquiry.

Notes

1. Some of the cultural references and the location of the ashram beside the Koshi river suggest that 'Kirāta' should in this instance be taken to mean 'Limbu'. However, BP's knowledge of the culture of 'Kirātas' is said to have been limited, and it is suggested that his main informant on

this matter was his fellow-prisoner, Divan Singh Rai (personal communication, Novel Kishore Rai, 1998), so perhaps no exact correspondence between the two terms need be sought.

2. Rex Jones identifies the Bijuwā, who may be a woman or a man, as one of the two principal categories of Limbu priest, the other being the Phedāngmā. The Bijuwā's functions include killing the fire spirit that may come to destroy a house, killing the spirit of evil death, averting jealousy, conducting the ceremonies that must be performed after a case of incest, interceding with his master spirits, and acting as a medium (in Hitchcock and Jones [1976], 1994: 58, 59).
3. Some commentators try to draw a parallel between this episode in the novel and the short-lived resistance by the Congress Party to King Mahendra's 1960 coup.
4. *Manuvā* related to the Sanskrit *manuṣya*, and used here to mean something like *inner man.*
5. *Samjhautā:* agreement, understanding, comprise.
6. Jones states that 'Limbu of the Terhathum area worship a number of deities taken from the Hindu pantheon, such as Mahādeo (Śiva), Durgā (Kālī), and Viṣṇu Bhagāuti. (Hitchcock and Jones 1994: 40)

References

Acharya, Narahari, BS 2053 [1996/7], 'Biśveśvarprasād Koirālāko Sumnimā Upanyāsle Prastūt Gareko Jīvan-Darśan', in Jivanchandra Koirala (ed.), *Biśveśvarprasād Koirālā Samālocanā ra Bicārmā,* Kathmandu, pp. 167–75.

Bhattarai, Bishnukumar, bs 2053 [1996/7], 'Sumnimā Jalāeko Prasaṅgmā, in Jivanchandra Koirala (ed.), *Biśveśvarprasād Koirālā Samālocanā ra Bicārmā*, Kathmandu, pp. 207–11.

Chatterji, Bhola, 1990, *B.P. Koirala. Portrait of a Revolutionary*, Calcutta: Minerva Associates.

Hitchcock, John T. and Rex L. Jones (eds), 1994 [first edn. 1976], *Spirit Possession in the Nepal Himalayas,* New Delhi: Vikas Publishing House (reprint).

Koirala, Bishweshwarprasad, BS 2054 (1997), *Jel Jarnal,* Lalitpur: Jagadamba Prakashan.

———, BS 2051 (1994/5), *Sumnimā: Kirāt Deśko Euṭā Kathā,* Kathmandu: Sajha Prakashan (fourth ed.), [First ed. Varanasi: Prasahant Prakashan, BS 2027 (1970/71)].

———, 1997, *Sumnimā,* translated into Hindi by Kali Prasad Rijal, Kathmandu: Pilgrims Book House.

Mishra, Kiran, 1994, *B.P. Koirala Life and Times,* New Delhi: Wishwa Prakashan.

Misra, Shashi P., 1985, *BP Koirala. A Case Study in Third World Leadership*, Bhubaneswar and Varanasi: Konark Publishing House.

Pradhan, Krishnachandra Singh, BS 2043 (1986/7), *Nepālī Upanyās ra Upanyāskār*, Kathmandu: Sajha Prakashan (second ed.), [first ed. BS 2037 (1980/1)].

Rai, Indra Bahadur, BS 2050 (1993/4), *Nepālī Upanyāskā Ādhārharū*, Kathmandu: Sajha Prakashan (second ed.), [first ed. Varanasi: Dipak Press, 1974].

Rayamajhi, Sangita, 'Sumnima: Woman or Agent?' in *Across*, No. 1, May–July 1997, pp. 10–12.

Subedi, Rajendra, BS 2053 (1996/7), *Nepālī Upanyās Paramparā ra Pravṛtti*, Varanasi: Bhumika Prakashan.

Yagyanidhi, Dahal, BS 2053 [1996/7], 'Sumnimabhitrakī Nepāl-Āmā', in Jivanchandra Koirala (ed.), *Biśveśvarprasād Koirālā Samālocanā ra Bicārmā*, Kathmandu: pp. 181–4.

Comments

MARTIN GAENSZLE

During my search on the narrative tradition of the Mewahang Rai in the Arun Valley, it soon became clear that the figure of Sumnimā (or Somnima, as it is pronounced) is of a central significance, not only in the local context. When I was told that B.P. Koirala had written a novel with that title, I was, of course, curious. But back then, in the '80s, it was not possible for me to obtain a copy. Fortunately the situation has changed now, and I am glad that Michael Hutt has devoted his attention to this interesting and important text, which certainly deserves a wider audience. What I will do in this commentary is supply some further information on the mythological heritage of the Rai, which may further clarify the symbolic values used by Koirala, and above all, may enable us to better understand the Rai's own perspective and their possible reasons for opposition.

I will begin with a summary of the widely known myth of Sumnima and Paruhang, as it is recounted among the Mewahang Rai in Sankhuwa Sabha District (see Gaenszle 1991: 257–63). Closely related versions have been found to exist among the Thulung (Allen 1976: 36–53), the Chamling (Ebert, personal communication), the Kulunge (own inquiries). No such myth is reported for the Limbu[1]. This suggests that the myth might be a pan-Rai tradition.

The primordial snake deity, Nagi, had brought about the creation of the first living being and descending from this there was a line of divine females whose only consort was the wind. When Sumnimā, the daughter of Ninamma Ridum, had reached maturity, she decided to seek a husband. But there were no males, only the wind. Sumnimā wanted to go to the wind, but her mother warned her, as this was her father. In order to find out what to do Sumnimā is advised by her mother to go on a mountain and call the wind by whistling. If the wind lifted up her skirt this would mean that she could go to him. If it blew it tight around her legs, she should not.

The latter happened, and so it was clear that Sumnimā had to look elsewhere. Her mother eventually tells her about Paruhang, who lived up in the sky, and advises her to meet him. A bird (brown hill prima) is sent to fetch him, but Paruhang is so ugly (because of a huge goitre), that Sumnimā is shocked and refuses him.

Eventually Paruhang resorts to a trick. He dries up all water of the world and leaves his semen on a colocasia leaf. Sumnima is about to die of thirst, when she is lead to the colocasia leaf and drinks this liquid.

Following this she becomes pregnant and in due course gives birth to a variety of species: the thorny creeper, big and small kinds of bamboo, trees, tiger, bear, monkey, and finally, First Man.

We do not know what version of the myth B.P. Koirala had heard about, but it is likely that his fellow prisoner Divan Singh Rai was acquainted with a similar story, which eventually may have triggered the writer's imagination.

A number of structural parallels and inversions indicate that Koirala took up the myth's basic ideas. Also in the Rai myth Sumnimā is described as a very human, down-to-earth kind of figure. In fact, she is the first being who develops feelings such as desire for a spouse, emotions of love and hate, and has a strong will of her own. Paruhang, on the other hand, is a heavenly being (he lives in the sky and in some versions is identified with Jupiter or Venus, (cf. Allen 1976: 40), and he is someone who can control the waters of the world. These qualities, it seems, are echoed in Koirala's figure of Somadatta who as a true seeker of spiritual power, practises severe penance, i.e. tapas (literally 'heat').

Both stories tell about an unequal partnership: there is some kind of attraction, but a true union is impossible, because the two protagonists are different. But there are also inversions. In the myth Sumnimā is the frightened by the sight of her potential spouse. He is ugly, or just too strange (significantly, in one version Paruhang is identified with Shiva and a reason for his ugliness is said to be his appearance as a naked, ash-smeared, intoxicated ascetic). In the novel, however, it is Somadatta who is frightened by Sumnimā, because of her sensuousness.

There are no doubt many differences in the stories. Though both deal with the impossibility of a sexual union and an unusual kind of procreation, the styles of the narratives and the developments of the plots are rather divergent. This is not the place to go into a detailed comparison. Rather, I will point out the fundamental differences between the two kinds of narrative, in order to clarify the possible reasons for the Rai's contestation.

It must be emphasized that the Rai myth is part of the *muddum,* the sacred oral tradition of the Kiranti groups, which is the foundation of their culture and identity. The myth is part of a larger narrative which deals with the primordial events of creation. There is indication that these myths were once integral to ritual recitations, as in some instances it is still the case. The Sumnimā/Paruhang story recounts a major cosmological event: it describes a first rudimentary (albeit incomplete) form of marriage and, in particular, the origin of the variety of species, so important for the subsistence economy of the Kiranti. To this day, the Mewahang Rai, for example, perform a dance during the harvest celebrations in autumn, in which these various species as well as Sumnimā and Paruhang are enacted in a cheerful manner.

The novel, on the other hand, is a modern genre, and B.P. Koirala makes use of the indigenous tradition of the Rai in order to tell his own story of a philosophical, psychological or ethnic conflict, and its possible resolution. (I personally think that the various readings concerning the nature of the conflict are not necessarily mutually exclusive.) It may well be that some Rai have felt offended by this appropriation of their sacred tradition in the writings of a Brahman. Though such use of indigenous traditions and their deliberate transformation is a common technique in modern literature, it can also be perceived as an instrumentalization. And especially when the purpose remains unclear, this is bound to be seen as problematic.

Besides this, there are a number of features in Koirala's depiction of the Kiranti, which derive from creative imagination than from ethnographic fact and may therefore be resented by the community as a misrepresentation of their culture.

The Kiranti are described as sensuous, body-focused, and almost hedonistic. This, of course, is a wild exaggeration. It is true that the Kiranti are, for example, less obsessed with purity and have a more positive attitude toward meat-eating and alcohol consumption than the Brahman, but to depict them in the way Koirala does must be seen as a symbolic contrast, rather than an adequate description of culture. Similarly, it is not true that the Kiranti have a matrilineal or even matriarchal society (even though the myth projects this into the past). All Kiranti groups we know of have clear patrilineal features, even though matrilateral filiation may also play a role in some contexts. Also the picture Koirala gives of Kiranti religion is somewhat projective. Sumnimā's bathing and ornamenting of Somadatta in the mountain lake has no parallel in contemporary ritual practice. Though there are pilgrimages to sacred mountain lakes in the company of shamans which include ritual baths, these are more for purification than for indulgence. The figure of the Bhill (actually a 'tribal' community in Gujarat) is clearly artificial in this context: it seems to symbolize 'tribal religion', the plume costume perhaps alluding to shamanism.

In sum, what Koirala depicts here is an idealized and stylized image of Kiranti culture, partly based on ethnographic facts, but mainly derived from literary imagination. No doubt, the novel is full of sympathy for this 'noble savage', but the problem is that the Other is not taken as different in its own right, but rather it is seen as an inversion of the Self. In this respect it may be compared to early European depictions of other cultures which often have similarly inverted the image of one's own society (Kramer 1977). It has, of course, to be kept in mind, that Koirala writes not as an ethnographer but as a novelist.

It seems that Koirala's vision has drawn resentment from both Kiranti as well as Brahmans, as both groups have reasons to feel misrepresented. But the crucial point in the story is their mutual relationship. The narrative can also be read as a parable of ethnic interdependence. Whereas for most of the time it was the Janajati who emulated the Parbatiya (in the process called Hinduization), the novel indicates that the time may have come that the Parbatiya have also something to learn from the Janajati. In Koirala's vision, however, both groups are of unequal strength and one is absorbed by the other.

Not surprisingly, this vision is too problematic to become an accepted symbol of national integration. But perhaps the novel's time is yet to come. It is interesting in this context that in 1996 there were plans to produce a movie based on the book. Deepak Rayamajhi intended to be the director and ironically, Manisha Koirala the granddaughter of B.P. Koirala was to play the role of the Kiranti girl Sumnimā. It is not entirely clear why the plans did not materialize. Some say there was not enough money. But perhaps the project was (and still is?) too risky.

Notes

1. Though a primordial couple is also documented for the Limbu (Sagant 1976: 78ff.), the story is apparently quite different. However, we have still relatively little ethnographic knowledge on Limbu mythology.

References

Allen, Nicholas J., 1976, 'Studies in the Myths and Oral Traditions of the Thulung Rai of East Nepal', Oxford (unpublished dissertation).

Gaenszle, Martin, 1991, *Verwandtschaft und Mythologie bei den Mewahang Rai in Ostnepal. Eine ethnographische Studie zum Problem der 'ethnischen Identität'*, Wiesbaden: Franz Steiner Verlag.

Kramer, Fritz, 1977, *Verkehrte Welten: Zur imaginären Ethnographie des 19. Jahrhunderts*, Frankfurt: Syndikat.

Sagant, Philippe, 1976, 'Becoming a Limbu Priest: Ethnographic Notes', in John Hitchcock and Rex Jones (eds.), *Spirit Possession in the Nepal Himalayas*, Warminster: Aris & Phillips, pp. 56–99.

Washing your Neighbour's God

Buddhist Royal Ritual in Fourteenth Century Himalayan Kingdoms

WILLIAM B. DOUGLAS

The Khasas, or western Mallas, appear in the medieval Newar chronicles as periodic raiders who also worship local deities. From inscriptional evidence and Tibetan chronicles, we know that these Khasas were a medieval Buddhist dynasty of western Nepal whose kings made donations at Bodh Gayā and Lhāsa, as well as at Buṃgamati. Bugama Lokeśvara, known today by his Newar name of Buṃgadyaḥ, or as Rato Mātsyendranāth, was one of the only Indian Lokeśvaras to survive past the thirteenth century. On the basis of Newar sources, I argue that Khāsa kings had a specific relationship to Buṃgadyaḥ, comparable to that of Newar Mallas themselves, and that it arose from their dynastic participation in Indian Buddhism. The fourteenth century Khāsa worship of Buṃgadyaḥ foreshadows the seventeenth century Newar cult in Lalitpur.

Towards a History of Bugama Lokeśvara

Buṃgadyaḥ, or Bugama Lokeśvara as he is known in the Sanskrit sources, has usually been studied as a specifically Newar deity. Up to the twelfth century, however, Newar Buddhism was part of a much wider system of medieval Indian Buddhism, and Buṃgadyaḥ has a history in Indian Buddhist iconography (see below). From the thirteenth through the fifteenth centuries, following the collapse of Indian Buddhism in its heartland, it is well known that the Kathmandu valley functioned as a surrogate source of Indian Buddhism for Tibetan pilgrims. Tibetans had long ago laid the foundations of a new form of Vajrayāna, quite distinct from the Indian. Yet the one-time Indian Buddhists of the Kathmandu valley had themselves to evolve an independent local form of Buddhism, and Buṃgadyaḥ became thereby the most important Buddhist deity of the Kathmandu valley with his own purāṇa, the *Guṇakāraṇḍavyūha*. For a time, he even becomes a royal Lokeśvara in a manner traceable to his Indian origins, though not until the seventeenth century.

It is tempting to see this process happening in a vacuum, or indeed as wholly caused by the vacuum resulting from the sudden loss of the major monastic complexes and pilgrimage sites in India. That this is not entirely so has already been adumbrated by Todd Lewis' account of the interplay between Newar and Tibetan Buddhists (Lewis 1996). Other Buddhists of the late Indian vintage, such as those of Kaśmir or Bengal, were similarly cut off from pilgrimage sites and meeting places, but continued to travel among the remaining Buddhist polities.[1] Whole Buddhist courts went underground; the erstwhile king of Magadha hid in the woods when the *turuṣka* troops came through (Roerich 1989: 6). The Śrī Laṅkan saṅgha did somehow keep up a presence at Bodh Gayā for an astonishingly long time, well into the fifteenth or sixteenth century, and we encounter occasional courageous pilgrims travelling from Bengal to Magadha[2] and onwards; but these are very much the exception. The Khasas of western Nepal were one such Buddhist kingdom slowly cut off from the centres of pilgrimage in Magadha, and as they shifted their interests into the Himalayas they encountered and worshipped the Lokeśvara in the Kathmandu valley.

The only source for records of Khāsa visits to Kathmandu valley is a cluster of late fourteenth century chronicles, two of which make up a text published as the *Gopālarājavaṃśāvalī* (GRV) (Vajrācārya, Dhanavarja and Malla 1985) and third, the Kaisher Vaṃśāvalī (KV).[3] The first (V^1) and second (V^2) sections of the GRV are distinguished by language; the former is corrupt Sanskrit and the latter early Newari.

As the evidence in this paper comes from a wide range of sources, it is difficut to present the argument in distinct blocks. I will begin by looking at the ritual bathing of Buṃgadyaḥ by Malla and Khāsa kings in the thirteenth and fourteenth centuries, then consider Buṃgadyaḥ himself and, finally, sketch the Khasas' own history and their relation to Buṃgadyaḥ.

Ritual Bathing of Buṃgadyaḥ

There are three recorded instances between 1200 and 1400 CE in which kings bathe Buṃgadyaḥ. From 1226–34 ce, the Tibetan scholar Dharmasvāmin lived in the Kathmandu valley, and he gives an account of the Buṃgadyaḥ *yātrā* (journey) which describes the bathing ritual. In 1313 CE, the GRV records that Khāsa king Ripumalla performed the bathing ritual. The GRV again records that in 1370 CE, Jayasthitimalla goes to Lalitpur and washes Buṃgadyaḥ.

The Account of Dharmasvāmin

Dharmasvāmin's account is short but pithy. Although he does not give an exact year, his description of *yātrā* is consistent with later sources in all details except the timing; the king at the time was Abhayamalla (1216–55). According to Dharmasvāmin (p. 6) the image of Buṃgadyaḥ was taken on procession 'on the eighth day of middle autumn month.[4] People made offerings to it during the month-long procession,[5] particularly the king and courtiers'.[6] They offer *pañcāmṛta*, pouring it over the head of the image, then bathe the image.[7] It is recalled to the temple on the seventh day of the following month, and cleaned and repainted by tantric priests called Hang.du, probably the same as the modern Pañjus.[8]

Ripumalla's Visit

Form GRV V²43 ka.

sa 433 phālguṇa kṛṣṇā pāḍā khaśiyā rājā ripumalana bugaṃsa hnavanaṃ yāña sahraṃ ādinaṃ duṃtā gvalam bhāhrasa prasa coñā yendeñcetasa bāhraṃ savatī[9] bhoja yānā dina 18 vasarapā lissa//

Translation:

In NS 433, on the first day of the dark half of Phālguṇa, the Khāsa king Ripumalla performed the bathing (ritual) of Buṃga,[10] making presents of a horse and such. He pleased the deity of Gwala (Paśupati), the deity[11] of the caitya at Yende, and offered a feast for all. After eighteen days he left.

Ripumalla, it seems, performs a smaller ritual than Abhayamalla; there is not mention of the yātrā here. There is some evidence that this is a calendrically fixed ritual (see table 1).

Jayasthitimalla

From GRV V[2]56 kha.

490 vesāṣa[12] śuddhi śrīśrījayasthitirājamaladesa, yarhaṃ manigala smastasana jātrā bijyācarā tom lu toraṇa vṛndanamāla khāsyaṃ vaṃśāhra lāsyaṃ, duṃvijyācakam manigalasa tava tava mīsa pramukha nāyakasana le cāsyaṃ le cāsyaṃ lunaṃ argha yāñā syeṣṭha pramukhaṃ jayat mulamīsa //

Summary:

In NS 490 Vaiśākha śukla 3 (April 1370), Jayasthītimalla goes to Lalitpur for the procession of Buṃgadyaḥ.[13] He washes the deity, after offering oblations from a golden [pot].[14] In translating the chronicle, K.P. Malla (Vajrācārya, Dhanavajra and Malla 1985: 159) takes the passage to mean that the nobles of Lalitpur offered Jayasthiti an oblation, while Petech (1984: 134) has Jayasthiti give gold to the nobles; but in context it clearly means that Jayasthiti led the nobles of Lalitpur, with Jayata Mulamī foremost, in bathing the deity. This takes place at the time when Jayasthītimalla is anxious to exert his authority over Lalitpur, having already fought several skirmishes. He is not officially crowned king of Bhaktapur (let alone Lalitpur) for some ten years more, but this is an important recognition of his authority—further asserted in the following passage, in which he executes some thieves from Lalitpur.

To Bathe

Three separate languages contribute words for washing here, and it is important to be sure that meaning in each is clear.

Tibetan

In Dharmasvāmin's Tibetan, the phrase is *sku.khrus.gsol.ba,* a term meaning 'to administer a bath', (pp. 592a, 51b) with the connotation of a religious ritual. Dharmasvāmin is our most specific source, for he describes the entire ritual: anointing with the five nectars, subsequent rinsing, and the consumption by the participant of the resulting prasād.

Sanskrit

In Sanskrit, the term is *snāpayati,* leading to New. *Hnavanaṃ yāye.* Thus, in the GRV (43a) entry concerning Ripumalla, we find the term *hnavanaṃ.*[15]

The term *argha,* appearing in the 1370 record, means both a liquid oblation and the pot from which it comes (Manandhar 1986: 8b). *Argha* in this case probably refers to the *pañcamṛta* itself; Locke (1980: 202) notes this in the worship of Amoghapāśa, but the order is unnatural in the GRV passage; one washes the deity after pouring the *pañcāmṛta.* See the *Amoghapāśahṛdayadhāraṇī,* where a particular mantra is described as the *arghāsana-snāna-mantrādyalaṃkāra-gandha-puṣpa-dhūpa-cchatra-dhvaja-patākā-bali-dīpa-mantraḥ* (p. 322).

Newari

The verbal noun *cāsyaṃ* comes from *cā-ya. Cā-ya* according to Jorgensen (p. 59a, s.v. cāyal) and the lexicon in the printed edition of the GRV (Vajrācarya, Dhanavarja and Malla 1985: 171b) simply means 'to wash'. *Cāsyaṃ* is a rinsing or washing.

Correlating Evidence for the Bathing Ritual

It is difficult to piece together a complete picture of the medieval ritual just from these descriptions, but there is plenty of material for comparison. Locke provides an excellent ethnographic account of this bathing ritual at Jana Bāhāḥ (Locke 1980: 68–9, 204–8, 328–9) which Bruce Owens subsequently expanded and corrected. There is also substantial support for the bathing ritual in Buddhist textual sources.

Locke does not appreciate the continuity of the evidence for the medieval bathing ritual as it applies to Buṃgadyaḥ, but he does connect Dharmasvāmin's account with descriptions given by the Chinese pilgrims to India, and to chapter II of the Bodhicaryāvatāra. He groups the Indian accounts and textual sources together with the ritual described by Dharmasvamin as Mahāyāna, in contrast to the late medieval and modern ritual which he describes as Vajrayāna (1980: 209). The literary connection, at least, was well known to earlier Newar Buddhists. The first chapter of the GKV, a work which elsewhere contains substantial extracts from the BCA, describes worshipping the image of Avalokiteśvara using fragrant water, hymns, and such in just the manner of the older work.

pañcāmṛtaiḥ paṃcasugandhitoyair ye snāpayanti pramudā triratnaṃ/ mandākinīdivyasugandhitoyaiḥ snātvā sukhaṃ te divisaṃ ramante// (I.103)

The GKV and Dharmasvāmin's account agree on the use of the five nectars (*pañcāmṛta*). The BCA, a text written well after the advent of the Vajrayāna which nonetheless stays entirely within Mahāyāna topics, does not mention them. It is a Vajrayāna category, and their use in Buṃgadyaḥ rituals is a clear signal that we are indeed looking at a ritual of the Vajrayāna. Indeed, for information on the pañcāmṛta, Dharmasvāmin refers the reader to the *Ratnāvalī*, a commentary on the *Kṛṣṇāyamāritantra.*[16]

Timing of the Yātrā

Finally, we must consider the shift in calendrical position for the festival. In Dharmasvāmin's account, the timing of the festival, from the eighth day of the middle autumn month to the eighth day of the following month, corresponds to injunctions in the *Guṇakāraṇḍavyūha* to perform the ritual[17] of Amoghapāśa on the eighth day of the bright half of Śrāvan or Kārttikā (*śuklāṣṭamyām viśeṣtaḥ* I.165c; *māseṣu śrāvaṇe śreṣṭhaṃ kārtike ca viśeṣataḥ* I.166ab). By the mid fourteenth century, however, the Buṃgadyaḥ *yātrā* has clearly shifted to Vaiśākha *kṛṣṇa prathama.*

Not only do we have at least two timings just for the Malla kings, an autumn observance in the 1230s but a late spring observance in the 1350s, there are also multiple traditions of Lokeśvara around the valley, each of whom has a bathing ritual and each of which takes up a distinct calendrical slot. The ritual in Jana Bāhāḥ takes place in Pauṣ; that at Nala in Phālguṇ, and the Lokeśvara of Cobhar is bathed in Caitra. On present evidence all of these Karuṇāmaya Lokeśvara cults postdate that at Buṃgamati, although each has a story giving ancient origins. The only Lokeśvara consistently identified as older than Buṃgadyaḥ is Cakwadyaḥ, resident in Tanga Bāḥāl; he is said to be the original Lokeśvara of Lalitpur, but his ritual has been largely submerged into that of Buṃgadyaḥ, and his rituals are performed at the same time.

What emerges here is that these are calendrically fixed rituals. It is not clear why the yātrā of Buṃgadyaḥ shifted from fall to spring, but it is clear that the festival was tied to a specific *thiti* at all times. This was apparently also true for the early Khasas, as we shall see.

Buṃgadyaḥ

The most famous shrine of the peculiarly Newar form of Avalokiteśvara known as Karuṇāmaya is at Buṃgamati, near Lalitpur; and the god—or Bodhisattva—resident there is known as Buṃgadyaḥ, one of a set[18] of Lokeśvaras all of whom can be called Karuṇāmaya. The name 'Karuṇāmaya' appears to gain popularity with the *Guṇakāraṇḍavyūha*, a text composed before 1550 as a māhātmya of the Amoghapāśa Lokeśvara at Buṃgamati.[19] During the period we are considering here, the late thirteenth and early fourteenth centuries, Buṃgadyaḥ transformed from a figure who had been known across India to a specifically Newar figure.

Evidence for Indian interest in Buṃgadyaḥ comes from two eleventh century manuscripts of the *Aṣṭasāhasrikā Prajñāpāramitā* studied by A. Foucher, Cambridge Add. 1643 from Nepal and a Pāla manuscript, Asiatic Society of Bengal A. 15. Among various deities and famous shrines, the manuscripts list many Lokeśvaras and Lokanāthas.[20] While Buṃgadyaḥ appears only in the Pāla manuscript, and the image there looks nothing like the *mūrti* actually found at Buṃgamati, he is perhaps the only one of what must have been a well-known group of famous Lokeśvaras who still exist today. He is only identifiable from the label, which reads '*nepāle bugamalokeśvaraḥ*'. The illustration is an iconographically accurate representation of the particular Lokeśvara who is identified with Buṃgadyaḥ that is, a red Padmapāṇi Avalokiteśvara. Dharmasvāmin notes particularly that the Tibetans favour Svayaṃbhū, while Bukham (Buṃgadyaḥ) is well known to the Indians.

His roots lie in the Mahāyānist Lokeśvara worship of the Pāla period and the Vajrayāna cult of Amoghapāśa with its Poṣadha fast. The Poṣadha fast, specifically a lay fast, was widely propagated in India, Nepal and Tibet. Of more interest to us here, however, is the public and specifically royal aspect of the Lokeśvara cult.

Buṃgadyaḥ as a Newar National Deity

These are the three documented instances of bathing Buṃgadyaḥ from 1200 to 1400. However, we also know that the Newar Mallas took part in his yātrā four or more times (including Dharmasvāmin's account). Indeed, the right to take part in the yātrā was contested between rivals for political legitimacy. Building on categories which Gérard Toffin and Bruce Owens use for the later Mallas in the Kathmandu valley, we can distinguish between the personal deity (*iṣṭadevatā*) of a particular ruler, the lineage deity of a dynasty (*kuladevatā*) and a national deity (*rāṣṭriyo devaḥ*).

Although Buṃgadyaḥ does not attain to the status of a *kuladevatā* of the Lalitpur Mallas until the seventeenth century, his status as a national god with royal patronage is already clear in Dharmasvāmin's account, and it is confirmed by account from the fourteenth century in the GRV. Between 1300 and 1400 we have at least 3 records for Malla observances of the festival.[21]

NS 457 Āṣāḍha śukla 2 (June 1337). In 1337, during a contest for power between the Kaśi and Karṇāṭa factions,[22] Gopālacandra of the Kaśi side is prevented from entering Manigal (Patan) during the procession of Buṃgadya[23].

NS 490 Vaiśākha śukla 3 (April 1370) (mentioned above). Jayasthiti's visit in 1370 is part of a long-term strategy to win over the Lalitpur nobles and assert his authority there.

NS 507 Vaiśākha śukla 4 (April 1387). By 1387, Jayasthiti's presence at the yātrā[24] is affirmation of his authority across the valley after the death of Rajalladevī, and he is accompanied in the procession by an old Bhonta rival here apparently acknowledging his authority[25].

Lokeśvara and the Throne

Although there were Lokeśvara cults right across later Indian Buddhism, the comparative work to establish a consistent character has not yet been done. However, one aspect which is repeatedly encounterd is a close relation between royality and Lokeśvara. Lokeśvara or Lokanāth is the object of royal devotion in various Pāla inscriptions, and also in minor courts under Pāla influence. For example, in an inscription found at Bodh Gayā of the Gāhaḍavalā king Jayacandradeva from the tenth century, there is a long eulogistic poem to Lokeśvara.[26] Even in Śri Laṅka, John Holt argues that there was a 'sleeping' cult of Avalokiteśvara very much on Mahāyāna lines centred around Kandy which had been introduced as early as the ninth century, and that this particular cult gives rise to the royal protective figure Nāth Deviyo in the Gampola period.[27] The Javanese state of Śrī Vijaya[28] and the Khmer complex at Angkor Wat are further examples which, however, need careful study.[29]

There is a substantial body of work on the relation between the saṅgha and the throne in Theravāda countries. However, the absence of any recent kingdoms organized on Indian Mahāyāna lines makes it difficult to offer a contrasting picture; we must rely on inscriptional, art historical, and textual sources. In fact, the best source of material is the relatively recent historical data for the Lalitpur monarchy. While this makes closer study of the medieval material that is much more interesting, it also raises the threat of circularity if we try to use comparative evidence to enrich what little we do have for the medieval rituals.

We might imagine that a later Mahāyāna model of kingship would resemble the medieval rituals for non-Buddhist states[30] or be mutually implicated with Śaiva state rituals.[31] Certainly in the Kathmandu valley, the Lokeśvara rituals of the later Lalitpur Mallas are deeply interwoven with both Śaiva and Vaiṣṇava elements. Minimally, we can look for the following:

A Distinctive Royal Pūjā

While Lokeśvara is a public figure with a wide basis for his cult, royal participation should be demarcated, by date, place, restricted access, or perhaps just ostentation.

Affirmation of Royal Status

The ritual should confer or confirm royal status, in the manner of the *rājābhiṣeka* or *puṣpābhiṣeka* of the Mallas.

Identification with the Person of Lokeśvara

In so far as Lokeśvara, especially in the form of Amoghapāśa, is a Vajrayāna deity, the ruler may undergo a tantric identification of himself with Lokeśvara, such as is exemplified in monumental imagery from Cambodia and Java.

The Malla observance of the Buṃgadyaḥ yātrā fulfils some, but not all of these criteria. Access to participation in the bathing ritual within the yātrā was reserved for nobles and the king, and was controlled by the dominant faction. Even in the later ritual of Buṃgadyaḥ the ostentatious presence of the king is necessary for the climax of the festival and the showing of the *bhoto,* symbol of the king of the nāgas. Jayasthiti, although he does not identify himself with Karuṇāmaya, is called '*budhervvaṃśāvatāra kalijuge*', an incarnation in the lineage of Buddha for the Kali Yuga (Vidyavinoda 1914). Thus, for the Mallas we have evidence of a distinctively royal pūjā, and a rather formulaic identification with the Buddha. However, the Śaiva Mallas did not use a Buddhist consecration ceremony.

The Khasas

Ripumalla is the second of four Khāsa kings recorded in the GRV. At least one other, his uncle, is known to have visited Buṃgamati and made donations there, and there is the possibility that the two later Khāsa visitors also took part in the ritual life of Buṃgadyaḥ.

The Dynasty at Ya.rtse

From the evidence in inscriptions and Tibetan chronicles, the Khasas were clearly a late Indian Buddhist polity. In the Tibetan chronicles, they are the royal family of Ya.rtse, one of the kingdoms in western Nepal who follow on from the three sons of Ñi ma mgon, exiled from central Tibet when the original diffusion of the Dharma was suppressed. It is probable, however, that they are not lineal descendants from that family, although the Tibetan tradition respects them as such. Rather, they are an Indian dynasty which takes hold in the region of western Nepal and Kumaon. At about the point when they emerge into Indian historical sources they begin consistently to use the suffix *calla*, which eventually becomes *malla*; in western sources this family is often referred to as the western Mallas to distinguish it from the Mallas ruling in the Kathmandu valley at the same time. In Bodh Gayā inscription (Petech 1980; Tucci 1956) of a feudatory, Aśokacalla is called the king of the Khāsa country, and this term or variants of it occur in the GRV. The term is preserved in the phrase *khās kurā* which refers to the Nepāli language.

The Khāsa capital was at Semjā or Ya.rtse, in western Nepal, just northwest of Jumla in one of the river valleys that cuts into the edge of the Himalayas. To the north is Mount Kailash; to the east is Dolpo. The Kathmandu valley is somewhat less than 400 kilometers to the east.

The most complete and best known source for the lineage of the Khasas is the Dullu inscription of Pṛthivīmalla, dated to Śāka 1279 (1357 CE). This has been the subject of considerable attention, first by Tucci, then Naraharinath, and finally Petech.[31] The inscription claims to offer an exhaustive account of the dynastic history as far back as one Nāgarāja. In fact, as Petech has ably proved, the inscription is an attempt to legitimate the recent annexation of the throne of Ya. rtse by Pṛthivīmalla's father, the ruler of Pu 'rang. It is possible to corroborate the Dullu inscription with other evidence; the account of the Dullu inscription is reliable up to Pṛthivīmalla's father, at which point it falters.[32] It is thus possible to establish the names and some of the dates with confidence, as illustrated in figure 1.

Evidence for the first five Khasas, from Nāgarāja to Krādhicalla, is mostly lacking. From the time of Krācalla (fl. 1220s) the Khasas appear to be a vigorously expanding Vajrayāna polity for the next hundred years. Their inscriptions and those of their vassals appear in Indian sites, with Buddhist epithets, sometimes specifically Vajrayāna. The Tibetan chronicles describe pious donations and

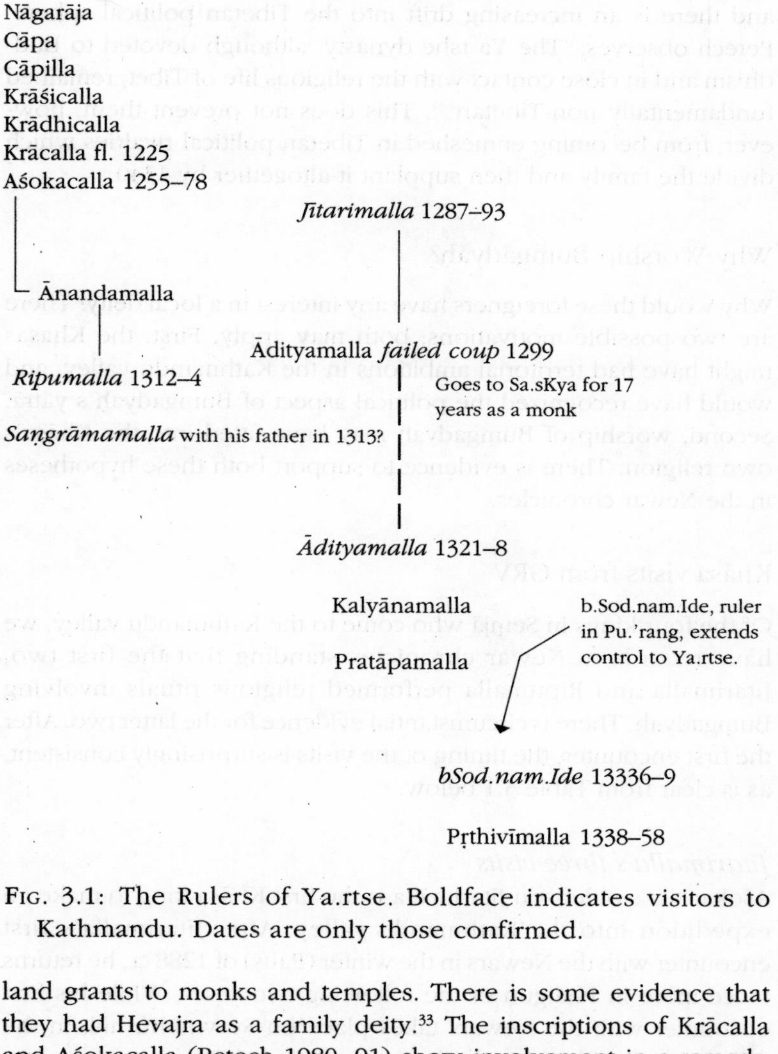

FIG. 3.1: The Rulers of Ya.rtse. Boldface indicates visitors to Kathmandu. Dates are only those confirmed.

land grants to monks and temples. There is some evidence that they had Hevajra as a family deity.[33] The inscriptions of Krācalla and Aśokacalla (Petech 1980: 91) show involvement in a remarkable effort of the later thirteenth century to reconstruct the Indian Buddhist pilgrimage site at Bodh Gayā after its destruction by Central Asian mercenaries in the late twelfth century. However, after Aśokacalla the evidence for Khāsa activity in the Indian plains diminishes. They begin to appear as raiders in the Newar chronicles, and there is an increasing drift into the Tibetan political sphere. Petech observes, 'The Ya tshe dynasty, although devoted to Buddhism and in close contact with the religious life of Tibet, remained fundamentally non-Tibetan'[34]. This does not prevent them, however, from becoming enmeshed in Tibetan political rivalries which divide the family and then supplant it altogether by 1340.

Why Worship Buṃgadyaḥ?

Why would these foreigners have any interest in a local deity? There are two possible motivations; both may apply. First, the Khasas might have had territorial ambitions in the Kathmandu valley, and would have recognized the political aspect of Buṃgadyaḥ's yātrā. Second, worship of Buṃgadyaḥ may have fitted into the Khāsa's own religion. There is evidence to support both these hypotheses in the Newar chronicles.

Khāsa visits from GRV

Of the four kings in Seṃjā who come to the Kathmandu valley, we have records in Newar chronicles standing that the first two, Jītarimalla and Ripumalla performed religious rituals involving Buṃgadyaḥ. There is circumstantial evidence for the latter two. After the first encounter, the timing of the visits is surprisingly consistent, as is clear from Table 3.1 below.

Jītarimalla's three visits

Aśokacalla's older son Jītarimalla is the first Khāsa king to make an expedition into the Kathmandu valley. After Jītarimalla's first encounter with the Newars in the winter (Pauṣ) of 1288 CE, he returns twice more in Phālguṇ of the following two years. While his first encounter with the Newars takes place on Svayṃbhū hill, in the following years he visits both Svayaṃbhū and Buṃgamati.

First visit: NS 408: From GRV V[1]26 kha

paścāt khaśiyā vavaḥ// rājā jayatāri prathama praviṣṭaḥ samvacchara cāri saya āṭha pauṣa māse/ sāhmaṃgusthāne khaśiyā abūṭha saya pātayitvā rāṣṭra sarvva vane sevitam khaśiyā tena palāyitam loka svasthane svasthānasthitam//

TABLE 3.1. Correlating GRV I and II records of visits to Buṃgadyaḥ

GRV section I		GRV section II		
Folio	date	folio	date	Khāsa king
26 kha	Ns 408			Jītarimalla
26 kha	Ns 409 Phālgun śukla 13			Jītarimalla
		40 ka	NS 410 Phālgun Kṛṣṇa pratipadā	Jītarimalla
		43 ka	NS 433 Phālgun Kṛṣṇa pratipadā	Ripumalla
		44 kha	NS 441 Caitra śukla 2	Ādityamalla
27 kha	448 Caitra śukla pūrṇimā	46 ka	NS 448 Phālgun śukla saptamī	Ādityamalla
		48 ka	NS 54 Bhadra śukla saptamī	? arrives
		48 ka	NS 454 Phālguṇa Kṛṣṇa Pratipadā	? leaves

Translation: The Khasas came from the west. In 408, the king Jītari entered [Nepal] for the first time in the month of Pauṣ. The Khasas were at Svayaṃbhū,[35] and one hundred died. The entire nation fled to the forest. Therefore the Khāsa retreated and the people returned to their own homes.

The first contact is violent. It must have been written in retrospect ('the first time'), and we do not discover why the Khasas were at Svayaṃbhū. The Kaisher Vaṃśāvalī is less informative:[36]

samvat 408 pauṣa māsa jayatārī praviṣṭa prathamam//

Translation: Jītari visited for the first time in Pauṣa of the year 408.

Second visit: NS 409 Phālguṇ: Continuation of GRV V[1]26 kha

tasya samvacchara pravartate phālguṇa māsa śukla trayodaśī/ punaḥ dvitīya jayatārī praviṣṭaḥ// grāmādi agnidāham karoti syeṃgu ceta prasthapati/ bugmalokeśvaradraśānam śrīpaśupatiprasanam svasthena svarāṣṭragamanam bhavati//

From the Kaisher Vamśvalī.[37]

samvat 414 phālguṇa māsa dvitīyā vāra praviṣṭa khaśiyā pravesa//

Petech takes this passage in VK to refer to the third incursion, although it obviously refers to the second[38].

Summary: In Phālguṇ of the the next year, Jītāri again entered [the valley] a second time, on the 13th of the bright half of the month. He burned villages. At Svayaṃbhū he dedicated a stūpa, then took darśan of Buṃgadyaḥ. He makes an offering at Paśupati and then leaves for home.

The third visit. NS 410 Phālguṇ: The first and second are recorded in V^1 and VK. In V^2 there is a record of a visit by Jītāri in NS 410. From GRV $V^2$40 ka

sa 410 phālguṇa kṛṣṇa pradīpadā jayatāri vasyaṃ liṃ tela navakvātha kāyā vugandevala payisarapambhaṇḍāra duṃtā/ gvalvaṃsa pachima dvāraṇa dumvisyam thavalāna aṅkāla visyam svāna chāyā uprabātha paścima dvārasa ṭayā thva liva gāma dvāko me coyā liṃchi yarhaṃsa garha yāṅa māṅā garha macālva//

Given the specificity of the dating it seems safe to assume that this records a distinct, third visit.

Summary: Jītārimalla raids or conquers Nuwakoṭ before coming to Buṃgadyaḥ at about the same time he had the previous year, and makes offerings. Subsequently he goes to Gvalaṃ (=Deopatan), and enters from the west. He leaves, placing something on that same gate, then sets fire to several villages[39] and proceeds to a fort in Lalitpur for one month, where (following Malla) he is unable to breach the fort of Māṇa.

It seems from these records that Jītarimalla is learning about the Newars with each encounter, and after the first clash, he returns for two years in a row at almost exactly the same date. Both times he worships all three significant deities in the valley, and by his third visit he is setting up camp in Lalitpur and staying for months rather than weeks.

Aśokacalla's younger son, Ānandamalla, follows his brother Jītarimalla onto the throne but the royal family appears to divide between the descendants of these two brothers. When Jītarimalla's son Ādityamalla tries and fails to take the throne, which passes to Ānandamalla's son Ripumalla, he flees to Sa skya and lives as a monk for 17 years, outlasting Ānandamalla's line and returning to assume the throne.

Ripumalla

Although Ripumalla was apparently a powerful and respected Khāsa king, the only Indian evidence we have for Ripumalla are graffiti from 1312 CE at Lumbini and Kapilavastu, naming him and his son Samgrāmamalla.[40] In the spring of 1313 he was in Lalitpur for the bathing ritual of Buṃgadyaḥ, as described above. Ripumalla and his son were apparently on a pilgrimage tour, passing first through Kapilavastu and Lumbini and then the valley of Nepal.[41] It appears to have been a peaceful visit; certainly the GRV does not record raids or conquests under Ripumalla's name. However, bathing Buṃgadyaḥ ought to have been a highly political ritual if performed by a king. Saṃgrāmamalla, his son, is not mentioned in the GRV, but as he was with his father on pilgrimage, he was probably with him at the ritual bathing. Evidence for Ripumalla's political dominance, however contested in his own sphere, is not lacking. He fought off a palace coup to take the throne. Although his cousin and rival Ādityamalla remained in Sa skya, he is remembered in the Tibetan annals as reasserting Khāsa influence in India as well as donating generously in Lhāsa.[42]

The date on which he performed this ritual is the same date recorded for his uncle 23 years before.[43] While there is considerable consistency between Jītarimalla's second two visits and Ripumalla's visit—so much so that they could have performed the same ritual on the same tithi, the first day of the dark half of Phālguṇ, all three times—this consistency breaks down with the later Khasas. Ādityamalla arrives somewhat later, in Caitra, both times and bSod.nams.lde actually leaves on this same tithi. If there was a calendrical ritual, either at the Buṃgadyaḥ temple or perhaps proper to the Khāsa family rituals, it is lost after Ripumalla.

Finally, in a manuscript colophom from Śaka 1370 (=1314 CE), Ripumalla is referred to as *rājarājeśvara lokeśvara śrīripumalladeva.* (60) We may cautiously take this as evidence that Ripumalla was identified with Lokeśvara in the Indian Buddhist style.[44]

Ādityamalla

When eventually he does gain the throne, the Newar chronicles do not record any religious activity for Ādityamalla in the Kathmandu valley; rather, in his two spring visits of NS 441 (= 1312 CE) and NS 48 (=1328 CE) he raids settlements in and around the valley and makes a more serious attempt on control in Lalitpur. During his first visit he attacks a royal fortress in Bhaktapur. In NS 448, he attacks Nuwakoṭ in mid-February, Pharping five days later, then proceeds to Lalitpur where he imposes fines and lays siege, unsuccessfully, for 22 days.[45]

bSod. nams. 1de

The last Khāsa to raid the Kathmandu valley is probably bSod.nams.1de, the expansionist ruler of Pu 'rang; the GRV does not name him. bSod.nams.1de was not actually a descendent of any previous Khāsa, but the Newars, like the Tibetans, accept him as a Khāsa ruler. Unlike in previous records, the Khasas arrive over winter in the valley, arriving by Bhadra of NS 454 (1334) and only leaving in February of the next year. The surprising thing about the GRV entry describing this visit is that no mention is made of the arrival of the Khasas. Instead, the Khasas are only mentioned when they kill a noble (the Sakhupati Rājā) sent to Lalitpur; and by the time they leave in the spring, they have killed forty other men.[46]

There is no direct evidence that either of the later invading Khasas worshipped any of the Newar deities; we do know that they were Buddhists closely tied to Tibet. That consistency in the timing of the earlier visits which suggests a fixed ritual is lacking for the later Khasas. They may simply have abondoned the fixed worship of Buṃgadyaḥ because of difficulty of access, or discovered or founded alternative sites for this worship in western Nepal or Tibet. This does not rule out an optional worship at the shrine of Buṃgadyaḥ, and indeed given the consistency of the earlier Khasas it would not be surprising to find independent evidence that their descendants had made pious donations to Svayaṃbhū and Buṃgadyaḥ.

Conclusion

I proposed above a set of three characteristics we would expect in a dynastic cult of Lokeśvara: a distinctive pūjā, identification with Lokeśvara, and some sort of a rājābhiṣeka. For both the Mallas and at least the earlier Khāsās, two of these apply. The Mallas actively controlled access to the Buṃgadyaḥ yātrā, and the ritual of oblation with the five nectars and rinsing, is well established. Jayasthiti, although he does not identify himself with Karuṇāmaya in the manner of the later Lalitpur Mallas, is called 'an incarnation in the lineage of Buddha'[47]. For Abhayamalla, Ripumalla and his son we have reference to a similar bathing ritual, as well as evidence of identification with Lokeśvara. Was Ripumalla's bathing of Buṃgadyaḥ a claim to sovereignty in the valley of Nepal? It is clear that other members of his dynasty moved from simply raiding to setting in for long sieges and occupying sections of Lalitpur for months at a time. It is also clear that participating in the bath and yātrā of Buṃgadyaḥ was as much a political as a religious act for the indigenous dynasty. Yet the consistent difference between the timing and scale of the Khāsa and Malla observances suggests that the Khāsa observances, while being important for their own political rituals, were not a territorial attempt to co-opt the Lokeśvara rituals of the local dynasty.[48]

The Khasas may well have had territorial ambitions in or around the valley of Nepal, but their observances are detached from the Newar yātrā of Buṃgadhyaḥ, and it is the scale and ostentation of the yātrā which give it political force in the valley. The Malla kings, for whom Buṃgadyaḥ is a powerful and popular national deity, must worship him although they are not Buddhist. The Khasas, who are Buddhists and who do appear to have a dynastic cult of Lokeśvara, worship a famous and old Lokeśvara who is not their local national deity. In neither case, therefore, can we expect to see a *rājābhiseka* as part of the ritual. The Mallas had their own Śaiva ceremony. The consistent timing of the first three Khasa observances at Buṃgamati suggest that for some time there was a calendrically fixed ritual, quite possibly scheduled according to the ritual year of the Khāsa court, which was transplanted to Buṃgadyaḥ as the Khasas were themselves squeezed out of the lowlands. Whether or not there was such a fixed ritual, it is clear that the Khāsa observances were not a claim to sovereignty in the valley of Nepal, but part of their own dynastic ritual whose intended sphere of effect was extensively all of Buddhist India and intensively their own state of Ya.rtse. For a time they borrowed the institutional charisma of this famous Lokeśvara in order to sustain the dignity of their own dynasty.

Notes

1. So, for example, in the Aśokacalla inscription of LS 51, we find mention of the Khāsa court pandit *Kaśmīrapaṇḍita-bhadantābhayaśrī* (correcting from *bhadantagucapathī*) in Vidyavinoda (1914). Abhyaśri is not mentioned in Naudou (1968).
2. Vanaratna (1384–1468), a monk of Bengali origins, was oriented in Magadha, trained in Śri Laṅka, taught in Tibet, and eventually settled in Lalitpur.
3. The KV was discovered by Petech and is included in the edition of the GRV.
4. *ston.zla 'bring. po'i tshes.brgyad.la phyi.rol.du*.
5. The actual duration of the festival is slightly unclear. According to Dharmasvāmin it is brought out on the eighth day and returned on the seventh day of the following month, but the festival lasts a half-month. There may be some confusion arising from the division of Newar months into light and dark phases.
6. *bha.ro,* a Newari word possibly derived from Skt. *variṣṭa* [Manandhar 1986] gives 'bhāradāra: king's men; courtiers, high government officials.' See mhn (p. 190).
7. *sku.khrus.gsol.nas*. See § 2.4.
8. See Locke (1980), p. 254, n. 14. Cf. also the reference to the 'White Handu' in Lewis (1996), p. 155, dating from 1076 CE.
9. The transcription in Vajracarya Malla (1985) has *savati* against the manuscript.
10. In *bugamsa*, Petech takes the -sa suffix as an ON locative, but he misses the sense of the passage completely mhn (p. 108). Malla however takes it as honorific; e.g., *deva kumārasa* at 60a and *bhāhrasa* in this passage.
11. Taking both *bhāhra and bāhra* as from *bhaṭṭāraka;* cf. the glossary entries at Vajracarya Malla (1985), p. 182a and the preceding note on the value of *sa*. This conception of a person resident in the caitya has been detailed by G. Schopen in various essays.
12. Vaiśākha.
13. GRV V² 56kha. Although Buṃgadyaḥ is not mentioned by name, K.P. Malla and Dhanavajra Vajrācārya both take this to be the Buṃgadyaḥ yātrā. The timing corresponds to later evidence, and the use of the term *argha* clinches the translation.
14. See §2.4. Usually argha would mean either an oblation or the flask from which the *pañcāmṛta* comes, that is, a flask used for oblations; but here it could mean a flask for water, in which case we must read 'Jayasthiti

washed the deity with water from a golden flask.' In K.P. Malla's translation (and that of Dhanavajra Vajrācārya), the Lalitpur nobles offered Jayasthiti oblation from the golden water-pot. See Vajracarya Malla (1985), p. 159. This is confusing the terms for bathing and oblation, as well as ignoring the ritual context.

15. There is inscriptional correlation for this usage in an inscription of NS 793 in Tanga Bāhāḥ, see Locke (1980), p. 399. David Gellner assures me that this is the term still used to denote the ritual bathing of an image.
16. Gellner (1992), pp. 301–2 has used the case of modern Newar Buddhism to put forward a model of negotiating between esoteric and exoteric meanings of a ritual which is also helpful in understanding both the medieval form and its Indian precursor.
17. This refers specifically to the poṣadha-vrata.
18. Usually said to be four.
19. The name Buṃgamati or Bugama is not mentioned in the text, and on internal literary evidence the text's focal figure is Karuṇāmaya rather than Buṃgadyaḥ specifically. However, as late as the nineteenth century Nāth yogīs from Jodhpur seeking the text devoted to Buṃgadyaḥ (in this case, as Matsyendranath) and his yātrā were given the GKV.
20. See [iconbouddh] and discussion in Douglas (1997).
21. Petech infers further instances, for instance in Vaiśākha of NS 448. [mhm {p. 111}] I am reluctant to include these as certain, when the dating of the festival itself is being established. The supposed participation of Jayarudramalla in NS 433 [mhn {p. 109}] is a misreading; see Vajracarya Malla (1985), pp. 99, 146 for better translations.
22. GRV V[1] 27kha–28ka and Petech [y mhn {pp. 118–9}].
23. GRV V[2] 49kha and see Petech [y mhn {pp. 118–20}].
24. GRV V[2] 63Ka-kha.
25. See Petech [y mhn {p. 152}] on Jayasiṃha Rāṃa of the Rāmavardhanas.
26. [jayabodhgaya] This inscription may be influenced by the *Lokeśvaraśatakam* of Vajradatta.
27. Holt (1991), and discussion in Douglas (1997).
28. The pathfinding discussion in [Mus 1935] needs revision in the light of archeological and theoretical advances that make a more rigorous discussion of the relation between Mahāyāna Buddhism and the throne possible.

    One problem is simply where to begin looking. There are isolated textual sources, but (for instance) the 13th chapter of the *Suvarṇaprabhāsa Sūtra* [Bagchi 1967, Vajracarya 1988] has no ritual content at all; the final chapter of the GKV is concerned with the welfare of the kingdom and is addressed to a king but again lacks any ritual.
29. Thus see, for instance, Dirks (1993), pp. 38ff.

30. So in Java, for example, by the mid-thirteenth century, Vajrayāna and Śaivism have been mixed together, such that King Vishnuvardhana, dies in 1268 and his ashes are divided between two shrines. At one (Chandi Melri) he is worshipped as Śiva; at the other (Chandi Djago) he is Amoghapaśa. Hall (1981), pp. 81ff.
31. GRV V[1] 29ka; Vajracarya Malla (1985), p. 131. The Lalitpur Mallas following Śrīnivas identified themselves as children of, or incarnations of, Lokeśvara.
32. See [gpy], Tucci (1956), and Naraharinath, as well as the discussion of the succession and Sa skya influence in Vitali (1996), pp. 456ff. The inscription attempts to legitimate the effective absorption of the Ya.rtse throne into that of Pu 'rang; but the Blue Annals, among other Tibetan sources, notes that the Ya.rtse dynasty has in fact ended. The succession from this point onwards is rather hazy.
33. He is named in two separate inscriptions, one belonging to a family feudatory of about 1288 CE [Vidyavinda 1914] and a second of Ādityamalla in 1316 CE [Adhikary 1988].
34. For Krācalla, see the problematic inscription in Atkinson (1884), LS 74 of Sāhanapāla, LS 83 of Puruṣottamasiṃha (which [Adhikary 1988] leaves out), and if Petech's objections are not well founded then we must also consider the two trident inscription noted by Prinsep at JRAS V: 340 and 482.
35. Taking *abuṭha* for *abhūt*, following A. Sanderson.
36. mhn (p. 227), and Vajracarya Malla (1985), p. 219, f. 10.
37. Petech says here, 'VK gives the date 414 for the second invasion, which is a palpable mistake.' [y Mhn {n. 3, 102}] He takes the date to be a error for 410, which see below. In fact, from the GRV it would appear that the second visit (*dvitīya vāra*) came in 409 Phālguṇ; the mistake is probably not scribal, but factual.
38. mhn (p. 227) and Vajracarya Malla (1985), p. 219, f. 10.
39. *dvāko* should probably be read as *dakwo* = *'all'*. The proceeding phrase (dumvisyamĪchāyā) is obscure; Malla reads it as describing offerings at Paśupati, and Petech avoids translating it. The term *uprahātha* may refer to a mark or inscription placed above the western gate.
40. Adhikary (1988) (App. B xiii) citing from Naraharinath (1958), p. 26 and Naraharinath (1956), p. 80.
41. gpy (pp. 93–4) The existence of graffiti naming Ripumalla is not conclusive proof of his presence, but the fact that there are two of them in the same year is strongly suggestive.
42. Richardson (1977) cited in gpy (p. 93).
43. As the GRV reads, it could be describing either the date in which he sacked Nuwakoṭh, or the date on which Jītarimalla took *darśan* of Buṃgadyaḥ; the verb (*kāyā*) is a conjuct form. See the discussion above.

44. I have not yet seen similar evidence for any other member of the dynasty, which would confirm the identification with Lokeśvara as a dynastic trait.
45. The first visit is recorded in GRV $V^2$44 ka; the second begins in GRV $V^1$27 kha, is described in VK 12, continues and ends in GRV $V^2$46 ka.
46. GRV V248 ka. It is possible that the reason there is no ruler named is that the Khasas involved were not raiders, but something more like a garrison put in place in 454, or even a well-armed trading community.
47. See 3.2 above.
48. If Petech is right to take V^2 45 kha as referring to the yātrā of Buṃgadyaḥ this would be mere weeks after Ādityamalla's last visit to Lalitpur.

References

Adhikary, S. M., 1988, *The Khāśa Kingdom: A Trans Himalayan Empire of the Middle Ages*, Jaipur–New Delhi: Nirala Publications.

Atkinson, Edwin T., 1884, *The Himalayan Districts of the North-Western Provinces of India: Volume XI. North-Western Provinces Gazetteer.* The Himalayan Districts covers vols. X-XII of the *North-Western Provinces Gazetteer*, Allahabad: North-Western Provinces and Oudh Government Press.

Bagchi, S., ed., 1967, *Suvarṇaprabhāsasūtra,* Buddhist Sanskrit Texts 8, Darbhanga: Mithila Institute.

Dirks, Nicholas B., 1993, *The Hollow Crown: Ethnohistory of an Indian Kingdom;* 2nd edn, Ann Arbor: University of Michigan.

Douglas, W.B., 1997, 'History and Cult of the Guṇakāraṇḍavyūha', Unpublished Master Thesis, contains edition and translation of chapter 19 of the GKV.

Foucher, Alfred, 1905, *Étude sur l'iconographie Bouddhique,* Paris, Bibliothèque de l'Ecote des Havtes Etudes 13.

Gellner, David N., 1992, *Monk, Householder, and Tantric Priest: Newar Buddhism and its Hierarchy of Ritual, Cambridge Studies in Social and Cultural Anthropology 84.* Cambridge: Cambridge University Press.

Hall, D.G.E., 1981, *A History of South-East Asia*, 4th edn, London: Macmillan.

Holt, John, 1991, *Buddha in the Crown: Avalokiteśvara in the Buddhist Traditions of Sri Lanka*, Oxford: Oxford University Press.

Lewis, Todd T., 1996, 'A Chronology of Newar-Tibetan Relations in the Kathmandu Valley', in Siegfried Lienhard (ed.), *Change and Continuity: Studies in the Nepalese Culture of the Kathmandu Valley*, 149–66. Orientalia, VII. Turin: CESMEO.

Locke S.J., John K., 1980, *Karunamaya: The Cult of Avalokitesvara-Matsyendranath in the Valley of Nepal*, Kathmandu: Sahayogi Prakashan.

Manandhar, Thakur Lal, 1986, *Newari-English Dictionary*, New Delhi: Agam Kala Prakashan.

Mus, Paul, 1935, 'Barabuḍur: les origines du stūpa et la transmigration. Essai d'archéologie religieuse comparée. Sixième partie: Genèse de la bouddhologie mahāyāniste', *Bulletin de l'E'cole Française d'Extrême Orient* 34, pp. 175–400.

Naraharinath, Yogi, 1958 (Śāka 1880), *Rudrākṣaraṇya Māhātmyam*, Kathmandu: Tārak Bahādur Shāha.

________, 1956 (2013 VS), *Itihāsa Prakāśa: Volume II*, Kathmandu: Itihāsa Prakāśaka Saṃgha.

Naudou, Jean, 1968, *Les Bouddhistes Kaśmīriens au Moyen Age*, Annales du Musée Guimet: Bibliothèque d'Études LXVIII, Paris: Musée Guimet.

Petech, Luciano, 1980, 'Ya-T'se, Gu-ge, Pu-raṅ: A New Study', *Central Asiatic Journal* XXIV, pp. 85–111.

________, 1984, *Mediaeval History of Nepal*, (c. 750–1482), 2nd thoroughly revised edn Serie Orientale Roma LIV. Rome IsMEO.

Richardson, Hugh E., 1977, 'The Jo Khang Cathedral of Lhasa', in Alexander MacDonald and Y. Imaeda (eds.), *Essais sur 1'art du Tibet*, 187ff, Paris: CNRS.

Sanyal, Niradbandhu, 1929, 'A Buddhist Inscription from Bodh-Gaya of the Reign of Jayaccandradeva- V.S. 124x', *Indian Historical Quarterly* V, pp. 14–27.

Tucci Guiseppe, 1956, *A Preliminary Report on Two Scientific Expeditions in Nepal*, Rome: IsMEO.

Vajrācārya, Dhanavarja and Kamal Prakash Malla (eds and translation), 1985, *The Gopālarājavaṃśāvalī*, Nepal Research Centre Publication 8. Also contains the *Kaisher Vaṃśāvalī*, Weisbaden: Franz Steiner Verlag.

Vajrācārya, Āśākāji, (ed. trans. and comm.), 1988, *Suvarṇaprbhāsa Sūtra*, Lalitpur: Nepāla Buddha Prakāśan.

Vidyavinoda, Vinoda Vihari, 1914, 'Two Inscriptions from Bodh-Gaya', *Epigraphica Indica* XII, pp. 27–30, 2 plates included, Edition of Aśokacalla, LS51 and Aśokacalla, LS74.

Vitali, Roberto, 1996, *The Kingdoms of Gu.ge Pu.hrang According to mNga'.ris rgyal.rabs by Gu.ge mkhan.chen Ngag.dbang grags.pa*, Dharmasala: Tho.ling gtsug.lag.khang lo.gcig.stong 'khor.ba'i rjes.mdzad sgo'i sgrig tshogs.chung.

Comments

Véronique Bouillier

The Argument

William Douglas' argument focuses upon the deity Buṃgadyaḥ: what was his ritual of worship and who were performing this ritual. The Newar Malla kings worshipped Buṃgadyaḥ as their tutelary deity and the bath was a state ritual. But some kings, the western Mallas, also came to the Valley and performed a *puja* to Bungadya around the fourteenth century. Why?

In fact we have this testimony only for two western Malla kings: Jitarimalla came as a raider three times and, among fights and destructions, made a visit to Buṃgadyaḥ two times in AD 1289 and 1290; then Ripumalla came in 1313 but only as a pilgrim. All the three worships were made in Phālguṇ, thus their religious calendar was different from the one of the Newars. Douglas's conclusion is that the cult of Buṃgadyaḥ by these western Mallas is related to their own worship of Lokeśvara as a state deity in their Karnali kingdom.

I focus my comments on the topic of religious affiliation of the Khāsas and also on Lokeśvara.[1]

The Khāsas, a Medieval Buddhist Dynasty?

My first comment is on the strong affirmation that the Khāsas were a medieval Buddhist dynasty. The fact that they were supporting Buddhism is quite certain but they were not only Buddhist, as they were also supporting Hinduism, building temples and praying Hindu gods.

Here are some examples and a few quotations.

First from somebody not mentioned: Prayag Raj Sharma. He made a survey of the art and architecture of the Karnali Basin, around

1970, and described, of course, many stupas but also many temples in the *śikhara* style of the Kumaon Katyuri period. He says that:

The sectarian character of the temples can be exactly determined only in a few cases. In the temples of Kimugaon, Ukhadi, Mehelmudi, Manma and Chilkhaya, the Śivalingas are still intact inside the cellas. . . . Similarly, the flame-shrines of *Sirasthān, Nābhisthān* and *Pādukāsthān* and the double-shrines of Dullu Chaur as well as the temple of Manma show a four armed Gaṇeśa (1972: 22).

On the basis of architectural and sculptural remains as well as inscriptions, P.R. Sharma comes to the following conclusion about Punyamalla's and Pṛthivīmalla's inscriptions (mainly the one on the Dulluh Kirtisthambha in AD 1357).

The gods invoked in the inscription in order to ensure the perpetuity of the landgrant show that the same honour is bestowed on the brahmanical gods as to the buddhist. . . . In the Dullu Kirtistha bha the inscription begins with an invocation to Gaṇeśa. Other relevant analogies in it are drawn from the brahmanical pantheon. Yet the chant of *om mani padme hum* persists at the top of the inscription [with a drawing of a stupa, I think]. This tells of remarkable spirit of harmony and acceptance between the two faiths propagated by the rulers of the kingdom with the least prejudice (1972: 18).

I now quote Adhikary (1988). He also says that 'Buddhism seems to have been the court religion of the Khasa Kingdom'. But he adds: 'however there was no discrimination between Hinduism and Buddhism. The Khasa kings were extremely tolerant in the matter of religion. The Brahmans declared the Khasa rulers as the living incarnation of divine Viṣṇu. . . From the epigraphic evidence, it appears that Hinduism was also gaining ground in the court of the Khasa Kingdom since the reign of Krāchalla' (early thirteenth century, 1207–23). And Adhikary comments on the Baleśvara inscription of Krāchalla:

The Baleśvara temple inscription of Krāchalla provides an example of the religious toleration of the Khasa rulers. The inscription mentions Krāchalla as an ardent devotee of Lord Buddha. At the same time they equally revered Ekrudra Baleśvara, the Hindu deity, by offering worship and donating lands. The inscription states: 'The donor of lands gain the favour of Āditya, Varuna, Brahma and Viṣṇu as also of Soma, Hutasana and the god holding the trident'. (1988: 84)

This confirms the religious orientation of the Khasa rulers to both Buddhism and Hinduism, in my opinion as having a common tantric background.

In fact I find a confirmation of this double orientation in Douglas's argument since in all the cases of worship in the Kathmandu valley by the Khasas, they not only paid a visit to Bungadya but also to Paśupati. There was never an exclusively Buddhist pilgrimage or worship. Ripumalla as well as Jītari (second and third visit) worshipped Buddhist as well as Hindu deities, and Buṃgadyaḥ does not seem to be more important than Śiva Paśupati. They surely got legitimation and 'borrowed the charisma' of Lokeśvara but also of Paśupati.

A comparison with the raiding visit of Mukunda Sen can be interesting, even if this invasion occured much later (end of the sixteenth century) than what is mentioned in the *Gopālarāja Vaṁśāvali,* as Mahesh Raj Pant (1981) has shown. The different accounts of this invasion give many details about the worship of Buṃgadyaḥ by Mukunda Sen who invaded Lalitpur during the bathing ceremony of the god, and seeing the power of the deity gave him a silver necklace. This worship did not stop him from destroying many temples afterwards and thus provoking the anger of Paśupatinath.

The Personality of Buṃgadyaḥ

Who is Bunga? How is the identification with Avalokiteśvara made? I think Bungadiya was a very local name (form the Newari word: Bunga, pond, spring) and the question is as follows: is Buṃgadyaḥ an old local deity later on encompassed by Avalokiteśvara, or is Buṃgadyaḥ just the local name of Avalokiteśvara?

As Douglas argues, the link of Avalokiteśvara with kinship is conspicuous everywhere in South Asia and thus his importance for the Khāsa kingdom is not surprising.

Locke gives us a long list of examples of royal worship of Avalokiteśvara, beginning with the Indian king Harsa: 'When Harsa was requested by his ministers to ascend the throne, he went to the statue of Avalokiteśvara to seek guidance. He came to realise that it was the will of Avalokiteśvara that he should devote himself to the affairs of the state' (1980: 411). We have also the example of

Cambodia with Angkor and the status of the Bayon. And also: 'The rulers of Yunan from the tenth to the thirteenth centuries worshipped Avalokiteśvara' and he became the tutelar divinity of the ruling family. In Tibet, the Dalai Lama is considered to be an incarnation of Avalokiteśvara (*Ibid*.: 413).

But according to Locke nowhere in the Buddhist world is there such a profusion of different forms of Avalokiteśvara as in the Kathmandu valley. This multiplicity as well as the characteristics of Avalokiteśvara explain how easily Avalokiteśvara can be seen as an encompassing and syncretic deity. His main characteristic is his compassion and his ability to take different forms, to incarnate under various aspects to be accessible, to teach, to give guidance to every sort of people. He has male and female aspects, he can be any other god in disguise. His link with Śiva in a tantric background is quite obvious and well illustrated by this custom related by Locke, of putting a bone ornament on Buṃgadyaḥ's head on the day of Śivarātri (*Ibid*.: 418).

This leads us to a later period, much later than the Khāsa encounters but important for understanding how Hinduism and Buddhism combine around Avalokiteśvara, or how Avalokiteśvara became one with Mātsyendranāth, the Nāth Siddha, the guru of Gorakhnāth, the lord of fishes or more exactly 'He whose lord is the lord of fishes' (White 1996: 223).

We can perhaps find a transition from Avalokeśvara to Matsyendranāth with Lu¥-pā: a ninth century Buddhist Siddhācārya, known in the Tibetan *Grub-thob* (a fourteenth century translation of a twelfth text by Abhayadatta: 'Caturaβ¥tisiddha pravṛtti', Acts of the 84 Siddhas) and whose name means 'Venerable red-fish' (id.: 224). His name Lu¥pāda figures in an old Newar song as the one of the deity Buṃgadyaḥ (Loke 1980: 426).

We know that Avalokiteśvara was represented at least once in a fish form: at Ratnagiri in Orissa, the bust of multiplated Avalokiteśvara image was found to be superimposed upon the image of a large fish (White 1996/7: 224).

As a conclusion to this comment on Hinduism and Buddhism and the figure of Lokeśvara, here is one instance of Lokeśvara as a pivot, a linchpin of a religious change from Buddhism to Hinduism. There is a monastery in Karnataka (Kadri near Mangalore) with Lokeśvara status set in AD 968. This monastery is now the abode of Nāth Yogis who tell that the Nāth converted from Buddhism to Hinduism after the collapse of their monastery. The main temple is dedicated to Mañjunāth, and in its middle, the statue of Lokeśvara and the inscription 'the image of the god Lokeśvara was placed in the beautiful *vihāra* of Kadirikā' in AD 968. Local tradition says that Mañjunāth appeared in the form of a three-faced image of Loknāth to the three yogi gurus Gorakhnāth, Matsyendranāth and Íār ganāth (White 1996: 94; see also Mitchell 1990: I, 458).

To return to Nepal and to the Hindu-Buddhist problematic, in a recent account of the coming of Matsyendranāth in the valley, we find the usual story of Gorakhnāth and the drought but with some differences. Some Nepali pilgrims pass Gorakhnāth and say: 'King of Yogis Mahendra Deva (sic) is the ruler of Nepal. He has embraced the Buddhist faith and he has told us to do so. . . He is giving us great discomfort. It would be a favour if you come to Nepal and help us. . . Gorakhnāth went to the outskirts of the town of Lalitpatan and settled down beside the bank of the river Bagmati. . . . He performs austerities and says, "The rain will not fall as long as I sit here." It does not rain for three years. The king learns about him, and consults astrologers who answer: "Great king, he will not get up from his seat until the oppressions that are falling on the followers of Matsyendra cease". The king organizes a great procession with the image of Matsyendra on a chariot to make Gorakhnāth stand up and salute his guru. The rain fell and the king was ashamed of his evil actions and fell at Gorakhnāth's feet and begged: "King of yogis, forgive me. From now on, no oppression will befall the followers of Matsyendranāth". But the king is not true to his word. He still persecutes the Hindus, thus Gorakhnāth plans to remove him from his throne and to give the kingship to one of his devotee's sons Vasant. After some episodes, Vasant is adopted by Mahendra Deva and becomes king (it was during the fifth century, like the Vasant Deva in genealogies), introducing the cult of Matsyendra and the procession' (Digby 1993: 66–8).

This is my Śivamargi presentation of your Buddhamargi otherness.

Notes

1. Though I will not comment on precise historical points or the translation, I wonder if the translation of *argha* as done by K.P. Malla and D. Vajaracarya cannot refer to a kind of *abhisekha*?

References

Adhikari, S.M., 1988, *The Khasa Kingdom*, Jaipur: Nirala Publications.

Digby, Simon, 1993, 'The Cycle of Gorakhnath', manuscript.

Locke, J.K., 1980, *Karunamaya,* Kathmandu: Sahayogi Prakashan.

Mitchell, G., 1990, *The Penguin Guide to the Monuments of India,* London: Viking.

Pant, M.R., 1981, 'King Mukund Sen's Invasion of Kathmandu Valley', *Regmi Research Series*, vol. 13, no. 12 and ff.

Sharma, P.R., 1972, *Preliminary Study of the Art and Architecture of the Karnali Basin, West Nepal,* Paris: CNRS.

White, D.G., 1997, *The Alchemical Body,* Chicago: University of Chicago Press.

From Cultural Hierarchies to a Hierarchy of Multiculturalisms:

The Case of the Newars of the Kathmandu Valley, Nepal

David N. Gellner

Multiculturalism has become a much publicized term and its study an academic growth industry in recent years. Vertovec (1998) cites a plethora of 'multicultural' textbooks on everything from the arts and grief management through banking to—most surprisingly to those who might have supposed that at least some areas of enquiry would be culture-blind—mathematics. Particular arguments for or against multiculturalism grow from specific political and cultural contexts. Charles Taylor's (1994 [1992]) influential formulation advocating a procedural liberalism acknowledging collective goals has its roots in Canada's Quebec problem, as he himself admits. All the same, there is a broad structural similarity to the way in which the advanced capitalist states of North America, Europe, and Australasia face similar problems of devising more inclusive institutions and practices for previously marginalized minorities, even if the solutions are very different.[1] Everywhere there is a shared multicultural assumption that—in whatever is the chosen relevant domain (and the possibilities, as Vertovec shows, are almost endless)—cultures should be treated equally. In pursuing and institutionalizing this idea, the so-called 'pluralist' states, such as Trinidad, Mauritius, and Indonesia, may be said to have 'got there first'. In the case to be discussed in this paper, however, it is the influence of the rather later global (and western-dominated) ideology of 'mulitculturalism' which is making itself felt.

The formulation 'all cultures should be treated equally' begs a number of important questions. Taylor is particularly hostile to the idea that all cultures should be presumed *a priori* to have generated products of equal value (Taylor 1994: 68–9), since it undermines the possibility of any criterion by which such a judgement could even be made. Taylor may find such a demand philosophically incoherent, but, as the case considered below will, I hope show, the demand is none the less heartfelt and springs from political circumstances which have analogues in many other parts of the world. More to the point, the formulation assumes, as Taylor himself seems to do that 'there are other cultures and we have to live together. . .' (*ibid*.: 72; cf. p. 66). In other words, he assumes that the world is divided up into separate cultures, that everyone has their own, and that—exceptional cases aside—it is only in recent times that societies are becoming 'increasingly multicultural' and 'more porous' (*ibid*.: 63). In fact, the 'one person, one culture' model is highly misleading even today and *a fortiori* for premodern times. The preindustrial world, as described by historians and anthropologists, provides evidence of a vast range of kinds of cultural allegiance, with people switching back and forth between 'cultures' combining more than one cultural identity in different ways, or changing gradually—or occasionally suddenly—over time.[2]

An important and relevant conceptual distinction, grounded in solid ethnographic fieldwork, has been advanced by Gerd Baumann in his book, *Contesting Cultures* (1996), which describes competing discourses of 'community' in the west London suburb of Southall. His main theoretical point is that there are two discourses which many people, especially activists, are capable of moving between almost seamlessly, depending on context: Baumann calls them the official discourse and the demotic discourse. According to the official discourse, Southhall is made up of five 'communities' (Sikhs, Hindu, Muslims, Afro-Caribbeans, and Whites) each of which (my summary):

1. has its own culture,
2. is structurally equivalent to other communities,
3. is—for all important purposes—internally homogeneous,
4. should respect each other's community, and
5. should be treated equally.

In the demotic discourse, by contrast, it is openly or implicitly acknowledged that each so-called community is riven by differences, often radical, and that there are other identities which powerfully cut across those of the five official communities. However, the official discourse survives, and indeed flourishes, because it is the only acceptable language in which claims to resources can be made in a nation-state committed (a) to the equality of all its citizens, and (b) to accepting the legitimacy of some communally inspired demands. It will be seen below that many of the debates between ethnic activists and others in Nepal are precisely about what is and should be acceptable 'official Nepalese discourse', with many ethnic activists themselves having doubts about whether caste organizations should be admitted to it.

The modern discourse of multiculturalism, in asserting that all cultures should be treated equally, implicity allows that cultures are not in fact equal and have not been treated equally. In the nineteenth century such unequal treatment was assumed by many people to be the only right and proper one. For example, it was considered both natural and good that the stronger and more 'civilized' English culture and language should displace Welsh and Irish in Britain, or that German should replace Slave tongues in central Europe. This hierarchical view of cultures as more or less 'civilized', more or less 'evolved', was fully in tune with the generally evolutionist background of nineteenth-century thought. It is, I would judge, still the predominant folk view of many, perhaps most, in western societies today. It is directly challenged by multiculturalism, and is openly avowed today only defensively or as part of Baumann's 'demotic discourse'. Even if many people believe in the hierarchical view, most realize that it is not 'politically correct' to say so in public.

Premodern Nepal and India, with their complex combinations of castes, religions, and other forms of community, provide still another form of the hierarchical organization of cultural difference. It would be misleading to conceptualize caste systems as hierarchies of ethnic groups, as Barth was tempted to do.[3] In fact castes within a specific geographically bounded locality share a great deal, just as north Americans of supposedly different 'ethnicity' in fact share a great deal. The crucial differences between the two situations, as will be described below, are that in premodern Nepal the multicultural assumptions—that (a) every person belongs to one and only one community, and (b) these communities should be treated equally—were conspicuously absent. The transformation of Newar identities that the present essay seeks to chart is precisely the attempt, encouraged by global egalitarianism as expressed through UN initiatives such as the Decade of Indigenous People begun in 1993, to introduce these two assumptions and impose them on a highly complex set of existing social arrangements. These arrangements were the outcome of centuries of praxis on the basis of the very opposite assumptions, namely, that (a) because of the sheer variability in and opacity of local practice, people can be members of several overlapping and contextually defined communities, and (b) difference implies hierarchy.

Themes and Paradoxes of Newar Identity

Sylvain Lévi (1905 I: 28) once famously compared the Kathmandu valley to a 'laboratory' where the history of medieval India could be seen working itself out (he was thinking in particular of the relationship of Buddhism to Hinduism, and the gradual eclipse of Buddhism in a context where kings were invariably Hindu). In the same way, within its small compass the valley could also be taken as a kind of 'laboratory'—or at least as a manageable case study—for observing the development of linguistic and cultural nationalism in South Asian context and the effect this has on long-established modes of 'ethnic' accommodation.

The Newars like to think of themselves as the indigenous people of the Kathmandu valley, but no one—not even the most ardent Newar cultural nationalist—believes that they all derive historically from one place or one gene pool. They are one people, with a common language and culture, but they are divided into twenty or more castes, each of which has its own myth of origin. They speak a

Tibeto-Burman language, but it is one that has been influenced at every level by the Newars' incorporation for at least 1700 years within the north Indian cultural world dominated by Indo-European tongues. Newar culture is very deeply South Asian, but many politically active Newars, particularly those favourable to communism, see themselves—at least in the relevant political contexts—as closer to the Chinese (as do some members of other Tibeto-Burman-speaking groups). The Newars are not defined by their practice of a religious tradition that marks them off from their neighbours: some of them are Buddhist, some are Hindu, and some, perhaps around half of them, respect and participate in the traditional practices of both religions.[4] The Newars are most definitely an urban population (even Newar villages have an urban 'feel') with a sophisticated artistic and literary heritage. But they are a minority (5.6 per cent) within the present kingdom of Nepal dominated by the Parbatiyas (Bahuns, i.e. Brahmins, and Chetris, i.e. Kshatriyas, are the two main Parbatiya high castes).[5]

The Parbatiyas' language, Nepali, is the official tongue; it is estimated that about one third of all Newars have adopted Nepali and given up speaking Newari (language loss is even higher among other groups, such as Magars, Thakalis, and Gurungs: Whelpton 1997: 59). In old-fashioned accounts of the kingdom of Nepal and in modern discourses descended from them, the Newars are often, quite misleadingly, lumped together with ethnic groups of hill regions, such as the Gurungs and the Magars, and thought of as a 'tribe' (see Table 4.1). Just how small the Newars are in South Asian

TABLE 4.1: Major castes and ethnic groups in Nepal according to the 1991 census (total population 18.5 million). See Whelpton (1997).

Parbatiyas		*Hill minorities*		*Plains (Tarai) groups*		*Others*	
Bahun	13	Magar	7	Tharu	6.5	Muslim	3.5
Chetri	18	Newar	5.6	Yadav	4		
Untouchables	9	Tamang	5.5	(+ many small			
		Rai	3	castes and 'tribes')			
		Gurung	2.4				
		Limbu	1.6				
Total	40		25		31		4 = 100

terms can be illustrated by the fact that any Newari newspaper would be delighted with a regular circulation of 3,000, whereas the south Indian Malayali daily, *Manorama*, has a print run of 9,00,000.

The coexistence of Buddhism and Hinduism within the Newar population—their sharing of cults, holy sites, pantheons, ritual practices, and religious concepts—might be seen as a paradigmatic case of 'communal' or 'religious harmony'. I have described this coexistence in terms of two key concepts: *multivalent symbols* (the sharing of cults and practices while naming and evaluating them differently) and *parallelism* (the existence of different but formally equivalent cults and practices) (Gellner 1992: ch. 3). The general context is one in which Hinduism and Buddhism are *in competition* with each other while simultaneously *sharing* fundamental assumptions both about religious salvation and the means to get it, and about the organization of social life. Thus solidarity or exclusion, equivalence or competition, can be stressed according to context or need. Some groups and individuals have a much greater stake in stressing equivalence than other, and they have found their point of view progressively disenfranchised. But most Newars do not assess each item of their culture and ask themselves if it is Hindu or Buddhist. (Such assessment, where it occurs, tends to be an ad hoc process). This religious coexistence has given rise to a pervasive government and even popular discourse of 'religious harmony' (*dharmik sahishnutā*) which, as discussed below, is propagated in school textbooks, tourist literature, and political speeches as characteristic of the country as a whole. Nepal is supposed to be simultaneously both a model of religious harmony and a Hindu state.

Such cultural paradoxes, if paradoxes they really are, were happily tolerated—and for the most part went unnoticed—in premodern times, when most ethnic identities, and Newar identity especially, were largely implicit. In the modern period, especially the panchayat era (1960–90), the state has propagated the idea that Nepalese citizens should have a single overarching national identity, and much rhetorical effort has gone into 'building nationalism' (*rāstriyatā*), as well as into propagating 'development' (*bikās*).[6] Both in the panchayat period and today the state is officially Hindu (to the frustration of many Buddhist and ethnic activists). Unlike in India, there is a single (Hindu-based) legal code, even for Muslims (Gaborieu 1993). Traditions in general are considered a valuable part of the nation's cultural heritage, but caste distinctions are no longer backed by the power of law. In the panchayat period distinctiveness was encouraged only in a folkloric sense; any political usage of ethnic or caste distinctions was illegal. The decennial national censuses recorded, but did not publish, figures for caste and ethnicity (these were released for the first time after 1990). Religious affiliation was regularly recorded, but only one answer was allowed: for many groups and individuals it would have been more ethnographically accurate had they been permitted to return both 'Hindu' and 'Buddhist' answers simultaneously, but this was not an option. For others 'Hindu' was a misleading label, used as the default option. However, at the same time, although listed as equal alternatives on the census form, the official position was that Buddhism, Jainism, and Sikhism were 'branches' of Hinduism, a view hotly contested by many Buddhist activists as demeaning. Islam and Christianity were more of a problem, and proselytization was strictly illegal.

Since 1990 it has been possible for activists to form organizations and register them. Religious practice has become much freer and apparently the Christian churches are booming. As will be discussed below, this has led to a great efflorescence of caste-and ethnic-based groups, where earlier only cultural and religious organizations were tolerated. All of these have had to wrestle with the same problem: their cultural and historical heritage includes numerous ambiguous, cross-cutting, and overlapping identities which have to be sorted out, rationalized, ignored, or 'reformed' in order to produce consistent, context-free, and legally enforceable criteria of identity. Such ambiguities were arguably a pervasive, and highly valued, feature of premodern Nepal and, though they played a larger part in preserving communal identities, their sheer complexity, contextuality, and locally fixed terms of reference, were powerful factors inhibiting 'ethnic' conflict.[7] These same ambiguities today represent a severe problem, requiring creative solutions, for modern activists, whether acting on an intra-Newar stage or on a broader inter-ethnic one. These problems are discussed below.

Who is a Newar?

The Kathmandu valley now houses the capital of the country, so it is both the centre of Nepal and the home of the Newars. Unlike other valleys of the 'middle hills', it is not a steep V-shape with only rare flatter areas suitable for intensive rice agriculture. It is a roughly circular bowl that was once a lake, both according to geologists and according to local mythology. Consequently its soil is deep and rich, and apparently inexhaustible, however, much is taken out to make bricks for the ever-expanding greater Kathmandu conurbation. From at least the fourth century CE, and almost certainly for some centuries before that, this rich farmland enabled the valley to support a degree of cultural elaboration (based on South Asian—Hindu and Buddhist—models) and numbers of ritual and artisan specialists that were simply inconceivable elsewhere in this part of the Himalayan foothills. This agricultural base enabled kingdoms to develop which then controlled the lucrative trans-Himalayan trade between Tibet and India; consequently the Newars count many merchants and businessmen among their number, and there have been Newar traders and artisans settled in Tibet for many centuries. This culture of the valley, with its famous pagoda temples, wood-carving, religious art, and festivals, is today usually thought of as typically Newar (as in the book by Macdonald and Vergati Stahl: *Newar Art: Nepalese Art during the Malla Period*).

The Newars of today think of the Malla kings of the thirteenth to eighteenth centuries as 'their' 'Newar' kings, displaced by the Parbatiya dynasty of the present ruler in 1796. But the Malla kings did not call themselves 'Newar'. The term seems to have been reserved for those high-caste, mainly Hindu, Kshatriya groups now collectively known as 'Srestha'; furthermore, we only have historical evidence for the term from the middle of the sixteenth century. Well into the nineteenth century the expression *sristha newa/niwa* was a kind of pleonasm. Only Sresthas were referred to in this way. Other castes were either not thought of as Newars at all, or thought of as Newars only in a secondary sense, for example, in that they spoke *newā-bhāy*, 'the language of the Newar', i.e. Newari. As in France, where the name of an elite (the Franks) eventually expanded its reference to include the whole population, so it happened with the term 'Newar'.[8]

This has led to a situation which I have dubbed the Srestha Paradox (Gellner 1986). The Sresthas were once thought of as the real Newars, the Newars *par excellence* (and in fact often still think of themselves in this way[9], even though others are contemptuous of their easy hybridity). But today they are the very Newars *least* likely to speak 'the language of the Newar' and *most* likely to be deliberately de-Newarizing their children by speaking Nepali to them, sending them to English-language boarding schools, and turning them, as they see it, into good citizens of modern Nepal and skilled performers in the global economy.

This old usage that restricts the label 'Newar' to Sresthas and denies it to other Newari-speaking castes still survives in many places in the hills, where Newar artisans and shopkeepers are found in bazaar towns throughout the kingdom and Newar peasants along its old trading routes. In these bazaars neither the Buddhist Sakyas and Vajracarya (frequently goldsmiths, Np. Bādā) nor the Khadgi butchers (Np. Kasā) are referred to as Newars. The same restrictive usage survives also in peripheral parts of the Newar heartland beyond the rim of the Kathmandu valley itself, e.g. in Panauti (Barré *et al.* 1981: 25n. 5). Even in the very centre of Newar culture, the three cities that were the capitals of the three Malla kingdoms in the eighteenth century—Kathmandu itself, Lalitpur, and Bhaktapur—the two essential castes at the very top and bottom of the Newars' internal hierarchy, the Brahmans and the Dyahla (untouchable sweepers), do not think of themselves as Newars. They speak of 'the Newars' and do not include themselves in this, even though other Newars think of them inclusively in many contexts.[10]

It is interesting to note that many ordinary Parbatiya in the valley think of Newar as one bloc and are unaware that there are specifically Newar Brahmans (it is true they are very few in number, but all Newars know of their existence). I have known Parbatiyas indignantly to reject the phrase 'Newar Brahman' as a contradiction in terms: 'everyone knows' that there are Newars (primarily Sresthas) and Brahmans (the very numerous Parbatiya Bahuns who make up some 12 per cent of the country's population) and never the twain shall meet: indeed the top prizes within the Establishment are often fought over between Sresthas and Bahuns. Many Newar Brahmans themselves are quite happy to go along with this perception. They have adopted the same surnames as some Parbatiya Brahmans (such as Rimal, Sharma, and Subedi) and they have switched within four or five generations from being Newari-speaking (and often monolingual) to being overwhelmingly Nepali-speaking.

It should be clear, then, that there are important caste cleavages within the Newars and no serious account of Newar identity can be given without taking these cleavages into account. A simplified model of the Newar caste hierarchy is given in Table 4.2 (the details vary from settlement to settlement).

Not only are there important cleavages in terms of status among the Newars, there are also very significant differences between Newars in different parts of their 'homeland', the Kathmandu valley and its surrounding areas, especially the Banepa valley on its eastern edge. Local connections are strong, and there are dialectal differences severe enough between east and west of the valley to ensure that many Bhaktapur or Dhulikhel Newar visiting the capital prefer to speak in Nepali rather than run the risk of raised eyebrows at their rustic accent and variations in vocabulary. Even between Kathmandu and Lalitpur, which now form one continuous conurbation straddling the Bagmati river that runs between them, there are considerable differences in attitudes, as well as differences in accent that locals can detect.

Even if we define Newars in the most modern and inclusivist manner, there have always been others who are universally agreed *not to* be Newars living in their midst. There have been Kashmiri Muslim traders established in Kathmandu, for example, since at least the sixteenth century. There have been some Indian, Hindu groups, for example Jha Brahmans, who have always remained apart from the Newars and vehemently deny being Newars even when they speak Newari. Many other groups from India did get absorbed into the Newar caste hierarchy, often as 'caste sub-groups' within a pre-existing caste (Gellner 1995a: 19–22). Around the edge of the valley there are Tamangs, as well as many smaller groups who have an ambiguous relationship to the Newars (Toffin 1981). It was the Tamangs who provided the labour reserve that supported the trade and building of the valley elite. Even before Prithvi Narayan Shah conquered the Kathmandu valley in 1769 there were many Parbatiyas settled in their scattered homesteads within the valley and knowledge of their language, now called Nepali, was widespread. Since 1769 their number has grown and the valley is home now to almost as many Parbatiyas as Newars.

Since 1951, and the collapse of the Rana regime, there has been massive immigration to the valley: of refugees from Tibet, of hill people settling in the capital, and of poor Indian labourers as well as numerous skilled Indian tradesmen (electricians and barbers, example). In short, Kathmandu and its suburbs are now multi-ethnic, multi-religious, and highly complex places: the Newars are no longer secure in their own place. In the words of K.P. Malla, Professor of English at Tribhuvan University and himself a high-caste Hindu Newar, 'With his social and cultural fabric of life slowly being destroyed, the average middle-class Newar of Kathmandu today feels like a displaced Nawab of Lucknow after the Loot. He feels like an alien in his own home pushed too hard against the wall by ever-stiffer social and economic competition with some 20,000 in-migrants every year' (1992: 24).

From an emic or internal point of view there is no doubt that this captures well the alienation and disadvantages perceived by the Newar. Furthermore, the pace and degree of change, and the massive increase in the intensity of interchange with the outside world, have led to a significant degree of disorientation or 'anomie' on the part of middle-class youth in Kathmandu, according to Mark Liechty's recent study (Liechty 1994). However, from an etic or outside viewpoint, the Newars are actually *part* of the establishment. This is brought home very vividly in Todd Ragsdale's account of education in a Gurung village. Questions for the national exams—held throughout the country for those in class 3 for the first time in 1974—presupposed knowledge of the religious geography of the Kathmandu valley. This obviously favoured Newars and Bahun-Chetris living in, or familiar with, the capital and its environs (Ragsdale 1989: 152–4). A recent, highly sophisticated statistical analysis uses data from the 1990 census in order to assess different ethnic groups' average quality of life along three axes: life expectancy, literacy and educational attainment, and standard of living. The Newars come out as the group with the highest quality of life in the whole country (Thapa 1995). There is, then a radical disjunction between the Newars' own sense of disadvantage and other ethnic groups' perceptions of the Newars' elite status.

TABLE 4.2. Simplified model of the Newar caste hierarchy

(1) Priests:	(1a) Brahmans (Rajopadhyaya, Dyahbaju)—Hindu
	(1b) Vajracharyas (Gubhaji) and Sakyas—Buddhist
(2) Patrons/landholders:	(2a) Sresthas—mostly Hindu
	(2b) Tuladhars (Uray)—Buddhist
(3) Agriculturalists:	Maharaja, Dangol, Suwal (Jyapu)
(4) Artisans and ritual specialists:	numerous small castes
(5) Milksellers/butchers :	(water-unacceptale but not untouchable): Khadgi (Np. Kasai)
(6) Sweepers (untouchable) :	Dyahla (Np. Pode)

Note: This is an idealized model showing the main distinct kinds of social positions; as in all caste systems many, in some cases most, members of the caste in question do not follow the traditional profession which is the focus of their identity. The Hindu/Buddhist distinction loses importance in the middle and lower parts of the hierarchy. For more detail on the criteria used to make these discriminations, see Gellner (1995a: 16–19).

For Newar activists, including their target audience of young and educated Newars, the question of how to define a Newar is a pressing one. They have no distinctive religion (some are Hindu, some Buddhist, and there are even converts to Christianity and Islam among their number today). Although there are certain 'typically Newar' festivals and rituals, there is none that is observed universally among them. This means that it is usually language that is used as a criterion (see appendix 3 for the Newa Guthi's definition). But activists have to face the fact that many Newars outside the Kathmandu valley no longer speak Newari and, even more galling, many educated mothers within it, especially among the Sreshtas, now systematically speak Nepali to their children. This happens even in the families of some Newar activists themselves.

For the New Year 1117 according to the Nepal Samvat (November 1996), a magazine called *Nasañcā,* published from Panauti, asked five leading figures in the Newari language movement the same three questions:

1. What is the (defining) sign by which one may recognize Newars and what should we do to ensure it survives?
2. Are Newars abandoning Newari because they have to or because they want to?
3. It is said that Newars have aroused others while they themselves remain asleep. Is this true and, if so, why?

The first author, Baldev Juju, is an interesting case, a Rajopadhyaya Brahman who is happy to claim to be a Newar (unlike most of his caste fellows). His answer to the first question was that there are three signs for recognizing Newars: (1) culture/customs (*samskrti*), (2) language, and (3) feeling pride in being a Newar. This answer has the virtue of invoking multiple criteria, which are hierarchically arranged, so that one can be more or less of a Newar. It recognizes that there are both objective and subjective aspects to being a Newar, and that it is, like most such identities, an evaluation. Furthermore, it corresponds rather well (though this is implicit) to three major divisions among the Newars: (1) those who live outside the valley and have a residue of Newar customs (performing the *bel* fruit mock marriage for their daughters, worshipping the god Bhimsen, having death *guthis* to ensure cremation) but do not speak Newari; (2) those Newars within the valley who observe the customs and speak the language (among themselves if not to their children) but for whom the active assertion of Newar identity is largely irrelevant to their everyday life; (3) Newar activists, a small and divided group of 1200 people who organize literary conferences and demonstrations, petition the government, try to mobilize others, and publish poems, plays, novels, magazines, and newspapers in Newari.[11]

Stages in the Development of Nationalism

On the basis of eastern Europe, Hroch (1985) has specified three stages through which ethnic nationalist movements pass. Initially, there is a romantic concern with carrying out essential historical and folkloristic studies of a given culture. The intellectuals who do these studies may or may not themselves belong to the group. In the second stage the intellectuals begin political campaigns for recognition of their chosen language and/or culture. In the third stage the movement acquires mass support from classes such as peasants and workers who were previously indifferent to it. As a model of a historical process and for comparative purposes, this has some merit. In certain circumstances the first two stages may be combined. In the Newar case, there is a sense in which the first two stages were inverted.

Among the Newars the earliest activists were concerned, not with recording Newar customs (that came later), but with celebrating and teaching the language. As a caste society, literacy was traditionally the preserve of the high castes, so it is hardly surprising that most of the earliest Newar intellectuals concerned with Newari and Newar culture were from the Srestha caste. It was precisely among them that there first emerged (perhaps as early as the mid-nineteenth century) the practice of speaking Nepali to their children—particularly to the boys, so that they would have an advantage in obtaining government employment. Today the practice is very widespread among all castes and nearly universal among Srestha of the three big cities. Among the high caste and aspiring middle class, only a slight distinction is made between girls and boys today: both must achieve academically, and the marriageability of both sexes is improved by academic attainments. A model of Newari-language competence by generation for urban Sresthas would be very similar to that produced by McDonald (1989: 352–3, n. 4) for the Breton language: great-grandparents, especially female, being comfortable only in Newari, and their great-grandchildren understanding nothing but Nepali; in the intervening generations the grandparents would use Newari among themselves but Nepali to their children and the parents are likely to have a good passive understanding of Newari, but to prefer not to use it unless they have to. The difference with the Breton situation lies in the existence of castes. Since other castes have not so universally abandoned speaking Newari to their children, there are frequently contexts where otherwise Nepali-speaking Sresthas are forced to participate actively in speaking Newari. And indeed there are many non-Newars (Bahuns, Chetri, Tamangs) brought up in Kathmandu who are fluent (but rarely literate) in Newari because it is used so often in public even though it has no official status.

The immediate concern of the first Newari cultural nationalists of the 1920s and 30s was to discourage their fellow Newars from speaking Nepali to their children. In the words of Yogbir Singh (a Newar poet and activist), they had to counteract the feeling that speaking Newari made one 'like a Jyapu', i.e., the Maharajan peasant caste, the largest group among the Newars. This has been the dominant theme of the Newari language movement ever since. The movement has therefore attempted modestly to attack elitist or hierarchical thinking; but it has not really been populist. It is true that the 'Jyapu' are often said to be the 'true Newars' both in the sense of the truly autochthonous people of the valley and in the sense of the most culturally conservative. But that has not led to any cult of the simple peasant, any intellectual affection of peasant ways. Disdain for physical labour and for simplicity of manners and language goes too deep for that.[12] In so far as traditional ways were extolled by Newar activists, it was, until about 1994–5, usually the elaborate cultural forms typical of the high castes that were held up as a model.[13] The argument aimed especially at high-caste Sresthas was not that Newars ought to imitate the authenticity of the illiterate peasant, but that they ought *not* to betray the highly sophisticated traditions and language of their own (high-caste) forebears.

However, when the state, mass media, or tourist hotels require Newar representatives for the folkloric display of Nepalese dancing, Jyapu (Maharajan) dances and drums are often used, thus reconfirming the association between Newarness and peasant ways. Ironically, the most popular 'Jyapu–Jyapuni' dance, involving the flirtatious gyrations of a male and female dancer, is Newar only in that the dancers wear traditional Maharajan dress: the dance itself, shown innumerable times to tourists, and nowadays even used at revivalist cultural shows organized by Newars themselves, seems to have been modelled entirely on those seen in Hindi movies.

Since 1994–5 there has been a sea change in this generally anti-populist stance of Newar cultural nationalism, but significantly it has been brought about by Jyapus themselves, through their own organizations which are discussed below. These do indeed hold programmes that involve the glorification of peasant culture. For example, on the visit of the German President in November 1996 numerous ceremonial 'gates' (*dhwakā*) were erected on the main roads along which he and his wife were to be driven; in Lalitpur, nearby a conventional gate put up by the local municipality, the Lalitpur-based Jyapu Samaj built a gate elaborately decorated with old-fashioned hand-held farming implements, with straw shoes (now rarely seen), and locally produced vegetables. The parents of the young men (and occasionally women) who organize such events are (or, perhaps more frequently, were) peasants, but they themselves are not. Thus, the furthest that Newar intellectuals go in the direction of populism is to say that every group should maintain its own traditions, and to allow that the Maharjans or Jyapus should do so particularly, given their past history of exploitation and their centrality to Newar culture. So far as I know, however, no one has suggested that simplicity, or rough manners, are in themselves signs of greater authenticity.

The political framework within which the Newar language movement has had to operate has changed considerably (see Gellner, Pfaff-Czarnecka, and Whelpton 1997). Under the Ranas (1846–1951) they would expect little mercy. Being an activist for Newari was equivalent to being a political activist (many, it is true, were both). Many, if not most, of the early Newari writers spent periods in jail where they composed some of their best-known poetry. Although there was some overlap between Buddhist and Newari activists, it would be wrong to see the activists for Newari as solely or even predominantly Buddhist (Toffin 1993: 196). Even under the Rana regime, and continuing thereafter, there has been a complex relationship between Buddhist allegiance and Newar cultural nationalism. As far as *activists* go, there has, in most cases (and despite some prominent exceptions), been a marked preference *either* for Buddhist *or* for Newar cultural nationalist activism (Gellner 1986). Both types of activisms have arisen in opposition to the dominant nationalist discourse and ideology of the Nepalese state. As Pratyoush Onta (1996a, 1996b) has shown, this discourse was borrowed in large part from the nascent ethno-nationalism of Nepalis in Darjeeling. It celebrated 'Gorkha bravery', military conquests, Nepali hardiness and independence. But in taking the discourse over from Darjeeling, the contributions of *janajāti* (especially Gurung) soldiers and heroes were edited out. It is this 'brave Nepali' narrative that is celebrated in the National Museum at Chauni, Kathmandu, with its portraits of Nepali monarchs in martial poses and displays of their weapons and the weapons captured from their enemies. There is no place for the hill groups here, except as subaltern ranks in the army. And there is no place for the Newars at all, except as the effete and cowardly inhabitants of the Kathmandu valley vanquished in 1768–9 by Prithvi Narayan Shah the Great, Father of the Nation.

Under the panchayat regime (1962–90), this discourse continued and was synthesized with that of economic development (bikās) under the dynamic leadership of the king. Parties were banned, and the main justification for this was the encouragement they would give to 'communal', i.e. ethnic, competition. Indirectly, however, there is some evidence of an ethnic aspect to political competition. During the brief period when parties were permitted before the establishment of the panchayat system, support for the Gorkha Dal and Congress Party in Lalitpur in 1958–9 seems to have come from Parbatiyas and Newars respectively. Furthermore, the founders of Nepalese Communist Party in the 1950s were predominantly high-caste Newars, for all that today the Communist parties are run overwhelmingly by Parbatiya Bahuns. On the part of the government, Newari was subtly undermined and denied official recognition. Newari and Hindi news broadcasts on the radio were discontinued in 1965. A point system governed the selection of subjects for the SLC (School Leaving Certificate). It was devised in a such a way that few students would ever study Newari formally because to do so would mean excluding too many other, mainstream, subjects. The same applied to other 'local' languages which were, on paper, part of the optional curriculum, such as Maithili and Bhojpuri, and the situation does not seem to have changed since 1990. Nonetheless, despite this official position, numerous literary movements and conferences, as well as local cultural organizations, were formed. A contributing factor was that all formal party political activity was banned. Under the cover of cultural organizations, with varying degrees of overtness, criticism of the government could be expressed.

With the collapse of the panchayat system in 1990 an entirely new situation has arisen. The new constitution of 1990 refers to Nepal as 'multiethnic' and 'multilingual', a radical departure from previous practice. To the great disappointment of Buddhist activists, the word 'multireligious' is not used and Nepal remains an officially Hindu kingdom. Section 26, subsection 2, of the Constitution reads as follows:

> The State shall, while maintaining the cultural diversity of the country, pursue a policy of strengthening the national unity by promoting healthy and cordial relations amongst the various religions, castes, tribes, communities

and linguistic groups, and by helping in the promotion of their languages, literatures, scripts, arts and cultures. (Constitution 1992: 17)

This gives some kind of constitutional support to multiculturalism. At the same time, the constitution makes it clear that Nepali has a special status as the 'language of the nation', all the others being merely 'national languages' (*ibid.*: 4). The constitution also bans political parties which discriminate against potential members on the grounds of religion, caste, tribe, or language or which are religious, communal, or separatist in tendency (*ibid.*: 97).

Within these constraints, political parties are now legal and political debate is open. This means that cultural organizations have to fight for attention in a much more open political and cultural marketplace. There is the further problem, which faces all of them, of whether or not they should align themselves with one of the major political parties. Some Newar activists have argued that the time is now ripe for Newar cultural organizations to cast off their habitual antipathy to political engagement; others reply that this can only lead to Newars fighting Newars. A common compromise argument is that Newars should enter political parties and strive for positions of power, but they should do so only as individuals and this should have no implications for whatever cultural organizations they belong to. Some Newar organizations, such as the Jyapu Mahaguthi, have gone so far as to ban those active within political parties from holding executive office, though they are welcome to join as ordinary members.

Newar language activists have been disappointed to discover that it was not just the panchayat regime which held their aspirations in check. The panchayat system, it is true, defined itself in terms of a single homogeneous national identity which necessarily implied suppressing ethnic demands, as far as practicable. But, quite independently, there are powerful economic forces working for the homogenization of culture and for language loss. These have been barely affected by the new political dispensation which permits the freedom to organize and gives official recognition (through as yet, no financial support) to languages other than Nepali.

The General Context: NEFEN, Antibrahmanism, Government Response, Economic Conditions, Bahun Backlash

The events of the revolution of 'people's movement' of 1990 are by now well documented.[14] What is perhaps little appreciated is the extent to which ethnic feelings were involved in the revolt, within the Kathmandu valley, probably outside it as well. Be that as it may, it is certain that in the new, more open atmosphere since 1990 there has been a great flowering of ethnic activism. Among Magars and among the Rais and Limbus, it is often expressed in far more extreme form than among the Newars. There is a Magar Liberation Front, a Khambuwan (Rai) Liberation Front, and a Limbuwan Liberation Front, but, so far, no Newar equivalent. Maoist-inspired violence began in the far western hills after the fall of the Communist government in 1995. Since Rolpa, the district where there have been the most disturbances, has a Magar majority, it is likely that Magar ethnic resentment has played some role in this, along with economic backwardness and Bahun ideological leadership. By 1997, however, the Maoist disturbances had spread to 18 districts, preventing local elections from being held there and presenting the government in Kathmandu with a very serious problem indeed. In view of its wide diffusion, any straightforward interpretation of the Maoist movement in purely ethnic terms must be an oversimplication.

Such extreme rejectionist stances apart, there is a common concern among ethnic activists to achieve greater recognition of, and resources for, cultural, religious, and linguistic differences. The main forum that has been established to push these issues is the Nepali Janajati Mahasangh, which calls itself the Nepal Federation of Nationalities (NEFEN) in English. It is a confederal umbrella grouping, initially founded to bring together groups representing different minorities on the national level. The etymology of janajāti is significant: NEFEN uses it to refer to groups which were designated 'tribes' in the past, and are more neutrally referred to as 'ethnic groups'.

The rise of the neologism janajāti since 1990 is an evidence of the radical changes in political and ideological climate.[15] It comes from Sanskrit roots meaning 'people'—jana, 'kind'/'species'—jāti. The latter part, jāti, is sometimes used to mean 'people' or 'ethnic group' as opposed to castes (*jāt*).[16] But, since jāti is simply the Sanskrit origin of jāt, jāti is also often used as a politer term for caste. The addition of the prefix jana-, however, makes it clear that 'caste' is *not* what is meant. The ethnic activists mostly prefer now to use the term, janajāti, and they translate it as 'nationality' (except that, since 1993, in order to fit in with international human rights discourse, they simultaneously gloss it as 'indigenous people' (all the [non-Hindu] 'nationalities' are indigenous peoples).

A minority of ethnic activists reject the term janajāti and talk of the 'Mongolians', thereby defining the minorities they wish to speak for in racial terms. The more sophisticated activists realize that this is problematic, given the very mixed racial origins of many Nepalese groups. On the other hand, this way of viewing things has the merit of crude simplicity, and it seems that many people in the hills accept the view that the Nepalese population is basically divided into two groups. In the past these were referred to as Khas (the Bahuns and Chetris, now known as Parbatiyas/Parbates) and the *matwālīs* ('alcohol-drinkers'). Today the *matwālīs* are frequently referred to in Nepali using the English loanword 'Mongolian'. The untouchables in practice form a third bloc or group, but it is no coincidence that they are often left out of accounts altogether.

It is surprising, perhaps, that this same view of Nepal's population as divided into two different racial and cultural groups is propagated in government-approved textbooks. For instance, lesson 14, 'Cultural Heritage of Nepal', in *Our Social Studies, Book 5* (intended for students in class 5), begins:

> The people of Nepal belong to two major races—the Aryans and the Mongolians. So, the culture of Nepal is composed of the social customs and traditions of these two races. (Timothy and Uprety 1994: 75)

After a sentence which reiterates one of Nepal's claims to national pride, its history of never having been conquered or colonized, it continues:

> The most important feature of Nepali culture is religious harmony between Hinduism and Buddhism. The two major religions of Nepal get equal respect from the people. . . (*ibid.*)

While it is never explicitly stated, the association of 'Aryans' with Hinduism and 'Mongolians' with Buddhism is clear. It is an association and opposition that activists too make use of, as discussed below (cf. appendix 1).

Finally, Nepali nationalists, who seem fewer and more embattled than in the Panchayat period, do not accept the term janajāti and would most certainly not accept the translation of it as 'nationality'. When referring to such groups, they prefer to use alternative terms, such as jāti (see above), *sampradāya* ('tradition', especially religious traditions), *samudāya* ('community), or the neutral *samuha* ('grouping'). The negative term used to translate 'communal feeling' derives from *sampradāya: sāmpradāyik bhāvanā.*[17] (Any movement on behalf of one group has to be permanently on its guard against the accusation of communal bias, and it will invariably argue that strengthening their group will simultaneously strengthen the nation.) Many Newar activists, especially those opposed to the leftists, prefer to see Newars as a samudāya or jāti, and not as a janajāti or rāstra.

When NEFEN was first set up, any group could join but very quickly the rules were changed so that only one organization per janajāti was allowed, in line with multiculturalist logic. This, of course, immediately leads to a problem, acute and quite explicit in the Newar case, of who has the right to speak for the group in question. (Among the Newars there is also the debate about whether they belong with the janajāti groups in NEFEN at all, as just described.)

The UN's declaration of a Decade of Indigenous People starting in 1993 led NEFEN and similar activists to come together and recast their demands in these internationally approved terms. There is a slight problem here in that 'indigenous' is translated as ādivāsī which implies that the people concerned have always lived in Nepal, whereas most of the groups affiliating to NEFEN have well-known myths tracing their origin from elsewhere, often Tibet, but sometimes India. One response to this is to gloss over the difference between ādivāsī and janajāti. Another is to propose a complex definition of 'indigenous' for the Nepalese context, with a whole series of criteria which oppose the 'indigenous to the dominant Hindus; the final criterion is simply that the group itself should claim to be indigenous' (see appendix 1).

NEFEN faces two basic problems in attempting to mobilize the ethnic groups of Nepal. The first is the sheer diversity of the different peoples it claims to represent: it is not just that each group is different from the others; there are also very significant cultural and linguistic differences *within* all the larger groups. The second major problem is, if you like, the same as the first, but specifically in the sphere of religion. The NEFEN diagnosis is that there is a simple religion called Hinduism, elements of which have been adopted in recent years to different degrees by Nepal's ethnic groups. According to NEFEN, Hinduization is a relatively simple process that can, equally simply, be acknowledged, regretted, and put into reverse. If this view of Hinduism and Hinduization were correct, it would be possible perhaps to generate a series of modern identities around Buddhism or 'animism' as opposed to the Hinduism of the dominant Brahmans and Chetris.

As far as the present situation is concerned, the root problem as diagnosed by NEFEN is something called 'Brahmanism' (*bāhunvād*). This blanket accusation covers both the disproportionate presence of individual Bahuns (Parbatiya Brahmans) in all elite positions (parliament, judiciary, bureaucracy, university posts, leadership of political parties) and the alleged disproportionate *ideological* influence of Bahuns. This latter is blamed for the continuing official position of Nepal as a Hindu kingdom in the new constitution of 1990, despite vociferous protests from Buddhist and ethnic activists and a massive demonstration in the capital while the constitution was being drafted. Brahman influence is also blamed for the introduction of compulsory Sanskrit in secondary schools (1993), and the introduction of Sanskrit newscasts on Radio Nepal (1995).

Part of the problem for NEFEN is that Hinduism is not merely a thin and recent veneer on the timeless culture of the indigenous people of Nepal (this is especially obvious in the caste of the Newars). The truth is that Hinduism goes much deeper, and is a much more complex phenomenon than NEFEN's ideologues can allow. The harder ethnic activists push in demanding that people give up 'Hindu' practices, such as the national festival and holiday of Dasain, the more they marginalize themselves from ordinary people. Even where self-conscious members of an ethnic group agree that they are not Hindu, traditional religious practice is so pluralistic (drawing on both 'tribal' shamanism and on Lamaism, for example, as among the Gurungs) and combines so many cross-cutting influences that any simple definition or ideological dogmatism creates divisions, not unity.[18] In the country as a whole, there is no religious, cultural, or linguistic boundary or symbol that aligns all others against the two dominant castes. Indeed, 9 per cent of the hill population, the 'untouchables', is excluded from NEFEN as 'too Hindu'. Consequently it appears unlikely that the ethnic activists will manage to put themselves at the head of a massive popular movement.

This does not mean, however, that they will not be a significant force, and may have considerable influence on a future government which included the UML. In fact all parties have shown that they take the 'ethnic vote' very seriously, even if their actions in government have not lived up to all the hopes of the activists. Thus NEFEN's published account of its third National Congress (May 1996) records that the prime minister, Sher Bahadur Deuba, officially opened the Congress and spoke; other speakers included the leader of the RPP, Surya Bahadur Thapa, leader of the NWPP, Narayan Man Bijukche, as well as Devendra Mishra of the Sadbhavana Party.

It is instructive to contrast the fates of two different projects pushed by ethnic activists: an ethnographic museum and a Janajati Academy. The establishment of a national ethnographic museum had been one of the demands of NEFEN (see appendix 1) and it was agreed by the cabinet in one of the last acts of the Congress-RPP coalition government of 1995–7, despite some doubts about whether the controversial term, janajāti, should be in the title of the museum. The proposals were made acceptable by the fact that *all groups* within the country were to be included. The plans for the museum envisaged a separate house for each group built in its own traditional style, with representatives of the group carrying out traditional crafts in it. To the 61 janajāti groups, the main Parbatiya caste groups were added, making a total of 69. The Academy, by contrast, was intended for janajātis alone, and it seemed much more uncertain whether this could come into existence, despite having been the object of an official government working committee. Part of this had to do with the large quantity of development funds that it was envisaged the Academy would control. But also crucial was the fact that it was bound to adopt an exclusivist definition of janajāti, thereby barring both Parbatiyas and caste Hindus of the Tarai from its development initiatives.

What the success of the Ethnographic Museum and the failure (so far) of a Janajati Academy show is that the government is likely to seek to placate the 'ethnic vote' by symbolic measures, but cannot risk a genuine shift of resources or major institutional change. Multiculturalism is increasingly stressed, without legally binding dispensations for 'distinct societies', 'scheduled tribes', or reform of the upper house. A sign of increasingly multicultural practice is the essentially symbolic move of having the news on Radio Nepal in ten different regional languages.[19] The Royal Nepal Academy's journal, *Sayapatri*, publishes articles on language and culture in all the languages of Nepal, along with Nepali translations either by the author or someone else. Even the Royal Palace seems to have acknowledged the trend by reviving in early 1997 an old slogan that now seems to have more than tinge of multiculturalism about it: 'Unity in Diversity is the Unique Attribute of Monarchy' (*Anektāmā ektā rājtantrako visesatā*). It is, then, interesting and somewhat ironic that in the governments towards the end of the Panchayat period there seemed an attempt to have some kind of ethnically balanced council of ministers. Today, by contrast, when governments have taken some tentative steps towards multiculturalism, cabinets have been noticeably unrepresentative of the ethnic make-up of the country.

Whether or not such political initiatives come to fruition, it seems that NEFEN and similar activists have already had a considerable impact culturally: exactly how much influence they may be having, on students for example, has not yet been studied. What is certain is that there are many more activists openly publishing (for instance, magazines with titles like *Indigenous Outcry*) and openly organizing than there were before 1990.

The context in which the activists work is essentially urban.[20] And for many this means Kathmandu. Kathmandu has gone through enormous demographic and structural changes in the last 20–30 years. Land prices, population, and the cost of living have soared. Part of this has to do with foreign aid and Nepal's position as an independent nation. As an international capital it has attracted large numbers of foreigners on high salaries. There has been

TABLE 4.3. Variations in the extension of the term janajāti (The non-exclusive Museum usage is the most bizarre. NEFEN's that with the widest currency at present.)

Who are janajāti?	All 69 groups in the country (as in the Ethnographic Museum)	All 61 non-Parbatiya groups (as in the Janajāti Academy definition)	all non-Hindu groups (as in the NEFEN definition: currently c. 30)

considerable immigration both from the hills and the plains. There have been Tibetan refugees and 'returnee' Nepalis from Darjeeling. And many Indians, both labourers and skilled craftsmen, have moved to the capital, where it is widely acknowledged that Indian workers are willing to work longer hours, for lower wages, while doing better work and taking less time off (for festivals or *guthis*, for instance).

Furthermore, there has been the inexorable inflow of modern ideas, either directly, or mediated by India. All educated Nepalis read the Nepali language. They also understand Hindi through exposure to the Hindi cinema and Hindi magazines. Hindi and Nepali are sufficiently similar, especially in their standard written forms, that literacy in Nepali effectively means literacy in Hindi also. In this medium they are made aware of new ideas very quickly. From the mid-1980s it was possible to see videos in private parlours throughout the city; these made available all kinds of pirated videos from Hong Kong. Nowadays fluency and literacy in English are also seen as a *sine qua non* of success, hence the explosion of English-medium private schools in and around the capital.[21]

Since 1989 there has been TV in the capital. In addition to Indian TV which people are able to watch outside the limited hours of Nepalese broadcasting, it has, since 1991, been possible to pick up Star TV, as well as several channels showing continuous Hindi pop and movie song videos broadcast from Hong Kong by satellite. Since 1996 cable television that offers even more channels, has been widely available in the capital. One of the local satellite companies now offers an hour of Newari TV programming a week. Also since

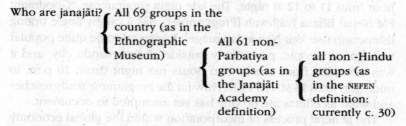

1996 there has been an FM radio station, with programming predominantly in English, with Nepali second. However there are also Newari programmes for half an hour in the afternoon, and for an hour from 11 to 12 at night. The late night programme, 'Goodnight FM Nepal Bhasa Jyājhwah [Programme]', has a catchy jingle urging listeners to use 'our Newar language'. It appears to be quite popular with young people, particularly outside of Kathmandu city, and it was extended from one to two hours per night (from 10 p.m. to midnight) from 14 March 1997. How far the programme really reaches and what its effects are no one has yet attempted to document.

The general process of incorporation within the global economy has of course been going on for a very long time, but the speed with which links are now made is unprecedented. As discussed above, local activists now react within months to UN initiatives, initiatives set up with very different situations in mind (that of the native Americans or Australian aborigines, for example). These are then translated into local terms and a programme of action formulated and texts published in both English and Nepali.

The globalization of the economy has had another, very unfortunate effect. Nepalis working for foreign companies or UN agencies can earn up to NC 60 or 70, 000 per month on a regular salary, and more than double that on an occasional 'consultancy' basis. A civil servant with some seniority might expect to be on 5 or 6,000 per month. An MP receives about the same, with a totally inadequate housing allowance if he comes from outside Kathmandu. A graduate just out of university, with no other training or experience, will, if employed by a foreign NGO, immediately be earning several times what his teachers were getting. The teacher's salary, meanwhile, is simply inadequate to support his family. If he has more than two children, his salary will probably not even pay their school fees (since only the poor now send their children to the state schools).

The disparities between what one 'needs' (at least NC 10,000 per month for a basic middle-class lifestyle, I was told in January 1996) and what government employees get, and between what foreign-employed employees get, have long been there. But the degree of difference, and the consciousness of its inevitability, seemed to have reached new heights by the mid-1990s. And this has, of course, a corrupting effect. Government servants and teachers are no longer just forced to take bribes in order to feed their families. They must now absent themselves from their offices for long periods in order to carry on other business altogether (private consultancies, if they are lucky enough to have them). '[T]elevision ownership', comments Liechty (1994: 290), 'was among the main requirements for anyone with even vague aspirations to membership in the broad middle class'. The same goes for private education.

The so-called English boarding schools have mushroomed throughout the Kathmandu valley. Even ordinary Newar peasants in outlying villages seem to have deserted the state schools and spend NC 6–700 per month per child on private schooling. Liechty reckons that there are over a thousand schools and campuses within the ring road alone.[22] Many middle-class parents now send their children to boarding schools in India; many billions of Nepalese rupees exit the country every year to pay the fees. Going on to college in Nepal is seen as second-best; all upper middle-class Nepalis in the capital aspire to go to universities in the USA, and if possible to stay on and work there as well, at least temporarily (Liechty 1994: 60–1).

There has been, then, in the last fifteen years an explosion of glitzy commercialism spreading far beyond the elite Rana families who were once the only Nepalis to be able to aspire to motorcars or to foreign lifestyles. English-language education is seen as the way to get on and speaking English is equated with knowledge and intelligence. Even Newari language enthusiasts making formal speeches in self-consciously 'pure' Newari cannot stop themselves from using the occasional English word in mid-sentence.

The high profile of Newar activism of various sorts, to be described below, has generated a kind of reaction or backlash on the part of Parbatiyas, particularly Bahuns, within the Kathmandu valley, and this too is part of the general context within which such activism operates. Some Newars complain that the aggressively political attitude of certain Newar activists and organizations has meant that Bahun civil servants in government offices will say, 'Go over there, there's a Newar over there who can deal with you'. An extreme written statement of the anti-Newar point of view can be found in the collected essays of Umabhadra Khanal, mostly published in the *Gorkha Express* newspaper (in Nepali) and reissued in his book *Leaves from the Nim Tree* (Khanal n.d.). (I was assured by a Bahun acquaintance that what Khanal had written many others were thinking or saying in private.) Khanal argues that the nine-month Communist (UML, 'United Marxist-Leninist') government of 1994–5 did not, as pro-Congress sources conventionally claim, 'UML-ize' the country, but rather it 'Newarized' it. This is an astonishing claim about a government that had seven Bahun Ministers out of eight (The eighth was Padma Ratna Tuladhar, a Newar). This very same government was seen by ethnic activists as evidence of the pervasive dominance of Brahmans. In another essay Khanal argues that the capital should be moved from Kathmandu, not just because of the endemic lack of water and space there, but mainly in order to get it away from Newars.

The Internal Politics of Newar Activism

The most high profile Newar activism is, perhaps inevitably, conducted in the capital, Kathmandu. The localism of Newar culture ensures that Kathmandu initiative are often ignored or seen as irrelevant, even just over the river in Lalitpur or up the hill in Kirtipur, let alone in Bhaktapur or in villages of the valley. But on the big issues activists of all these places agree, even if they find it difficult to work together.

One of the earliest demands of Newar activists, articulated by the first Newar cultural nationalist, Dharmaditya Dharmacharya, was that their language, known in English and Nepali as Newari, should henceforth be called by its honorific title, Nepal Bhasa ('the language of Nepal'). This plays on the fact that the Kathmandu valley was traditionally, and even today for many, is called 'Nepal' and the official extension of this name to the whole of the country is very recent (going back only to the 1920s and 30s). The authorities have always been reluctant to grant this, presumably because it would appear to give Newari a special place in the country and therefore a special claim on government resources. Newar activists assert that the last act of the UML government of 1994–5 was to recognize this demand; but it was never enacted, and the radio continues to refer to 'Newari'.

In a similar fashion, Newar activists have pressed the government to recognize and adopt as the nation's official era, the Nepal Samvat.[23] The campaign goes back in its present form to 1979. The Nepal Bhasa Manka Khalah was founded in 1979, as the New Year 1100 according to the Nepal Samvat approached, in order to bring together numerous locally based cultural and literary organizations. It had the brilliant idea of inaugurating an annual motorcycle rally around the three cities of the Valley both to celebrate the New Year and to demand official recognition for the Nepal Samvat (this rally is still the Manka Khalah's main annual activity). Over the years the arguments for adopting the Nepal Samvat have become increasingly complex. They began from the point that this is a genuinely indigenous era, whereas the Vikram Samvat, which is the official calendar at the moment, has no basis in Nepalese history, but was adopted from India only in this century by Chandra Shamsher (Rana prime minister from 1901 to 1929). Activists also claim that the refusal to countenance the Nepal Samvat, and the panchayat regime's insistence on referring to it as the 'Newar Samvat', were indicative of a general refusal to allow that non-Parbatiyas were full citizens and that their culture was an equal part of the nation's heritage. Such arguments often become very academic, picking over the details of how inscriptions were dated from the fifth century up to the present day.

The New Year (Mha Puja) procession attracted large numbers of young men, who circulated on bicycles, motorbikes, small tractors with trailors, taxis, and trucks. The route chosen imitated a religious pilgrimage and emphasized the unity of the valley. It was very noticeable and disruptive. Slogans in favour of Newari ('If the language survives, the jāti will survive') were chanted alongside those calling for recognition of the Nepal Samvat. It was a highly visible statement and the procession has come to be known as *bhintunā* in Nepali, from the Newari word for 'good wishes', because a frequent chant ran *nhugu dañ yā.. bhintunā* (new year's. . . good wishes!). The success of the demonstration spawned similar processions in other cities of Nepal, and Newar activists in the late 1980s argued, in a sophisticated way, that the campaign for the recognition of Nepal Samvat had nothing to do with the language issue. It was not, they claimed, a specifically Newar demand, but one that was shared by activists all over the country.

The leader of the Nepal Bhasa Manka Khalah is Padma Ratna Tuladhar. A naturally shy and retiring man, who is however a mesmerizing public speaker, he was persuaded to stand for the national assembly in 1986 and was elected from a constituency in the heart of Kathmandu. Padma Ratna never joined, and has still never joined, any political party. He became famous for his outspoken criticisms of the panchayat system, made even within the national assembly, as well as for his hatred of corruption and absolute personal incorruptibility. In a climate where politicians of every part of the spectrum are known for accepting bribes, and where it is a normal part of both political and bureaucratic life, this reputation has gained him an enormous popularity. Padma Ratna, Newar activists claim, 'made a present of Kathmandu to the Communists'. It was his influence, they say, that enabled the Communists to win eight out of ten seats in the valley in 1991 and ten out of ten in 1994. As proof, they cite the fact that the UML adopted Padma Ratna's symbol, the sun, as their own. In the UML government, as minister of health and labour, Padma Ratna became the only Newar in a cabinet of eight (the other seven were parbatiya brahmans). But even then he did not join the Party. He argues that he is temperamentally unsuited, since he always says what is on his mind, and would make a bad party member (Gellner and Sharkey 1996: 42).

Officially, political support for Padma Ratna was organized by the Padma Ratna Sahayog Samiti (the Padma Ratna Support Committee) and officially the Nepal Bhasa Mankah Khalah remained unaligned. There was opposition within the Mankah Khalah to Padma Ratna combining his presidency of the organization with such political involvement. Many members of the Mankah Khalah did indeed campaign for the Communists in various elections, but the formal Mankah Khala position was that this was 'in their personal capacity'. However, from the outside such distinctions are not made, or are dismissed as academic, and it is widely believed that the Nepali Bhasa Manka Khalah itself provided support and electoral activists for Padma Ratna both under the panchayat regime and afterwards. It came to be seen as a leftist organization and contributed to the image of Newars as predominantly leftist (based originally on the strongly leftist reputation of the two Newar towns of Bhaktapur and Kirtipur). Many Newar are in fact Congress Party supporters, including many of those prominent in the Newar cultural nationalist movement. They were very unhappy at the way in which Padma Ratna was able to control the Manka Khalah and, as they saw it, lead it into his political line. There were struggles over the control of the Manka Khalah, and though individuals were allowed to join, as well as organizations (as had originally been the case), they were never able to vote for its leadership. The price of stability in the leadership of the Manka Khalah seems to have been that many activists left and formed separate organizations.

One of the most successful of these new organizations, at least initially, was the Newa Guthi, set up in 1994. It aimed to be a more democratic organization open to all Newars on an individual basis, rather than, like the Nepal Bhasa Manka Khalah, principally to groups. It was supposed to operate on the principle of one member, one vote. It also wanted to be apolitical; in other words, it was reacting to the widespread perception that the Manka Khalah was a leftist and anti-Congress organization.

However, in 1995 there was a further split within the ranks of the Newa Guthi, occasioned by the infamous 'cow issue' (*gai kānd*). When Padma Ratna Tuladhar was a minister in ULM minority government of 1994–5, he was invited to a human rights meeting. As a long-standing human rights activist he said many of the things that he had said before, including that it was infringement of the human rights of communities such as the Tamangs and Muslims not to be able to eat beef in a country which prides itself on its religious harmony and tolerance. This was interpreted by his Congressite opponents in Kathmandu as meaning that he favoured an end to the ban on cow slaughter in Nepal and Padma Ratna was attacked as a way of embarrassing the Communist government. The issue was then picked up by Hindu activists both in India and Nepal. An Indian Hindu fundamentalist came to Janakpur and made a speech demanding that Padma Ratna be slain. Tension rose in Kathmandu when Hindu activists called for a city-wide 'strike' (*bandh*, literally means 'closure'; it is a common leftist tactic and effectively means the closing down of all shops, public transport, and private vehicles, under the threat of violence from the activists who have called the strike). Anti-Hindu ethnic activists supported Padma Ratna and threatened violence if the strike went ahead. Mediation efforts were organized at a local hotel and at the last minute the strike was called off.

Under the leadership of Santa Bir Tuladhar, the Newa Guthi came out in defence of Padma Ratna at what appeared to be a critical time. However, others, led by Hitkar Bir Singh Kansakar, a highly respected headmaster and long-serving Newar activist, considered this political involvement incompatible with the Newa Guthi's policy of political non-alignment. So they left and founded the Nepal Bhasa Prajatantrik Khalah, which is pro-Congress. The Newa Guthi itself split, for largely personal reasons, which were later represented in political terms, in 1995, so that now there are two rival Newa Guthis. A similar split occurred within the Newari daily, *Vishwabhumi*, in 1995. For a short time two rival versions of the same paper with the same masthead came out; subsequently the majority of the editorial staff, who had left, began to publish the *Sandhya Times*. This too was initially a personal financial battle, which later came to be seen, at least by some, in political terms.

Towards the end of 1995 yet another organization was formed, the Newa De Dabu (Newar National Forum), the aim being to bring all the different Newar groups together, although the leading representatives of the Nepal Bhasa Prajatantrik Khalah declined to attend. Even among those who did attend, there was some suspicion, because many of the activists prominent in the Nepal Bhasa Manka Khalah also held high positions within the Newa De Dabu. One informant used the simile of the elephant, which has two sets of teeth, one for show and one for biting, the point being that the Newa De Dabu was in effect a front organization, only seemingly non-political, through which the Manka Khalah would continue to pursue its leftist agenda.

Whatever the justice of such fears, it is certain that since the end of 1995 there has been considerable debate within activist circles on what the Newars are. Are they a rāstra (nation), jāti (ethnic group/people), janajāti (ethnic group/tribe/nationality), or samudāya (community)? Should they or should they not begin to organize on a political basis? For instance, Malla K. Sundar, a prominent journalist, one-time editor of the now defunct but once highly influential Newari weekly, *Inap*, argued in a three-part essay in the *Sandhya Times* that the non-political, literary, and linguistic focus of the Nepal Bhasa movement had been suited to the conditions of the panchayat system, but had failed to produce a general sentiment of attachment to the language (Sundar 1995). Others who argue that the Newars are really a 'nation' imply that the Newars should not be campaigning alongside the other ethnic groups of Nepal in NEFEN, but pursuing their own path to some kind of political autonomy. A common argument is that, because the Newars have castes providing every service within them, they are potentially self-sufficient, and this makes them a 'nation'.

In general, the fiercest nationalists tend to be on the left. Those Newars are politically on the right, or are at least anti-leftist, tend to prefer to define Newars as a jāti or samudāya. Thus Pradip Man Shrestha, editor of the pro-Congress weekly, *Desaymaru Jhya*, argues that the Newars cannot be a janajāti because the constitution makes it clear when it mentions them in section 27.10 (cf. note 14) that it is talking about oppressed (*pichadiyekā*) communities, which by no means can apply to the Newars; and that they cannot be a 'nation' because they have no specified territory (Shrestha 1997). His position can be taken to be close to that of the Nepal Bhasa Prajatantrik Khalah. An alternative term, samudāya, is used predominantly by the Nepal Newa Samaj, a national organization set up in 1994. It is led mainly by Newars, originally from outside the valley who are now based within it. It organizes seminars and meetings which are run in Nepali, not Newari. It is both pro-Newar and pro-monarchy. It has a large number of businessmen among its organizers, whereas valley-based movements tend to have businessmen as titular heads and contributors rather than as activists.

The Nepal Newa Samaj provides a home for the older activists. It has a disproportionate number of Sresthas among its members. This is partly because Sresthas predominate outside the Kathmandu valley; but it is also because its loyal, 'patriotic' position expresses far better than the oppositional, leftist stance of other activist groups the feelings of the majority of the older generation of educated Srestha Newars, both within and outside the valley. Among the first generation of Newar cultural nationalist poets, those who came from a Buddhist background, such as Chittadhar Hridaya, tended to write only in Newari, whereas those from a Srestha background, such as Yogbir Singh, wrote in Newari, Nepali, and Hindi equally. They felt equally a part of north Indian culture. Their successors today, such as Sahitya Mohan Joshi, may have, for the most part, abandoned

Hindi, but they continue to write equally in Nepali and Newari, for which they may sometimes be roundly criticized by other pro-Newari activists. Among the Sresthas more widely, there is, as noted above, the greatest openness to Parbatiya culture and the greatest stress on loyal service to the crown.

The Rise of Caste-Based Organizations

An aspect of the same process of 'ethnic self-discovery' has also seen a less remarked upon rise of 'caste self-discovery'. In modern terminology castes, on the one hand, and ethnic groups or 'nationalities', on the other, are quite different sorts of group. Castes are supposed to exist *within* a population and to represent an occupationally specialized *segment* of it (even if, in fact, the members no longer perform their hereditary profession). To be a caste is to exist in relationship with other castes with a different identity.[24] By contrast, ethnic groups or 'nationalities' are *whole* populations which, though they may in fact exist in economic interdependence with other groups, do not need to do so.

This western and sociological distinction between caste and ethnic group has in effect been adopted by the modern activist of Nepal. Caste is, in the dominant public discourses, not something to be encouraged; it is true, though, that specific 'traditions' certainly are thought to be a 'good thing', worthy of preservation, and it may even be recognized that these are often specific to particular castes. Ethnic groups, on the other hand, are thought to be of a very different order. Traditionally, as many anthropologists and others have noted,[25] there was only one term, jāt, or, in its more Sanskritic form, jati. Literally meaning 'birth', it referred to any hereditary descent group, caste, sub-caste, surname, clan, or even lineage. That no fundamental distinction was recognized between castes and ethnic groups was a crucial fact enabling the absorption of tribes or other marginal groups into the system as castes. Thus, neither in official policy, as expressed in the influential Legal Code of 1854 (Höfer 1979), nor in popular usage was there any distinction between caste and ethnic group. Ethnic groups were simply treated like castes.

In the period since 1990, whereas some activists have organized as 'nationalities'/'ethnic groups', others have made use of the same modern means of organization on behalf of castes. It may perhaps be yet another paradox that, while the Newars have been surprisingly (at least to some) slow at organizing as an ethnic group or 'nationality', they are probably relatively ahead of other groups in Nepal in the development of modern caste-based organizations. Among the Newars, there are so far organized bodies representing the Brahmans, Vajracaryas, Kansakars, Maharjans (Jyapu), Nakarmis, Manandhars, Citrakars, Tandulkars, Khadgis, and Kapalis.[26] Of this list, the Kansakars are not a caste but what I call a caste sub-group within the Uray.[27] The Uray of Kathmandu have set up an ad hoc committee, but have yet to publish their aims and rules, or to register their organization officially. Both Brahman and Vajracarya organizations are focused more on religion (vedic Hinduism and vajrayana Buddhism respectively) than on caste identity as such. Of the others, the significant fact is that, the Jyapu/Maharjans apart, they are all relatively small castes; indeed four (Nakarmi, Manandhar, Tandulkar, Citrakar) are from bloc 4 (see Table 4.2) which is composed entirely of such small castes.

To explain this contrast between small and large castes among the Newars, and why the Maharjans (Jyapu) are a partial exception to the rule, it is necessary to explore the contrast a little further. Large Newar castes have tended to be fissiparious. In the past the largest caste, the Maharjans, rarely married between the three large cities of the valley. Maharjans in Bhaktapur considered themselves purer than those elsewhere.[28] City Maharjans considered themselves superior to the Maharjans of the villages. Within the overall caste there were various grades of status, indicated by titles such as 'Dongol', 'Singh' and 'Suwa(l)', all of which are still used as surnames. These grades did not rigidify into endogamous sub-castes, but were none the less often thought of in a hierarchical fashion. In Lalitpur the Maharjans also had a problematic relationship with the potters (Kumha, Awale, Prajapati), who were considered by some to be part of the same caste as the Maharjans and by others to be lower caste.[29] Such contested grades of status were typical of the larger castes. The Sresthas, the dominant Kshatriya group, were even more diverse and complex than the Maharjans/Jyapu, with, in the cities, two broad, and supposedly endogamous, sub-castes, the Chathariya and the Panchthariya; there were, moreover, various groups of village Sresthas, some considered higher than others, and numerous subtle grades of status within all of these.

In short, there was no way in the premodern period that the large castes could come together and express unity in an organized fashion. Perhaps the only approximation to it was those ritual occasions when all Sakyas and Vajracaryas of the valley could be present to receive offerings in their role as Buddhist monks (the Samyak festival). But this did not generate cooperation in any other sphere, and in matters of marriage and status they were as sensitive to differences between city and village, between kinds of monastery, and between Vajracarya and Sakya, as the Maharjans.[30]

The real difference, then, is between large castes such as the Sresthas, Maharjans, and Sakyas and Vajracaryas, where the numbers were sufficient to generate competition and fission, and very small castes where it was necessary for all the members of the caste to stick together. They had to do this because of the necessity for brides. Maharjans of Lalitpur marry overwhelmingly within Lalitpur. They do not need to recognize Maharjans from outside, or did not, until recently. There was no need for institutions bringing together Maharjans of Lalitpur and Kathmandu and it was possible for each of them to be confident in their superiority to the other. By contrast, Napits, Citrakara, Newar Brahmans (Rajopadhyayas), and many similar small castes must marry throughout the valley. Their small size meant that it was possible to have a valley-wide caste council with considerable powers, and in some cases these did indeed exist.[31]

In the case of the Manandhar caste this cohesiveness was helped by the fact that the majority of them are concentrated in the city of Kathmandu. Where such caste councils existed in the past, and have remained in force, it has been possible, at least in some cases to build on the achievements and institutions of the past. In the caste of the Manandhars, the Kendriya Manandhar Sangh has been expanded to include the Manandhars of Bhaktapur, who were not traditionally part of the caste council based in Kathmandu.

Most of the caste organizations try to have annual meetings. When the caste is small this can potentially include all members of the caste. Among the Manandhars there was a pre-existing tradition of an annual caste feast at the Buddhist shrine Svayambhu. The annual meeting is now used as an occasion for giving prizes to

Manandhar children who have done exceptionally well in the SLC (School Leaving Certificate), or for other scholarly achievements; to hold children's races; and to reach an agreement on caste rules, e.g. for 'reforming', i.e., slimming down, the observance of life-cycle rituals in order to prevent wasteful extravagance. On other occasions some caste organizations also run free mobile health clinics, on the lines of other charitable groups, such as the Lions Club or some Buddhist groups.

In the case of the larger castes, it must be difficult to bring together in any effective way such disparate populations. The Maharjans, furthermore, have the problem of just how widely they should open their doors. The Vyanjankars of Lalitpur, who have always been regarded as of lower social status and have been held at arm's length by local Maharjans (Gellner and Pradhan 1995: 163–7), want, for understandable reasons, to enter the Jyapu Mahaguthi. After an initial period of hesitation, the Mahaguthi has followed the lead of the Lalitpur Jyapu Samaj which has accepted them as Jyapus, a decision which might have been seen as controversial only a few years earlier (for the Jyapu Samaj's definition of 'Jyapu', see appendix 2).

A similar problem occurs with the Uray: should they or should they not include in their organization the Rajkarnikars (sweet-makers), many of whom now live in Kathmandu, are very rich, and intermarry with the Tuladhars? As far as old-fashioned Uray are concerned, they are not Uray at all, but members of a different caste, some of whom traditionally eat chicken meat, a sign of low caste. It is true that the Rajkarnikars are one caste sub-group of a larger caste cluster from Lalitpur, all of whom intermarry. The other Lalitpur sub-groups are Tamrakar (copper-workers), Silpakar (stonemasons), and Varahi (carpenters). The (Lalitpur) Tamrakars are Hindu, i.e. have Brahman domestic priests, whereas the other sub-groups are all Buddhist, i.e. have Vajracarya domestic priests. It is also true that these Lalitpur Tamrakars traditionally ate chicken, even when their Buddhist caste fellows did not. However, Rajkarnikar intermarriage with the Uray has been going on long enough, and in recent times has occurred in sufficient numbers on an arranged basis with respectable Tuladhar lineages, thus establishing that it is not simply a question of the occasional irregular union. A married B, B married

C, and C married D, even though A and B would never consider marrying D.[32] There is here the kind of radical ambiguity which until recently could be, and in fact was, easily accommodated: some believed firmly that Rajkarnikars were not Uray, and others that they were, but there were sufficient potential brides available for both points of view to coexist. However, a modern Uray organization has to take a stand on the question: are they Uray or not? The present ad hoc committee seems to have come up with an ingenious solution. The Uray organization will in the first place only be for Uray of Kathmandu. It is allowed that the Rajkarnikar are Uray, but since they are originally from Lalitpur, and still have all their ritual links in Lalitpur, they will have to wait until the Uray organize on a national basis before they can join.

Many Newar activists are dismayed by the appearance of these caste movements. Keshab Man Shakya, in an article published in December 1995, referred to them as 'clannish polarization' and further said:

> Caste organizations will certainly bring mental satisfaction and material gain to the members of that caste. However, the diversity of caste organizations confuses the issue of Newar unity. This is further complicated by slogans calling for a Newar nation, which are unclear. Could it be that this diversity is a true reflection of Newar plurality? It is undeniable that this 'clannish polarization' complicates Newar politics, but the question is: How are we going to make sense of this polarization? Obviously it is proof of [intra-] Newar conflict. (Sakya 1995)

The particular activist subsequently became reconciled to the existence of such organizations and indeed encouraged their incorporation within the Newa De Dabu (Newar National Forum) during its second national conference in Narayanghat in 1996. Other Newars, particularly Sresthas, remain deeply unhappy about these caste organizations, particularly the Jyapu Mahaguthi with its claim that Jyapus are the original inhabitants of Nepal, and its stated aim of restoring Jyapu pride from centuries of high-caste oppression. Its size and potential power is an uncomfortable reminder of intra-Newar divisions and of a traditional caste hierarchy that many activists would prefer to see wither away without discussion.

It is striking that Newar activists reproach the organizers of these caste organizations in exactly the same way as nationalist writers attack Newar activists and others. The ethnic activists reproach the caste activists with pursuing unnecessary, atavistic divisions and weakening ethnic/national solidarity (in this case, of the Newars). The caste activists answer in exactly the same way as the ethnic activists do when faced with the identical reproach by Nepalese nationalists: the larger group will be *strengthened,* not weakened, by the self-conscious assertion of its constituent parts. Strong caste organizations which make people proud of their own traditions will make for stronger, more confident Newar ethnic identity, rather than threatening or undermining it. In just this way, ethnic activists respond to the charge that they are weakening the nation: it is only by dealing responsibly with past ethnic inequities, making people confident, and ensuring that they are treated equally, that the nation will be made stronger, and not by pretending that differences do not exist and are not important.[33] Thus in *Nepālmā Jana-Jāti Samasyā (Nationalities Question in Nepal)*, published before the 1990 Movement, Sitaram Tamang wrote in reply to the official (panchayat system) labelling of any ethnic cultural organization as communal and a threat to 'nationalism' (rāstriyatā):

> It is only when all nationalities/ethnic groups (janajāti) enjoy an equal chance to economic development and when the protection of their religion, language, culture, and social respect is ensured to all nationalities—only then will the country's 'nationalism' [i.e. national identity] be strong. (Tamang 1987: 65)

Furthermore, to justify what they are doing, both the Jyapu Mahaguthi and the ethnic activists draw in similar ways on a common political rhetoric of Nepal's cultural richness. An official government calender quotes King Birendra: 'National culture/customs and traditions are the pride of an independent nation'.[34] Newar activists argue that Nepali culture that is the nation's pride, and which tourists come thousands of miles to see, is in fact Newar culture, with its rich history, elaborate temples and beautiful art and architecture. In exactly the same way, Jyapu activists argue that Newar culture is overwhelmingly preserved by the Jyapus and that they are the central and indispensible actors in its public manifestations.

I began this section by talking about caste organizations in general, and have ended by discussing specially the Jyapu Mahaguthi. It is clear that the Jyapu Mahaguthi is, by virtue of the size of its potential following, different from other Newar caste organizations. It has had most success within the city of Kathmandu itself, and has built links to villages to the west and south of the valley. But in the other two big cities of the valley it has had difficulty in establishing its leadership. In Lalitpur there is now a separate Jyapu organization for the city alone, which is unaffiliated with the Mahaguthi, even though some people are members of both. Bhaktapur remains a world apart; there is the particular problem in this case that the agriculturalists of Bhaktapur refuse the Newar label 'Jyapu' altogether.

At this point one is tempted to recall the marked introversion and territorial basis of Newar social organization. As Gérard Toffin (1984: 216) put it, in his *magnum opus* on Newar society, 'each localized fragment of caste tends to become individualized and autonomous in relation to the overall caste hierarchy.' In Quigley's words, 'Unambiguous affiliation to a locality, rather than the south Indian alternative of kinship, provides the means by which the status of one's affines may be guaranteed and, most importantly, publicity demonstrated' (1986: 94). Thus, '[i]n theory, and still very much in practice, Newars marry Newars not only of their caste but of the *local* sub-caste' (Quigley 1987: 160; original emphasis). The very existence of the Jyapu Mahaguthi is evidence of the relative decline of this extreme introversion, but it still has to struggle against this. In addition to this, any large organization in post-1990 Nepal is faced with the pressures of politicization; as will be discussed below, this is a major factor in the internal politics of Newar activism. So far the Mahaguthi has avoided alignment with either of the major political parties, but the danger that it might be perceived to be so is ever-present in the minds of its organizers. The small Newar castes do not have to fear this. Their small population means that no one is tempted to use their caste organizations as a vehicle for their political ambitions.

What the rise of caste-based organizations, which Newar activists have had to take seriously, shows is that the multiculturalist ideal is taken up as far as the largest cultural unit that can support it. There is in fact a hierarchy of multiculturalism, as summarized in Table 4.4.

TABLE 4.4. A hierarchy of multiculturalisms among the Newars

National level:	69 or 61 'castes and ethnic groups'
Local level:	Newar caste groups (not all organized but potentially 20–25)
Caste level:	Different groups within the Jyapu (Awale, Vyanjankar, Maharjan etc.) or within the Uray (Tuladhar, Kansakar, etc.)

Conclusions

Following the revolution of 1990, Nepal found itself, as far as public life was concerned, in a position somewhat analogous to the countries of the ex-Soviet bloc after the fall of Communism. In Nepal there were no parties; in the Communist countries there was only one party. But the effect was similar. There was a hegemonic official ideology and certain unwritten 'rules of the game' which everyone understood. Professional advertisement was possible without being politically active, provided one did not get involved in oppositional activities, and providied one kept one's opinions to oneself.

Once the multi-party system was introduced, all this changed. Suddenly everything is political and every appointment is determined by party political affiliations.[35] Every trade union and every professional association is either riven by party political factionalism or has already split into two, aligned with the two main political parties, Congress and the UML. The rewards for belonging to the 'right' faction at the right time are great, and the struggle is correspondingly fierce.

It is, therefore, no surprise that Newar organizations feel the effects of this all-pervasive factionalism, nor that the fault lines between organizations should reflect party alignments. Even when disputes and splits occur between Newar activists for primarily personal or economic reasons, the dispute tends to be interpreted in party political terms. It is normal to accuse one's opponents of trying to 'Congressize' (*kāngresī karan*) the organization, or conversely to 'UML-ize' (*emālī karan*) it. That is why Newar cultural and caste activists expend much time and ingenuity trying to prevent such politicization of their organizations. They are aware that if it happens, or is believed to have happened, the organization will split into (at least) two separate factions.

Public space, ruled by law (however unreliable that may seem from an outsider's perspective), is a much more hospitable place for such organizations than before 1990. Proper registration of an organization remains vital. It is striking that where there has been a split, those who are the losers in terms of public recognition and allegiance still console themselves, if they can, that *they* have the registration and legal title to the organization.

Law is also relevant because of the need to have legally enforceable rules. This requires criteria of inclusion and exclusion to be made explicit, context-free, and unambiguous. Creative solutions which enabled Newars to be both Hindu and Buddhist, or Buddhist at one time and Hindu at another, or to be both Uray and not Uray, are no longer possible—at least, not in the world the activists are building. This process of Weberian rationalization applies also to the question of who is a Newar. In the past, difference was highly valued and the Newari language was a kind of invisible shared heritage. Nowadays, difference is a problem—it is this very combination of cultural difference and inequality that the philosophical work by Charles Taylor, mentioned at the beginning of this paper is intended to address. Taylor wishes to grant some justice to cultural nationalist demands even where they might infringe to some extent on an individual's right to choose in cultural matters. Most controversially, in Quebec all parents not from an Anglophone background are denied the right to send their children to an English-speaking school, in the name of preserving the collective 'nation'. There are two problems with Taylor's formulation, as I see it, both of which are recognized in Appiah's comments on Taylor (Appiah 1994). The first is that he takes what Baumann has dubbed 'the official discourse' as the whole of the matter. *Recognition* of—i.e. granting respect to—cultural identities of those deemed to be their bearers is inevitably an attack on their individual autonomy and replaces 'one tyranny with another' (Appiah 1994: 163). So far no one in Nepal has suggested that Newars should not have a choice of where to send their children to school, though the issue might arise if the activists' dream of having state-funded primary schooling in the mother-tongue were ever to materialize. Taylor's perspective ignores the fundamental sociological difference between activists, who have chosen to make the politics of recognition the core of their own identity, and the 'lay' majority, for whom such issues are not so salient.[36] By ignoring the distinction it allows the activists' definitions to be imposed on the others, denying the latter the choice the activists themselves had.

The second problem with Taylor's formulation is that it de-emphasizes the oppositional nature of ethnic identity. That identities are dialogic was one of Taylor's point, but the implications of this are not followed through. It is a truism of anthropological observations about modern politicized identities that they emerge in opposition to, and in competition with, others; in many cases this competition is with the state as representative of majoritarian cultural values. In such a situation, one group's success becomes *ipso facto* the other's failure, a zero-sum aspect to ethnic competition that is all too familiar to those trying to nudge Protestants and Catholics in Northern Ireland towards some kind of political accommodation.

If there is a specifically Nepali model of ethnic accommodation it is the traditional one based on hierarchy, requiring a king advised by Brahmans to settle disputes. Today that model is in full retreat before two alternatives:

1. The view of all Nepalis as equal citizens, with no formal recognition of collective units (different cultural traditions celebrated merely as heritage and folklore);[37]
2. The multicultural position that ignoring ethnic identities simply institutionalizes Parbatiya, and especially Bahun, privilege, so that, in order to strengthen the nation, collective ('ethnic' or 'national') identities must be given formal recognition.

Adherents of the first view see all ethnic attachments as threatening national unity. Adherents of the second view argue that it is only by strengthening the components of the nation that the nation itself will be strengthened. The multiculturalists are clear, however, that all groups must be treated equally, and not ranked in a hierarchy as before; and as I have described, the very same logic applies *within* the Newars, in dealing with the organizations that have sprung up to represent different Newar castes. It brings with it all the essentialist political problems of defining the relevant groups and determining the level of resources they should be permitted. It is these political problems which no doubt have prevented anything more than symbolic moves in the multiculturalist direction by the Nepalese government so far.

Notes

1. The fear that multiculturalism may imply the collapse of the society as a whole has been most strongly articulated in the USA, though those fears have been convincingly argued to be overstated (Lindholm and Hall 1997).
2. Among the older anthropological sources, one could cite Leach (1954), Southhall (1969), Spencer (1965), and Barth (1969). Two excellent introductions to the anthropological literature as a whole are Eriksen (1993) and Banks (1995).
3. Barth (1969: 27). Dumont (1980) remains the most effective critique of this view.
4. Hinduism is numerically and officially the dominant religion of Nepal and Newar Hindus can visit shrines and celebrate festivals with non-Newars. Newar Buddhist shrines are worshipped also by adherents of Tibetan Buddhism (e.g. Tamangs, ethnic Tibetans, Bhutanese on pilgrimage).
5. At the same time Newars constitute about half of the population within the Kathmandu valley. Of the total population of 18.5 million (1990 figures), Bahuns form 13% and Chetris nearly 18% (if the small Thakuri of royal caste is included with them). Parbatiya low castes (ex-untouchable tailors, blacksmiths, and cobblers) make up a further 9%. Although high-caste Parbatiyas are only about 31% of the country as a whole, they represent about 45% of the people of the middle hills, the culturally and politically dominant part of the country (i.e. excluding the people of the Tarai).
6. See Gaborieau (1982) and Pigg (1992) on the ideology of the Panchayat regime and development respectively.
7. This should not be taken to imply that severe conflict on 'communal' or 'ethnic' grounds could not occur in premodern times, for all that religious purism was less strong then, as Bayly (1985) convincingly shows.
8. The same process has been identified with the ethnic terms 'Sinhala' in Sri Lanka (Gunawardena 1990), and 'Mahratta' in Maharastra, India (O'Hanlon 1985: 17–21).
9. In November 1996 a young Srestha woman (who had certainly been brought up speaking Nepali and now works in a casino), when asked if she was a Newar, replied (in English), 'Yes, I am a typical Newar'.
10. By a further paradox, however, in recent years Dyahla children attending school with other Newars have adopted 'Newar' as a surname. My guess is that most other Newars have not yet noticed this.
11. I do not mean to suggest by this that only activists feel proud in being Newars, nor that these three groups are hermetically sealed (far from

it), but merely that Baldev Juju's criteria for Newar identity reflects some highly significant sociological cleavages.

12. Bista (1991) was, in part, a critique of this kind of hierarchical thinking, which it blamed on 'Brahmanism', and as such had *succès de scandale* in Kathmandu.
13. Clair Burket (1997) has described the in-built cultural elitism in the way that even a 'folk' art, the paintings of Maithil women, is perceived.
14. See Raeper and Hoftun (1992), Dhakal (1992), and Brown (1996).
15. It is said that the first use of the term janajāti was in the book *Tamba Kaiten* by Sant Bir Lama (Darjeeling, 1959). It was not in general use in the 1980s. Even now it is confined to intellectual and political circles.
16. Thus the English version of the 1990 Constitution systematically renders jāt as 'caste' and jāti as 'tribe'. The Constitution only uses the word janajāti when referring to 'backward' communities and there it is translated simply as 'group' (cf. section 6).
17. Of all these terms, only sampradāya was generally in use in premodern times, when it designated specific religious traditions. On the other hand, sampradāyik bhāvanā is, it is safe to say, a modern neologism coined to translate the modern concept, 'communal feelings'.
18. For an exemplary study of the mutual, 'dialogic' definitions of lama and shaman among the Gurungs high up the Marsyangdi river, see Mumford (1989). For higher status lineages of Gurungs further south, living adjacent to Bahun-Chetris, one would have to add the figure of the Brahman priest as well.
19. Only Newari, Sanskrit, and Nepali are heard throughout the country. News in Maithili, Rai, Gurung, Magar, Limbu, Bhojpuri, Awadhi, Tharu, and Tamang is heard only in one of country's four development zones where the population in question is concentrated. All other programming is in Nepali.
20. An exception here would be those educated activists who have taken to the hills in sympathy with the Maoist movement and those of the Mongol National Organization whose base is in the far eastern hills. But it remains true that political and ethic activism is predominantly the preserve of educated urban dwellers.
21. See Liechty (1994) for a discussion of youth perceptions of English-medium education.
22. Liechty (119: 56). He also analyses the reasons why it is such a good investment for those who own the schools: low start-up costs, the need to provide an outlet for unemployed but educated members of the family, and a seemingly unlimited demand for the product with little consumer knowledge about quality.
23. On the background of the Newar cultural nationalist movement, see Gellner (1986, 1997). For a useful discussion of similar ideas among the Gurungs, see Des Chene (1996).

24. Cf. N.J. Allen (1997: 309): 'One cannot be a caste without being part of a caste "system"'.
25. Höfer (1979: 112–13), Burghart (1996[1984]: 251–3), Gellner (1986: 114) Lecomte-Tilouine (1993: 46), Whelpton (1997: 52), N.J. Allen (1997: 304–5).
26. This list was collected by Rajbhai Jahkami in a paper presented at the second Newa De Dabu conference in 1996 (Jahkami n.d.).
27. On the distinction between a sub-caste, which is usually and/or ideally endogamous, and a 'caste sub-group', which is not endogamous, see further Gellner (1995a).
28. Nepali (1965: 167). To be ethnographically absolutely precise, the Bhaktapur agriculturalists do not even accept the label 'Jyapu' (preferring the Nepali *kisān*, 'peasant'), nor do they use the surname 'Maharjan'.
29. These divisions are discussed at greater length in Gellner and Pradhan (1995).
30. In Kathmandu, but not in Lalitpur, marriages between Sakyas and Vajracaryas are considered irregular.
31. Even this stark contrast between large and small castes has an exception: the small caste of Kapali-Jogi death specialists has a smaller, stigmatized, and endogamous sub-caste that performs ritual functions for them (Gellner 1995c: 281).
32. Taking A as Uray lineages refusing to countenance marriage with Rajkarnikars, B as lineages that have intermarried with them, C as Rajkarnikars, and D as the other three sub-groups based in Lalitpur, Tamrakar, Silpakar, and Varahi.
33. This argument was implied in the title of William Fisher's (1993) piece: 'Nationalism and the Janajati: Diversity in Ethnic Identity Strengthens Nepali Nationalism'.
34. *Rāstriya samskrti ra paramaparā svatantra rāstrakā gaurav hun*.
35. A friend related a recent incident he observed in the far western hills where a minister telephoned from Kathmandu to ensure his candidate was selected for a peon's position [peons fill the lowest rung in offices and other workplaces in Nepal and are illiterate dogsbodies, though in practice they are often influential and knowledgeable]. (Justice 1983).
36. See McDonald (1989) for a sensitive ethnography of Breton nationalism which focuses on, and provides very detailed justification of this distinction between activists and 'ordinary' people.
37. There were 'class organizations' (*bargīya sangathan*) under the panchayat regime, corporate representative groups for youth, peasants, workers, women, and ex-soldiers, but these were increasingly marginal to the operation of the system as time went by, and they no longer exist today.

APPENDIX 1

The Definition of 'Indigenous' and *Janajāti*

In March 1994 'the National Council on Indigenous People of Nepal' was held in Lapsiphedi, Kathmandu. There were representatives of all the constituent organizations of NEFEN and various other interested parties. The recommendations and suggestions were subsequently adopted by NEFEN at its second annual Congress in May 1994. Recommendations fell under three main headings. The first, on definitions, will be quoted in full:

The definition of indigenous peoples of Nepal—'The Indigenous Peoples' refer to those communities—

(i) which possess their own distinct and original lingual and cultural traditions and whose religious faith is based on ancient animism (worshipper of ancestors, land, season, nature), or who do not claim the Hinduism enforced by the state, as their traditional and original religion.

(ii) those existing descendants of the peoples whose ancestors had established themselves as the first settlers or principal inhabitants in any part of the land falling within the territory of modern state (Nepal), or and who inhabit the present territory of Nepal at the time when persons of different cultures or ethnic origins arrived there and who have their own history (written or oral) and historical continuity.

(iii) which communities have been displaced from their own land for the last four centuries, particularly during the expansion and establishment of modern Hindu nation state and have been deprived of their traditional rights to own the natural resources (Kipat communal land), cultivable land, water, minerals, trading point etc.).

(iv) who have been subjugated in the state's political power set-up (decision-making process), whose ancient culture, language and religion are non-dominant and social values neglected and humiliated;

(v) whose society is traditionally erected on the principle of egalitarianism—rather than the hierarchy of the Indo-Aryan caste system and gender equality (or rather women enjoying more advantageous positions)—rather than social, economic and religious subordination of woman, but whose social norms and values have been slighted by the state;

(vi) which formally or informally admit or claim to be 'the indigenous peoples of Nepal' on the basis of aforementioned characteristics.

> Though 'indigenous peoples' and 'nationalities' are restively not synonyms but, however, all the 'nationalities' seem to be the 'indigenous peoples' in the context of Nepal.

(Indigenous 1994: 2--3; punctuation and spelling as in original)

Under the other headings (*ibid*.: 4–8) the meeting called for many different things, but inter alia for

- history to be 'rewritten' by analysing 'the formal and informal agreements and treaties that were entered into between the indigenous groups and the then colonizing state power (that emerged in the nineteenth century under the banner of 'National Unification').'
- primary education in the mother tongue.
- revision of school curricula and discontinuation of compulsory Sanskrit.
- the right to take the civil service exam and to defend oneself in court in one's mother tongue.
- a secular constitution.
- state support for customary women's rights.
- an 'Ethnographic Museum of Indigenous Peoples of Nepal'.
- compensation for violations of indigenous people's traditional rights to natural resources and trade routes.
- the establishment of a 'Commission for the Economic Development of Indigenous Peoples' and for reservations for indigenous people in state employment and higher education.
- bilateral agreements with foreign countries to ensure that, just as Gurkha soldiers may not be used against any Hindu community or state, so also they should not be used 'to suppress the national and indigenous peoples' liberation movement in any part of the world'.
- an end to the 'trafficking of women from indigenous groups for prostitution purposes'.
- an end to child labour.
- the right to self-determination of Nepal's indigenous peoples.
- the conversion of the upper house of parliament into a 'house of nationalities'.
- reservations for women of indigenous groups in parliament.

In its report of 1996 the governmental working committee set up to recommend a Nepal Foundation for the Upliftment of Nationalities (*Nepāl Janajāti Utthān Pratisthān*) stated that

> *janajāti* are groups with their own mother tongue and traditional customs that do not fall within the tradition of the Hindu four *varnas*; they can be recognized by the following characteristics:
>
> (1) they are known by their own separate group culture;
> (2) they have a traditional language, religion, rites and customs;
> (3) they have their own written or oral history;
> (4) their traditional social organization is based on equality;
> (5) they have no decision-making power in the politics and government of modern Nepal;
> (6) they are the original or principal inhabitants (*ādivāsī vā mulbāsī*) of Nepal;
> (7) they have a sense of collective belonging;
> (8) they have their own traditional geographical territory;
> (9) they do not fall within the Hindu caste system of four *varnas*;
> (10) they make the claim to be janajāti's.

A list of 61 groups fulfilling these criteria was drawn up.

APPENDIX 2

Caste-Based Organizations: Who is a Jyapu?

From a pamphlet of the Jyapu Mahaguthi Ad Hoc Central Committee:

Main Motivation

The Jyapu Mahaguthi is an organization that takes on board the fact that all the country's castes, languages, and cultures are free and equal and brings together the Jyapu caste (jāti). It is a free and autonomous guthi that attempts to replace feelings of caste inferiority with those of pride, inequality with equality, and communalism with good will. It is not a political organization. It will remain aloof from political movements.

Aims

(a) to unite on a national level all Jyapus from the Kathmandu Valley, wherever they may be earning their living; to raise caste awareness; and in so doing to bring them on the road to the development of the country;

(b) to develop, preserve, and carry out research on the origins of the Jyapu caste, its religion, culture, life-cycle rituals, festivals, occupations, customs, etc.;

(c) to advance the development of the Jyapu caste by freeing it from economic, political, religious, and intellectual domination;

(d) to protect and develop Nepal Bhasa, the mother tongue of the Jyapu caste; to work to increase the feeling that 'we are Jyapus, we are Newars, and we are Nepalis'.

The 'Jyapu Mahaguthi National Anthem (*de mye*)', by Rajbhai Jahkami (as printed on the back of the flier inviting participation in the Mahaguthi's programme for the day of Laksmi Puja, November 1996):

Today the Jyapu caste is assembled
It has broadcast the name of the Jyapu Mahaguthi
The Jyapu caste is coming today
Wearing the flower of caste pride.

Language and culture are called dharma
They are the signs of our caste
    The beautiful flowering of our caste
    Is the pride of our nation.

Making sure our caste survives
It is the distillation of our ancestors
    The dharma of our ancestor is called karma
    It is our lifeblood as human beings.

Yes! Jyapus are the aborigines (ādivāsī) of Nepal
As Jyapus we are Newars
    Full of pride as Nepalis
    Outstanding in arts and skills.

Yes, we are industrious workers of the soil
Guardians of the nation's culture
    Flying the flag of our caste
    Together let us resolve to survive.

The Lalitpur-based Jyapu Samaj defines a Jyapu as follows:

In this organization 'Jyapu' shall be understood to refer to local inhabitants of the municipality of Lalitpur who earn livelihood today either by agriculture or by other means but are descended from the aboriginal inhabitants (ādivāsī) whose main profession was agriculture, and who speak Nepal Bhasa (Newari) as their mother tongue, and who have the dhime bājā (large drums) as their main custom. (article 2.ka)

APPENDIX 3

Criteria of Newarhood

Extract from the rules of the Newa Guthi (20/9/1995)

5. Main Aims of the Guthi

- working within the current laws of the land, to arouse all Newars from their slumbers in order to make them feel pride in being a Newar;
- without allowing any place to communal opinions, and putting aside all discrimination on the basis of caste, religion, politics, or any other dispute, to make all Newars united and of one mind;
- to uplift (*jāh cwanhyāketa*) Newars;
- even if customs are diverse, to make use of Nepal Bhasa, which unites all Newars, and cause others to use it;
- to encourage the various dialects of Nepal Bhasa and to encourage the use of Nepal Bhasa in ordinary conversations between Newars;
- to cause Nepal Bhasa and customs to survive in a form suitable to the times;
- to take necessary steps to (fulfil) the rights of Nepal Bhasa and Newars under the present constitution;
- to organize or support the organization of libraries and schools of Nepal Bhasa in order to advance the cause of Nepal Bhasa;
- to support or to work towards strengthening Newars in the economic field;
- to carry on and get to carry on the indispensible work investigating and analysing Nepal Bhasa and Newar culture;
- to support and carry out the meritorious work advancing the cause and strengthening the living Newar nation (rāstra) and culture;
- to bring out and help others bring out books and papers which propagate Nepal Bhasa and culture;
- to help build a Newa House so that Newars may live economically and in accordance with Newar culture;
- to establish, and help others to establish, good relations between

the various groups and people who are working for the upliftment of the Newar nation;

- to help establish a Newa Dhuku [trust] in order to coordinate the economic support which is being used for the advancement of Newars, Nepal Bhasa, its literature, art, and customs;
- various other activities, whatever is necessary for the bringing together of these various aims.

6. Form of Membership in the Guthi

In this guthi there will be seven kinds of members:

(1) member; (2) life member; (3) associate member; (4) deputy member; (5) guest member; (6) institutional member; (7) honorary member.

7. Conditions of Membership

7.1 Members and Life Members

Any Newar who fulfils the following conditions may be a life member of the guthi:

(1) speaks Nepal Bhasa in own home;
(2) speaks Nepal Bhasa with other Newars;
(3) when the Guthi so decides, gives at least one hour per week for Guthi work;
(4) possesses Nepalese citizenship;
(5) is at least 16 years old.

7.2 Associate Members

A Newar who uses Nepal Bhasa at home and with other Newar but cannot give time for the work of the Guthi may be an associate member of this Guthi.

7.3 Deputy Member

Any Newar who does not know Nepal Bhasa but wishes to help in the achievement of the main aims of the Guthi may be a deputy member.

7.4 Guest Member

Any person who, though not a Newar, is well disposed towards the Guthi and helps it may be a guest member.

7.5 Institutional Member

Any association, group, guthi, forum, etc. which is connected to Nepal Bhasa, Newars, their literature, art, or culture, and which works in such a way as to further the main aims of the Guthi, may be an institutional member of the Guthi.

7.6 Honorary Member

If the Guthi so decides, any person who makes real efforts to propagate and protect Nepal Bhasa, literature, art and culture, and the Newar nation, may become an honorary member.

APPENDIX 4

Prominent Newar Newspapers and Organizations

Details of Selected Newspapers and Magazines in Newari (with perceived political affiliations where known)

Nepal Bhasa Patrka (daily) (1955 [2012]–1984) (circulation 3–400) eds. Phatte Bahadur Singh, Padma Ratna Tuladhar.

Inap (weekly) (12/1/1983–16/11/1994) (circulation c. 2200) (non-aligned leftist) ed. Malla K. Sundar.

Rajmati (weekly) (1983–23/7/1996) ed. Dharma Ratna Sakya.

Visvabhumi (daily) (1987–) (circulation grew to 11,000 at the height of the People's Movement of 1990; now down to *c.* 1500) (non-aligned) ed. 1987–90 Ashok Shrestha, 1990– Sushil Bir Singh Kansakar.

Sandhya Times (daily) (1995–) (circulation *c.* 3000) (pro-UML) ed. Suresh Manandhar.

Hisi (monthly '*Reader's Digest*' style magazine) (1994–) (circulation *c.* 3000) (first published from *Visvabhumi*, now from *Sandhya Times*) ed. Ramesh Kaji Sthapit.

Desaymaru Jhya (weekly) (23/1/1994–) (circulation *c.* 1700) (pro-Congress) ed. Pradip Man Shrestha.

Nasana (weekly) (27/4/1997–) (pro-Samyukta Jan Morcha) ed. Omkareshwar Shrestha.

Jhigu Sa (weekly) (29/7/1997–) ed. Kiran Muni Bajracharya.

Selected Organizations

		Founder/Leader
Nepal Bhasa Parisad	1951	Cittadhar Hridaya
Cwasa Pasa (Friends of the Pen)	1950	Prem Bahadur Kansakar
Nepal Bhasa Manka Khala	1979	Padma Ratna Tuladhar
(confederal grouping of local Newar cultural and literary groups)		
Jyapu Mahaguthi	1993	Bipendra Maharjan/ Rajbhai Jahkami
Newa Guthi (1)	1996 (1994)	Santa Bir Singh Tuladhar
Newa Guthi (2)	1996 (1994)	Durga Lal Shrestha
Nepal Newa Samaj	1994	Dil Bikas Rajbhandari

Nepal Bhasa Prajatantrik Khalah	1994	Hitkar Bir Singh Kansakar
Newa De Dabu	1995	Bhakti Das Shrestha
Newa Mahaguthi	1997	Nati Maharjan
Newa Khalah	1998	Mukti Pradhan

Notes

I would like to thank K.P. Malla, Johanna Pfaff-Czarnecka, Declan Quigley, Anil Sakya, Keshab Man Sakya, John Whelpton, and participants in seminars at the Martin Chautari, Kathmandu (January 1997), at ICES conferences in Cochin (April 1997) and Oxford (January 1998), and at the European Bulletin of Himalayan Research Workshop in Paris (September 1998) for comments and suggestions. I am particularly grateful to the ICES, Colombo, for its generous and broadminded sponsoring of this research, and for permission to republish this article here.

References

Allen, N.J., 1997, 'Hinduization: The Experience of the Thulung Rai', in Gellner, Pfaff-Czarnecka and Whelpton (eds.).

Appiah, K.A., 1994, 'Identity, Authenticity, Survival: Multicultural Societies and Social Reproduction', in A. Gutman (ed.), *Multiculturalism: Examining the Politics of Recognition,* Princeton: Princeton University Press.

Banks, M., 1995, *Ethnicity: Anthropological Constructions,* London: Routledge.

Barré, V., P. Berger, L. Feveile, and G. Toffin, 1981, *Panauti: Une Ville au Népal,* Paris: Berger-Levrault.

Barth, F., 1969, 'Introduction', in F. Barth (ed.), *Ethnic Groups and Boundaries: The Social Organization of Culture Difference,* Bergen/London, Universitets Forlaget: George Allen & Unwin.

Baumann, G., 1996, *Contesting Culture: Discourses of Identity in Multi-Ethnic London,* Cambridge: Cambridge University Press.

Bayly, C.A., 1985, 'The Prehistory of "Communalism"? Religious Conflict in India, 1700–1860', *Modern Asian Studies* 29: pp. 177–203.

Bista, D.B., 1991, *Fatalism and Development: Nepal's Struggle for Modernization,* Calcutta: Orient Longman.

Brown, T.L., 1996, *The Challenge to Democracy in Nepal: A Political History.* London: Routledge.

Burghart, R., 1996 (1984), 'The Formation of the Concept of Nation-State in Nepal', in C.J. Fuller and J. Spencer (eds.), *The Conditiona of Listening: Essays on Religion, History and Politics in South Asia,* Delhi: OUP.

Burkert, C., 1997, 'Defining Maithil Identity: Who is in charge?', in Gellner, Pfaff-Czarnecka, and Whelpton (eds.).

Des Chene, M., 1996, 'Ethnography in the *Janajāti-yug:* Lessons from Reading *Rodhi* and other Tamil Writings', *Studies in Nepal History and Society* 1 (1), pp. 97–161.

Dhakal, G.P., 1992, *Jan-āndolan: 2046* [in Nepal], Lalitpur: Bhupendra Purusha Dhakal.

Dumont, L., 1980, *Homo Hierarchicus: The Caste System and its Implications* (complete revised English edition). Chicago: University of Chicago Press.

Eriksen, T.H., 1993, *Ethnicity and Nationalism: Anthropological Perspectives,* London and Boulder: Pluto.

Fisher, W., 1993, 'Nationalism and the Janajati: Diversity in Ethnic Identity Strengthens Nepali Nationalism', *Himal* 6 (2), pp. 11–14.

Gaborieau, M., 1982, 'Les Rapports de classe dans l'idéologie officielle du Népal' in J. Pouchepadass (ed)., *Caste et Classe en Asie du Sud (Purusārtha* 6). Paris: EHESS.

Gaborieau, M., 1993, *Ni Brahmane, ni Ancêtres: Colporteurs Musulmans du Népal,* Nanterre: Société d'ethnologie.

Gellner, D.N., 1986, 'Language, Caste, Religion and Territory: Newar Identity Ancient and Modern', *European Journal of Sociology* 27, pp. 102–48.

——— 1992, *Monk, Householder, and Tantric Priest: Newar Buddhism and its Hierarchy of Ritual,* Cambridge: Cambridge University Press.

——— 1995a, 'Introduction', in Gellner and Quigley (eds.).

——— 1995b, 'Sakyas and Vajracaryas: From Holy Order to Quasi-Ethnic Group', in Gellner and Quigley (eds.).

——— 1995c, 'Low Castes in Lalitpur', in Gellner and Quigley (eds.).

——— 1997, 'Caste, Communalism, and Communism: The Newars and the Nepalese State', in Gellner, Pfaff-Czarnecka, and Whelpton (eds.).

——— n.d., 'Ethnic identity or Kshatriya identity? The Newars in History'.

——— and D. Quigley (eds.), 1995, *Contested Hierarchies: A Collaborative Ethnography of Caste among the Newars of the Kathmandu Valley, Nepal,* Oxford: Clarendon.

——— and R.P. Pradhan, 1995, 'Urban Peasants: The Maharjans of Kathmandu and Lalitpur', in Gellner and Quigley (eds.).

——— and G. Sharkey, 1996, 'An Interview with Padma Ratna Tuladhar', *Himalayan Research Bulletin* 16 (1–2), pp. 37–46.

——— J. Pfaff-Czarnecka, and J. Whelpton (eds.), 1997, *Nationalism and Ethnicity in a Hindu Kingdom: The Politics of Culture in Contemporary Nepal,* Amsterdam: Harwood.

Gunawardena, R.A.L.H., 1990, 'The People of the Lion: The Sinhala Identity and Ideology in History and Historiography', in J. Spencer (ed.), *Sri Lanka History and the Roots and Conflict,* London: Routledge.

Höfer, A., 1979, *The Caste Hierarchy and the State in Nepal: A Study of the Muluki Ain of 1854*, Innsbruck: Universitätsverlag Wagner, Khumbu Himal series 13/2, pp. 25–240.

Hroch, M., 1985, *Social Preconditions of National Revival in Europe*, Cambridge: Cambridge University Press.

Indigenous 1994, *Indigenous Peoples of Nepal Towards Self-Identification and Re-establishment* (Proceedings of the National Consultation on Indigenous Peoples of Nepal), Kathmandu, National Ad Hoc Committee for International Decade for the World's Indigenous Peoples, Nepal.

Jahkami, R., n.d., 'A Brief Introduction to Newar Caste Organizations', (in Newari), paper presented to Newa De Dabu conference, Narayanghat, 1996.

Justice, J., 1983, 'The Invisible Worker: The Role of the Peon in Nepal's Health Service', *Social Science and Medicine* 19 (3), pp. 193–8.

Khanal, U., n.d., [c. 1995], *Nimkā Pātharu* [Level of the Nim Tree], Kathmandu: Mrs S. Khanal.

Lama, Santbir, 1959, *Tambā Kaiten*, Darjeeling.

Leach, E.R., 1954, *The Political Systems of Highland Burma*, London.

Lecomte-Tilouine, M., 1993, *Les Dieux du Pouvoir: Les Magar et l'Hindouisme au Nēpal central*, Paris: CNRS.

Lévis, S., 1905, *Le Népal: Etude Historique d'un Royaume Hindou* (3 vols.), Paris: Leroux: Reissued 1986, Kathmandu and Paris: Raj de Condappa, Le Toit du Monde, and Editions Errance.

Liechty, M., 1994, 'Fashioning Modernity in Kathmandu: Mass Media, Consumer Culture, and the Middle Class in Nepal', PhD, University of Pennsylvania, Ann Arbor: UMI 9521066.

Lindholm, C. and J. Hall, 1997, 'Is the United States Falling Apart?', *Daedalus* 126 (2), pp. 183–209.

McDonald, M., 1989, *We are not French! Language, Culture, and Identity in Brittany*, London: Routledge.

Macdonald, A., and A. Vergati Stahl, 1979, *Newar Art: Nepalese Art during the Malla Period*, Warminster: Aris and Phillips.

Malla, K.P., 1992, 'Bahunvada's Myth and Reality', *Himal* 5 (3): pp. 22–4.

Mumford, S.R., 1989, *Himalayan Dialogue: Tibetan Lamas and Gurung Sharmas in Nepal*, Madison: University of Wisconsin Press.

Nepal, G.S., 1965, *The Newars: An Ethno-Sociological Study of Himalayan Community*, Bombay: United Asia Publications.

O'Hanlon, R., 1985, *Caste, Conflict, and Ideology: Mahatma Jotirao Phule and Low Caste Protest in Nineteenth-Century Western India*, Cambridge: Cambridge University Press.

Onta, P., 1996a, 'Creating a Brave Nepali Nation in British India: The Rhetoric of *Jati* Improvement, Rediscovery of Bhanubhakta and the Writing of Bir History', *Studies in Nepali History and Society* 1 (1), pp. 37–76.

Onta, P., 1996b, 'Ambivalence Denied: The Making of *Rastriya Itihas* in

Panchayat Era Textbooks', *Contributions to Nepalese Studies* 23 (1), pp. 213–54.

Pigg, S., 1992, 'Inventing Social Categories Through Place: Social Representations and Development in Nepal', *Comparative Studies in Society and History* 34, pp. 491–513.

Quigley, D., 1986, 'Introversion and Isogamy: Marriage Patterns of the Newars of Nepal', *Contributions to Indian Sociology* (N.S.) 20, pp. 75–95.

————, 1987, 'Ethnicity without Nationalism: The Newars of Nepal', *European Journal of Sociology* 28, pp. 152–70.

Raeper, W. and M. Hoftun, 1992, *Spring Awakening: An Account of the 1990 Revolution in Nepal*, Delhi: Viking.

Ragsdale, T.A., 1989, *Once a Hermit Kingdom: Ethnicity, Education, and National Integration in Nepal*, Kathmandu: Ratna Pustak Bhandar.

Sakya, K.M., 1995, 'Newar Disunity and Newar Politics' [in Newari] (two parts), *Sandhyā Tāims* 25–26/12/95.

Shrestha, P.M., 1997, 'The Newars are *jāti*, not a *janajāti' Desaymaru Jhyāh*, 2/1/97.

Southall, A., 1969, 'The Illusion of Tribe', *Journal of Asian and African Studies* (Leiden) 5, pp. 28–50.

Spencer, J., (ed.), 1990, *Sri Lanka: History and the Roots of Crisis*, London: Routledge.

Spencer, P., 1965, *The Samburu: A Study of a Gerontocracy in a Normadic Tribe,* London: Routledge & Kegan Paul.

Sundar, Malla K., 1995, 'Newar must now go foward politically' [in Newari] (3 parts), *Sandhya Taims* 17–19/12/95.

Tamang, Sitaram, 1987, *Nepālmā Jana-jāti Samasya (Nationalities Questions in Nepal)* [in Nepali], Naya Bazaar, Kathmandu: Sushri Tamang.

Taylor, C., 1994 (1992), The Politics of Recognition', in A. Gutmann (ed.) *Multiculturalism: Examining the Politics of Recognition*, Princeton: Princeton University Press.

Thapa, S., 1995, 'Human Development and the Ethnic Population Sub-Groups in the 75 Districts in Nepal', *Contributions to Nepalese Studies* 22, pp. 181–92.

Timothy, C. and N.P. Uprety, 1995, *Our Social Studies, Book 5*. Thapathali, Kathmandu, Ekta Books and Stationers.

Toffin, G., 1981, 'L'organization sociale des Pahari (ou Pahi), population du centre Népal' *L'Homme* 21, pp. 39–68.

————, 1984, *Religion et Société chez les Néwar du Népal*, Paris: CNRS.

————, 1993, *Le Palais et le Temple: La fonction royale dans la vallée du Népal,* Paris: CNRS.

Vetovec, S., 1998, 'Multi-Multiculturalism', in M. Martiniello (ed.), *Multiculturalism in Two Societies: Belgium and Great Britain*, Utrecht: ERCOMER.

Whelpton, J., 1997, 'Political Identity in Nepal: State, Nation, and Community', in Gellner, Pfaff-Czarnecka, and Whelpton (eds.).

Comments

GÉRARD TOFFIN

Three points of this interesting paper will be discussed here: the sense of Newarness and paradoxes of Newar identity'; the politics of Newar identity and the internal context of Newar activism, especially since 1990; and, finally, the rise of caste-based organizations.

Sense of Newarness and Paradoxes of Newar Identity

Gellner emphasizes correctly that in pre-modern times Newar identity was mostly implicit, as elsewhere in the Nepalese hills. It must be recalled in this connection that the term Newar itself dates back only as far as the seventeenth century and that, in the old usage, it was restricted mainly to high Hindu castes, especially Shrestha; other Newari-speaking castes were denied it. As noted in some of my works, this usage still survives today, at least partly, or was surviving some decades ago. I agree with what is said about the heterogeneity of the Newars. Clearly, important cleavages exist within this group. Newars are divided among numerous castes; some of them are Hindus (or call Hindu priests), the rest Buddhist. From the physical point of view, they are disparate population. Local cleavages are also important: all Newarologists know the strong sense of difference among Newars attached to small territories and to the boundaries of the former Malla kingdoms.

Three factors, at least, explain the rise of Newarness from the eighteenth century onward and its increasing expansion during the last decades of the twentieth century:

1. Reaction to the Gorkhali conquest of the Kathmandu valley and resentment to having been relegated to a second position in the political sphere.
2. Massive immigration: Parbatiyas, Tamangs, Magars, and more re-

cently Indians have settled in great numbers in the valley. As stressed, the Kathmandu valley is becoming more and more multi-ethnic, multi-linguistic, and the capital looks increasingly like an international, cosmopolitan city. The revivalist movement of the Newars, their glorification of the past, has obviously something to do with this new solution and the feeling of becoming a minority.

3. The so-called 1990 revolution and the restoration of a parliamentary system have opened the way to a more open political system where ethnic claims can be expressed.

The chief paradox of the Newar campaign for better recognition is that this group is among the richest in Nepal. Newars have a high standard of living, and are still part of Establishment.

The Politics of Newar Identity and the Internal Context of Newar Activism, Especially Since 1990

The historical sketch of Newar cultural associations, closely parallel to the hill tribes ethnic movement, is very useful. Four of these are primarily mentioned: Nepal Bhasa Manka Khala, founded in 1979; Newa Guthi, set up in 1994; Newa De Dabu, in 1995, whose aim is to bring all the different Newar groups together; and Newa Samaj, set up in 1994, led mainly by Newars originally from outside the valley, with a high proportion of Shresthas among its members. This phenomenon raises a host of problems, some of which I would like to point out.

These organizations have first to be placed into the Newar internal context, so conflictual in nature. Are these groups representative of the Newar population? What is their real impact? We know that the Nepal Bhasa Mankha Khala is able to mobilize huge mobs for their annual motorcycle rally around the three cities in the valley to celebrate the Newar new year and the adoption of the Newar era as the official era. But what about the three other groups? What is the number of sadasyes of these associations, the number of active members, the proportion of women, and so on?

Gellner stresses the pervasive influence of political factionalism in these Newar associations as well as in other spheres. The two factions are, of course, the UML and the Congress. As is well known, nothing is simple in this matter. In many cases, these factions, related to the political life of the country, obviously have a strong economic base. It is not just by chance that Jyapu peasants have for a long time been communist supporters, and that Shresthas, traders and often land-owners, in general support the Congress or the monarchy. However, it is also true that these political oppositions might seem incoherent with modern politics. As a matter of fact, being pro-UML or pro-Congress is still related to caste. That is why wealthy Jyapu peasants, having their own workers, many of them Indians, may still feel disadvantaged and defend UML theories. Gellner refers to the politization of conflicts. But these politics still derive, to a great extent, from pre-modern habits. Caste is often rejected as an alien system, adopted long ago from the Hindu world, but it still controls religious thought and hierarchy. The politization of social relations is perhaps just a new or another form of the old factionalism.

The Rise of Caste-based Organizations

I turn now to the last part of the paper, related to the rise of caste-based organizations. As is correctly stated, this movement is in contradiction with most of the Newar ethnic revendications.

We are facing here what can be called a process of ethnization or tribalization of caste. The Jyapus claim to be the aboriginal inhabitants, adivasis, of the valley. They pretend to have better preserved the most ancient Newar traditions (this is sometimes true) and to be less influenced by 'Indian civilization' than the other Newar castes (in this concern, they underestimate the impact of the Indian Buddhist great tradition among them). These claims closely parallel those of the hill tribes, such as Tamangs or Kirantis. The difference is that Jyapus have been included in a more global society made up of a number of Newar specialized castes. Seen from the overall social system, they form just a part of the total Newar organization and not an entity in itself. Jyapus now increasingly tend to refuse to assume their traditional caste duties towards upper castes. They refuse to act as messengers or to carry goods or gifts during festivals and rituals performed by Shresthas or Udas. These old obligations, related to their inferior status, are presently considered to be humiliating, and are therefore rejected. Consequently, the Jyapus tend to act more like an ethnic group than like a caste. Such a process, called 'substantialization of caste' by Louis Dumont, is a clear indication of the progressive disintegration of the old order and of a loss of the sense of relations which characterized the traditional Newar caste system.

What about representation of the self? It is interesting to note that the word Jyapu is still contemptuous for many persons in the valley. Inspite of this, Newar peasants are proud to be Jyapu, a large caste by its population but of relatively inferior status within the caste system. Accordingly, Jyapus marry mostly within their caste and are not so attracted by intercaste marriages. The process of upward mobility, Jyapus marrying Shrestha girls, described by Colin Rosser in 1966, is true for the eastern part of the valley of Kathmandu, where Jyapus are heavily influenced by Hindus (in Sankhu and a Panauti for instance), not for Kathmandu, Patan, and the southern villages of the valley. Is this phenomenon new? I am not so sure. During my fieldwork, I came across some examples of solidarity among Jyapus, towards other castes, which indicate that such a sense of unity already existed some decades ago.

Until now, the rise of caste-based organizations among Jyapus has not altered the traditional social structure. First, as Gellner noted, the importance of the territorial basis within the Jyapu Mahaguthi is still prevalent in everyday matters. Local affiliation to the central branch of the organization is always problematic and tends to be nominal. Second, the membership has until now been mostly restricted to men. I saw some young women during Mahaguthi meetings, but they were so shy that they did not dare to speak. Besides, as soon as they marry, they stop participating in the association. I was amused to read in the Lalitpur Jyapu Samaj pamphlet quoted in appendix 2, that this Samaj defines Jyapu as the caste which, among other things, 'has dhime baja drums as their main custom'. As you know, these drums are played only by men. In fact, the traditional music, so important in the Jyapu social structure, excludes women and is ideologically male dominated. This raises the question of the relationships between identity and gender, a point which has not been dealt with in detail.

Notes

1. I am especially interested in what is said about the Jyapus, the Newar peasant caste. I am still conducting research on this group and it is among them that the Newar caste organizations are presently the stongest.

Differences and Distances

Contested Ethnic Markers in Local and National Communities

JOHANNA PFAFF-CZARNECKA

Culture can establish bridges, or, on the contrary, it can erect forceful barriers between groups of people. The outcome depends largely upon the given context in which the social actors—more or less consciously—choose specific attitudes towards people they consider different, for instance towards people belonging to other caste or ethnic goups. In situations of conflict, the signs of avoidance, highlighting difference, or distance acquire an importance. Within relatively short spans of time, strategically important signs can be interpreted anew, or they may acquire additional conditions. Three issues are of significance in such circumstances. First, the very fact that with changed circumstances established meanings and signs can be re-interpreted makes thorough inquiries necessary: we have to ask when crucial shifts in meanings of established symbols take place, and what kind of meanings are especially prone to contestations. Secondly, when we examine the processes of production of new meanings and inquire into the processes of re-interpretation of signs in situations of ethnicity formation, it is interesting to see how local negotiations, say, within villages or among the members of particular groups are affected by discourses and actions beyond the 'local' context, coined for instance in the national centres. The third set of questions pertains to the conditions and the actual processes underlying the coining and/or the re-interpretation of meanings, making for a particular use of symbols.

Ethnicity speaks a complex language. Social actors incorporate various cultural and religious elements when involved in identity politics, when, seeking to express their grievances or to formulate their projects. Prone to 'capture' are religious elements, rituals, specific habits and customs, historical notions, ritually important sites, cultural notions considered (by some people) as elements of the national culture, dress, and others. Usually such elements become ethnic markers when publicly contested by members of those groups feeling excluded from particular notions, especially when trying to define themselves in opposition to values and symbols embraced by those in power. Indeed, in Nepal specific cultural or religious notions were turned into ethnic markers only after the ethnic activists sought to define their identity *in reaction* to the prevailing public images of the national society and of the minorities in particular. Especially since the year 1990, various ethnic activists in Nepal have been publicly challenging the cultural and religious forms of the dominant Hindu groups. Such actions came as a surprise in view of the fact that until 1990, minority issues as well as the general theme of ethnic accommodation in Nepal have been perceived—by and large—as devoid of conflict.

Unfortunately, only few accounts of the forms of co-existence of people belonging to different caste and ethnic groups in Nepal exist, let alone regarding the signs used in everyday interactions as well as during special occasions. As is well known, until the year 1990, Nepal has generally been described—in official rhetoric, but also by scholars—in rather harmonious terms. Her multi-ethnic nation has been eagerly depicted as 'wild garden in which numerous wild flowers have been growing, since centuries' (see Sharma 1992). While until 1990 social anthropologists—mainly foreign—have been concentrating upon the ethnic populations[1] (see Dahal 1993)[2]—only seldom indicating the possible conflict potentials with the *tagadhari*-groups, the focus of inquiry has radically shifted in the aftermath of the so-called 'revolution' of 1990.[3] From this moment onwards, accounts of conflicts across the ethnic borders have rapidly proliferated due to at least two reasons. The first lies in the changed climate within which scientific research occurs: until the end of the 1980s, any hints at potential social conflict by (foreign) scholars had been actively discouraged by the authorities.

The second reason is the actual increase of overt conflict situations in the aftermath of the 1990-'revolution'. While ethnic conflicts occurred long before the 1990-awakening its success has opened a Pandora's box of old grievances, leading to contestations of their public displays deploying pejorative symbols. The social movements depicted by the term 'ethnicity formation' are especially geared towards symbols expressing unity within groups, simultaneously stressing difference and distance towards the others. Notable are also negotiations within particular groups when the very bases of unity and/or self-definition come under a conflict-laden scrutiny (see Gellner 1997).

Why do such shifts come about? James Scott's concept of moral economy helps us to understand the current dynamics of ethnicity formation. Scott (1976) urges us not to be taken in by appearances, such as displays of ethnic harmony because within specific power arrangements the subjugated sections of a society have to display compliance to specific symbols displayed by the superordinate. Only when power configurations change does the real nature of these seemingly binding symbols come to light. The fact that specific symbols have been associated with former power arrangements can induce social actors challenge them publicly, once the power shifts. In the later sections of this chapter, I shall focus on such recent endeavours. Before doing that, it may be useful to assess the scope of symbolization in the inter-ethnic interactions in Nepal.

Overt and Covert Signs in a Multi-ethnic local society in Central Nepal

Most symbols and other signs used in everyday encounters as well as on special situations, for instance during rituals, fall into the category of 'what goes without saying' (Bloch). Largely taken for granted, the signs organizing the local requirements of differentiation and of distantiation form a kind of a ***hidden agenda*** in inter-ethnic and inter-caste encounters. Or, to be more precise, some of the signs have belonged to the *hidden agenda* until recently, but have been put into question in recent years—since the movement when the ethnic and low-caste activists have started to examine interactions and the silent signs, declaring some of them as symbols of oppression, and/or as devices misrepresenting their cultures.

Life in local settings characterized by a group of people belonging to various ethnic and/or caste groups is highly semiotized. It is hardly surprising that within microcosms so thoroughly dominated by Hindu norms and values, great efforts have been made—especially by those ranking high within the Hindu hierarchy—to express difference and distance in the idiom of superiority and inferiority.[4] But generally, people tend to read signs given through dress as well as through adornment in order to determine their relative standing (see also Srinivas 1972).

The use of symbols in the central-Nepalese village of Belkot where several caste and ethnic groups live in close proximity is one case in point (proxemic signs). Until a decade ago, the interactions highlighting difference and distance here seemed to be self-evident and binding. Some of the signs such as the attire, housing structures, or forms of behaviour were immediately visible. Other forms could only be deduced and could not be taken as signs in the precise moment of their enactment. In retrospect, when they became contested they eventually turned into symbols. One such example is the use of common wells.

Among the most visible signs is, of course, the *appearance* of persons. The Nepalis are very well trained in 'reading' each other's signs as expressed through dress, jewellery, and other accessories (for comparable inquiries in India, see e.g. Béteille 1972). In quotidian village life such signs get ignored because personal intimacy makes such signs seem unnecessary and therefore invisible. But strangers encountered on village paths are closely scrutinized, and if their identity cannot be immediately determined by a mere glance the person is directly asked a question relating to his or her identity. Differences indicate caste and/ or ethnic belonging. In central Nepal high-caste people do not wear black with the exception of vests—a new addition in the male attire—while this colour is common among the low-castes. The members of ethnic groups display different attitudes in their dressing style. In Belkot, the Magars and Newars are dressed in the same way as the high-caste Parbatiyas (though the Newarnis do not wear nose-ornaments), whereas many Tamang still wear hand-woven woollen fabrics which are cut differently from the Parbatiya clothes. During the 1980s, often when the villagers were heading to offices in the near-by district capital, they could witness state officials testing the Tamangs because of their distinct dressing-style. External signs do not pertain solely to the ethnic/caste belonging, but also to status, especially to the marital status of women. It is widely known that in central Nepal high-caste widows do not wear red and do not wear non-metallic jewellery while unmarried girls must not wear the *pote*.

Another set of signs is apparent in the *interactions* in private as well as public spaces (on this concept, see KcKim Marriott 1976; Dumont 1966). In private places, the treatment of guests is especially significant: guests visiting high-caste households are either admitted into the houses, or kept outside; outside, they are either admitted to the veranda or kept away from it. Those invited to eat in the kitchen are either asked to eat at the same level with the householder, allowed to the level where the children eat, or allowed to sit only in a corner—at a secure distance from the hearth where the rice is cooked. The look of the domestic compounds, the animals kept in the yard (usually, but not as a rule, only those animals that the household members are allowed to eat are kept), the allocation of the entrances as well as the small tectonic barriers between the compounds can be 'read' as signs—either symbolizing the particular status of the inhabitants, or the necessary distances to be kept from the neighbours belonging to lower ethnic groups or castes. For instance, the Brahmins guard the entrances into their kitchens from the view of passers-by more carefully than the members of other groups.

In public situations, the temples, offices, schools and tea shops make people adopt special forms of interactions. The tea shops are especially interesting because food is served—which makes temporarily for stronger rules of avoidance. As in the private house, the rules of distantiation pertain also to access into tea shops. For an outsider, the distances kept by people considered 'low-caste' may be scarcely visible, but they are in fact to be seen as forceful barriers. Distances of just 20 centimetres can express deep social cleavages. Most striking is the behaviour towards the low-castes. They are not only made to remain outside the tea shops; the tea served to them is either poured into special vessels which are only used by the low-caste customers, or it is served in the ordinary glasses which have to be cleaned by the low-caste customers themselves. A clear-cut expression of Hindu hierarchy is the order in smoking cigarettes and water-pipes (*hukka*). Whenever several persons join in smoking one cigarette, it is always passed from a person of higher ranking towards the next ranking person. . . until it lands at the feet or in the palm of a low-caste person. The hukka is not only handed down from a 'higher' to the 'lower' person; depending upon the relative status of the smoker, the user may only be allowed to use parts of the hukka. (see also Höfer 1979)

Ritual occasions provide another arena for expressing differences and distances in interactions. Generally, rituals make for well-defined spatial arrangements of the involved persons, including the access to the ritually sensitive spots. Rituals make people express the relative standing through bowing and through the patterns of giving and receiving the tika (for instance, the Brahmin priests may not touch their Tamang *jajmans* when they are to give them a tika; on tika-exchanges on Dasain, see especially Bennett 1983). Rituals require special arrangements for the distribution and eating of the sacrificial food. Due regard is paid to the order in which the members of particular castes and ethnic groups are seated and served.

Particular ritual events make for special adaptations as shown in the case of the adjustments between the Magars and their Brahmin neighbours. The Magar hamlet of Belkot is situated near several Brahmin households. All the neighbours share the same well. In everyday situations this fact does not call for any particular adjustments. It is gender rather than caste and ethnic group membership that orders the interactions. This order changes when the Magars kill pigs and cook pork on ritual occasions: they are then not allowed by the Brahmins to use the common well. Drinking water is usually stored in advance; washing is done at a distant water-source. This arrangement indicates that particular practices of distantiation may help to maintain friendly neighbourly links between people belonging to different caste or ethnic groups. This arrangement as such is not a sign, but it has acquired the status of a signal in Belkot when recently, 'all of the sudden' the Magars decided to 'read' it as a demonstration of power differentials to their disadvantage.

The most impressive displays of hierarchies and distances occur during the Dasai celebrations, when members of various castes and ethnic groups are united through patterns of a ritual division of labour, on one hand, and when they are divided among themselves by rules of distantiation on the other. The Dasai celebrations as they have been celebrated in Belkot until the second half of the twentieth century, consist of an elaborate ritual sequence, with ritual specialist acting as the protagonists throughout the first nine days of the festivities, and with local power holders playing the major role on the last day. By and large, Belkot's festivities conform to the broader pan-Indian tradition of Durga puja celebrations. They contain, however, some particular aspects along with specific 'local meanings'. Neither the ritual nor the local specificities can be described here (see Pfaff-Czarnecka 1993; 1998), but two instances are of special interest in relation to the symbolic practices: first, the co-operation of the ritual specialist, consisting of the Dasai priest (a Brahmin); a temple priest (a Brahmin); the village servant (*naike*—a Newar); a man who fasts together with the Dasai priest, who lives together with the Dasai priest in the Dasai house, who performs the sacrifices and carries the sword (*upasye*—a Magar) as well as the leader of the orchestra (*kotwal*—a Damai). The joint activities can be (and have been over a long period) 'read' as forceful manifestations of local unity—notwithstanding caste and ethnic divisions. This notion is also enhanced by the opportunity provided to the various actors to 'use' the ritual setting for action important to individual actors or collectivities taking part in the festivities—for instance ritually linking one's own lineage to the deity worshipped during Dasai, or pointing to a particular importance of one's group within the local society.

The second instance evoked in Belkot's Dasai pertains to the ritual ordering displayed during celebrations. Especially on the tenth day, the relative status of the different castes and ethnic groups living in Belkot is displayed, reflecting, among other things, the prevailing power relations. On this day, a goat is sacrificed in the morning. Its head is put on a leaf plate and placed in the Durga puja house. Outside, Brahmins gather and they read from the *Devi-Mahatmya.* A crowd gradually assembles in and around the sacrificial ground. Inside the ritual house the priest worships the objects symbolizing the goddess. After the ritual objects, including the last goat's head, are brought and arranged outside the ritual house, the priest gives the first tika to the political village head (i.e. to the *dware* under the Ranas and to the *pradhan panc* until 1983). Afterwards elaborate tika exchanges between the ritual specialists begin, leaving the village head in the centre with the villagers coming to him to receive the tika, to bow, and to offer a gift. The special signal character to Dasai in Belkot was demonstrated by the fact that before the panchayat period (i.e. before 1962) all villagers had to attend the celebrations, to bow in front of the dignitaries, to receive tika from them, and to present them with gifts of prescribed items and in prescribed amounts. As we shall see the Dasai celebrations in Belkot are currently 'read' afresh, that is, as a particularly oppressive situation on the occasion of which ritual ranking and actual power structure reinforce one another.

Re-reading and Re-interpretation of the Established Signs: Local and National Examples

The recent actions by various ethnic and low-caste activists cast a new light upon the prescribed interactions and the signs invoked in them. What could earlier be interpreted either as outcomes of prolonged acculturation processes (see Pfaff-Czarnecka 1997) or of fascinating cultural devices allowing for peaceful accommodation, in multicultural settings emerges, at least to some extent, as a ground of cultural struggles over the politics of representation. Signs described above as forms easing the mutual interactions tend to transform partly, into symbols of oppression, of subordination, of enforced acculturation—as various ethnic and low-caste activists claim. While the ethnic markers expressing difference bear conflictual potentials, those markers expressing distance tend to enhance a harmonious co-existence. Strikingly, however, distances and differences can be expressed by the same markers—being put forward and interpreted differently by different set of actors—according to the social context. Elements which have been taken for granted over long time periods can emerge as powerful political symbols within comparatively short spans of time. On the other hand, elements highlighting conflict may lose their symbolic salience when re-interpreted, or when other cultural or religious elements are incorporated along with them. Let us consider some striking example of re-reading and/or of re-interpretation of cultural forms.

The Dasai celebrations in Belkot are one case in point. In 1986, the new political head of Belkot did not attend Durga puja festivities at any stage because he, a Tamang, opposed their communal performance. As a consequence, the 'political power' was represented by the village secretary who was a Chetri. That a Tamang was the elected leader of the village (pradhan panch) was a novelty. Until then the village head has always been a member from the twice-born castes. His decision not to participate in the event was a departure from Durga puja celebrations during the preceding periods under high-caste Hindus. Though the villagers were not any longer obliged to deliver any tokens (foodstuff) to the village headman in the panchayat period from the early 1960s onwards, a majority *felt* compelled to appear on the tenth day and to bow in front the pradhan panc.

It is noticeable that the Tamang opposed Durga puja immediately after they came to power, so this was already the fourth year in a row with this kind of conflict. Originally this opposition came especially from young, dynamic leaders of the Tamang community who had a radical vision of change in Nepalese society. Gradually they came to be supported in their opposition against the public displays of hierarchical relations on Durga puja by a very large proportion of the Tamang community. In the view of many Tamangs, nowadays actively expressed mainly by the younger generation, Durga puja is an expression of the Hinduist predominance within the Nepalese political system under the rule of the king and the dominance of his clients who belonged to the twice-born castes over the local society.

According to the Tamang leaders, by promoting the local cult in Belkot the rulers both expressed their religious feelings, and at the same time conveyed a message substantiating their worldly power while extending their possessions (see Burghart 1984). The local population was expected to acknowledge this fact by demonstrating its deference. Confronted with a specific symbol of the emerging political culture shaped by central rulers, the local élite (holders of administrative offices, priests, influential families) took the opportunity to express their loyalty, but also sought to substantiate, in turn, *their* power of elevated status, by linking their prerogatives to symbols related to the central rulers. The local population, subjects to the central rulers and to the local élite, was made to witness such endeavours. They were not merely invited but compelled to come, to bring tributes, to bow, and to watch. By displaying obedience they were forming a part of the festive background. Their presence served to assert the importance of those who were able to establish themselves as the focus of the celebrations.

While the high-caste members of the local community have been striving to make the festivities a resource substantiating their importance, the members of the hitherto low-ranking (by Hindu standards) ethnic community, the Tamangs, have undertaken action in order to stop the Durga puja celebrations altogether after they acquired political power. The Tamangs in Belkot made a conscious choice not to endorse the central values of the ritual even though, having attained political power, they could have turned the ritual order to their political advantage. Claiming, however, that the Durga puja ritual not only commemorates their political subjugation but also symbolizes their ritual inferiority within the Hindu hierarchy, the Tamang leaders have decided to boycott the entire complex: the Tamangs have chosen to 'read' Durga puja as a symbol of their oppression within the Hindu realm. It is remarkable that after a period of over 200 years of a seeming accommodation within a ritual complex, they wanted to effect a break with the past. Let us note in passing that in other parts of Nepal, members of non-Hindu communities have taken to performing purification rites on the occasion of Dasai, that is in order to wash away the sin loaded upon Nepal in the course of the animal sacrifices conducted on the occasion of Dasai (Paul 1989).

Since at least two decades, low-castes are opposing their treatment in tea shops. That they were made to use either special cups, or that they were made to wash the cups themselves unlike other customers has increasingly become a bone of contention not only in Belkot, but also in other central Nepalese villages (see especially the film *Makai* by Garlinski and Bieri; Blustain 1977). Another contested sign is the dress. While the Parbatiya attire of *kurta-surval* seemed to be replacing the earlier forms of clothing, there is an effort to encourage the wearing of 'traditional' clothes made from local material and the local human resources, corresponding well with the notion of self-sufficiency at the grassroot level.

All over Nepal a process of 'exodus from South Asia' can be observed. The major feature of this process is to reject Hindu notions as intrinsic components of ethnic cultures. Alan Macfarlane's (1997) account of the activities among the Gurungs is probably most relevant (for similar process among other ethnic groups, see especially Krämer 1996; B. Campbell 1997; Gaenszle 1997; and Russell 1997). The two related cases are the re-interpretation of the ethnic chronicles as well as the re-assessment of the social structure of one's own group. Both cases are related because they are put forward as instances representing a thorough critique of Brahmanic practices. Gurung activists who have acted as Alan Macfarlane's informants endorse a common pattern visible in Nepal. Brahmin priests are blamed for having distorted the *vamsavalis* and for having misrepresented ethnic cultural forms. On 13 March 1992 Macfarlance received in Cambridge (UK) a fax sent from Pokhara (west Nepal) signed by Gurung activists, informing him that at the national relay earlier that year the Gurungs had formulated several resolutions: (1) Gurungs' history has been written and distorted by the Brahmins; (2) there exist no higher and lower Gurung clans; (3) the traditional Gurung priests have been Pachyu and Klabri, the Lamas came later.

Four elements are salient. First, the insistence upon equality within the Gurung community put forward in the claim that all Gurung clans are equal (but see Höfer 1979). Secondly, equality also manifests itself in the insistence upon equal importance of marriage with the matrilateral cross-cousin as much as with the patrilateral cross-cousin. The idea of the exodus from South Asia manifests itself in the revised version of the vamsavalis. Gurung activists claim that contrary to the earlier depictions they did not migrate into the Nepalese territory via India, but that they came from Mongolia. Thirdly, they stress the special importance of the Bön religion. The fourth element highlights the interaction between the ethnic activists and the scientific community: among the reasons why Alan Macfarlane was confronted with all this information was that he and Sarah Harrisson were working at that time on the translation of the famous monograph on the Gurungs by Bernard Pignède into English. While criticizing the Brahmins, the Gurungs activists have pointed out that Pignède's analysis of their culture tended to impose a South Asian perspective on them. They stressed that Pignède was Louis Dumont's student who has perceived all of South Asia through the prism of Hindu values.

An examination of the recent efforts of Gurung activists reveals the following. What becomes a symbol (of cultural oppression; of political subjugation) does not appear to have been public issue in the previous one or two decades. It might have been an issue, but was hardly ever raised at a national or even a local public forum. We could claim that overt conflicts were more or less absent before the 1990 'revolution'. But caution has to be exercised in saying this. Haven't there been overt conflicts, or did we, social anthropologists of western as well as of Nepalese provenance, just fail to record and to analyse them? The film *Makai*, my own data on overt disputes during the Dasai celebrations, Paul's statement about the Buddhist activists' reactions to the animal sacrifices and some other examples have all been recorded before the 1990 movements. One can assume, therefore, that similar instances have occurred in the past.

The second inference relates to the shift in emphasis on specific elements and of rendering them prominent. What seemed to go without saying a decade or so ago, currently acquires new connotations. Signs which formerly were hardly noticed emerge as new, important tools in conflictual situations. The description of signs and rules in interactions given in the first part of this paper can easily appear as a naive description of specific modes of ordering under the conditions of a clear cut hegemony, while currently cultural displays and mutual encounters turn into contested grounds. What is striking in these processes—this is my third inference—is a certain kind of homogeneity in the cultural debates observed throughout Nepal which brings us to the topic of the national, international, and local exchanges in the cultural production of meanings.

The Cultural Production, Reactions, Common Patterns, Role Models, and the Importance of the (inter) National Audiences

What accounts for the shift in orientations of signs? The increasing salience of ethnicity formation in Nepal is a widely observed phenomenon, and the processes of ethnicity formation are all about symbolization. The easier it is to coin one sign as standing for the internal unity as well as a sign for mobilizing action, the more it is likely to be used in politics of representation. Signs comprising positive (identity marker) as well as negative (opposition to other groups) connotations acquire a strategic importance. Further, symbols are especially effective when they can also be transmitted to audiences which are not directly involved in particular conflicts. Therefore, querying the reasons for the shift in the use and in the interpretation of symbols, enables us to answer crucial questions relating to ethnicity formation.

It is still impossible to assess how the ongoing endeavours to redefine the politics of representation in the national context will impinge upon cultural manifestations of different groups. Growing interest in one's own culture, the search for origins, new cultural projects, public discussions of culture, cultural comparison and cultural competition come about through a variety of processes. Partly, members of minorities react to earlier neglect of their cultures in official rhetoric. Furthermore, tactical manoeuvres by activists may result in highlighting particular symbols at the expense of others. Also, searching for roots of one own community may be pursued as a hobby among intelligentsia. While struggling for rights and resources some members of minorities have taken recourse to 'cultural' arguments. At the same time, some members of the majority, notably the supporters of Hindu organizations, seek to preserve the status quo in a counter-movement. It is not possible to discern one single tendency for cultural change, or one major factor underlying the unfolding processes. In order to understand the current processes of symbolization it is important to acknowledge the public character of the ongoing endeavours. The activities of organizations and their individual exponents indicate the nature, direction, and discontinuities of the broader process. Since the 1990 movement, the previously neglected, marginalized, or even suppressed groups and orgnizations have been able to act within a new legal framework. At least in theory, all Nepalese citizens are invited to participate in the development process: as clients to welfare, through party politics, and also as concerned citizens with access to the public sphere.

At the same time, it has become obvious that minority formation has been closely connected to the politics of representation. If we envisage the public sphere as being an arena where any civic action can be subjected to public scrutiny, one is immediately confronted with the question as to the actual share of the ethnic population involved in *cultural politics*. One may ask whether the majority of members of the Nepalese minorities know that they are being represented by their leaders on public occasions, and whether they agree with the way in which they are represented, or whether they comply with the objectives particularly stressed by their self-appointed spokespersons. There are very often village teachers or learned opinion-makers exposed to the national, and—increasingly—international politics of representation who are in charge of defining issues on the local agenda, of re-shaping symbols and of popularizing them. The great interest in the vamsavalis, to take one example, is related to the special interest of the learned men who are informed about the measures taken by other activists. Interestingly, the interest in the vamsavalis has grown among several ethnic groups, by and large as a uniform process.

The simultaneity of assimilation to a new, dominant culture and revitalization of one's own old one results in a paradox: the search for distinction and uniqueness creates somehow a unifying factor in the national perspective, as if those seeking to distinguish themselves are striving to establish a common denominator at the same time. This is one of the outcomes of the national exchanges in which well-educated activists play a prominent role. Such exchanges tend to result in shared models of action: when activists of particular groups successfully start to put forward specific notions, there is a tendency that similar practices will be adopted by other groups: rejection of Hindu notions, re-interpretation of the historical accounts, social and cultural reforms, a greater care in religious expression, including the erection of new religious structures, or even invention of a new script. All of these measures can mean endorsement of specific cultural elements, but the politics of reaction may not be overlooked: after a century-long subjugation under Nepalese rulers encouraging or even enforcing (especially after the collapse of the Rana regime) the adoption of the cultural-religious elements of the Parbatiyas, most ethnic activists are eager to reverse the trend of the cultural change.

Whenever cultural forms are made official or public, specificities or 'inconsistencies' fall prey to the different process of cultural translation. Traditionalism tends to simplify tradition for the same reason. Traditional elements to be displayed are selected after culture is subjected to careful scrutiny. If shamanism—fascinating for foreign tourists but embarrassing to many among the Nepalese intelligentsia—is to be considered an intrinsic part of the tradition, shamanism without blood sacrifice may appear as a compromise solution in the process of adopting a progressive outlook (see Ramble 1997). Several accounts (see Gellner, Pfaff-Czarnecka and Whelpton ed. 1997; Krämer 1996) reveal that within minority groups, discussions about valid versions of their cultures abound. Diverse sections of ethnic groups, guided by their elite, differ in their visions of what is to be understood as the 'cultural content'. While cultural purists opt for retaining practices disapproved of by others, reformers advocate modifications in ritual practice.

Let us finally look at the audiences for whom the politics of representation are partly intended. Minority representations are a pertinent factor in the present political process in Nepal. They indicate the scope of an emerging pluralism corresponding to the enhanced access of citizens to ongoing debates. However, pluralism does not preclude inequality, especially where the decision-making process is concerned. In the present field of popular representation, new forms of differentiation are likely to emerge and old inequalities may well be reinforced. Second, the emerging public sphere is a contested ground. Institutionalized rules governing the ways in which 'potential issues are kept out of the political process' (Lukes 1974: 21) and 'control over political agenda' (ibid.: 25) are being produced and reproduced. In the process of minority formation in Nepal, the public sphere is simultaneously moulded by the international aid scene, international 'capital', international audiences (tourists, religious disciples, see Ramble 1997; Burkert 1997), members of the ruling groups and their clients (as a counter-movement) as well as various spokesmen for minorities promoting sectional visions. In pursuing these interests, current values which guide action are being negotiated. In the present context, a particularized notification of ethnicity emerges as a political resource since it serves various interests such as the new 'development discourse', the new entrepreneurial culture, the western 'dream' of authenticity—especially of archaic communities—presently invoked in the aid scene, the power-holders' image as politically progressive, and the minority leaders' newly acquired role of intermediaries as a new type of political resource. Certainly, in the complex and contested public sphere, a variety of cultural manifestations confront each other. That the politicization of ethnic difference should be affected by such a variety of factors making for a proliferation of ethnic repertoires comes as a surprise—probably not only to the foreign analysts, but to those involved in ethic politics as well.

Notes

1. There are exceptions, however: Bennett (1983); Campbell (1978); Gaborieau (1977); Stone (1977); Gray (1980); Ramirez (1996); Höfer (1979); Pfaff-Czarnecka (1989).
2. Rather, forms of harmonious co-existence were stressed by authors indicating the economic interdependence between different groups (von Fürer-Haimendorf 1971) or showing how prolonged contact situations have made for cultural adaptations, as described for instance by Höfer (1986).
3. See especially Gellner, Pfaff-Czarnecka and Whelpton (1997).
4. Dumont (1966) uses the term *séparation*, but *distance*, as we shall see below, seems more appropriate.

References

Baumann, G., 1992, 'Ritual implicates "Others": Rereading Durkheim in a Plural Society', in D. de Coppet (ed.), *Understanding Ritual*, London and New York: Routledge.

Bennett, L., 1983, *Dangerous Wives and Sacred Sisters*, New York: Columbia University Press.

Béteille, A. (ed.), 1969, 'Caste in a South Indian Village', in A. Béteille (ed.), *Social Inequality*, Hammondsworth, Penguin Books.

Bista, D.B., 1991, *Fatalism and Development: Nepal's Struggle for Modernization*, Calcutta: Orient Longman.

Bloch, Maurice, 1992, '*What goes Without Saying: The Conceptualization of Zafimaniry Society in Conceptualizing Society*', Hrsg. Adam Kuper, London: Routledge, pp. 127–46.

Blustain, H.S., 1997, *Power and Ideology in a Nepalese Village*, Unpublished PhD Thesis, Yale University.

Burghart, R., 1984, 'The Formation of the Concept of Nation-State in Nepal', *Journal of Asian Studies* 64(1), pp. 101–25.

Burkert, C., 1997, 'Defining Maithil Identity: Who is in Charge?', in D. Gellner, J. Pfaff-Czarnecka, and J. Whelpton (eds.), *Nationalism and Ethnicity in Hindu Kingdom: The Politics of Culture in Contemporary Nepal*. Amsterdam: Harwood Academic Publishers.

Campbell, J.G., 1978, *Consultations with Himalayan Gods: A Study of Oracular Religion and Alternative Values in Hindu Jumla*, Ann Arbor: Human Relation Area Files.

Campbell, B., 1997, 'The Heavy Loads of Tamang Identity', in D. Gellner, J. Pfaff-Czarnecka, and J. Whelpton (eds.), *Nationalism and Ethnicity in Hindu Kingdom: The Politics of Culture in Centemporary Nepal*, Amsterdam: Harwood Academic Publishers, pp. 205–35.

Dahal, D.R., 1993, 'Anthropology of the Nepal Himalaya: A Critical Appraisal', in C. Ramble and M. Brauen (eds.), *Anthropology of Tibet and the Himalaya*. Zürich: ESZ 12.

Dumont, L., 1966, *Homo Hierarchicus: Essai sur le système des castes*. Paris: Gallimard.

________, 1979, *Homo Hierarchicus: Le système des castes et ses implications*, Paris: Gallimard.

Fürer-Haimendorf, Chr. v. 1971, 'Tribes and Hindu Society', *Contributions to Indian Sociology* 5, pp. 24–7.

________, 1971, 'Status and Interaction among the High Hindu Castes of Nepal, *The Eastern Anthorpologist* 24:7–24.

Gaborieau, M. 1977, 'Systèmes traditionels des échanges de services spécialisés contre rémunération dans une localité du Népal Central', *Purusartha* 3, pp. 1–70.

Gaenszle, M. 1997, 'Changing Conceptions of Ethnic Identity among the Mewahang Rai', in D. Gellner, J. Pfaff-Czarnecka, and J. Whelpton (eds.), *Nationalism and Ethnicity in Hindu Kingdom: The Politics of Culture in Contemporary Nepal*, Amsterdam: Harwood Academic Publishers, pp. 351–73.

Gellner, D., 1992, *Monk, Householder, and Tantric Priest: Newar Buddhism and its Hierarchy of Ritual*, Cambridge: Cambridge University Press.

________, J. Pfaff-Czarnecka and J. Whelpton (eds,), 1997, *Nationalism and Ethnicity in a Hindu Kingdom: The Politics of Culture in Contemporary Nepal*, Amsterdam: Harwood Academic Publishers.

Gellner, D., 1997, 'Caste, Communalism, and Communism: Newars and the Nepalese State', in D. Gellner, J. Pfaff-Czarnecka, and J. Whelpton (eds.), *Nationalism and Ethnicity in Hindu Kingdom: The Politics of Culture in Contemporary Nepal,* Amsterdam: Harwood Academic Publishers.

Gray, J.N., 1980, Hypergamy, Kinship and Caste among the Chetris of Nepal, *Contributions to Indian Sociology* (N.S.) (14)1: 1–34.

Höfer, A., 1979, *The Caste Hierarchy and the State in Nepal: A Study of the Muluki An of 1854,* in Khumbu Himal, Innsbruck: Universitätsverlag Wagner.

________, 1986, 'Wieso hinduisieren sich die Tamang?' in B. Kölver (ed.), *Formen Kulturellen Wandels und andere Beiträge zur Erforschung des Himalaya,* Sankt Augustin: VGH Wissenschaftsverlag.

Inden, R. and R. Nicholas, 1977, *Kinship in Bengali Culture,* Chicago: University of Chicago Press.

Krämer, K. H., 1996, *Ethnizität und Nationale Integration in Nepal: Eine Untersuchung zur Politisierung der ethnischen Gruppen im modernen Nepal,* Stuttgart: Franz Steiner Verlag.

Krauskopff, G. and M. Lecomte-Tilouine, 1996, *Célébrer le pouvoir: Dasai, une fête royale au Népal,* Paris: Editions CNRS.

Lukes, S., 1974, *Power: A Radical View,* London: Macmillan.

________, 1977, 'Political Ritual and Social Integration', in S. Lukes (ed.), *Essays in Social Theory,* London and Basingstoke: Macmillan.

Macfarlane, A., 1997, Identity and Change Among the Gurungs (Tamu-mai) of Central Nepal, in *Nationalism and Ethnicity in Contemporary Nepal: The Cultural Politics in a Hindu Kingdom,* Amsterdam: Harwood Academic Publishers.

Marriott, McKim, 1976, 'Hindu Transactions. Diversity without Dualism', in B. Kapferer, (ed.), *Transaction and Meaning. Directions in the Anthropology of Exchange and Symbolic Behavior,* Philadelphia: Institute for the Study of Human Issues, pp. 109–42.

Paul, R. A., 1989, *The Sherpas of Nepal in the Tibetan Cultural Context,* Delhi: Motilal Banarsidass Publishers.

Pfaff-Czarnecka, J., 1989, *Macht und Rituelle Reinheit: Hinduistisches Kastenwesen und Ethnische Beziehungen im Entwicklungsprozess Nepals,* Gruesch: Rüegger.

________, 1991, 'State and Community: Changing Relations of Production after the Unification of Nepal', in H.J.M. Claessen and P.V.D. Velde, (eds.), *Early State Economics,* Political and Legal Anthropology, Vol. 8. New Brunswick and London: Transaction Publishers.

________, 1993, 'The Nepalese Durgaapuujaa Festival, or Displaying Political Supremacy on Ritual Occations', in C. Ramble and M. Brauen (eds.), *Anthropology of Tibet and the Himalaya,* Zürich: ESZ 12.

________, 1997, 'Vestiges and Visions: Cultural Change in the Process of

Nation-Building in Nepal', in D. Gellner, J. Pfaff-Czarnecka, and J. Whelpton (eds.), *Nationalism and Ethnicity in a Hindu State: The Cultural Politics in Contemporary Nepal*, Amsterdam: Harwood Academic Publishers.

Pfaff-Czarnecka, J., 1998, A Battle of Meanings: Commemorating Goddess Durgaa's Victory over Demon Mahisaa as a Political Act', *Asiatische Studien* (Hrsg. J. Helbling) 52(2), pp. 575–610.

Ramble, C., 1997, 'Tibetan Pride of Place, Why Nepal's Bhotiyas are not an Ethnic Groups', in D. Gellner, J. Pfaff-Czarnecka, and J. Whelpton (eds.), *Nationalism and Ethnicity in a Hindu State: The Cultural Politics in Contemporary Nepal*, Amsterdam: Harwood Academic Publishers.

Ramirez, P., 1996, 'Luttes d'influence dans l'empire de la Déesse', in G. Krauskopff and M. Lecomte-Tilouine (eds.), *Célébrer le pouvoir: Dasai, une fête royale au Népal*, Paris: CNRS, pp. 209–39.

Russel, A., 1997, 'Identity Management and Cultural Change: The Yakha of East Nepal', in D. Gellner, J. Pfaff-Czarnecka, and J. Whelpton (eds.), *Nationalism and Ethnicity in a Hindu State: The Cultural Politics in Contemporary Nepal*, Amsterdam: Harwood Academic Publishers.

Scott, J.C., 1976, *The Moral Economy of the Peasant: Rebellion and Subsistence in Southeast Asia*, New Haven and London: Yale University Press.

Sharma, P.R., 1992, 'How to Tend this Garden', *Himal* 5(3), pp. 7–9.

Srinivas, M.N., 1972, 'The Caste System in India', in A. Béteille (ed.), *Social Inequality*, Hammondsworth: Penguin Books.

Stone, L., 1977, *Illness, Hierarchy and Food Symbolism in Hindu Nepal*, HRAF.

Williams, R., 1984 [1976], *Keywords. A Vocabulary of Culture and Society*, London: Fontana Paperbacks.

Comments

MARIE LECOMTE-TILOUINE

J. Pfaff-Czarnecka has chosen to discuss the interpretation of signs according to context, and stresses that it is important to understand the shift of meaning of signs within a local and a broader context. Those signs which are used to define one group are the so-called ethnic markers and she rightly argues that they are highlighted by activists in reaction to the prevailing public use of them. She emphasizes how harmony rather than potential conflicts was described in the multi-ethnic Nepalese society before 1990 and how the focus of inquiry shifted afterwards to conflicts. And I think that she rightly criticizes the fact that potential conflicts underlying the apparent harmony of this multi-ethnic and multicaste nation have not been adequately studied in the past.

Its seems to me that the main reason for the change in the way Nepalese society is viewed lies in an apparent radical change within the studied society itself, the new freedom of the press and the multiplication of local 'ethnic publications' which followed. All these phenomena are obviously linked to the post-'revolution' period. To take the Magar journals as an example: *Gorākh* was first published in 1991, *Lāphā* and *Soni*, in 1992, *Sār* and *Gyāvaṭ* in 1993, *Kānung lām* as well as *Janajāti Manca* and *Im* in 1995. These journals, as well as the meetings organized by the associations which publish them, are the main media of ethnic contestation and of the building of 'ethnicity'. In a way, conflicts are thus made concrete and obvious.

I will discuss Pfaff-Czarnecka's examples of reaction against traditional values and meaning, with the help of facts I observed and these Magar publications.

The fact that the Magars cannot use water from the public well when they perform pig sacrifice, is now becoming an ethnic marker in Belkot. This first claim is particularly interesting, because the Magars themselves are accustomed to taking ritual precautions when they perform pig sacrifice, which is also in a sense polluting for them. It seems that the need to oppose themselves to the Brahmins led the Magars to change their own conception of the pig sacrifice. Through such a tiny detail the author has highlighted one of the most central *object à penser* of the Magar culture, and I would like to discuss it in more detail. The place of the pig in the Magar society seems indeed to be very central and ambivalent. We know that its consumption is usually prevalent among the southern Magars and restricted or forbidden among the northern, if we can still employ this occidental classification of the Magar groups who themselves speak instead of eastern and western Magars, a better suited geographical delimitation. Among Magars with northern clan names in Gulmi district, the pig is held responsible for landslides and hail sent by the offended mountain gods. In the same district, the Saru clan of southern origin from Musikot perform in great secret a pig sacrifice outside the palace, but they do not consume its flesh, offering it to the low castes. Of course, this could be the result of Hinduization, but even in Pyugha village of Syangja district, where pigs are consumed every day, the Magars do not use pig excrement as manure because they say it is repelling, sticky, and too close to human excrement. The pig is very often qualified as a *pāpi*, sinner or sinful, animal. A very common tale about the origin of the Magars is that they were Thakuris who started to eat pork, whether for local ritual obligations or to expel the Muslims who were purchasing them. It is true that this story has now assumed another form: that the Magars saved the Thakuris and Brahmins with their pigs, thus preventing the Muslims from purchasing them further north. In this new story the Magars are not a degraded high Hindu caste but a local group whose secret weapon is this disgusting animal. In their recent writings, the Magars indeed emphasize how well they received the Hindus, offering them shelter and food and how they were deceived by them. But Hinduism is all-embracing and it seems hard for the Magars to escape it and to promote the pig as a special ethnic marker specific to them. Indeed, for the Hindus, the incarnation of Vishnu in the form of a wild pig is held in great sanctity, a fact which puzzles the Magars. Anabir Somai Magar thus wrote about the Hindus and their Varāha god: '. . . touching a wild pig is impure for them. Thus they think that they are higher than god himself'. It is, on the other hand, symptomatic that the consumption of the cow is not a Magar revendication: symptomatic of their deep Hinduization and of the fact that the Magar ethnic movement is principally held by southern Magars.

The second point discussed is the fact that the Tamang local headman refused to participate in the Dasai celebrations. His attitude, I think, may be interpreted in different ways. First, as Pfaff-Czarnecka said, it can be understood as a boycott of a nation-wide festival, which links every local centre of power to the central one in a Hindu way. But this man chose to be elected in the panchayat system, and by this very act, he did not refuse to be a political representative in a Hindu kingdom. On the other hand, the Belkot ritual unity as described, does not traditionally include the Tamangs: indeed the Brahmins act as priests, a Magar endows the royal function and they are helped by Newar and Damai servants. These ethnographic details diminish the Dasai boycott decided by the Tamangs and I am tempted to ask several questions.

Aren't the functions of the traditional Dware headman and of the pradhan panc different in nature? Rather than the administrative power of the person elected at the head of the panchayat, isn't another kind of ritual power displayed during Dasai in which the Tamang headman had no place structurally? It is significant in this regard that the author notes that the twice-born office holders like to present themselves as if they *were* Dware. And that the Kshetri village secretary gave the *ṭikā* mark instead of the Pradhan panch. An important question, therefore, is: were the Dware of Kshetri origin? If yes, in one sense, the Tamang Pradan panch left the traditional structure unchanged, although he had the administrative power. Another question about Dasai is important to consider: did the Tamang pradhan of Belkot make an individual and conscious choice, or did he follow nation-wide janajati instructions?

In this regard, the Magar case is more complicated than the Tamang one, because, as shown with the Belkot example, the Magars are at the heart of the traditional sacred function of Dasai. Nevertheless this boycott of Dasai has also been promulgated by different Magar journals, *Lāphā* in particular, following an action initiated by the eastern Kirants. As far as I know, this call had little effect among the Magars, probably because no other structure was given instead.

The last main point discussed is the rejection of Hindu notions as intrinsic components of ethnic cultures, with the example of the informants of Alan Macfarlane who criticize the Brahmanic lecture of their society. Here, the author pinpointed a fundamental element of the formation of ethnic identity, that is the reconstruction of one's own history. First, I would like to stress that given the lack of written documents, the history of Nepalese tribal groups is particularly prone to ideological manipulations. And I must say that I have doubt about the authenticity of the newly discovered 'secret genealogies' of the Gurungs, compared to the nineteenth century's 'false ones', especially when they indicate Mongolia as a place of origin. To understand this new ideology, we can take again the case of the Magars. The building of their history is very tormented because they can hardly find cultural specificities which are their own, except two languages (the Magaranti and the Kham) which few of them can now speak and the idea of an ancestral territory, outside which many of them live today.

Like the other tribal groups of Nepal, the Magars consider themselves as a janajati (a term difficult to translate, which, according to the Nepali Brihat Shabdakos designates groups like the Nagas and the Kusundas who live on slash-and-burn agriculture or a group living on one territory, and which is usually translated as nationality nowadays), as the Adibasi (first occupants) and claim a special status as owners of the earth, which is in fact their traditional way of acquiring power in one place. It is symptomatic that they call themselves *Bhumiputra*, the sons of the earth and *Bhumipita*, the fathers of the earth, this earth that, as they say, was 'imbued with their sweat and blood, which was modelled by them to their convenience, and which was named by them'. The right to a territory is thus acquired by the direct action on earth and not by the authority over the people who inhabit it. In their ideology, this first action on earth is given forever and they are shocked, for instance, by the renaming of places, like the city of Tanahun which became Nagarpalika, feeling that they are 'erased' by this.

The janajati define themselves negatively and with regards to the caste system as 'the people who do belong to the four jāt (Brahman, Kstratriya, Vaisya and Sudra)'. But this, of course, does not explain who they are and the Magar turn themselves to physical anthropology and racial theory for this. The janajati are hence described as Mongolians, dominated by the Hindu Aryas, with a precise description of the physical appearance of each race: the Magar claim that they are not a jāt (caste) but a *prajāti* (race)—the English translation being given by them. In fact it seems to me that it is mainly from this physical anthropology that the newly found origin in Mongolia stems. I leave the reader to imagine what excesses can result from this race-based anthropology, augmented by racist remarks directed towards the Brahmins.

In fact, through their writings, the Magars seem to be in a state of distress, feeling that nothing was left of their own past except their physical appearance. Let me take for example an article published in *Janajati Manca* where the author expresses his feeling that Gorakhath was a Magar god before the conquest of Gorkha by Drabya Shah. I think that the fact that he feels so should by itself be taken as in important token, but his demonstration has no historical base at all and relies precisely on an ethnic marker, maize, as opposed to rice. For him the fact that Gorakhnath is offered maize bread is an indicator of his Magariness, since this food is specific to this group, forgetting that maize was anyway not introduced before the seventeenth century in Nepal, that is, much later than Drabya Shah's conquest. Our ancestors, he continues, have forgotten to tell the real name of the god to their descendants while the Hindus gave him a new name and wrote books about him: 'In these conditions', he adds 'how can we know what the Magar culture was?' I could multiply the examples, like the Sorathi Nac, which is shown as a typical Magar song and dance, whereas it is sung in Nepali and relates the story of a baby girl along the Yamuna river. These details should indicate by themselves an Indian origin, even if one ignores that the very same story is sung all over Uttar Pradesh and Bihar and probably originated in Gujarat (Catherine Servan-Schreiber, personal communication). Nevertheless the Magars consider this song as theirs and perform it in their meetings as an ethnic marker. The Tihar festival is another example. Classified as one of the Magar festivals, it was, according to several Magar authors, established by the Magar king Balihang who is mentioned in the Tihar Bhailo songs. It should be noted that the Khas of western Nepal who also sing during Bhailo 'King Bali has sent us', claim that it is the king of Jumla who is referred to and that more generally, Bali is the name of the famous demon-king of Hindu mythology, who is clearly referred to during the Tihar rituals of the Bahun-Chetri. This situation is typical of the Himalayan region where the same god or cultural tradition may be raised to the status of an ethnic marker despite its common belonging, by elaboration of specific myths which links it closely and exclusively to each different group.

To mark real distance from those who are considered as the dominant groups, the Magars had no choice other than to invent a specific tradition, and this is what they have done by publishing complicated manuals of Magar Buddhist rituals, or by creating an alphabet. The Magar associations now promote the Akka lipi, the Brahmi script, because in the complicated historical reconstruction of one of their thinkers, M.S. Thapa, they are the original Licchavi and Briji speakers whose script was the Brahmi. So, in their eager return to the very origin of things, they chose to 'reintroduce' it. Now the study of this difficult new alphabet is encouraged while Sanskrit is severely rejected as the secret arm of the Brahmins to keep their superiority in the exams. Programmes in Magar on television and radio are asked for, while broadcast in Sanskrit is said to be 'the manifestation of the hate of the Hindu Arya against other groups'. Obviously, the Magars cannot escape defining themselves in reaction to, and on the model of , their disturbing Other, the high caste Hindus, while they remain significantly silent about the low castes, although often described by villagers as endowed with a power of attraction which defies the caste system.

The radical change displayed within Magar society seems to follow the very old mechanism of Sanskritization, but in a new mode of relation with their group of reference, the Bahun-Chetri. In a sense, we could say that in the past the Magars were aiming to become Bahun-Chetri and that with their new strategy their aim is now to become equal to them: identification has shifted from an ontological or natural register to a positive one. Nevertheless the Magar's new revendications remain within the limit of what is acceptable for a modern Hindu person of high caste as the role of the king, the sacrality of the cow and most important, the untouchable status of the low castes are not questioned. The shift of meanings of the ethnic markers remain thus limited to what is acceptable to the dominating other.

Bahuns

Ethnicity without an 'Ethnic Group'

GIL DARYN

This chapter discusses the caste (or ethnic?) identity of Bahuns in the remote 'village of Thamghar'[1] in central Nepal, where I conducted one and half years of fieldwork. In this village, Bahuns who constitute the vast majority of the 280 families, live together with a few Chetri[2] families, a minority of untouchable artisan castes (Damai, Kami, Sarki) and a handful of Baran and Gharti[3] families.

My main argument is as follows: much of the scholarly attention given to ethnicity has been devoted, unjustly I suggest, to the definition of an 'ethnic group' and its application to social analysis. I would like to argue that Bahuns, who do not view themselves as a group, nor meet the usual anthropological definition of an 'ethnic group', were so classified and are generally seen as a group by outsiders (other Nepalese 'groups' and scholars). I would like to propose that the reason for this discrepancy between self and outside ascription is mainly due to the 'ethnic relationships' a Bahun has with others, whether Bahun or not. Moreover, the case of Bahuns demonstrates the way in which social situations with a strong ethnic element, or ethnicity in general, do not depend upon the existence of an 'ethnic group'. This may have a number of implications for a general discussion on ethnicity. I shall conclude this paper by suggesting that abandoning the concept of the 'ethnic group' enhances analysis of dynamic processes with an ethnic element.

Anthropologists have devoted much effort to try and define different kinds of groups: corporate groups, quasi groups, ethnic groups and others. In the case of ethnic groups, the literature is scattered with futile attempts to define what an ethnic group is alongside numerous cases that exemplify the inapplicability of such definitions. I will not go over these examples here as I am sure that the reader is familiar with many of them.[4] I argue that the concept of 'ethnic group' ceased to be helpful as an analytical tool once rigorous definition was sought and where it was used as an empirical test for the existence of such 'groups'. Ethnicity so it seems, has at times become falsely dependent upon the existence of an 'ethnic group'.

Returning to the Bahuns in Nepal, we find a situation where although Bahuns do not view themselves as a group, nor fit any definition of an ethnic group, they are seen by outsiders as such. Moreover, if we try to employ one of the most frequently used definitions, that of Anthony Smith (1991), who defines an ethnic group as a named human population with shared ancestry myths, histories and cultures, having an association with a specific territory and a sense of solidarity, we soon come to the conclusion that Bahuns do not fit this definition. 'Bahun' is mainly an outside ascription. Kumai (originally from Kumaon)[5] and Purbia Bahuns (eastern Bahuns) may share some ancestry myths but not the same history; Bahuns are not associated with a specific territory and have no sense of solidarity.

It may not be surprising that self-ascription may be different or in conflict with external perception, yet both are not only valuable but indeed correspond to diverse realities. However, in this case, the outside view that points towards the existence of Bahuns as a social entity and not only as a category is incorrect, as I will argue below. I shall first briefly describe how Bahuns are viewed by outsiders, that is by other Nepalese and foreign scholars, and then try to penetrate their 'emic point of view'. I shall further try to explain the aforementioned tendency of other Nepalese to make the misleading fusion between Bahuns as a 'category' and Bahuns as a 'group'. Either independently or together, many different groups and Nepalese scholars depict Bahuns as a separate group and place them in the hub of contemporary ethnic discourse in Nepal, accusing them of being responsible for perpetrating most of Nepal's ills. The list of publications and expressions of such views is long, starting maybe with Gopal Gurung's book in 1985, the establishment of NEFEN which is a confederate grouping of ethnic organizations representing 21 ethnic groups, Dor Bahadur Bista's book published in 1991 etc.[6]

While Bahuns are viewed by fellow Nepalese as a distinct ethnic group, Euro-American scholars are more cautious in attributing them this separate status. Foreign scholars tend to view Bahuns as part of a larger ethnic group that includes other castes such as the Chetris and the untouchable artisan castes that accompany them. All are, supposedly, of Indian origin and belong to the category of Parbatiya.[7]

The Bahuns of Thamghar do not view themselves in any of the above ways. For Bahuns the term Parbatiya signifies a connection to a geographical region (the mountains) and not to a specific social group. The villagers' use of self-identificatory categories is flexible and changes according to the specific context and the level of perceived knowledge and intimacy the interacting participants are taken to have, especially according to the governing principle of Bahun life, the hierarchy of ritual purity. Hence, Bahuns identify themselves as belonging to the Bahun jati[8] in the presence of Magar, or Rai[9] out of the village, but in the village they differentiate between Jaisi and Upadhyaya[10] Bahuns. Jaisis view themselves as Bahuns but the others (Upadhyaya, Chetri and other lower castes) ascribe the title of Bahun exclusively to those who are entitled to perform a puja (sacrifice), that is to Upadhyaya Bahuns. Among themselves, Jaisi or Upadhyaya Bahuns identify each person as a member of a specific *kul*[11] (Subedi, Adhikari, Banjara and the like). I need only briefly mention here that within the category of Bahun, villagers further differentiate not only according to the sub-castes of Jaisi or Upadhyaya, but also between the aforementioned Purbia Bahun and Kumai Bahun. Historical and other differences apart, it is important to note that both Purbia and Kumai Bahuns mutually view each other as belonging to the lowest ritual status because of their supposed history of inter-marriage with Muslims.

It seems that for a Bahun all of the above categories except the kul are too broad a self-ascription. These broad categories are used while interacting with people who are taken to be unfamiliar with Bahun inner division, or to denote lower ritual status groups as a whole, since their inner divisions do not make a difference. Indeed, the existence of an intricate categorization up to the level of the kul indicates that each category makes a difference and separates people. Hence it is no wonder that these broader categories of Parbatiya, Bahun, Purbia, Upadhyaya and Jaisi, which become relevant only in certain situations, are not significant for everyday life and are too broad to evoke the feeling of solidarity required to generate any kind of collective action.

The category of 'village', which abounds in ethnographic literature, has little significance for the villagers in Thamghar, as has been mentioned with regard to the Indian village by Dumonnt and others.[12] I use Thamghar here in the same way as it is used locally, to demarcate a certain geographical region. Thus, when I mention 'the village of Thamghar' or Thamgharians, I mean roughly the people who happen to live within the above area (where I conducted my fieldwork and in the absence of any better term), but it is important to understand that this title bears little significance for the people themselves. The reason for this is that boundaries of caste and clan usually extend beyond the boundaries of Thamghar, and there are other varied and more significant divisions of this area into smaller geographical units such as the modern division into wards. The category of 'village' is used by Bahuns to refer to a group of houses belonging to one kul (clan), ideally separated geographically from other such 'villages'.

In Thamghar, when we come to consider the extent to which the kul may be a significant social unit for a Bahun, we find that although membership of a kul is a minimal requirement, a pre-requisite for every villager, legitimizing individual presence and making the person sociable, one hardly finds expressions of solidarity, unity or communal action related to the kul. This is because the bone (*hard*)[13] connection that members of a kul share comes into play mainly under negative circumstances, such as cases of extreme pollution (*jutho*) arising from death, birth or improper sexual relations. The annual gatherings for a kuldevta puja (clan god sacrifice) are more often than not occasions that give rise to deep animosities within the kul and, as a result, many such pujas are celebrated separately by different households on the same day. However, in Thamghar, the custom of making endless distinctions and categorizations goes well beyond the level of the kul, to the joint family level and at times even beyond that, and thus at any possible group level one hardly finds any expression of solidarity, unity or communal action of Bahuns in Thamghar.

This being the case, a discrepancy becomes apparent: Bahuns resist anthropological definition as an 'ethnic group' and do not feel part of one, yet they are clearly seen as an 'ethnic' or a distinct 'group' by outsiders. I would like to suggest that it is the 'ethnic relationships' a Bahun has with others which lie at the root of this discrepancy. For the moment I shall leave 'ethnic relationship' undefined and only mention that this relationship clearly includes what Barth (1969) has called 'boundary maintenance' and actively making divisions and distinctions in social interaction.

Apart from rare occasions in some of the kuldevta pujas,[14] Bahuns are constantly involved in 'ethnic relationships' with each other and with everyone else. Maintaining such relationships and distinct identity is held as indispensable to Bahun survival in the world. Hence a social situation that includes the presence of a village Bahun is a situation where strong 'ethnic relationships' are developed, and these intense relationships render Bahuns collectively an 'ethnic group' to non-Bahuns and scholars alike. However these very relationships make, from a Bahun point of view, any notion of being part of a group irrelevant. Thus we have a situation where intensive 'ethnic relationships' exist and people feel a strong ethnic identity in the absence of a defined 'ethnic group' in the usual anthropological sense.

What I mean by ethnic relationships becomes clear if we view them through what I call an ethnic process, which consists of three dynamic, interconnected and mutually influential elements. The order in which these elements are presented does not imply a difference in importance nor any evolutionary argument. On the contrary, I should like to maintain that an 'ethnic process' may be invoked by any of the elements, but that there may be little sense in viewing them separately.

The first element is the mutual acknowledgment or assumption of a '*shared difference*' concerning one or more of the following: origin, collective name and history, language and/ or other cultural traits or manners, territory, cosmology or a certain ideology, economic/ political/environmental or other circumstances, interests, and motivation. A shared difference may at times be the only thing the interacting parties acknowledge as common. This is not to be confused with the usual assumption of a difference common to a group, as distinct from another such group. The second element is the existence of distinctive *identity*. The third element is involvement in an 'ethnic *relationship*'. 'Ethnic relationships' may include a whole range of possible relationships between individuals (and 'groups'), that have some kind of social notion or effect, are influenced by the existence or formation of a certain distinctive identity and developed through the acknowledgments of a shared difference.

The presence of these three elements, which generate and influence one another, may indicate the existence of an 'ethnic process'. Indeed, the 'ethnic process' in which Bahuns are involved may only be illuminated by analysis that starts with 'ethnic relationship' instead of the 'ethnic group'.

The above broad and flexible 'definition' of ethnicity in terms of relationship opens the possibility of recognizing 'ethnic processes' within a variety of social units or elements which would not otherwise be accepted under the prevalent categorization of 'ethnic groups' or 'ethnic'. Against the claim that the above 'definition' may be too broad or unbounded, and allows other socially unrelated phenomena to be regarded as ethnic, I would answer that this is probably unavoidable but that it should in fact be welcomed, as it may bring to light phenomena formerly neglected.

The above view of ethnicity is influenced by and is a different form of the views expressed by many scholars. Sharing the unease of others in trying to define the group studied, my view is influenced mainly by Barth's (1969) and Eriksen's (1993) understanding of ethnicity. However, my approach is very close to that of Leach (1964) who, recognizing the problem of definition, also identified the need to keep such concepts fluid and unbounded. Finally, my views are influenced by those challenging the concept of 'society' as a useful theoretical tool, as argued by Marilyn Strathern (1994, 1996). Most criticism levelled against the use of the term 'society' in social theory is probably also applicable to 'ethnic group', as the latter appears to be derived from the former. Although I do not claim that 'ethnic group' may not be a useful term in certain contexts, I do suggest that the specific way in which it was used, as an analytic tool to define groups, and its derivatives—the indispensable connection between an 'ethnic group' and both 'ethnicity' in general and 'ethnic identity' in particular—obscure social reality and at times may be a major obstacle to social analysis. Thus I suggest that the study of ethnic processes, at least in certain cases, fares better without it. Viewing 'ethnicity' in terms of relationships which are part of a social process does away with its false dependency or confinement to the theoretical category of the 'ethnic group/unit/community', and may facilitate our discussion of what it entails for people who are involved in, or are indifferent to such a process.

I shall end this chapter by examining one possible future scenario in Nepal, in which Bahuns may play a leading role. I hope to show how the application of the 'ethnic process' suggested above which does not depend on the concept of the 'ethnic group' facilitates our understanding of this phenomenon.

Young Thamgharian Bahuns[15] go through a transformation while in Kathmandu. The words of Manmohan Subedi (26) who teaches in one of Kathmandu's boarding schools illustrate this clearly. Commenting on his life outside the village, he said 'when I go to Kathmandu I leave my *janai*[16] at home'. Indeed, young Bahuns in the city voluntarily reject village norms when they go to Kathmandu to work and study. Rejection of village norms is not only evident symbolically in their shaving their moustaches and cutting their *tuppi* (scalp-lock), but in a wholly intentional breach of most of the numerous purity taboos strictly observed in the village.

The new identity that young men from Thamghar adopt in Kathmandu is of modern, liberal, educated and wealthy young men or, in other words, the opposite of what they perceive to be the identity of a villager. This dichotomy between 'the village' and 'the city', inculcated through the contents of the formal education system, as embodied in village schools[17] is vivid in their minds. The term 'villager' carries strong connotations of the parochial Hindu way of life and its numerous divisions. As young Bahuns choose to shift their allegiance to the modern, developed society, which they imagine exists in Kathmandu, almost anything they view as 'villageness' is rejected. The connection with the kul serves as their only bridge with the village, yet home visits are rare and most young men do not care to participate in the annual kuldevta puja. Unlike the Bahun intellectuals residing in Kathmandu, young Bahuns seem practically to ignore the contemporary ethnopolitical discourse of Nepal, and most of them have never bothered to read Bista's *Fatalism and Development* (1991).

If in the village we can imagine Bahuns taking part in an ethnic process as described earlier, with intensive relationships and mutual influence between the three elements mentioned, in Kathmandu it is totally absent. The feelings and motives that in the village led to endless differentiation are in Kathmandu substituted by ideas of 'modernity' and equality. In place of intensive 'ethnic relationships' in the village, we find none in Kathmandu and instead of the strong distinctive identity we find a dormant Bahun identity

This dormant Bahun identity in the city may be awakened by the current escalation of ethnic discourse in Nepal and the growing opposition to Bahuns. It is interesting however, to note that it is precisely the absence of 'ethnic relationship' of caste and the identification with an ethos of equality which makes young Bahuns in the city prone to take part in a new set of 'ethnic relationships' with strong political expression,[18] than for such expression ever to develop in Thamghar. If this was to happen, Bahuns will probably not suffer from a lack of solidarity, as in 'the village', a solidarity which will be based on feelings of equality and shared interest, shared adversity and common motive. If such changes were to occur, it is conceivable that young Thamgharian Bahuns would join forces with other young Bahuns, including Kumais, and other Brahmans from the Terai or west Nepal, possibly together with Bahuns who have resided in Kathmandu for more than a few generations, some of whom already view themselves as part of a distinct 'ethnic group'[19]. It is also possible that some Newar[20] Brahmans who do not consider themselves Newars[21], will find that joining such a movement may provide a path towards their desired acceptance as Parbatiya Bahuns.

Indeed if this were to happen, it would exemplify a situation where an external influence on members of an 'external category', that of Bahuns, generates an 'ethnic process', which transforms the category into a politically active group opposing its external creators.[22] Furthermore, such a situation provides another example where abandoning the concept of the 'ethnic group' enhances analyses of the dynamic ethnic process involved.

Notes

1. The reason for the use of inverted commas is to imply the non-existence of such a social unit. It will be used for the present purpose until further clarification below.
2. The title Chetri is the Nepalese translation of the Indian caste Kshatriya, warrior caste.
3. Both of Tibeto-Burmese origin.
4. See for example Mitchell 1956 on corporate groups, Naroll 1964 and Leach 1964 about 'cult unit', Moerman 1965, Barth 1969, Smith 1991, Eriksen 1993.
5. This way of describing the difference between Kumai and Purbia is of course a simplification of the debatable question of their origin.
6. See also Macfarlane 1997, Gellner 1997a, and Gellner, Pfaff-Czarnecka and Whelpton 1997.
7. If 'ethnic groups' are in general difficult to define (as was mentioned above), the Indian and Nepalese castes are particularly hard to delineate as such. Thus, Gellner is right in criticizing Barth's view (1969:27–8) of the caste system as a special case of a stratified poly-ethnic system, since it implies that there are as many ethnic groups as there are castes and sub-castes (Gellner 1997a: 16–7). What Gellner suggests seems to be in accordance with general scholarly attitude towards castes in Nepal, which sees a few castes as belonging to the same ethnic category. Hence Bahuns are often referred to as a subcategory within the larger ethnic group of Parbatiya Hindus. This may be evident in the numerous references to 'the Parbatiya' in the edited volume *Nationalism and Ethnicity in Hindu Kingdom* (Gellner, Pfaff-Czarnecka, and Whelpton 1997). While in some instances scholars would prefer to include the untouchable artisan castes within the Parbatiya (Gellner 1997a: 3–4, Gellner, Pfaff-Czarnecka and Whelpton 1997:35–6), in others, scholars feel the need to further differentiate and

exclude the untouchables by adding the title of high-caste Hindus to denote the upper castes of Bahuns, Thakuris and Chetri (Bennett 1983), (Pfaff-Czarnecka 1997).

8. Jat is the general term used by Bahuns to distinguish between groups (according to different categories like origin, ritual purity etc.), and in fact to make any kind of taxonomy relating to the world around them. For further discussion of the term jāt in India, see for example Dumont (1980).
9. Both of Tibeto-Burmese origin.
10. Jaisi are of lower ritual status than the Upadhyaya.
11. A kul is a lineage or agnatic descent group. A few different kuls construct a *gotra* that is an exogamous agnatic unit whose members are descendants of one seven mythical rishis. A certain *kul* name may belong to more than one gotra, although this is an exception. A kul also includes all women married to its members, but they usually have a second class status and are not fully trusted.
12. For example Dumont and Pocock 1957, Dumont 1980:160 and note 74b p. 391.
13. For further discussion about the 'bone connection' of kul members see Lecomte-Tilouine 1993.
14. Note the exception of young Bahuns in Kathmandu, described below.
15. This title is used here instead of the Nepalese term *yubakharu*, which is used loosely to refer to men of less than 30 years, usually single.
16. *Janai* is the sacred thread worn by Bahun and Chetri males.
17. This was also found by Pigg (1992) in relation to Nepalese village schools in general.
18. As was found in India, see Dumont 1980:225–7.
19. Notably Dr A. Raj, a Bahun intellectual and the author of the book entitled *The Brahmans of Nepal* in which he clearly views Bahuns as an 'ethnic group' opposing other 'hill tribal ethnic groups' (Raj 1996), and other Bahuns who collected and published vamsavalis (genealogies) in which they assert their distinctiveness.
20. A Tibeto-Burman speaking people, the original inhabitants of the Kathmandu valley.
21. The Rajopadhyaya Newar Brahmins who do their best to be accepted as Bahuns (Gellner 1997b:160).
22. Compare with a similar process in India described by Bailey (1963).

References

Bailey, F.G., 1963, 'Closed Social Stratification in India', *European Journal of Sociology*, Vol. IV, 1, pp. 107–24.

Barth, F., 1969, Introduction, in Barth, F. (ed.), *Ethnic Groups and Boundaries,*

The Social Organisation of Cultural Difference. Copenhagen: Scandinavian University Books.

Bennett, L., 1983, *Dangerous Wives an Sacred Sisters. Social and Symbolic Roles of High-caste Women in Nepal*, New York: Columbia University Press.

Bista, D.B., 1991, *Fatalism and Development, Nepal's Struggle for Modernization,* Calcutta: Orient Longman Limited.

Dumont, L., 1980 [1966], *Homo Hierarchicus,* Chicago and London: the University of Chicago Press.

Dumont, L. and Pocock, D.F., 1957, 'Village Studies', *Contributions to Indian Sociology,* I, pp. 23–42.

Eriksen, T.H., 1993, *Ethnicity and Nationalism, Anthropological Perspectives,* London, Boulder, Colorado: Pluto Press.

Gellner, D. 1997a, 'Introduction; Ethnicity and Nationalism in the World's only Hindu State', in D. Gellner, J. Pfaff-Czarnecka, and J. Whelpton, (eds.), *Nationalism and Ethnicity in a Hindu Kingdom, The Politics of Culture in Contemporary Nepal.* Amsterdam: Harwood Academic Publishers.

———, 1997b, 'Caste, Communalism, and Communism: Newars and the Nepalese State', in D. Gellner, J. Pfaff-Czarnecka, and J. Whelpton, (eds.), *Nationalism and Ethnicity in a Hindu Kingdom, The Politics of Culture in Contemporary Nepal.* Amsterdam: Harwood Academic Publishers.

Gurung, G., 1985, *Hidden Facts in Nepalese Politics,* Kathmandu: Deurali offset.

Leach, E., 1964, 'Comment on "On Ethnic Unit Classification" by Rahul Naroll', *Current Anthropology* 5(4), pp. 298–9.

Lecomte-Tilouine, M., 'The Proof of the bone: Lineage and *devali* in Central Nepal', *Contribution to Indian Sociology (n.s.),* 27(1), pp. 1–23.

Macfarlane, A., 1997, Identity and Change Among the Gurungs (Tamu-mai) of Central Nepal, in D. Gellner, J. Pfaff-Czarnecka, and J. Whelpton, (eds.), *Nationalism and Ethnicity in a Hindu Kingdom, The Politics of Culture in Contemporary Nepal.* Amsterdam: Harwood Academic Publishers.

Mitchell, C., 1956, *The Kalela Dance,* Manchester: Manchester University Press, Rhodes-Livingstone papers, no. 27.

Moerman, M., 1965, 'Ethnic Identification in Complex Civilization: Who Are the Lue?', *American Anthropoligist,* 67, pp. 1215–30.

Naroll, R., 1964, 'On Ethnic Unit Classification', in *Current Anthropology,* 5(4), pp. 283–91.

Pfaff-Czarnecka, J., 1997, 'Vestiges and Visions: Cutural Change in the Process of Nation-Building in Nepal', in D. Gellner, J. Pfaff-Czarnecka, and J. Whelpton, (eds.), *Nationalism and Ethnicity in a Hindu Kingdom, The Politics of Culture in Contemporary Nepal.* Amsterdam: Harwood Academic Publishers.

Pigg, S.L. 1992, 'Inventing Social Categories Through Place: Social Representations and Development in Nepal', *Comparative Studies in Society and History*, 34(3), pp. 491–513.

Raj, P.A., 1996, *Brahmins of Nepal*, Kathmandu: Nabeen Publication.

Smith, A.D., 1991, *National Identity*, London: Penguin.

———, 1997, 'Structure and Persistence of Ethnic', in Guibernau, M and Rex, J. (eds.), *The Ethnicity Reader, Nationalism, Multiculturalism and Migration*, Cambridge: Polity Press.

Strathern, M. 1994, 'Parts and Wholes: Refiguring Relationships', in Borofsky, R. (ed.), *Assessing Cultural Anthropology*. New York: Mcgraw-Hill, Inc.

Strathern, M., 1996, 1989 debate: The Concept of Society is theoretically obsolete, Part I, for the Motion (1), in Key *Debates in Social Anthropology*, Ingold, P. (ed.), London: Routledge.

Comments

PHILLIPPE RAMIREZ

I am very glad to have the opportunity to comment on Gil Daryn's paper, as it brings to light some points that I have been trying to underline for a couple of years. Let me mention only two of them.

First Gill describes the term Parbatiya as an outside ascription. This is too rarely stated and I have not read it in the recent literature. Parbatiya is a word so commonly used in anthropological texts, or elsewhere, that the average reader naturally understands it as the designation of an ethnic group. It has to be remembered that this designation is not only exogenous to the people it is supposed to concern, but is also not assumed by them. Secondly, I totally agree with Gil when he states that the Bahun do not see themselves as an ethnic group. To my mind this affirmation can be applied not only to the Bahun but also to each component of the so-called 'Parbatiya'. Nor do the Bahun see themselves as being part of any ethnic group, that would associate them for example with culturally alike groups like Chetri, Thakuri, Kami, Damai, and Gaine.

Hindus of the Nepalese hills do not conceive that they form an entity distinct from other entities of the same degree. For them the world is divided into jāt at different levels: The Chetri are distinct from the Magar, the 'nepali jāt' from the 'amerikan jāt', the human beings from the fish. They are fully aware that certain jāt are very similar in their way of life and religion, for example the Bahun compared to the Chetri, or Damai to the Kami. These particular jāt keep up some closed social relations; however they do not conclude from this intimacy that they form a well defined category. This is particularly clear in their perception of the Magar jāt. In many localities, the Magars speak only Nepali, live the same life as their close Bahun-Chetri neighbours and interact very closely with them, including through marriage. In the eyes of these Bahun-Chetri however, their Magar neighbours belong to the same jāt and are not less Magar than the Magar of the west, the Kham for instance, who have an altogether different culture. So, to put it briefly, the Bahun or Chetri dissociate culture and identity. The cultural or even social characteristics of a group do not make it a jāt which is not contradictory with the deeply entrenched idea that to be born in a jāt gives somebody some particular abilities and trends.

This point of relationship between culture and identity in the Bahun conceptions leads to a problem. When a Bahun, or a Chetri, discusses with the anthropologist about a particular custom and says 'we do it this way', who are these 'we'? Is it the Bahun, a particular lineage, a domestic group, people of the surrounding area, Hindus of the hills, or Nepalese people? In another society, the anthropologist may suppose with little risk that the reference is the 'ethnic group'. Among the Bahun however, considering their vision of a world divided into multi-level jāt and considering as well their dominant position in the global Nepalese society, the references are numerous, without being contradictory. As in any assumption concerning identity, the logic here is deeply egocentric: 'we' may jointly signify 'our family, our lineage, the Bahun of this area, people of the district, and—the case may be—all Nepalese'. We face here the complexity of the Hindu identity, not only of the Nepalese Brahmins, but of all Hindus.

Thus, it is particularly necessary in the case of an assertion on identity by a Hindu, and even more by a Brahman, to determine which set of references have been in mind. Gil rightfully points to the multiplicity of 'self-identificatory categories' among Thamgar villagers: a Bahun may be either Kumai or Purbia, a Kumai either Upadhyay or Jaisi, an Upadhyay may be Adhikari, Banjare and so on. I would add that, according to the data I collected, these categories are not segmentarized, but interlacing: thus you may find Adhikari who are Upadhyay, others who are Jaisi and even an Adhikari Chetri. Moreover, an Adhikari Bahun and an Adhikari Chetri may belong to the same lineage or even be first degree agnates as a result of an hypergamic marriage. The consequence is that it is not sufficient that an Adhikari Bahun pretends to be Adhikari to assume that he is a Bahun. On the contrary, a patronym like Adhikari is reputed enough all over the kingdom for any Nepalese, whatever his extraction, to understand that Adhikari means Bahun–Chetri.

This leads to the question of *thar*. This notion is very important in Nepal and constitutes a discriminating criteria with no equivalent in India. Thar is a patronym corresponding to different entities according to the jāt of its holder, and which at least identifies his jāt. Among the Bahun, Chetri and Thakuri, thar corresponds to their patrilinear clan, i.e. somebody is commonly named after his clan: Koirala, Adhikari, Pande or even Shah are examples of such thar. Among most other groups, that corresponds to the name of the jāt, whatever the degree: Gurung, Shrestha, Gandharba, Tawa Lama and so on. There are some exceptions as the personal initiative of certain Upadhyay Bahun who choose to be called simply Upadhyay, or certain intellectuals or politicians who adopted a 'jāt-free' name, like 'Krisan' or 'Nepal'.

In the case of the Bahun–Chetri the role of the thar in the 'ethnic' interactions seems more than marginal, for at least two reasons. First, the number of Nepalese thar is limited enough to enable an easy estimation of the jāt. Knowing the thar is knowing the average status. Secondly, the thar is fundamental in expressing the membership to a descent group. To clarify his identity, somebody would prefix his thar with a second application, called the *prakār*, which refers generally to the locality of origin of his lineage: for example 'Nuwakote Adhikari'. The association of thar and prakār points to a segment of clan or even a lineage (kul), thus very precisely identifying a Bahun–Chetri in terms of descent and status, and even, in a regional context, his matrimonial and political affiliations. Such a reference to descent is extremely important in the identity of a Bahun, Chetri, or Thakuri. As for the social implications, even though the solidarity between agnates is not always very obvious—as Gil underlines—kul members generally maintain close relationships and very often meet collectively to take common decisions.

Finally, I would say that the ongoing debates in Nepal about ethnicity must not hide the fact that up to now the existence of a political entity corresponding to 'the Bahun' is largely a notion publicized by the ethnic movements, and I must say, also by *some* anthropologists and NGO workers. It should be remembered that what made the dominant position of the Bahun—from which the Chetri can not be reasonably dissociated—is not their solidarity against others but in fact the solidarity among members of clans and networks of clans, which provided powerful political machines. This is obvious when one considers the balance of power in the nineteenth century Gorkhali state, as well as the kin relationships inside the present political parties. As a matter of fact, the history of Nepal since the death of Prithvi Narayan could be summarized as a succession of conflicts between Bahun–Chetri clans, each followed by multi-ethnic support groups. Whatever the reality of a 'bahunvad' in the past, I will fully join Gil Daryn by concluding that it could well crystallize as a unified political force in the near future as a reaction to the so-called 'anti-Bahun' movements.

Identity and Power in a Conflictual Environment*

BEN CAMPBELL

In this chapter I explore a particular question of the environmental context of identities of self and other. With issues of the Himalayan environment having attracted international attention and prompted state-directed efforts to intervene in communities' environmental use patterns over the last few decades, it seems pertinent to ask how such interventions might interact with people's sense of self? If social relationships which postulate contrastive identities are presumably linked in some significant ways to the environments in which those identities are lived out, and if the relationships of access and control to those environments are then radically altered, some crisis of identities could be expected.

Commentators on the Himalayan environment tend to follow economic and political aspects of conservation policy implementation, but the issue deserves to be treated equally in terms of shifting ecologies of the self. Given the diversity of ethnic groups characteristically found in the Himalayan region, can culturally distinct human–nature relationships be identified? In asking this question I have sought to integrate cultural texts with embodied practices of environmental interaction.

* This research was supported by ESRC (R000237061)

Debates about how to protect the world's biodiversity have focused increasingly on the problem inherent in imposing the standard conservation model of 'wilderness', devoid of humanity, on to areas of the globe which are inhabited (Posey 1998, Cronon 1995). Nepal's initial phase of national park establishment adopted the wilderness model of minimal human encroachment somewhat uncritically, with the result that many communities immediately experienced an alienation from the affordances of their previously taken-for-granted environments. By the 1990s the conservationists' separation of society from nature came to be recognized as practically unenforceable, and conceptually suspect (Stevens 1997). Hence policies were introduced for participatory conservation, and 'buffer zones' were created in order to mediate between areas of uncontrolled human activity and strict nature protection.

One of the arguments for participatory conservation is that local or indigenous peoples have traditional concepts of oneness with nature, that merit consideration as being complementary to the goals of conservation (Ramble and Chapagain 1990, Müller–Böker 1995). I examine some aspects of kinship with the natural world (Ramble and Chapagain 1990:27) as expressed by Tamang-speaking communities situated within the Langtang National Park, central Nepal. The main argument is that Tamang notions of human selfhood are not radically separated off from those of other species. Social groups are like natural species, but they are not species in the Western scientific sense, and depend on often conflictual relationships with others for their reproduction. The Tamang understanding of interspecies conflict in the natural world suggests possibilities for the role of indigenous ecologies of the self in helping to think about the problems faced by attempts at nature conservation.

Natures of self and other

1. Tamang notions of self and other find their primary field of display and negotiation in the categorical and political ramifications of marriage. Exogamous groups of male and female parallel kin (*pamyung-busing*)[1] constitute the main foci of inclusive identity, as marked in specific gift exchanges at rites of passage. These exogamous groups define the core ontology of

'bone' (*nakhrit*)-sharing selfhood against other types, but in themselves these clan groups are infertile, and require the admixture of another's milk/flesh (*nye*) to produce legitimately whole human beings. Clans provide common bone substance which establishes a unity of natural type, but though the word jāt may be translated as 'species', clearly this is not as understood in western science. For the Tamang, human natural types are reproductively incomplete and depend on relations of exchange and hierarchical deference (including brideservice) with affinal others.

2. The quasi-naturalization of affinal self/other difference is continuous with the perceptual framework for looking at the non-human world. In mythical narratives natural species are attributed with similar desires for trans-species affinal alliance, and humans themselves can become entrapped by forest-dwelling anthropoids (such as *nyalmo*) to bear their offspring in virtual marriage by capture.[2] In the Tamang cultural imagination non-human species are endowed with human-like motivations of relationality. Cultural representations of human-natural species relations postulate interspecies communication and conflictual power relations.

3. Tamang representations of relationship to natural diversity do not amount to what Descola (1994) has referred to as a 'coherent canonical theory'. They are partial and contextually embedded. There is also a danger in presuming that cultural narratives can convey the ontological sense of what it is to dwell in a given environment. It is outside the scope of this paper to investigate the varieties of 'being' in nature which a more comprehensive treatment of the Tamangs' environmental selfhood would require, but what is pertinent to the theme is that a certain enforced rupture of connectivity to plants, animals and places has been effected through the national park's construction of nature as separate from society. The shortcomings of environmental protection are in part due to this incomprehensible rupture of the self from an environment populated by diverse natural selves.

There are layers of irony in the situation of the Tamang communities of Rasuwa District being subjected to the nature/society dichotomization introduced through the setting up of the national park. They are for instance perceived by plains people and city folk as archetypal mountain *jangali* people, who live in a particularly close relationship to the soil in that they do not practise the Hindu bodily rituals of bathing. They are then a people stigmatized by their embodied connectedness with nature, yet find themselves involuntarily divorced from it by the proscriptions of the department of national parks. The thinking of the conservationists is clearly to disenjoin perceived deleterious human activity from taking place in the forest. The key activities which have been banned are: hunting, slash-and-burn agriculture, pasture burning, and unlicensed harvesting of forest products.

A Walk in the Forest

When the park was created in the 1970s, registered agricultural fields were deemed outside the park's control. The abrupt juxtaposition of nature and culture at the field edge goes against both the pattern of use around village settlements, and the roaming habits of wild foragers of human crops. An idea of the progressive gradations of human-forest interaction can be conveyed in a brief account of a walk I took with some children in October last year above the village of Tengu.

[I] was followed by a posse of children from the school including Pasang and Timara's youngest daughter and Ranimaya's son. We walked up through the potato-harvested fields (and there's some mustard) and found it pretty near impossible to get over the walls that Bangali had build around his Lamrang fields. Quite an undertaking for the protection of his spuds.

The children continued to follow me and asked 'what is he looking at?' when I stopped to try and recognize which ever tree. Their interpretation was that I must be looking for fruit and said 'meme pulna tsaba? ['grandfather do you want to eat pulna'[3]]. They found a pulna tree which only had unripe '*ching*' fruit. The pulna fruit is a bit smaller than a pingpong ball with a dimpled outer casing.

They saw some more *poldung nyet* red berries high up. Then they wanted to take me to a *kado* [walnut] tree they knew of. Timara's wife was coming down through the woods with a load of firewood and watching a flock of sheep and goats. The sheep have already been shorn. I noticed some of them eating *banmara* [forest killer, *Eupatorum adenophorum*] which is growing even under considerable canopy. I walked on a bit more and the children started saying '*meme tur ta nuy, chyen khaba, timnyu khaba, timnyu ya bale tsungjim toba*' ['grandfather don't go up there, leopards come, rhesus macaque monkeys come, the monkeys take hold of your arms and legs and beat you']. I then descended back down to the top of Bangali's walled fields where Tarshya and Amanyela were cutting firewood from branches of thicket fencing beside the wall.

I asked Ama and Timra's wife if there had been a visit from the boar hunters[4] this year. They said they had come last year and killed a boar on some fields, just one. They had shot more in Bharku and Shyabru. The villagers have to go and ask for the hunters to come.

The village children delight in wandering through the secondary forests beyond the field edges, where wild fruits trees grow on abandoned slash-and-burn fields of previous generations. The stone walls we had to climb over are now an essential feature of potato farming, as although national park hunters can be summoned annually to cull the growing population of wild boars, they never manage to stop the problem of crop damage. The prohibition on pasture burning has also made it impossible to control the spread of banmara, which though I noticed some of the sheep and goats nibbling it, prevents the regrowth of trees and grasses. The generation of villagers who remember the time before the park frequently express a sense of disempowerment in relation to the condition of the forest margins. They once engaged with this environment through periodic burning of excessive non-pasture weeds, which resulted months later in the aesthetically pleasing flush of green grasses on the shrub-forest floor.

In the typical secondary forest where children learn in groups to gather fruits, (and the walnuts they play with, like marbles, and exchange as gifts), collect firewood and watch livestock, they develop their familiarity with species and spatial distribution. The immediate secondary forest is their play area, but they had clearly internalized the sense of not wandering too far for fear of lurking dangers, such as leopards and monkeys.

Although children are taught to be fearful of large beasts, they are also exposed to myths which tell of relationships between the beasts. They are made aware that natural powers depend on certain qualities and characteristics, and that even powerful creatures have shortcomings and weaknesses, or, at least, that their powers are not insurmountable, and the seemingly great can be overcome. Cunning and deceit are important tactics for children to learn in outwitting foes (human and non-human alike). Status difference in natural hierarchies of power is an arena for contesting wills. The stories children hear present a congress of creatures that include people pitting their wits for an upper hand.

Older villagers informed me there used to be not just leopards but tigers (*taa*) in the forest too. Some were indeed man-eaters, but even these powerful beasts had to watch out for a particular enemy, as recounted in the following myth.

The Tiger and the Porcupine

A long time ago a porcupine chased off a tiger. An old man went hunting. The old man came face to face with the tiger. The tiger told the old man 'a porcupine chased me off. Kill that porcupine.' The old man struck the porcupine with a stick and killed it. The tiger said 'Don't tell anyone in the village. Don't talk [about it]'.

The old man returned home carrying the meat. He told his old woman 'Don't mention to the villagers we have eaten meat'. The next day in the morning the old woman went to fetch water. She went cleaning her teeth with a splint of wood. The neighbours carrying water asked 'what have you found then, walking along picking your teeth?' The old woman explained 'a porcupine chased off a tiger'. The tiger was in hiding. The tiger heard.

The next day the old man again went hunting. 'Why did you tell' asked the tiger. The old man said 'I didn't tell'. 'Your wife told' the tiger said. 'I am going to eat you now' said the tiger. The old man said 'Eat me from my head first'. 'I'll eat from you arse first' said the tiger. The old man crouched over. The tiger was about to eat him from his arse. Now the old man was frightened. His arse was palpitating. Then what did the old man say? 'The porcupine I ate yesterday is coming out'. Then the tiger said 'Hold on tight a bit, I'm running off.' As the tiger ran the old man said 'Run quickly, it's about to come out'. The tiger ran off, the old man's life was saved, and he returned home.

In mythical accounts animals are given the surprising power of speech along with sensitivities of pride and vengeance, but this is not to say that the story of the tiger and porcupine is devoid of accuracy in its portrayal of animal behaviour. The old man in the story in fact mimics the rear-end combative position of porcupines, which can be the undoing of the high and mighty tiger.

When irritated or alarmed, porcupines erect their spines, grunt and puff, and rattle their hollow tail quills. Their method of attack is peculiar. The animal launches itself backwards with incredible speed and, clashing its hindquarters against an enemy, drives its erect deep quills deep into it with painful or fatal results.

Mr R.C. Morris records how a panther was slain by a porcupine, its head pierced by the thrusting quills. There is yet another record of an almost full-grown tiger meeting its death by leaping on porcupine. Its lungs and liver were riddled with quills, and it could do little more than crawl away, to die a few yards from its victim.' (Prater 1971:216).

Another pertinent level of accuracy in the tale of the tiger and porcupine is the social envy and secrecy surrounding eating wild meat. These days it is even more important to conceal the consumption of hunted game. Villagers recall a bygone age when their musket-carrying, headmen grandfathers used to order water to be put on the fire, and before it had boiled returned with a pheasant or other prey. Now illicitly hunted or trapped meat is only shared among the most restricted social group of trusting neighbours and kin, 'our people' (*nyang ki mi*), who can be relied on not to tell. The occurrence of disclosure about infringements of park regulations to the authorities is feared for the incarceration and fines that follow. It introduces a degree of suspicious surveillance that plays into intra-village feuding, although the moral dimension to these suspicions is not so much to do with the ethics of hunting as the miserliness of not sharing.

The story thus brings together in one smooth narrative, the rivalry of powerful beasts, the cunning of natural mimicry to deceive a dominant threat, and human fickleness. The tiger's revenge is thwarted by the hunter's manipulation of the tiger's fear of a natural foe. Ingold writes of hunting societies animals where 'participate as real-world creatures endowed with powers of feeling and autonomous action, whose characteristic behaviours, temperaments and sensibilities one gets to know in the very course of one's everyday practical dealings with them' (1996:136).

Two weddings and a hypothesis

Among the narrative genres still current in Tamang villages of Rasuwa is a more royal-epic tradition known by the specific description 'the words of the king's palace'.[5] This strand of narrative tradition seems to be a subset of further myths, referred to by several terms, including the Nepali loan-words *arta* and *ugen*. These stories often invoke weird and wonderful species metamorphosis or human-nature interactions. They are clearly meant for entertainment (and prompt mirthful response when recited in company), but their comic force of the bizarre rests in some illumination of identities and relationships. In considering how to sketch out a cultural understanding of natural affinities within Tamang communities, these stories constitute an important source of imaginative exercise in the relationships of identity and being. What is particularly interesting in the stories presented below is the linkage made between marriage, nature and power. I would suggest that the existential problematic is a question of the difficulties involved in marriage partners having to come from other natural types, and the dilemma this presents of just how a match can be contemplated, particularly in the face of affinal resistance.

The Pumpkin

Back in the beginning of time, four *hal*[6] were sown with pumpkin. Only one pumpkin ripened. It was put on the ledge behind the fire. When someone said, 'Let's cook this pumpkin and eat it', it said 'Oh No! Don't eat me', 'This pumpkin speaks' said the people of the house. The father said he was going to plough with oxen, 'take hold of the plough handle'. The pumpkin was about to plough. The pumpkin ploughed up and down, and up and down.

The pumpkin decided to ask for the king's daughter in this place. The pumpkin went to the king's palace. The king said 'who's going to give a daughter to a pumpkin like this?' 'Will you give her or won't you?' the pumpkin said. What could be inside, what indeed. 'I'll make your palace fall down' said the pumpkin. It rolled about, up and down, up and down, and the king's house collapsed. Then the pumpkin asked for the king's oldest daughter. 'I won't go with the pumpkin' said the king's oldest daughter. He asked the second daughter, 'will you go with the pumpkin or not?' 'I won't go' said the second daughter. He asked the third daughter. The third daughter said, 'I'm not going with the pumpkin'.

He asked the youngest daughter, 'Well, what has my fate come to? I'll go to this pumpkin then', said the youngest daughter. They strung together some artemesia plants and brought her in carrying frame. They didn't carry the pumpkin, he walked wobbling along. Then there was an orange tree in fruit. The pumpkin's wife asked him if he could find an orange to eat. 'You will eat' he said, and his wife lifted him up into the orange tree. He jumped up and down, up and down, and an orange fell to the ground. The princess ate the orange.

'Hold out a cloth tightly, I'm going to jump down' said the pumpkin. He jumped and the cloth ripped apart. The pumpkin split open, and out of the pumpkin emerged a king like a god. They fried breads and went to the wedding at the father's house. When they got to the father of the bride's house, the older sisters asked 'where is brother-in-law?' He was concealed by the door on the balcony. The older sisters said 'bring out brother-in-law'. The day before they had the youngest sister going off with a pumpkin, now she had found a husband like a god.

The older sisters said 'Come on younger sister, let's go and look for lice in your hair'. They threw her in the river. The younger sister had given birth to a child previously. The child cried. The older sisters made a comforter of cloth, and gave it to the child to suck. Milk did not flow. The husband asked 'where have you gone and disposed of my wife? I'll lock you up if you don't bring my wife back'.

At the fireplace ledge chickens pecked, at the door threshold they crowed. 'Come here Mother Queen of Gold.' Her voice came from out of the river wanting to nurse the child. The mother of the child had been caught by a river demon (*nyambu*). The husband went to the blacksmith and a hammer was forged. Then he caught hold of the river demon with fire-tongs, and beat it with the hammer. He managed to free his wife and bring her back. The river demon died.

These are the words of the King's House.

Tamang Raja

Back in the beginning of time, a Tamang took a king's daughter. They exchanged tika marks. The king's daughter was happy with the Tamang.

After the wedding the father returned [home]. He sent a message to his daughter and son-in-law. And then the bride went to the palace of the king. 'Son-in-law will you obey my words or not?', he said. The daughter said, 'he will obey'. The father said, 'can you plough nine hal of land or not?' What did the wife say? 'Say you can do it', she said to her husband. 'I can do it, father-in-law', he said, thinking [he could] if the family of wild boars he saw the day before could be caught. He got the family of wild boars to plough up nine hal of land. They ploughed right up to the king's courtyard. The father told his daughter if she hadn't taught [her husband what to do], 'I would eat your husband'. The father was a snake in his lower body, and a man above (half snake, half man).

And then the father asked, 'can you eat nine *muri* of rice?' His daughter told her husband, 'say you can eat it'. 'Gosh! If we can catch the pigeons we saw yesterday this rice can be eaten'. 'Have you eaten it?', said the king. 'There wasn't enough food, it's all eaten down to the leaf'.[7]

'Now, can you put out a fire of nine score loads of wood with your own piss?' 'Say you can do put it out', said she. 'This no good whore has taught her husband. If you cannot do it I'll eat you', said the father-in-law. 'Gosh! If we can catch the monsters we saw yesterday swallowing a river, this fire could be put out', said the Tamang. 'I will put out the nine score loads of wood with my own piss'. The monsters he saw the day popped. 'The piss even caused a landslide, father-in-law. If you don't believe me go and see'.

Now the son-in-law had finished this, his father-in-law said, 'Can you bring down the milk of thunder[9] from the sky or not?' His daughter said, 'Tell my father you can bring it down'. 'Father-in-law I can bring it down', said the husband. 'This whore has taught her husband. If you can't I'll eat you' [said] the snake-below man-above. And so, could [the Tamang] climb to the top of the king's palace? His wife said, 'tell my father you can do it'. When he got to the top he looked all around. As he looked around, the memory of his father came to him, the memory of his mother came to him. 'Have you looked all around', asked the father-in-law. On his serpentine knee fell three tears from the son-in-law, on his father-in-law's knee. The [Tamang's] wife said, 'What can you say father, he has seen his home'. '*Thuk*![10] This whore has made this happen, it's spoiled' said the father. 'Gauri parbate Isur, give the father-in-law the milk of Mahadev'.[11] The son-in-law won, the father-in-law lost. The wife taught her husband to succeed. Her father did not find meat to eat.

These two tales offer contrasting attitudes of bride-seekers' to their affines, who in both cases are presented as dramatically different in nature to their marital partners. The pumpkin bounces up and down ploughing fields, harvesting oranges, and when revealed as human threatens his sisters-in-law for their devious schemes. He is on the one hand the ideal hard-working type, similar to an immigrant gothalo cow-herder in Tamang communities, who once they have demonstrated prowess as workers receive encouragement to find a local bride. On the other hand, his metamorphosis into a god-like king takes him from being a performer of brideservice, (who was not even carried to his wedding as grooms should be) to a technically adept slayer of man-eating river-demons.[12]

The Tamang who marries the snake-king's daughter, by contrast, is far more passive in character, and depends on his wife's cunning in harnessing other creatures' capacities to accomplish the humanly impossible task set him by the blood-thirsty father-in-law. Finally, it appears to be the Tamang's genuine humanity, his emotion of longing for home and his parents, that brings success in overcoming the last hurdle of producing symbolic drops of divine milk from the sky in his tears.

Leaving aside a fuller examination of the texts, I suggest that the two narratives can be seen as demonstrating the central dynamic of marriage to be one of negotiating difference. In both cases the affines are reluctant partipants to the alliance, and the mutual perceptions of otherness was overcome by force and compliance respectively. Both narratives revolve around weddings in which one of the partners is of non-human descent. This highlights the Tamang notion that even between non-mythical brides and grooms there is a coming together of different perceived natures. It is not therefore a case of recognized common being, of like and like, as conceived by the notion of endogamy,[13] that is needed for proper affinity, but the coming together of difference. Difference, however, appears to be celebrated by the two couples in question as they counter the resistance of the wider affines.

This Tamang idea of clan nature entails an 'other' notion of species to the 'scientific' version. It is one that cannot achieve auto-reproduction except by loss of humanity. Intra-clan marriage, however, many generations distant, is incest, or as the Tamangs say *klap soba*, 'to behave like a bull'. For Tamangs, the defining criterion of humanity is to recognize quasi-species difference among clans. This does leave a logical problem remaining as to where quasi-species difference gets so distant as to be questionably human at all. Many tamang myths seem to deal particularly with this dilemma of what happens when the affinal other is so other that the principle of attracted opposites invites monstrous encounters.

In both cases the marriages are also charged with violence. The sisters attempt to drown the pumpkin-prince's bride, and the snake-king intends to devour his son-in-law. Conversations about the history of the communities of Rasuwa illuminate the connection between marriage and violence, in that marriage between enemies is often positively represented. When it came to conflict between villages or rival (Ghale) clans, the fact of intermarriage enabled a discourse in which the enemies could be spoken of as *mha-busing* (sons-in-law and one's own clan sisters and daughters). Conflict is part of what makes a good marriage.

After the two weddings, now for the hypothesis. The key to understanding Tamang concepts of nature is to admit the fragility of the concept of Tamang society.[14] For a start, half the people I have been talking about would deny being Tamang at all. They are Ghale. Admittedly they speak a language they call Tamang, and share a common kinship terminology apart from a few Ghale-specific categories, but as a jāt they are assertively not Tamang. Indeed others who would categorically deny being Tamang include pockets of Gurung and Bei (Newar) and Sherpas of Helambu ancestry, who although they may marry with Tamang clans, remain distinct. Intermarriage in fact promotes the reproduction of distinctiveness, because marriage is explicitly about recognizing difference.

My hypothesis is therefore that asking the question whether there could be said to be Tamang concepts of nature should begin with the perceived natural underpinnings of social relations. It is not so much that social relations are projected onto a non-human world as that the social world is recognized as naturally diverse, and as part of natural diversity. The non-human world is not seen as an absolute other except in so far as human society is characterized as distinct by particular regulations of non-incestuous type, as opposed to the inability of animals to make such moral discrimination and maintain ethically correct inter-species relations.[15] There is thus no grand distanciation of society from nature, which Ingold (1993) argues, provides the legitimation for western society's control over nature. Rather, the environment is considered to be populated by a great diversity of beings, inhabiting the vast range between mountain tops and valleys, and, furthermore, these life presences can potentially be communicated with.

Engaging with Nature

This last point touches on issues in a debate over environmental perception carried on by Ingold (1992). He argues that, particularly regarding hunter-gatherer societies, anthropologists have too readily accepted the modern predilection for understanding environmental perception as filtered through cultural categories, to the neglect of direct interaction. From this point of view, to look for a culturally inscribed Tamang relationship with the environment would be a mistaken project, because the background presumption would be that culturally constructed meaning is imposed on an inert nature. This would neglect peoples' embodied direct perception of affordances from the environment, unmediated by cultural classification. The important lesson is perhaps not to substitute readings made from cultural texts for an understanding of the actions of people in direct environmental engagement. My point is that the Tamangs' narratives of nature and power imply a directly continuous engagement with their environment.

Ritual language in particular deserves to be appreciated as a technique of self-environment awareness. The chanting of place names in evoking ancestral migrations, or the mental journeys involved in reciting the sequences of sites of local territorial nature-spirits (*shyibda-than*) through the region, are examples of what Höfer (1997: 26) terms 'enumerative phraseology', that connects the ritual participant in the here and now to another time and place.

It is perhaps when direct environmental engagement fails to provide peoples' needs, or is excluded as a possibility by political constraints, that ritual language becomes a privileged means of achieving desired ends. The Tamangs invoke a 'time when people spoke with gods' (*lha deng mi batiba bela*) to recapture the direct communication they once are supposed to have been capable of, before a misunderstanding in the forest between a man and his spirit brother-in-law led to the severance of that communication.[16] Ruptures of personal relations within communities are referred to by the sign of 'not talking' (*tam apang*). In the condition of regulatory semi-detachment from their environment that has existed for two decades the Tamangs of the Langtang National Park are now reliant upon complex strategies of self-preservation, combining conspiracies of silence towards the authorities with deferential modes of supplication when caught eating a porcupine or carrying a load of bamboo too many.

Currently, however, the estrangement produced by the dichotomization of nature–society is now under review in the form of a policy of creating 'buffer zones' to acknowledge legitimate human–environmental engagement in the forest margins. To be fair, the situation in Langtang National Park in practice has never been as exclusionary as for instance in Chitwan, but after twenty years of the national parks having been run along the professed model of ideal minimum human encroachment on nature, at least in theory the radical dimorphic ideology of nature–society has been tempered by a recognized zone of interface.

The control over nature by the park authorities is for the most part a claim rather than a reality. The lack of adequate resourcing and poorly-motivated staff keeps the level of environmental surveillance to one of periodic rituals of enforcement, which assert the political relations of hierarchy between the park officials and villages. But beyond the matter of staffing constraints in a difficult terrain, from the villagers' point of view there is another sense in which the park authorities' claim to control is flawed. I mentioned previously the occasional visits of official hunters who come for the purpose of keeping the wild boar numbers under control. They only manage to kill a few beasts at most, and leave the villages disappointed. A nineteen year old young man explained why he thought the hunters were unsuccessful. He said the boars were protected by the territorial guardian of wildlife, *shyibda*. It was as if the hunters as outsiders do not have the adequate ritual connections for permission to kill the boars.

This perceived lack of adequate connectedness to the local sacred environment on the part of the park authorities underlines the problem of lack of understanding in the relationship with the local communities. The authority of the park is legitimated by the state and western conservationist financial donors, and is enforced by the military. But it has till now little consensual participation. I would argue that the Tamang discourses of engaged difference, of creative conflict, of dialogues across natural types provide an avenue for communicating disagreement. The trouble is this dialogue is too politically one-sided, and unlike genuine bride-seekers, the park in-comers have little to enter the danger-zone of negotiating mutual identities bilaterally.

Conclusion

What I hope to have done in here is to have located issues of human–environmental relations within understandings of the self as situated imperfectly and negotiably to the relational properties of the world. It will perhaps only be when the identities involved in human–environmental interaction are recognized as legitimately conflictual that the debate over biodiversity can truly begin, which will start from the basis of desire for mutual relationships between different qualities of nature. The Tamangs of the Langtang National Park do not have the scientific discourse to engage conceptually with issues of nature conservation. What they do have is an ecology of self that celebrates engagement with natural difference, which arguably resonates far more with the ranges of Himalayan biodiversity than an imposed categorical distanciation of society from nature.

There is some promising convergence in the fact that just as the modernist ideology of nature–society opposition in conservationist thought is transforming into a less dichotomized perspective in the concept of buffer-zone, so in anthropology the same opposition is being discarded. Ingold argues for a new ecological anthropology which would recognize that

> the relations with which it deals, between human beings and their environments, are not confined to a domain of 'nature' separate from and given independently of, the domain in which they lead their lives as persons. For hunter-gatherers as for the rest of us, life is given in engagement, not in disengagement, and in that very engagement, the real world at once ceases to be 'nature' and is revealed to us as an environment for people. (Ingold 1996: 150)

The tendency in the anthropology of Nepal is to assume that caste and ethnicity are the supreme defining frameworks of identity. It may well be that rhetorics of jāt offer a more exclusively articulated discourse than any other, but the proper anthropological problematic should be to contextualize such purified representations in the total complexity of peoples' lives, and evaluate whether these rhetorics are sustained by or contradict other elements of both verbalized and embodied being. Caste/ethnic identities could then be seen in a situated ontology that would include the self in a total environment that would contain all that we otherwise refer to as kin, community, language, religion, power, livelihood, property, territory, and so on.

The 'tribal' appearance of Tamang society emerges from a history of mutual distanciation from the state (Holmerg 1989), but the internal logic of Tamang sociality hinges on heterogeneity of social type and incorporation of others through affinity, and classificatory or 'fictive' kinship. The Tamang narratives of composite selves are irreducible to pure type and proclaim the principle of admixture, by which fact natural rivalries and coalitions are perpetually lived out.

Notes

1 My rendering of the Tamang language obeys no greater precision than attempting to follow my own fallible ear; apologies are here made to more linguistically proficient scholars. Due to the significant regional variations I make no attempt to standardize with other works on Tamang, but I have to acknowledge a profound debt to the corpus of 'meme' A. Höfer.
2. Campbelll n.d. and 1998.
3. Toffin and Wiart (1985: 133) list '*pulna*' as *Cornus capitata*, but mention it fruiting in April–May.
4. The hunters come from the department of national parks and wildlife conservation.
5. *Raja darbar ki tam.*
6. One hal is the amount of land one man and bullock team can plough in one day.
7. Plates made of leaves?
8. *Simbu*, a man-eating creature of voracious appetite.
9. This is a slightly unclear passage. The narrator told me that 'Gauri nye' referred to a female property of the sky, and that when thunder sounds it is a sign of 'Gauri, the milk of Lachmi'. Gauri, 'The Golden One', is the name of Parvati. O'Flaherty (1975) *Hindu Myths* p. 343; p. 168 refers to the sound of drums in the sky.
10. Spitting.
11. Mandeo (Mahadev) is the greatest divine presence in the landscape, worshipped at the lake of Gosainkunda, and the natural lingam at Shikar Besi, where milk is liberally poured as an offering.
12. Guru Rimpoche is also said to have killed these creatures, to make the landscape safe for people.
13. I have never come across any sense of group endogamy beyond purely de facto interests of neighbourhood preference. In practice up to a half of marriages may turn out to be village endogamous, but the point is there is nothing in the logic of Tamang marriage that speaks of in-group circulation, beyond the stated (parental) preference for marrying a child of the parents' cross-gender siblings. This seems to be

diametrically opposed to the Hindu practice of village exogamy combined with jāt endogamy.

14. The discussion here is about the Tamang speakers of Rasuwa. The arguments quite possibly do not apply elsewhere in Nepal, such as the inhabitants of Temal, Khabre Palanchok, some of whom have told me they are the pure Tamangs. In Rasuwa there is little certainty about 'pure' Tamangs. In Rasuwa there is little certainty about 'pure' Tamang'-ness, and perhaps the district is especially hybridized in this respect.
15. I discuss animals' moral treachery in 'Animals Behaving Badly: Talking about Wildlife and Conservation in Langtang National Park'.
16. Holmberg records the same myth in the Nuwakot section of the Trisuli valley (1989: 171).

APPENDIX

DangbDumshing deng chyen (The Porcupine and Tiger)

o dumshing tse chyen shurpee riiba tim. Kyekpa ghi shikari nibala. Kyekpa deng chyen khaDu tajim. Chyen tse pangjim kyekpa ta, 'Dumshing tse nga shurji, o Dumshing set klaago'. Kyekpa shya naaji tim ti juhim. Kuyu dsa ta pangjim 'nyang shya tsaba namsaba ta ta pango'. Kyekpa shya naaji tim ti yujim. Kuyu dsa ta pangjim 'nyang shya tsaba namsaba ta ta shetgo'. Namshodang shori kuyu dsa kwi naa nibala, shingal tse sa tso tsopji ni nibala ro. 'Kwi naabari khimse ma tse 'ta yangi e ta? Sa tsop tsopji pratiba. Kuyu tse shetjim, 'dumshing tse dhyen shurpala' pangji. Chyen dsa laajim hyen tibala ro, cheyen tse teehji. Ase namshodang kyekpa dsa pheri shikari nijim ro. Tale shéppa e tse?' chyen tse pangji. Kyekpa tse 'ngai ashetnyi'. 'E mring tse shetji' pangba ro. 'Nga derem e tsaba' chyen tse pangji. Kyekpa tse 'kra gyam tse tsau' pangji. Chyen tse 'baksa gysam tse tsaba' pangji. Kyekpa paphule tijim ro. Asem kyekpa tse pangjim 'tila tsabe dumshing yu-i lajim'. Asem chyen tse 'yam kongbale tsorro nga chonge'. Ase chyen chongji, kyekpa tse 'tsarle chongo, dongi laji'. Chyen chongji, keykpa-i jyan tarji, tim ti do yuji.

chinji.

Pumpkin (Parsi)

Dango kalbe sangbe diri, parsi dap sujim, hal pli sari, parsi ghi ghi no rojim, pusang guri ten khajim, 'tsu parsi yojim tsaba' pangimo parsi tse 'Abi! Atse!', parsi tse tam pangba ro, tim ki mi ma tse. Aba tse klap meebarinijim ro, darse tsu gorr ki yuri kinpinno, parsi tse klap mee laji. Tur chong chong, mur chong chon laji, klap meei parsi tse. Tsu palana klaari raja-i tsame rit doji, parsi raja darbarti nijim ro, raja tse 'tsu oteva parsi ta kala pimba tsame?' lajim ro. 'A prino apin?' parsi tam pangba taji nang ti ta muji, ta muji. parsi 'e darbar phup klaaba'. Parsi rrilji—mur chong chong, tur chong chong laji—raja-i rim phok tiji. Darse parsi raja-i tsame teba nyetji 'nga ani' tsame teba tse, parsi deng ani ro. Tsame Parang ta nyetjim. Saili tse 'parsi deng ani' lajim. Tsame chyangba ta nyetijim. 'Lo se ngala karma ta tale taji, nga derem tsu parsi ta niba' chyasngba tse. Chendi tsangji, doli ti naajim bajim ro. Mha parsi anaa, te rikliklik praba. Asem suntala dongbo robala, mring (parsi be tse) tsu suntala tsa myangsam nyetji parsi ta, 'tsaba' pangji ro, be tse kwetjim suntala dongbori ten pinjim.

Tur chong chong mur chong chong, suntala deejim sari. Rani tse tsaji suntala. 'Rumal ghi kongbale tsungo, nga chong yuba' parsi tse. Deeji, rumal pli shurmam, parsi tiijim, asem raja lha weeba dongji parsi tse. Gyena krangji aba maiti ta dochang ti nibala. Aba maiti tim ti doji, nanama tse nyetjim 'mha ka se?' Mrap guri, li guri, tsung tenji. Nanama tse 'mhatetto'. Tangshya parsi mrangji. chyangba ta niji, lha weeba-i pa yangji. Nanama tse 'anga prau' pangji, 'shyet chaa niba, pangji. Gendiri pit klaajim ro, anga, nanama tse. Anga chyangba tse kola ghi najim ro, ngondeng nabala. Kola kraaba ro. Nanama tse wen ki yokto soji, nye whaajim kolta. Nye ayunem. Te la pa tse nyetjim. 'Ngala mring kana hur klaa nijim?' Karpe laa (chuppa) ngala mring atetsam. Pusang guri naga mheme syau-syau, mrapsang guri nyau-nyau. 'Ye khau ama margyelmo' kola ta nye whaa khajim gendi nang tse khaji. Nyambu (sarpa) tse tsungbala kola-i ama. Kami tsa niji hodoro sojim ro, darse chimda tse nyambu nyeppa, darse hodoro tse pungji, te mring ngwetji, mring tet kamji ro, baji terem. Raja ghar ki tam tsu. Nyambu shiji.

Tamang Raja

Dangbo kalba sangbe diri, Tamang raja-i tsame kinjimo, Darse tika thalo lajim. Tamang pa ta raja-i tsame kushi partijim. Darse aba tse biha laji pitkhajim. Tsame deng mha ta samdar la khajim. Darse kuyu raja darbar ki tim ti nijim. 'Mha ngai pangbe tam nyenla o anyen' pangjim. Tsame tse 'nyenla' pangjim. Aba tse 'klap hal ku-i sa mee kamla o akham?' Be tse ta pangjim 'kamla pango' pangi pa ta. 'Kamla ashyang' pangjim. tila mrangbe Doga mheme upinsam. Hal ku-i sa Doga mheme mee pinji. Raja-i pindi samma mee pinji. Tsame tse lop apinsam 'ela pa tsaba' bas tse. Aba mur sarpa, tur mi (tet sarpa tet mi). Darse 'mla muri ku tsa khamba?' nyetji aba tse. Tsame tse 'tsa khamla pango'pangji pa ta. 'Ame! tila mrahgbe shyarwang mheme upinsam o tsu mla pilla. 'pijo? {Ken ayoa lapti sammet tsa chinji'. Darse tet kal ku-i shing e chuam tse set khamla?—meri pitsam. 'Set khamla pango' pangjim tsame tse pa. Aba tse 'tsu phtuik randi pa ta lop pinji'. Akhamsam tsabe pheri kyen tse. Darse 'Ame! tila mrangbe simbu (gendi klongbe simbu) upinsam, tsu me set khamba, shee' Tamang tse. Shing tet kal ku nyang ki chyam tse set beela. Tila mrangbe simbu kyol yuji 'chyam tse di no yerji ashyang. pati atisma chaa nyu'. Derem mha tsu chimba deng, kyen 'tsu kauri nye bee khamla wa akham'. tsame tse 'bee khamla pango aba ta' pangji. 'Kyen, ga bee khamla, pangi pa tse. Derem 'lo tsu randi tse lopala te-i pa ta'. Akhamsam tsaba mur sarpa, tur mi. Darse tur Darara dsori ni khamla o akham. be tse 'khamla pango aba ta' pangi. Dsori dobadeng lungba mrangji, mrangba deng mi abaa wala khaji, ama wala khaji. 'E tse lungba mrangba mrangji' kyen tse, kyen ki sarpa-i gyari mha ki mikli phum sum dee yujim, kyen ki gyeri. Be tse ta pangjim 'Abam ta pangba, ro-i lungba mrangshinla'. 'Thuk! tsu randi tse laji, nongji aba. Gauri Parbate isur, mandeo ko dudh sasure le deo lau. Mha daaji, kyen ta breeji, mring tse lopji pa daaji, shya tsa amyangni aba tse.

References

Campbell, B., n.d., 'Natural Affinities: Tamang Discourses on Biodiversity and the Kinship of Species'.

________ 1998, 'Conversing with Nature: Ecological Symbolism in Central Nepal', *Worldviews*, 2: 123–37.

________ 2000, 'Animals Behaving Badly: Indigenous Perceptions of Wildlife Protection in Nepal', J.J. Knight (ed.), *Natural Enemies: People–Wildlife Conflicts in Anthropological Perspective*, London: Routledge.

Cronon, W., 1995, 'The Trouble with Wilderness: or, Getting Back to the Wrong Nature', in Cronon, W. (ed.), 1995, *Uncommon Ground: Rethinking the Human Place in Nature*, Norton: New York.

Descola, P., 1994, *In the Society of Nature: A Native Ecology in Amazonia*, Cambridge: Cambridge University Press.

Höfer, A., 1997, *Tamang Rituals Texts II: Ethnographic Studies in the Oral Tradition and Folk-religion of an Ethnic Minority in Nepal*, Franz Steiner Verlag: Stuttgart.

Holmberg, D., 1989, *Order in Paradox: Myth, Ritual and Exchange among Nepal's Tamang*, Ithaca: Cornell University Press.

Ingold, T., 1992, 'Culture and the Perception of the Environment', in E. Croll and D. Parkin (eds.), *Bush Base: Forest Farm: Culture, Environment and Development.* Routledge: London.

________ 1993, 'Tool-use, Sociality and Intelligence', in K. Gibson and T. Ingold (eds.), *Tools, Language and Cognition in Human Evolution*. Cambridge: Cambridge University Press.

________ 1996, 'Hunting and Gathering as Ways of Perceiving the Environment, in R. Ellen and K. Fukui (eds.), *Redefining Nature*, Berg: Oxford.

Müller–Böker, U., 1995, *Die Tharu in Chitwan: Kenntnis, Bewertung und Nutzung der natürlichen Umwelt im südlichen Nepal*, Franz Steiner Verlag: Stuttgart.

O'Flaherty, W., 1975, *Hindu Myths*, Harmondsworth: Penguin.

Posey, D., 1998, 'The Balance Sheet' and the 'Sacred Balance': Valuing the Sacred Knowledge of Indigenous and Traditional Peoples', *Worldviews*, 2: 91–106.

Prater, S.H., 1971. *The Book of Indian Animals*, Bombay: Oxford University Press.

Ramble, C. and C.P. Cahpagain, 1990, 'Preliminary Notes on the Cultural Dimension of Conservation', Report no. 10. Makku-Barun Conservation Project Working Paper Publication Series, DNPWC/WMI.

Stevens, S. (ed.), 1997, *Conservation through Cultural Survival: Indigenous Peoples and Protected Areas.* Washington: Island Press.

Toffin, G. and Wiart, 1985, 'Recherches sur l'enthnobotanique des Tamang du Massif du Ganesh Himal (Nepal Central): les plantes non-cultivées'. *Journal d'Agriculture Traditionelle et de Botanique Appliquée,* XXXII.125–75.

Comments

ANDRAS HÖFER

Campbell's reflections are a highly stimulating attempt at offering a new perspective on the question of the relationship between the *perceptual* and the *effective* environment, as was first formulated by American enthnoecology more than forty years ago. For reasons of space, I shall refrain from dealing with the many points on which I fully agree with Campbell, and concentrate instead on three problematic issues, namely the nature–culture dichotomy, the interpretation of the narratives, and the quest for the 'environmental selfhood'.[1]

1. The first comment is meant as an ethnographic supplement to Campbell's findings. As he stresses, a nature–culture dichotomy is foreign to traditional concepts of the Tamangs in the upper valley of the Trisuli and has only recently been imposed by the national park project. As for the Tamangs of my fieldwork area in Dhading district, I can report that such a radical and obvious dichotomization does indeed appear to be absent. In common parlance, the Nepali word jaṅgalī ('of the jungle') is sometimes employed with the meaning 'uncivilized', 'ill-mannered' or 'brutish', but neither in modern colloquial Tamang nor in the more archaic language of the oral ritual texts of the shamans and exorcists do we find terms referring to a clear-cut division drawn between what would correspond to our notions of an autonomous, self-generating nature (*physis, natura naturans*), on the one hand, and of a man-made realm of culture and civilization (*nomos* and *techne*), on the other. In the conceptualizations of space underlying the rituals texts, the notion of 'wilderness' does exist, albeit only implicitly; to my knowledge, there is no collective noun for it.[2] Thus, particular high mountain regions, certain mountain peaks, hillocks, steep rocky slopes, forests, and so on do play an important role as numinous places, but terminologically they are not set in opposition to the area inhabited

and/or cultivated by humans. The opposition which is predominant is that between 'house' (or 'homestead', also synecdochically for 'settlement') and 'fields' (i.e. 'cultivated land').[3] Why this should be so in an intriguing question.

This is what we find in the rituals texts. However, a closer look at their wider context in general and at the traditional organization and treatment of the landscape in particular reveals a specific type of distinction.

There are numerous insular sanctuaries which constitute a kind of natural reserves and occur scattered in the landscape, situated on certain peaks, hillocks, slopes, in certain river gorges, at a spring or at the foot of a solitary boulder amidst the fields, and, which are regarded as residences of certain local gods known as 'guardians of the place', 'masters of the soil', 'masters of the lake', and the like. Both conceptually and etymologically, these *genii loci* are akin to the Tibetan *sa-bdag, ghzi-bdag* and *klu* (The king in Campbell's narrative number 3, who is half man and half snake, is a *nāga* or *klu*). Since these divinities are believed to have existed prior to the arrival of humans as cultivators, the relationship between them and humans is based on a kind of contract: the divinities, who also control natural phenomena, such as weather, floods, and landslides, demand worship in return for remaining neutral or even acting as guarantors of good harvest and prosperity. Any transgression of the rules of symbiosis, any infraction of the traditional 'natural' order of things—including sacrileges, such as the disturbance of the sanctuaries or a case of incest, as also the disturbance of social peace in the settlement by violence or continuous dispute, or even any radical deviation or conspicuous innovation concerning the cultivation of fields and animal husbandry—is likely to entail collective sanctions in the shape of natural calamities, epidemics, accidents, and the like.

In as much as the sanctuaries of such local divinities are holy in the sense that, except for rituals, access to them is prohibited, and that natural vegetation in and around them must not be cut down or otherwise utilized, one may say that in them, human engagement with nature is reduced to a minimum: the only engagement permitted is conservation. Nature is protected from humans by humans.[4] What we can conclude from the distribution and the treatment of such places is that the demarcation is not made in terms of separate zones, such as 'cultivated' versus 'non-cultivated' areas. Rather, it is only in such sanctuaries that nature as natural landscape finds its purest manifestation, preserves its original state, condensed as it were, into insular sites which are focal in the sense that it is from them that superhuman control is exerted over human intervention in the rest of the landscape, which has irreversibly been 'adulterated' precisely by this intervention, and where the boundary between nature and culture is blurred.

It is quite another question to what extent, or even whether at all, modern conservationist policies could take advantage of such patterns in traditional conceptualizations of the landscape in view of the overwhelming economic constraints resulting from demographic and other factors.

2. To be sure, it is not the human-nature relationship that seems to be central to the narratives numbered 2 and 3. It is one thing to say, as Campbell plausibly argues, that both infer that they mirror or describe a specifically Tamang perception of the human-environment relationship. Personally I am inclined at first to take the stories at their face value as works or oral art that are closed to the literary genre of the *grotesque* in that they highlight through 'exaggeration' the dangerous, extreme, or even absurd aspects implied in marriage alliance as a continuous negotiation of difference between wifetakers and wifegivers in a society which practises bilateral cross-cousin marriage. Anyone acquainted with a western Tamang community is at once reminded of the role-types of the towering, 'ever-demanding' father-in-law and the 'shy', 'ever-obliging' son-in-law, as they come to the fore in ceremonial behaviour on the occasion of visits and prestations, to mention just one of the aspects adumbrated by the stories. One is also tempted to see in the refusal by the elder sisters, in narrative number 2, and in the assistance given by the youngest sister in overcoming all the hurdles, one by one, a reflection of the protracted, processual character of western Tamang marriage (to the effect that the final wedding rite for a wife is often performed after her death), with the married-in woman gradually 'growing into' her role as mother of her husbands's children[5] and as housewife.

Furthermore, one cannot but agree with Campbell when he emphasizes interaction and conflictual engagement in the human-environment relationship (which is presumably valid, though to varying degrees, for all societies with a subsistence economy and stands in contrast to radical contemporary western conservationist ideology), but I cannot help being somewhat sceptical about the general applicability of some of his conclusions. If he sees a 'danger in presuming that cultural narratives can convey the ontological sense of what it is to dwell in a given environment', and if he warns against substituting 'readings made from cultural texts for an understanding of the actions of persons in direct environmental engagement'—then why should one resort to such narratives at all? Would not the observation of everyday action be sufficient?

Also, Campbell seems to contend that the narratives in question simply mirror (or rationalize, *a posteriori*) the principles underlying the Tamangs' 'directly continuous engagement with their environment', which implies, among other things 'creative conflict'—without providing a cultural classification that would mediate the peoples' perception and thus influence, as a feedback at least, their physical engagement with the environment. If this were generally true, there would exist, all over the world, far fewer group-specific preferences and avoidances in matters of taste, or attitudes towards animals, of the choice of substances for food and as *materiae medicae*, of body techniques, and so on, and probably also far fewer taboos on incest (whose definition varies from group to group). The point is that not all such classificatory rules, which selectively regulate (complicate or in a sense also simplify) the exploitation of natural resources and to some extent even the allocation of their products within society, can be derived directly, in a deterministic manner, from the pattern of the ecological adaptation of an individual group as we observe it at a given time. All this 'cultural stuff' does possess a certain degree of autonomy, in good part because being 'inherited' as tradition, it stems from past experience and as such tends to 'lag behind' present-day facts or objective requirements. To disregard this partial autonomy would also be tantamount to denying, among other things, the tendency of cultural discourse to aim at maintaining some consistency in classificatory logic through 'correcting' or 'completing' lacks of fit without empirical justification.

3. Campbell's call for focusing future research more on group-specific 'environmental selfhoods' as frameworks of identity is fully

justified in its own right. Nevertheless, however challenging such an enterprise may appear, I think we must be aware of its limitations. Even if we go beyond the interpretation of such narratives[6] and widen out scope to study a more or less complete corpus of beliefs and practices, traditional knowledge and traditional techniques (including nosology and therapy, hitherto rather neglected in ethnography), along with their linguistic articulation, the effort to extract from them some sort of ethno- or caste- or other group-specific 'morality' is likely to founder on the ethnographic complexity of the Nepal Himalaya in particular. Local units bearing one and the same ethnonym may be ethnically quite different types of ecological adaptation. It is also questionable to what extent the cultural data we collect among local groups mirror exactly their own individual type of ecological adaptation. After all, the high intensity of inter-ethnic and inter-local communication in the Nepal Himalaya has also resulted in borrowings of motifs, notions, interpretations, and vocabulary, and it may often turn out to be difficult to prove that a certain element or pattern was adopted from other groups simply because it fitted perfectly into the logic and ethos of the 'environmental selfhood' of the borrowing group in question. (Precisely the case of the western Tamangs; provides a striking example of the co-existence of different strands of traditions, including Tibetan Buddhism and Hinduism, which, albeit interconnected through attempts at mutual adjustments, cultural translations and hierarchizations, do not appear in a fully consistent and stable analysis). In sum, what we can expect are mostly instances of never-ending and ever-inchoate bricolages resulting from temporary efforts at conceptualization as part of numerous processes of negotiating discrepancies rather than settled structures of identity. Is 'environmental selfhood' not likely to turn out in the end to be even more dynamic and permeable a category than 'caste' and 'ethnic group'?

Notes

1. If I have misunderstood any of Campbells's conclusions the failure would be entirely mine.
2. In the texts in my collection, there are two archaic words that the informants rendered through 'jungle', 'dense forest', and that, according

to some of the contexts in which they occur, may perhaps also be interpreted as meaning 'wilderness'. The one is *rilunma,* a composite of the words for 'mountain' and 'valley', and the other is *rina:luṅ*, a composite of the words for 'mountain', 'forest' and 'valley', respectively.
3. That is, *khaṅsa* versus *syiṅsa* in the ritual language. The meaning of the latter word is identical with that of its etymon, namely *zhing-sa*.
4. As is well known, the existence of comparable sanctuaries is also among other groups and in other regions. It may suffice to refer here to the cult places of certain Hindu divinities, especially in the countryside, or to the idea of the 'sacred grove' in both Hinduism and Tibetan Buddhism.
5. The kinship term of address and reference used by the husband for his wife identifies the latter as the mother of the first-born child and is 'mother of X'. Until the birth of the first child, there is no term of address for one's wife, and when in the company of other, the husband usually refers to his wife simply as 'this woman'.
6. Just as, say, La Fontaine's animal fables alone would not provide sufficient evidence for a characteristically French 'environmental selfhood' in the seventeenth century, in the same way it would be hazardous to infer a mental orientation or 'worldview' from a number of Tamang narratives alone, and to presume that it is shared and internalized by virtually all members of a given community in which the stories were collected.

Dumji and Zhindak

Local Festival Performance and Patronage as a Crucial Source of Sherpa Identity

EBERHARD BERG

Sherpa culture is primarily rooted in the locality where it is both generated and given its particular shape. Sherpa identity seems to originate predominantly in this particular context. There it emerges primarily from the performance of several important religious festivals which are celebrated annually by all Sherpas of the local community.

In this chapter intended to direct attention to the question of how local groups mobilize, shape, and reaffirm Sherpa identity, I focus on Dumji, the most important annual religious festival held in the Sherpa locality. I attempt a short description of the Dumji festival that is performed in each locality according to a distinct tradition of its own. Moreover I want to highlight the Dumji festival in relation with patronage. It will be demonstrated in this context that the originally Tibetan *sbyin-bdag*—concept constitutes an important social mechanism upon which not only traditional, but also contemporary Sherpa culture rests. To begin with, however, some remarks on Sherpa identity seem to be appropriate.

Some Markers of Sherpa Identity

The Sherpa represent a small, ethnically Tibetan group in

Solukhumbu, who are adherents of the Nyingmapa tradition of Tibetan Buddhism. About 480 years ago they had migrated from eastern Tibet into their present settlement area. Within the ethnic and caste mosaic that is typical of the 'Hindu Kingdom of Nepal' the Sherpa represent a small, but very successful and probably the best-known ethnic group of Nepal's indigenous Tibetans. Owing to their deliberate engagement in the flourishing trekking industry in contemporary Nepal, the Sherpa represent one of the most 'westernized' ethnic groups.

In her recent innovative, provocative and highly acclaimed *Ethnography of Himalayan Encounters*, Vincanne Adams suggests '. . .that the idea of an authentic Sherpa must be revised; there are, instead, only virtual Sherpa' (1996: 237). According to her analysis, Sherpa identities are created through a mimetic process whereby Sherpas deliberately construct themselves in images that conform to '. . .the persistent anthropological and Western desire to find a site of authenticity beyond the Western gaze. . .' (p. 8). Adams' investigation focuses on how Sherpas mould their cultural identity in a transnational setting. As to her conclusion—'. . .their malleable and transnationally constructed identities. . .' (ibid. 239)—Adams does not only depict a chameleon–like Sherpa identity which may hold true for certain contexts; she also argues that there are 'only virtual Sherpas'.

Without any doubt the Sherpas' contemporary cultural identity is deeply informed by transnational forces. Yet what is obviously lacking in Adams' treatise is the demonstration of how Sherpas actually construct their identities either in transactions with others including westerners, or with other Sherpas.[1] Hence it has to be demonstrated how and in which frameworks of action Sherpas forge their identities within their own cultural setting.

In the context of the Nepalese nation-state, Sherpa culture, society and religion display a wide variety of 'identity markers' which clearly set them off against their different neighbours. The Sherpa share a sense of a common religion; they share a common name—*Shar pa*, i.e. 'people from the east'—which mirrors the fact that they see themselves as belonging to one ethnic group with a distinct tradition of its own; and they display a common interest and a solidarity in regard to other Sherpas.[2] In their dealings with others, their cultural or ethnic identity is not hidden;[3] in fact, they are proud of it. The internal diversity of Sherpa culture is not strong, but sufficient enough to establish a regional opposition between Khumbu and Solu Sherpas. Khumbu Yullha and Shorong Yullha, the two regional protective mountain deities, are seen as the focal point for the Sherpas' regional identity. Moreover, Sherpa society is embedded in a wider society that is distinguished by a markedly different Hindu culture. However, the policies of the Nepalese nation-state with regard to the Buddhist populations have seldom consisted in more than simple negligence or discrimination.

Religion seems to be the most important idiom in which Sherpa present themselves in their dealings both with Sherpas and with others including westerners. Most of their ritual celebrations are performed locally in honour of the powerful protective goddess and gods of the locality and/or the wider region. Trying to secure their benevolence, help, and protection, the Sherpas perform elaborate rituals for the worship of the protective deities in the local community as well as in the households. Most of these ritual enactments follow an already pre-existent Tibetan pattern; but they were moulded according to the specific local needs which arose from their new environment after their setting in Solukhumbu. According to Stein (1987: 153) these deities fulfil a highly functional role as they bind individuals to their social group in time and space. This can be witnessed, among others, in the performance of several religious celebrations which are staged annually in the local public arena, i.e. the village temple and its courtyard. In this context a wide variety of identity markers are put into dramatic play: specific food such as *thukpa, shakpa,* or *dildro* is distributed to the participants, traditional festive clothing is worn such as the *chuba*, the long ankle-length robe worn by women and men alike that is bound around the waist by a long sash; traditional jewellery such as corals, turquoise, and *dzi* stones is worn by the women; the *shyabru* (Tib. *shabs-bro*), the traditional Sherpa dance, is performed late at night by women and men alike when a religious performance comes to an end.

Dumji: A Short Description

Notwithstanding all the influential changes that have emerged in the context of the Sherpas' ongoing encounter with modernity[4],

Sherpa today continue to devote a considerable part of their resources to religious purposes. Thus religion still seems to be the most important idiom in which Sherpas present themselves in their dealings both with Sherpa and with others—Buddhist, Hindu caste and ethnic groups, and westerners.

The great Dumji festival is considered as the Sherpas' most important religious festival of the local community within the annual cycle.[5] It is held in the sacred centre of the locality, i.e. the *gomba* (Tib. *dgon pa*) or village temple. In contrary to its monastic counterpart—the famous *Mani Rimdu* dance drama—the Dumji festival belongs to the sphere of religious celebrations practised within the realm of the locality.[6] It is enacted by members of the locality; and it is performed for the well-being of the entire local community. Hence for the Dumji performance no representatives of 'high religion' from outside the local community are needed.

Dumji is presided over by Tantric village priests i.e. married clerics (Tib. *snags-pa*) whom the Sherpa refer to as lamas.[7] In most cases they are members of the local patrilineal clan, or clans that sponsor this religious event. The village lamas are supported by monks as well as by learned lay men who have received some monastic education as children, but who later married and began the life of a householder.

Dumji is performed annually, but in different localities at different times of the year. It is always the specific local tradition that has created a distinct shape of its Dumji celebration.[8] It is held from the end of February/beginning of March (at Sagar-Bhakanje/Solu) until the middle of May (at Pangboche) thus marking the annual beginning of spring and the onset of the yearly agricultural cycle, first in lower Solu, then in high-altitude Khumbu.

In popular understanding of the name Dumji, the Tibetan term *dhub chod* ('meditation'; 'offering') blends with *sgrub pa* ('to obtain a blessing, boon') (Das 1984 (1902): 334). The festival centres on offerings and requests to the gods as well as offerings and threats to the demons; and after a distribution of ritual foods to all present it closes with a 'long life' blessing ceremony (Sherpa *whong*, Tib. *tshe dbang*). In other words, Dumji represents a ritual ceremony performed to propitiate the deities by prayer and to worship them by meditation and offerings in order to secure their benevolence, protection and help while, on the other hand, exorcising evil forces from the local community. To accomplish all this the diverse ritual procedures that form distinct parts of celebration extend over a period of at least four or five days.

Notwithstanding the diverse local differences of the performance of the Dumji, the festival reveals a basic structure which has its roots in Tibet.[9] Mask dances (*cham*) in the temple courtyard performed by the officiating lamas and monks, and, in few cases of minor importance, by some lay people is the main characteristic of Dumji.[10] Another one is the ritual recitation of a set of Tantric texts by the officiants.[11] A very impressive feature is the ritual circumambulation of the sacred complex in the course of which the officiants worship the 'guardians of the four directions'. However, the present outline is concerned mainly with the diverse social aspects of the Dumji celebration.

The spectacular dramatic enactment of central episodes of their own history within the wider realm of Tibetan Buddhism which takes place on the third day is attended by all members of the local Sherpa clan or clans. For this occasion all the Sherpa lay people dress up in their best finery and gather in the gomba courtyard which is turned into the stage of the performance. There they form a highly responsive audience for a ritual celebration that the people themselves see as embodying the core of their culture. Visitors of neighbouring clans as well as few Tamang, Rai Hindu high castes, and usually all landless Kami who represent a marginal section of the local community, join the wider circle of the audience.

The Dumji performance involves three distinct forms of ritual worship; those of Guru Rinpoche, of the Sherpa's local mythical hero, and of a range of protective 'deities of place'—in this context primarily *yullha*, i.e. mountain-god, and *lu*, i.e. serpent divinity[12]. Thus the elaborate religious celebration combines both the ritual practices of 'high religion' and of local folk beliefs which are reflective of the history of the locality. It is Guru Padmasambhava, the Great Indian Guru, who represents the focus of the Dumji celebration. Like Guru Rinpoche this saint is universally revered by Nyingmapa Buddhists such as the Sherpas.[13] But actually it is a rich interplay of those three different elements which seem to be constitutive of the Dumji celebration.

An important aspect concerns the worship of the protective deities. It is a well-known fact that the Tibetans have populated their natural environment with a host of deities and spirits upon whom they feel dependant.[14] Both yullha and lu guarantee prosperity, power, health, success, and long life to the individual Sherpas and their household along with securing the general welfare and protection of the Sherpa communities of the whole region.

In fact, most of the Sherpas' ritual celebrations are performed locally in honour of the powerful protective goddesses and gods of the locality and/or the wider region (Tib.*srung-ma*).[15] Trying to secure their benevolence, help, and protection, the Sherpas perform elaborate rituals to worship them. In this context they follow an already pre-existent Tibetan pattern.[16] However, the ritual complex was moulded according to the specific local needs which arose from their new environment after immigration to Solukhumbu. According to Stein these deities fulfil a highly functional role as they bind individuals to their social group in time and space (Stein 1987(1962): 153). In Sherpa culture it is the Dumji festival that offers a vivid illustration of the important social function inherent in the worship of the territorial deities.

Zhindak and Dumji

In Sherpa culture, practically all communal festivals rest upon a social institution called zhindak.[17] Tib. *sbyin-bdag*—Skt. dānapati—is translated as patron, more especially a dispenser of gifts, a layman manifesting his piety by making presents to the priesthood (Das 1989 (1902): 939). The institution of the zhindak has evolved in Tibet.Originally it implied the historically and usually culturally highly important relation between a lama, the religious officiant/counsellor/spiritual preceptor as donee (*mchod gnas*) and the royal lay donor (*yon bdag*). Whereas the former provides the material support for the lama, the latter gives spiritual advice to the royal or princely donor. Even the relationship with the Mongols had been conceived in terms of this priest-patron relationship.[18] As to the donor his act of supporting the Dharma via making gifts to clerics is a means by which he gains merit (*bsod-nams*). Among the Sherpas the zhindak's sole function consists of donating money, food, clothing, a house or a plot of land. It must be noted, however, that this activity is not associated with any political power in the community. Moreover, the profane work such as the building of bridges and the repair work of mountain trails etc. is dependent on the individual Sherpa's choice to act as Zhindak in a particular case once or repeatedly.

Sponsorship for annual local celebrations such as *Dumji, Nyungne*, or *Losar* is considered to be one of the main communal duties. It rotates from household to household on either a mandatory or on a voluntary basis (Adams 1992: 542). As opposed to all other communal celebrations, however, sponsorship in the case of Dumji, being the most important festival in the local community that is actually attended by all Sherpa members, involves far more resources. The Dumji requires that sponsors provide massive quantities of food, drink, and money in some cases to the entire village community, in others to the officiating lamas, monks, and lay men only.

Each local community where Dumji is held, has a group of so-called *chiwa* (Tib. *spyi-pa*) which is translated by Das (1989 (1902): 807) as 'head, chief, leader'[19]; in this context it means 'the one in charge' of the organization of the Dumji festival. The chiwa's duties are manifold, the most important one being the care for the whole organization of the festival; this also includes the responsibility to act as the festival's 'peace-keeper'. Together with their wives and daughters the chiwas are responsible for the catering of either all the people present or of the officiating lamas, monks, and lay people only. Their wives also have to brew the *chang* weeks before the start of Dumji. Moreover, the chiwas have to do the necessary fund raising, the collecting of grain, the serving of tea, chang, and food either for the officiants or for the whole community present, provide the firewood for the temple kitchen, care for blankets and carpets for the officiants.

There are basically two different modes of sponsoring the Dumji. In some local communities all those households owning property have to contribute the same amount of money, food, and drink. The male household representatives act permanently every year as 'small Zhindaks, as the Sherpas themselves perceive it; in consequence, the expenses are relatively low. Contrary to that mode in other localities this duty has to be fulfilled by a group of—between two and twenty—householders in annual rotation. In the former case the *chiwas* act as organizers of the festival; whereas in the latter the organizers are identical with patrons.[20]

It is common knowledge among the Sherpas that it constitutes an important communal duty of the married householder to act as zhindak of the Dumji festival at least once, sometimes even twice in his lifetime. Provided the chiwas and the zhindak are identical, patronage in this context is a costly affair. Mostly people know quite a while beforehand when their turn as patron is likely to come; this knowledge is necessary as many householders have to save for a long time to be able to cover the expenses involved. If someone is not able to meet these obligations for some reason or other the order of rotation may be changed for some time. But permanent exemption from duty as a patron in this context is impossible as it implies the loss of full membership in the village community.[21]

Conclusion: *Dumji* and *Zhindak* in their relation to Sherpa communal identity

With my observations concerning the annual Dumji festival among the Sherpa I try to demonstrate the significance of the zhindak activity for the existence and well-being of the local Sherpa community. In the course of its performance the local people are bound into one frame of common action. Owing to this, social solidarity and unity in the local community is promoted and thereby the existing social order is reaffirmed and strengthened. Moreover, in the course of the Dumji membership in the Sherpa community by means of patronage is celebrated. Hence, the patron assumes a key role in the process of identity building in Sherpa culture. In my view is is predominantly in the context of the local religious celebrations such as the Dumji festival that Sherpa communal identity is moulded and given its particular character.

The office of the patron for the performance of the Dumji festival implies fairly high expenses as well as a lot of duties before, during and after the festival. But apart from those expenses and duties there are also certain definite advantages associated with the patron's job. Most important seems to be the fact that, at least once in their life time, it provides all men as representatives of the households, be they rich or poor, with the opportunity to act in a leading role in the context of a ritual celebration that mirrors the distinct history of the local sherpa community with the Nyingmapa tradition of Tibetan Buddhism. Due to this and the merit that accrues to the zhindak in organizing the Dumji festival, the office of the patron has been held in high esteem not only in the past but also in contemporary Sherpa society.

Indeed, Sherpa culture and society has been changing profoundly in the context of its highly successful involvement in the trekking and climbing industry. The recent growth of a Kathmandu-based 'middle class' that has adopted western values and patterns of consumption is only one aspect of this fundamental change. But it is this aspect that is coupled with some severe consequences for contemporary Sherpa culture and its future. Among others, this change affects the individual readiness among the Sherpas to act as patrons in support of 'high religion' and its monastic institutions. Instead of acting according to their traditional norms and values, the representatives of the new Sherpa 'middle class' prefers to spend its accumulated wealth within the domain of its own nuclear family. Reflective of this attitude is the constant complaint from the part of the Sherpa lamas that refers to the fact that the willingness to take the responsibility of the patron as 'dispenser of gifts to the priesthood' of 'high religion' has been severely on the decline since more than one decade.[22] Stevens (1993: 196) quotes a saying in Khumbu that is illustrative of this contemporary predicament of Sherpa culture: '. . .whereas once, when a Sherpa became rich, he spent his money on religion (thus accruing merit for his rebirth), he now builds a new house.' In consequence, nowadays almost all Sherpa monasteries in Solukhumbu are dependant on patronage either from the west or the Japanese.[23]

However, the recent decline of the readiness among the Sherpas to act as patrons does not hold true for the realm of the local community and its well-being. According to my information until now no Sherpa has dared to take the risk of the loss of full membership in the village community due his neglect of the duties associated with a Dumji patron. When it is their turn those who live in Kathmandu or abroad return home for the festival in order to fulfil traditional duties as patron for the local community; while those who happen to be absent during the festival provide a substitute to act on their behalf.

In conclusion it is the system of patronage that seems to constitute a crucial guarantee of both the flourishing of Sherpa culture and a distinct—local—Sherpa cultural identity even in the context of increasing change due to the forces of 'globalization'.[24] Moreover, as my observations demonstrate, Samuel's statement concerning religion as 'the field *par excellence* of continuity within Tibetan society' holds true also in the case of contemporary Sherpa culture (Samuel 1993: 150). Yet one might wonder whether the coming generation of Sherpa will continue to fulfil the traditional social obligations vis-à-vis the local community in Solukhumbu at a time when a considerable part of the Sherpa population will live in the Kathmandu valley and in several diasporas in the west.

Notes

1. In my view, Adams' 'authentic Sherpa' and the associated distinct cultural identity does exist and, in fact, can be encountered, the transformative power of the forces of globalization notwithstanding. Moreover the search for the 'authentic other' seems to be wholly obsolete, at least, in our contemporary era which is formed by the forces of globalization which produce phenomena such as 'cultural hybridity'.
2. According to Ramble (1997: 379) there is no 'sentiment' among the diverse Bhotiya groups in Nepal that they constitute a 'distinguishable ethnic category'. Among the Sherpas, however, this 'sentiment' is strong.
3. The 'impression management' of Tamang who, in specific contexts, pretend to be Sherpa, is the best-known example; in their few encounters with westerners, members of low caste groups such as Kāmis and Dāmais try sometimes to do the same.
4. According to V. Adams (1996: 17) in the particular context of the Khumbu Sherpas the 'encounter with modernity' is shaped by three decisive factors: trekking tourism, development aid, and anthropology.
5. It is difficult to understand why this complex religious festival has been fairly neglected by anthropological research. The only article on Dumji has been written by Paul (1979). But in my view due to his somewhat narrow Freudian approach the value of his investigation in this context

is rather limited. Exceptions are von Fürer-Haimendorf, C. (1964: 185–208); Funke, F. (1969: 115–37); and Ortner, (1978: 130).

6. Stein (1987(1962): 129–57) calls this complex 'La religion sans nom ou la tradition'; and Tucci describes it as 'folk religion' 1980 (1970: 163–212).
7. Unlike the other three orders in Tibetan Buddhism the Nyingma or Old Translation School is characterized not only by great monasteries and celebrates lamas and monks, but also by lay tantric practitioners who perform the ritual functions for the local community.
8. In Khumbu, Dumji is held in the gomba, i.e. the village temple complex, of Pangboche, Khumjung, Namche, and Thame; in Pharak it is held in Rimishung; and in Solu it is celebrated in Jung, Goli, and Sagar-Bhakanje. It is worth noting that there are many localities in Solukhumbu without Dumji; moreover, a Dumji can disappear such as in Sete; and it can also be newly established/invented', e.g. in Sottang, in Gumdel.
9. First day: 'site ritual', second day: 'dance rehearsal' without masks, third day: public mask dance, and fourth day *whong*, i.e. 'long life' blessing ceremony in the course of which the 'life force'/Tib. *tshe dbang*) is transferred to the entire community. The historical roots of this can be traced back to the time of the construction of Samye—around AD 770—the first monastery in Tibet; see Stein (1987: 128).
10. On the history of the Tibetan ritual dances (*cham*) see R. de Nebesky-Wojkowitz (1976); G. Tucci (1980: 150–1).
11. According to the distinct local traditions the number of Tantric texts varies from one to four. On the history of the tradition of the texts involved see Boord, M.J. (1993); and Mayer, R. (1996).
12. Whereas the yullha is the guardian of the territory whose abode is on the regional holy mountain, the lu is the (female) guardian of the purity of the soil and the streams, and of the houses and their hearths. On the local worship of the lu see Berg (1998).
13. Moreover, as Ramble has emphasized recently (1997: 388–9), Guru Rinpoche has been adopted as a 'symbol of unity' among the Himalayan Buddhists.
14. This is dealt with in a length by Nebesky-Wojkowitz (1993); see also Stein (1987: 129–57); Samuel (1993: 113; 158–70).
15. In her detailed inquiry into the realm of offering rituals to the host of gods, spirits, and demons in Sherpa belief, Ortner (1978: 128–56) gives a full description of the various aspects involved.
16. Among the Sherpas, just like among Tibetans, the most important of the protective deities are believed to dwell on mountain tops and in lakes. On the significance of territorial gods and their worship in the realm of Tibetan culture see most recently the articles by Buffetrille,

Diemberger, and Karmay in Blondeau and Steinkellner (eds) (1996); on the importance of territorial gods in Dolpo see Snellgrove (1992 (1967): 15); on the worship of mountain-deities and communal identity in eastern Nepal and southern Tibet see Diemberger (1994); on mountain cults and national identity in Tibet see also Karmay (1996).

17. The term *benefactor* is used in the important historical document on Sherpa clan history 'Ruyi or Report of the Bones' written by Chak Pon Sangye Paldjor, translated by M. Oppitz in his book *Geschichte und Sozial-ordnung der Sherpa.* Innsbruck: Universitätsverlag Walter: 32–49 and 73–100; see: 41. On the importance of the sbyinbdag in Dolpo see Jest (1975: 346).
18. Goldstein (1997: 3). On the 'priest–patron relationship' (Tib. *mchod-gnas* and *yon bdag*) see the comprehensive treatise by Ruegg (1995).
19. In Khumbu, instead of zhindak another term—*lawa*—is in use as well; see Fürer-Haimendorf (1964: 185–7). In another context, the Muktinath Yartung, Ramble (1987: 228) translates the term as 'steward'.
20. In both cases the names of the actors involved are recorded in a book called *tho*; Das (1989 (1902): 588): 'register, list'. And it is the 'temple-committee' (Tib. Sherpa *tshogs-pa*) that usually selects the chiwas for the next year's festival. This is done on occasion of the official chang test in the week before the onset of the Dumji.
21. Similar observations have been recorded by von Fürer-Haimendorf (1964: 187).
22. In this last book entitled *The Sherpa Transformed* (1984: 12) von Fürer-Haimendorf notes, among others, the considerable decrease in the efforts and resources spent on religious enterprises. This is wholly opposed to the 'great generosity for religious purposes' he described in his early ethnography (1964: 31).
23. Notable exceptions are to be found in Rimishung and Goli only. Adams (1992; 1996) emphasizes that Sherpa demonstrate a special capacity for deliberately recruiting westerners as patrons.
24. On the importance of patronage among the Tibetans in exile for the construction of Tibetan national identity see Kleiger (1992).

References

Adams, V., 1992, 'Tourism and Sherpas, Nepal. Reconstruction of Reciprocity', in *Annals of Tourism Research* Vol. 19: 534–54.

———, 1996, *Tigers of the Snow and Other Virtual Sherpas: An Ethnography of Himalayan Encounters,* Princeton: Princeton University Press.

Berg, E., 1998, 'The Sherpa Pilgrimage to Uomi Tsho' (forthcoming in *Himalayan Research Bulletin*).

Blondeau, A.M. and E. Steinkellner (eds.), 1996, *Reflections of the Mountain: Essays on the History and Social Meaning of the Mountain Cult in Tibet and the Himalaya,* Wien: Verlag der Österreichischen Akademie der Wissenschaften.

Boord, M. J., 1993, *The Cult of the Deity Vajrakila. According to the Texts of the Northern Treasures Tradition of Tibet (Byang-gter phur-ba).* Tring, UK: The Institute of Buddhist Studies.

Das, S.C., 1989 (1902), *A Tibetan-English Dictionary with Sanskrit Synonyms,* New Delhi: Asian Ed. Serv.

Diemberger, H., 1994, 'Mountain-Deities, Ancestral Bones and Sacred Weapons. Sacred Territory and Communal Identity in Eastern Nepal and Southern Tibet', in P. Kvaerne (ed.), *Tibetan Studies Proceedings of the 6th Seminar of the IATS Fagernes 1992,* Oslo: The Institute for Comparative Research in Human Cultures: pp. 144–53.

Fürer-Haimendorf, C. von, 1964, *The Sherpas of Nepal: Buddist Highlanders,* London: J. Murray.

________, (1984) 1989, *The Sherpa Transformed: Social Change in a Buddhist Society of Nepal,* New Delhi: Sterling Publishers.

Funke, F.W., 1969, *Religiöses Leben des Sherpa* [Reihe Khumbu Himal 9], Innsbruck/München: Universitatsverlag Wagner.

Goldstein, M.C., 1997, *The Snow Lion and the Dragon: China, Tibet, and the Dalai Lama,* Berkeley: University of California Press.

Jest, C., 1975, *Dolpo: Communautés de Langue Tibétaine du Népal,* Paris: Ed. du C.N.R.S.

Karmay, S., 1996, 'The Tibetan Cult of Mountain Deities and its Political Significance', in Blondeau/Steinkellner (eds.), pp. 59–76.

Kleiger, C., 1992, *Tibetan Nationalism: The Role of Patronage in the Accomplishment of National Identity,* Berkeley, CA: Folklore Institute.

Large-Blondeau, A.M., 1960, 'Les Pèlerinages (Sources Orientales III), Paris: Ed. du Seuil: pp. 199–245.

Mayer, R., 1996, *A Scripture of the Ancient Tantra Collection. The Phur-pa bcu-gnyis,* Oxford: Kiscadale Publ.

Nebesky-Wojkowitz, R. de., 1993 (1956), *Oracles and Demons of Tibet. The Cult and Iconography of the Tibetan Protective Deities,* Kathmandu: Tiwari's.

________, 1976, *Tibetan Religious Dances. Tibetan Text and Annotated Translation of the 'Chams yig'* C. von Fürer-Haimendorf (ed.), The Hague: Mouton.

Oppitz, M., 1968, *Geschichte und Sozialordnung der Sherpa* (Khumbu Himal, Vol. 8), Innsburck/München: Universitätsverlag Wagner.

Ortner, S.B., 1978, *Sherpas Though their Rituals,* Cambridge: Cambridge University Press.

Paul, R.A., 1979, 'Dumje: Paradox and Resolution in Sherpa Ritual Symbolism', in *American Ethnologist* Vol. 6, 2: 274–305.

Ramble, C., 1987, 'The Muktinath Yartung: A Tibetan Harvest Festival in its Social and Historical Context', in *L'Ethnographie* LXXXIII/No 100–101: 221–45.

———, 1997, 'Tibetan Pride of Place; Or, why Nepal's Bhotiyas are not an Ethnic group', in Gellner, D.N., J. Pfaff-Czarnecka, and Whelpton (eds.), *Nationalism and Ethnicity in a Hindu Kingdom: The Politics of Culture in Contemporary Nepal*. Amsterdam: Harwood Academic Publishers: pp. 379–413.

Ruegg, D.S., 1995, *Ordre Spirituel et Ordre Temporel dans la Pensèe Bouddhique de L'Inde et du Tibet: Quatre Conférences au Collège de France,* Paris: Edition-Diffusion de Brocard.

Samuel, G. 1993, *Civilized Shamans: Buddhism in Tibetan Societies*, Washington/London: Smithsonian Inst. Pr.

Snellgrove, D.L., 1992 (1967), *Four Lamas of Dolpo: Tibetan Biographies,* Kathmandu: Himalayan Book Seller.

Stein, R.A., 1987 (Org. 1962), *La Civilization Tibétaine*. Ẹdition Définitive, Paris: L'Asiathèque.

Stevens, S.F., 1993, *Claiming the High Ground: Sherpas, Subsistence, and Environmental Change in the Highest Himalayas,* Berkeley/Los Angeles/ Oxford: University of California Press.

Tucci, G., 1980 (Orig. 1970), *The Religions of Tibet,* Transl. from the German and Italian by G. Samuel, Berkeley and Los Angeles: University of California Press.

Comments

NICOLAS SIHLÉ

At the outset of her important but somewhat controversial presentation of 'Sherpas Through their Rituals', Sherry Ortner states her intention: 'to "open" Sherpa culture to the reader' notably through a number of significant rituals, which she sees as 'cultural peformances' (Singer), defined as 'rituals and other culturally formalized events, that the people themselves see as embodying in some way the essence of their culture' (Ortner 1978: 2–3).[1] In a recent article (1997), very much in the same 'interpretivist' vein as the book quoted by Berg (see p. xxx), Vincanne Adams explicitly takes some inspiration from Ortner's stance, in an attempt to analyse western presentations of Sherpas through the Sherpa concepts that apply to effigies in ransom rituals.[2]

Berg's point of departure is similarly very much in tune with Ortner's approach, in the sense that certain rituals are seen as a particularly efficacious gateway to some sort of Sherpa 'essence': the author claims that 'Sherpa identity . . . emerges primarily from the performance of several important religious festivals', and notably the Dumji'.[3] Anthropologists' delight in ritual analysis in general, and Ortner's authority in particular notwithstanding, one may note that this statement is by no means trivial, and one would have welcomed at least some supportive (theoretical, or preferably, ethnographic) elaboration about this '*primary*' character of collective ritual for the 'emergence' of Sherpa identity.[4] I shall return to the notion of identity itself below.

To come to the author's main point: the patronage of the Dumji appears to play a significant role for 'the existence and well-being of the local Sherpa community'. Through the community's common involvement, the 'social order is reaffirmed', and 'membership in the Sherpa community by means of patronage is celebrated'. Leaving aside the classic, functionalist argument of 'reaffirming the social order',[5] let us consider more particularly the latter point. As Berg states himself (fn. 26), Haimendorf's data are quite similar (compare with 1964: 186–7). Full membership in the village community implies taking one's part in the rotation of the chiwa (or *lawa* in Khumbu) function,[6] and to a certain extent is defined by this sharing in the community's investment in collective rituals. This appears quite clearly in what Fürer-Haimendorf describes as the Dumji's 'social function' of 'integration of new residents . . . . Once an immigrant has served as Dumji lawa he is truly a full member of the community' (1964: 207). We shall return to this point below.

For Berg, patronage is particularly crucial as a means of affirming one's community membership in those cases where the particularly high cost of the Dumji is shouldered by a few persons only (which means by their households), in annual rotation, instead of being borne by the entire community each year, as it also is the case for several Dumji festivals. In the former case, a chiwa is also called *jindak*, 'patron, donor'; in the latter in comparison, chiwa might be glossed as 'small jindak'. Although both economically and psychologically, the two situations are quite different, one might suppose that community membership in the latter case depends nevertheless just as much as in the former case, highlighted by the author, on the fulfilment of this important communal duty.[7]

If we take a brief look at other Tibetan societies of the Nepalese Himalaya, we get the impression that similar notions and institutions prevail quite widely. In the neighbouring Yolmo's Lama village, according to Clarke,

> [to] become a full village member involves taking a loan from the temple, part of which is paid back immediately, and on which annual interest is payable as contribution to the costs of temple-festival. Repayment of this loan is known as 'returning one's village membership' and would only be done if a person wished to leave the village permanently. (1980: 81)

Here also, collective ritual appears as a locus of community integration, by the means of its material organization.[8]

A detailed description of the economics of collective rituals is also to be found in Ramble's thesis on the Lubra community of *bönpo* householder priests (1984: chapter 10). In this case also, the rituals' material basis depends on the rotation of the duty of chiwa along with a complicated system of loans, called *jarchok*.[9] Similar systems again are to be observed in Dolpo.

As Berg mentions, the patronage of the Dumji enables a householder to 'act in a leading role' in an important community event: thus it is the same time an occasion for acquiring (at least temporarily) prestige. In this respect, Fürer-Haimendorf mentions that the competition for prestige and status between Dumji lawas has grown fiercer with the transition to a cash economy. However,

> [the] purpose of dispensing lavish hospitality is by no means sole[l]y the wish to gain prestige, but the dispensing of hospitality is believed to be also a source of religious merit. . . .For this reason the Sherpas feel obliged to accept gifts and even excessive offerings of food and drink, because by accepting them they give the donors a reason for gaining merit.

According to Fürer-Haimendorf, the importance of occasions such as the Dumji lie in 'the game of giving and accepting [as] a fundamental means of gaining religious merit as well as status' (1984: 98–9). This analysis, combined with Berg's own presentation, highlights the richness and complexity of events like the Sherpa Dumji festivals.

Maybe a brief word could be said about the concept of 'identity'. The author states that 'in the course of the Dumji membership in the Sherpa community by means of patronage is celebrated. *Hence* concerning the process of identity building in the Sherpa culture the patron assumes a key role' (emphasis added). There seems to be here some conflation between two distinct notions: on the one hand community membership (a question of legal status, of procedures for acquiring this status, and of rights and obligations that the status implies), and on the other identity (a question of boundaries between insiders and outsiders, and of how, or why, such boundaries are maintained (Barth 1969), or posited, constructed—be it by the group or by the outsiders. This is not to say that these two aspects are totally unrelated; but identity cannot be simply inferred from social institutions. As a construction, it becomes apparent mainly through discourse.[10]

Fürer-Haimendorf mentions that the Dumji has, among others, an integrative function, in the sense the recent immigrants designated as 'Khambas' (generally of Tibetan or Tibeto-Burman ethnic background) have been able to achieve social integration by taking up the role of lawa—the fact of being (for some of them) of inferior, '*khamendeu*' status, not being particularly an obstacle (1964: 36–7, 207).[11] He also mentions, in his second Sherpa monograph the interesting case of the Chetri (thus culturally, ethnically quite alien) schoolmaster of Khumjung, who had married a Sherpa and had become a permanent resident, and who was the first non-Sherpa to be allowed to assume the role of lawa for the local Dumji (1984:77–8, 98). According to Fürer-Haimendorf, this rare event was both the *sign* of a successful integration (p. 7), and the *basis* for hopes (by the schoolmaster) of [yet fuller?] integration (p. 98). Of course, it is doubtful whether he would thereafter be considered, or consider himself, a Sherpa; but we are talking here about 'communal identity'. Unfortunately, Fürer-Haimendorf's data provides insufficient evidence concerning the consequences of this (relative) integration in terms of identity: to what extent did the schoolmaster become a 'Khumjungwa' in local discourse? Conversely, one may ask: to what extent is a young Sherpa householder, who has not yet had the opportunity to fulfil his role as a Dumji patron, considered not an 'insider' of the local community?

The question of Sherpa (communal) identity cannot probably be understood without taking into consideration the traditionally rather open nature of Sherpa society towards immigration, yet with a lasting differentiation (at least at the global, ethnic level) between a core of original 'protoclans' and progressive 'layers' of peripheral 'accretions', consisting of more recent immigrants of various ethnic backgrounds, and concerning which, blanket terms such as 'Khamba' for instance apply (Fürer-Haimendorf 1964: 24–6, Oppitz 1974). One may wonder how decisive or binding the ideology of patrilineal descent really is. An analysis of how contemporary Sherpa communal identity is constructed would have to take into account, apart from the question of ritual patronage, the complex social and ethnic dynamics of integration and differentiation that take place at the communal level.[12]

Berg concludes his paper with some interesting observations and reflections on current social and religious changes in Sherpa society. Among others, he highlights the fact that although patronage by the Sherpas of their local monasteries appears to be on the decline, their involvement in sponsoring the annual Dumji festival shows no sign of decline, including among the Sherpas who have settled in Kathmandu, and who seem keen on maintaining their community membership.[13] One might want to suggest that the decisive factor in this lasting support of the Shar-Khumbu Dumji festivals could have nothing to do with religion (nor with the 'well-being' of the local community, as the author seems to imply): could it not be just a question of maintaining one's community membership?

I personally do not know the Sherpa (and I hope that I might be excused for addressing some comments, and even occasionally some criticism, to someone who knows them far better than I). I would like therefore to conclude by quoting an old tantric priest from Baragaon (lower Mustang), who had a saying—quite typical of the Tibetan sense of irony, in its fierce brevity—on the prosperous Sherpas' attitude towards religion. The saying runs:

> *Shar-gyi Khum-bu mar-gyi lung-pa yin/*
> *A-khi shi-na dkar-brgyan med//*
> *Khumbu in the east is the land of butter;*
> *if a father dies, there are no butter ornaments*[14]

Notes

1. Whether Sherpas have a notion of the essence of their culture is a debatable question, which may be left aside for the present. Actually, Berg seems to support a similar point of view: in his short description of the ritual, he writes that the Dumji is a 'ritual celebration that the people themselves see as embodying the core of their culture'.
2. This rather far-fetched argument may also be left aside for our present purposes. As for Adams' 1996 book, one cannot but subscribe to Berg's criticism of some of her radical formation concerning the notion of 'virtual' Sherpahood.
3. In order to differentiate the retroflex from the dental (voiced) occlusives, I write 'Dumji' (an alternative would be 'Drumji', according to the common transcription 'dr' of the retroflex), even if, since Fürer-Haimendorf, authors have generally kept the approximative renderings 'Dumji' or 'Dumje'. The Tibetan spelling is actually *sgrub-mchod* (*cf.* Tucci 1980: 132), its literal meaning being an offering ritual (*mchod-pa*) in which deities are produced, actualized (*sgrub-pa*). It is a common designation for particularly elaborate liturgical rituals of Tibetan

Buddhism.One should note in particular that whatever the festival's import for the local (lay) community, whatever the type of the officiating priests (be they monks as in the Mani Rimḍu or, here, tantric householder priests), a Dumji should not be confused with what Stein terms '*la religion sans nom*', or Tucci 'folk religion' (see fn. 3, in Berg's essay; the same confusion is made by Ortner 1992: 3). Tucci's inclusion of Buddhist textual rituals under the 'folk religion' heading, and his definition of the latter phrase, are not uncontroversial: one can refer to Blondeau's criticism (1985–86: 150, quoted by Macdonald 1987: 10–11).

4. The same comment could be ventured concerning a somewhat more general phrasing by the author, who claims (without particular substantiation): 'Religion seems to be the most important idiom in which Sherpas present themselves in their dealings both with Sherpas and with others including westerners'. One may actually refer to a similar statement, concerning the place of Buddhism in Tibet's 'national identity', by Ramble (1997: 380), a claim for which he provides some historical substantiation; however, it is unclear whether the question of Sherpa communal identity shows any significant similarity with the notions or process involved in that of Tibetan national identity.
5. I agree with Ortner that such assertions are not 'wrong' and certainly ritual plays an important role in keeping the system together . . . [but this perspective] is so broadly applicable that it tells one virtually nothing'. (1978: 4)
6. The similarities between the Shar-Khumbu and Baragaon situations suggest that Ramble's rendering of chiwa by 'steward' is most probably a better translation for the term than the one quoted from Das' dictionary ('head, chief, leader'). The same term (corresponding to the same function) is to be found in Yolmo also, for instance, although Clarke mistakingly took it for a contraction of *jindak* (Tib. *sbyin-bdag*), 'patron, donor' (Clarke 1980: 81).
7. It would be interesting to know what led to the establishment of these two different systems (economical determinations?), and how members of each of the two types of communities view the other system. Can the difference between the two be analysed, among others, in terms of more prestige-oriented *vs.* more egalitarian local communities?
8. G. Childs, at the 1998 seminar of the IATS in Bloomington, has described a very similar situation in Nubri, where annual readings of the Kangyur (bKa-gyur) section of the Tibetan Buddhist canon are financed by interests paid by households, which stem from a compulsory loan taken at the moment of the founding of the new house (forthcoming).
9. Maybe spelt *sbyar-tshogs*, 'combined accumulation', according to a suggestion by Gene Smith.

10. One interesting element in this respect that Berg mentions is the idea that the Dumji is seen by the Sherpas as 'mirroring' their specific history, and involving the worship of their local mythical hero(es). It is unfortunate that this theme, and its relations to conceptions of identity, could not be developed slightly more in the present paper.
11. Funke (1969) points to the fact that this, interestingly enough, is only the case in Khumbu: in Shorung on the contrary, only members of the original Sherpa clans are entitled to act as chiwas.
12. It would also have to clarify the nature of what E. Berg terms the 'local community'. One recalls that the patronage of the Dumji rituals rotates among households of a single village, but at least in two cases also among those of village groupings, such as those of the 'twin villages' of Khumjung and Kunde, or Pangboche and Phortse, which in this case are 'situated at considerable distance' (Fürer-Haimendorf 1964: 186, 206). Fürer-Haimendorf actually uses a specific term, that of 'parish', to designate the 'community' involved in the patronage of a Dumji festival (1964: 207). In Shorung (Solu), according to Funke (1969), the patronage of a Dumji is shared among all the households.
13. Fisher also gives a few interesting elements on the patronage of a Dumji by Sherpas residing in Kathmandu (1990: 138–9), on changes in the perception of the ritual's economics (*ibid*.: 169–70), and on perceptions of local religious change in general (*ibid*.: 139, 149–51, 158–9; see also p. 170, 183).
14. These ornaments are sculpted on the ritual cakes, tormas. The saying suggests the Sherpas could be stingy on the crucial occasion of their own father's death.

References

Adams, Vincanne, 1997, 'Dreams of a Final Sherpa', in *American Anthropologist,* vol. 99, n. 1, pp. 86–98.

Barth, Fredrik, 1969, 'Introduction', in F. Barth (ed.), *Ethnic groups and Boundaries, The Social Organization of Cultural Differences,* Boston: Little Brown, pp. 9–38.

Blondeau, Anne-Marie, 1985–86, 'Religions Tibétaines', in *Annuaire (Résumé des conférences et travaux)*, Paris, EPHE, V section, Sciences Religieuses, vol. XCIV.

Childs, Geoffrey, forthcoming, [Communication presented at the International Seminar of the IATS, Bloomington, 1998, to be published in the Proceedings].

Clarke, Graham E., 1980, 'Lama and Tamang in Yolmo', in M.V. Aris, Aung San Suu Kyi (eds.), *Tibetan Studies in Honour of Hugh Richardson,* Delhi: Vikas Publishing House, pp. 79–86.

Fisher, James F., 1990, *Sherpas: Reflections on Change in Himalayan Nepal*, Delhi: Oxford University Press.

Funke, Friedrich W., 1969, *Religiöses Leben der Sherpa*, Universitätsverlag: Wagner.

Fürer-Haimendorf, Christoph von, 1964, *The Sherpas of Nepal: Buddhist Highlanders*, London: John Murray.

——, 1984, *The Sherpas Transformed: Social Change in a Buddhist Society of Nepal*, New Delhi: Sterling.

Macdonald, Alexander W., 1987, 'Avant-propos', in *L'Ethnogrpahie*, tome LXXXIII, nos. 100–101 (special issue 'Les rituels himalayens'), A. W. Macdonald (ed.), p. 5–13.

Oppitz, Michael, 1974, 'Myths and Facts: Reconsidering some Data Concerning the Clan History of the Sherpa', in *Kailash, a Journal of Himalayan Studies*, Vol. 2, nos. 1–2, pp. 121–31

Ortner, Sherry B., 1978, *Sherpas Through their Ritual*, Cambridge, London, New York, Melbourne: Cambridge University Press.

——, 1992, *High Religion: A Cultural and Political History of Sherpa Buddhism* (reprint of the 1st edition: Princeton University Press, 1989).

Ramble, Charles, 1984, '*The Lamas of Lubra: Tibetan Bonpo Housholder Priests in Western Nepal*', Ph.D. dissertation, University of Oxford, Hertford College.

Tucci, Giuseppe, 1980, *The Religions of Tibet*, New Delhi: Allied Publications (translated from German and Italian by G. Samuel).

The Janajati and the Nepali State

Aspects of Identity and Integration

KARL-HEINZ KRÄMER

From its inception the unified modern state of Nepal has been the playground of high caste Hindu elite groups. Simultaneously the numerous ethnic groups and the lower Hindu castes were marginalized and prevented from active political participation. This status was codified by the *muluki ain* of 1854 and it was further intensified in recent times by the unitarian politics of King Mahendra's panchayat system.

It was only in the late seventies and early eighties that the growing self-consciousness of the ethnic elite led to the formation of ethnic organizations. The turning points were the students riots of 1979 and the national referendum of 1980 which led to constitutional changes undermining the conservative basis of the royal system. It became evident that political and social changes were possible through mass mobilization. Because of Nepal's ethnic diversity these ethnic organizations represented very small sections of society, even though their agendas were very similar in nature. So these organizations started informal talks which, in 1986, led to the formation of the Sarvajati Adhikar Manc (Forum for the Rights of All Nationalities).

A further step was the active participation of ethnic organizations in the people's movement of 1990, now under the name of Vividh Dharma, Bhasha, Jati tatha Janajati Sandharsha Samiti (Various Religions, Languages and Nationalities Action Committee). The ethnic elite not only wanted a change in the political system but also socio-political modifications and economic participation.

Beyond doubt, the political changes of 1990 have opened up broader scopes for Nepal's numerous ethnic groups. Many of them have formed organizations to preserve their cultural identity and to fight for equal rights and participation in the Nepali state. Starting with criteria like race, language, religion, and territory they have detected the importance of history of their respective groups, not all of which have been historically-formed entities, and, thus prove that they are part of the modern Nepali nation.

On the other hand, we have a Nepali state which until 1990 totally disregarded the multiethnicity of its society. It was during the elaboration phase of the new constitution that ethnic demands were presented in public. But there was no participation of ethnic groups in the decision-making bodies, neither in the political parties nor in the constitution drafting commission. So, the result was half-hearted. The Nepali state recognized the multiethnicity of society but it refused to introduce institutions and regulations for a broader participation of the disadvantaged sections of society.

Ethnic Arguments

The ethnic elite is trying to reconcile its groups with their cultural values but, at the same time, to look for new ways of interpreting tradition. Their first criterion is that of race. Most of Nepal's ethnic groups belong to the Tibeto-Mongolian stock. There are only a few Tarai groups having relations with Indian Mundas or Southeast Asian groups. By laying stress on their common Tibeto-Mongolian race the ethnic elite—who usually speak of Mongols or Mongoloids—not only point out their differences from the high Hindu castes dominating in politics, society and economy, but at the same time they also provide a common racial bond for Nepal's divergent ethnic groups.[1]

The second criterion is that of religion. It is claimed that all ethnic groups of the country are Buddhists or, at least, are influenced by Buddhist thought. This again brings them in contrast to the relative minority of high Hindu castes[2] who have declared Nepal to be a Hindu state. Different from race,[3] religion is one of the fundamental pillars of ethnic culture. Thus it would be an ideal starting point for ethnic reconciliation and for separation from the country's ruling elite. But the problem again is that it is not clear, as well. The mixture of religious thoughts and practices across ethnic boundaries has been even stronger than that of racial phenomena. The religious base of most ethnic cultures is not Buddhism but some kind of animism or shamanism which, within many ethnic cultures of the *pahad* region, has been overlapped by Buddhist influences with different intensity. Other ethnic groups, because of their long running contacts to neighbouring Hindu castes, have adopted a number of Hindu values and practices.

This historical overlapping and reciprocal influencing of religions has been intensified in modern times by the Nepali state through some form of guided Hinduization of society. This process already started in some of the principalities of western Nepal in pre-unification times, and it got its legal basis by the promulgation of the *muluki ain* in 1854. The ethnic elites regard this legalization of the Hindu social order as the principal cause for all inequalities in politics, economy, and society. To be non-Hindu becomes important in ethnic politics. Not animist practices but Buddhism can provide an important counterbalance when entering into discussions with the state Hinduism of the ruling elite.

Another pillar of the ethnic elite is language. All Tibeto-Mongolian groups speak Tibeto-Burman languages. This distinguishes them from the Indo-Aryan Hindu population speaking Nepali, an Indo-European language, as mother tongue. The language has been used by the Nepali state as one of the most important tools to enforce its Hindu politics. The government's statistics showed a steady decline of the number of people speaking ethnic languages while at the same time, the share of Nepali as mother tongue went up to more than 58 per cent in the census of 1981.[4] The current endeavour of the ethnic elite to revive its mother tongues and, if necessary, equip them with script and literature is based on the constitution's definition of the state as a multiethnic and multilingual one. This is often an arduous task in face of the lingual heterogeneity of many ethnic groups.

The ethnic elite demands an equal treatment of all languages in education, administration, judiciary and the media, since Nepali is a foreign or only secondary language for almost 50 per cent of the population. They do not object to the use of Nepali as *lingua franca* but to the special promotion of Nepali and Sanskrit to the detriment of ethnic languages. Language may be a cultural element but, using it as a fundamental argument in their dialogue with the state, the ethnic organizations make it a political one. This politization of the ethnic organizations is also forced by the Nepali state which has made language a political issue since the time of military unification and especially since the 1950s.

Ethnic organizations, having realized this, soon enter the next stage of the argument which definitely is a political one. If they talk about history, it is first of all not the history of their own group but the history of the Nepali state that they criticize and want to have rewritten. According to their argument the integration of the different peoples of the country is only possible if all ethnic groups are treated equally. There can be no talk of equality of all Nepali citizens as long as the official version of Nepali history, as it can be read in a steadily growing number of history books, is only a history of the ruling elite, in which the ethnic groups are non-existent. The written history of the country is a mirror of its social order.

The ethnic organizations believe that the history of the country, must bear witness to the great injustice inflicted upon the numerous peoples by the ruling elite in the past. Especially mentioned in this context are:

- deprivation of ethnic territories by the Nepali state,
- allocation of ethnic territories in favour of members of Hindu high castes,
- enslavement, subjugation, and indebtedness of once autonomous and self-sufficient ethnic peasants,
- systematic decomposition and dissolution of ethnic areas by settlement of members of Hindu high castes,
- deliberate cutting of ethnic areas by arbitrary drawing up of administrative borders,
- social and judicial incapacitation of ethnic groups by the discriminating law code of the *muluki ain*,

- introduction of caste values and prejudices into ethnic communities, which—with the sole exception of the Newars—had casteless societies before,
- withholding of every kind of education,
- exclusion from all government offices,
- non-participation in the politics and administration of the country,
- destruction of ethnic culture by perpetual state politics of Hinduization.

According to representatives of the ethnic organizations, the above have to be emphasized specifically without extenuation or reservation. Consequently, history becomes the strongest and most important basis for the formation of consciousness and identity among Nepal's ethnic groups. Their leaders argue that their situation can only be changed by a fundamental revision of Nepali history.[5]

But in order to rewrite the national history of Nepal, ethnic historiography is a precondition, for ethnic leaders to enter into discussions with the Nepali state about the abolition of inequalities. By setting the classical ethnic arguments—like race, language, and religion—into the historical framework they lose their exclusively cultural aspects and become political. It is in this historical context that ethnic groups change from cultural entities to nationalities, *janajati*, as they are called by the current ethnic leaders.[6]

Constitutional Regulations

The introduction of the new constitution in 1990 offered a chance to reconsider the state's politics of nationalism. How did the ruling elite use this opportunity? Article 2 of the constitution declares that all 'Nepali people, irrespective of religion, race, caste or tribe collectively constitute the nation *rastra*.' This sounds positive since no section of the population is excluded. But this positive aspect is revoked by article 4(1) which, on the one hand, concedes that Nepal is a multiethnic and multilingual state but, at the same time, defines the country as a Hindu kingdom (*Hindu adhirajya*). This definition as Hindu state is underlined by a number of symbols mentioned in the constitution like the flag and the coat of arms representing different aspects of Hindu myths and society.

Another important aspect of the constitution is the definition of Nepali as the language of the nation (*rastriya bhasa*) (article 6). Of course, the country is in need of a common language, and there is no other language as widespread as Nepali, but it is the mother tongue of only 53 per cent of the population according to the census of 1991. For the rest of the population, Nepali is some kind of a foreign language. Having only rudimentary knowledge of colloquial Nepali the others feel deprived of their fundamental rights guaranteed elsewhere by the constitution, especially in face of the ever growing Sanskritization of the high standard language to the detriment of indigenous terms.[7]

Thus the ethnic elites regard the national language, Nepali, as another symbol of Hindu high caste domination. Against the background of Nepal being a multilingual and multiethnic country, social tensions are on the cards as the political and social consciousness of ethnic groups is growing. The constitution has named the other languages as national languages (*rastriya bhasa*) without providing further specifications. That they are not meant for official use has quite recently been declared by the supreme court, when the District Development Committees (DDC) of Kathmandu, Dhanusha and Rajbiraj were prohibited from using Newari and Maithili respectively during their meetings.[8] Even Village Development Committees (VDC) comprising members of one single ethnic group only are not allowed to use their mother tongue.[9] Among the few positive reactions of the state is Radio Nepal transmitting short news programmes in ethnic languages, spoken by more than 1 per cent of the population, and that the Royal Nepal Academy has started to publish books in ethnic languages.

During the drafting phase of he constitution in 1990 the transformation of Nepal into a secular state had been demanded by ethnic and women organizations as well as by representatives of Buddhists, Muslims, Christians, and the so-called untouchable Hindu castes. But there had been a vehement opposition against this idea from Hindu traditional organizations[10], which had strong propagators within the then interim government, the greater political parties and sections of the press.

The chairman of the Constitution Drafting Commission and later Chief Justice, Vishwanath Upadhyaya, called all demands concerning religion, language, caste and ethnicity, which consisted of about 90 per cent of the public recommendations, as being of minor importance for a democratic Nepal, comparing them to communalism:

> Statements which foster communalism and sow the seeds of religious intolerance cannot be justified. Such improper tendencies, if not checked in time, will create obstacle in our efforts to establish a democratic constitutional system.[11]

That only a non-Hindu alignment is regarded as communal can be see from Article 112 (3) which denies the recognition of any political party or organization formed on the basis of religion, community, castes, tribe, or region. Must not the state itself be called communal because of its Hindu affiliation? This is further verified by the fact that after 1990, regional parties were recognized as long as they did not oppose the Hindu state, e.g. they Nepal Sadbhavana Party, but they were rejected whenever they opposed the Hindu state and supported the cause of ethnic groups like the Mongol National Organization.

Attitudes of Government and Political Parties

The Nepali political parties have always been dominated by members of the upper Hindu castes, especially by Bahuns. This fact, too, has its mooring in the historical development of unified Nepal, which now is so strongly criticized by the ethnic elite. Prithvinarayan Shah and his successors established their power on the support of a number of Bahun and Chetri families who, in return, got their share of political and economic returns. Later, when a new aristocracy arose with the ascent of the Ranas, those better-off families settled in the Tarai or in India, from where they could send their children to Indian schools. The children not only became educated but by actively participating in the Indian independence movement, they also got a political consciousness. It was this younger generation of expatriate Nepalis that in the late forties founded parties like the Nepali Congress and the Nepal Communist Party in India.

Since then not much has changed in the rank and file of the parties. The 1950s, sometimes called a phase of democratic experiments, has been more a time of restoration of royal power, especially under

King Mahendra, doing little to involve larger sections of society in the political process. Following a period of 30 years in the underground, the political parties of the 1990s are only just starting to become mass organizations. They are still dominated by a handful of now elder politicians of the early years. But the problem is that the inevitable regeneration of the parties is not taken as a chance of involve different sections of society within the party rank and file. In 1991, 37 per cent of the Nepali Congress candidates and 48 per cent of those of the CPM-UML were Bahuns and another 22 per cent among the former and 16 per cent of the latter were Chetris, even though these groups have only a share of 13 per cent respectively 16 per cent in the population of the country according to the census of 1991. Or to mention another figure, among the ministers of the two Girija Prasad Koirala cabinet, 50 per cent were Bahuns.

Another constitutional institution criticized by the ethnic organizations is the national assembly (*rastriya sabha*). In its current form, it is some kind of replication of the house of representatives (*pratinidhi sabha*), the latter nominating 35 of the 60 members of the national assembly according to the party strength in the lower house.[12] The ethnic elite, instead, want the national assembly to be a house of parliament where all population groups of Nepal are represented. In 1991, when the *rastriya sabha* was constituted for the first time, 40 per cent of its members were Bahuns, which is similar to the figures of the *pratinidhi sabha*.

This ethnic number game could be continued endlessly.[13] It proves that people of ethnic groups do not have equal chances of participation even in democratic Nepal. This was confirmed to the Rai and Limbu MPs of eastern Nepal, who said that they only have a chance at the local level but cannot figure in the central hierarchy of their parties. Most of the persons involved in ethnic activities are closer to left parties than to the Nepali Congress. The reason may be that the latter party is identifying more and more with the traditional forces of the country. The ethnic organizations want fundamental changes in state and society, and these do not seem to be possible with the Nepali Congress. In a society characterized by poverty and socio-religious inequalities the populace is looking for a kind of political representation that offers a vision of transformation.

The continuation of the Hindu state has been the most important maxim of both the conservative forces and the leading party politicians of democratic Nepal, because this alone guarantees their elite privileges. Secularism has always been identified with the lifting of the ban on missionary practices. There is talk of the decline of Hinduism, its eradication by Christian missionaries and, finally, the expulsion of Hindus from Nepal. On the basis of these practices by some of the numerous Christian aid organizations working in the country, fears are expressed of thousands of conversions to Christianity everyday.

But the discussion of the dangerous Christian missionary distracts from the negative attitude of the Hindu state towards the many indigenous cultures. In support of the Hindu state-religion the king and the politicians are courting Hindu dignitaries and sponsoring Hindu organizations and events.[14] One never hears a word about the danger of Christian missionary to the ethnic cultures, the Buddhist and the Muslims, not to talk about the danger of state Hinduism to these religions and cultures.

Conclusion

Nepal's ethnic groups still lack integration and participation in the modern democratic state. But their situation has, nevertheless improved when compared to the time of the *panchayat* system. The guarantee of fundamental rights is much stronger today. The rights of freedom of opinion and expression and the freedom to form organizations (article 12) have helped the ethnic elite to make their arguments heard among their own groups and in the general public.

The greatest problem is still the attitude of the Nepali state. There is hardly any organization outside the ethnic camp that can empathize with the ethnic point of view. An outstanding example are the human rights organizations which have come into existence in greater number. They may be talking about indigenous groups, but like the political parties they, too, are dominated by members of high Hindu castes, especially Bahuns. These people cannot understand the arguments of the ethnic leaders, since they have never learnt to view the Nepali state and society from the ethnic perspective because of the one-sidedness of the national education system.

Nepal must make the diversity of her ethnic groups, religions and cultures an essential feature of her nationalism. The unity of the nation can only be preserved, if the uniforming politics of the Hindu state is brought to an end, and if the constitutional declaration in the multiethnicity of the country is implemented by politics of integration and equal treatment of all groups of the Nepali society.

Notes

1. The elite do not mention that many of the current ethnic groups included under the same name are themselves the result of ethnic interbreeding, like the Newars.
2. The 1991 census for the first time gives statistical data concerning the country's ethnic composition. According to this census about 30 per cent of the population belongs to the high Hindu castes of Bahun and Chetri while 41 per cent are members of ethnic groups. (His Majesty's Government, Central Bureau of Statistics (ed.) 1993, *The Analysis of the 1991 Population Census (Based on Advance Tables)*, Kathmandu: Central Bureau of Statistics).
3. As mentioned above, racial boundaries are fluid; and this is true for ethnic groups as well as Hindu castes.
4. The decline of Nepali in the census of 1991 by 5.2 per cent may prove the falsification of data during panchayat times. This is confirmed by Rishikesh Shah who wrote:

    > A word of caution must, however be sounded with regard to population statistics of various ethnic groups. Their population figures are based on language identification rather than on the actual counting of heads belonging to different ethnic entities. In the collection of census data, the people are asked what their mother tongue is, and not to which of the ethnic groups they belong. This procedure might have caused some discrepancies, but more in the figures for ethnic groups in the hills than in the Tarai, because people of the hills who generally speak Nepali might have mentioned it as their mother-tongue no matter what ethnic group they belong to.

    (Shah, Rishikesh, 1990, *Politics in Nepal 1980–1990: Referendum, Stalemate and Triumph of People Power,* Kathmandu: Ratna Pustak Bhandar, pp. 109f.)
5. For further discussion of the ethnic demand for rewriting history, see the author's article: 'Requiring a Social History: Must Nepali History be

Re-written?', Paper written in honour of Wolf Donner on the occasion of his 75th birthday, Kathmandu: Pilgrims (in press).

6. For a broader discussion of this complex see the chapter on the meaning of history for the demands of the ethnic groups in Krämer, Karl-Heinz, 1996, *Ethnizität und nationale Integration in Nepal: Ethnic Untersuchung zur Politisierung der ethnischen Gruppen im modernen Nepal,* Stuttgart: Franz Steiner: 217–46.
7. K.P. Malla wrote in this context:

   > So the paradox of Nepali linguistic nationalism is that the broader the scope of Nepali, the less it sounds like a language of Nepal. Nationalism in Nepal, in so far as it is manifestly anti-Indian in orientation, is a self-defeating aspiration, particularly when one of its major foundations is Nepali, which is bound to be increasingly Sanskritized.

   (Malla, Kamal Prakash, 1979, *The Road to Nowhere: A Section of Writings 1966–1977,* Kathmandu: Sajha Prakashan, p. 144)
8. *The Kathmandu Post*, 19 March 1998. The petitioners had been members of high Hindu castes.
9. See § 11 of the Village Development Committee (working procedures) rules (*Nepal Recorder* 18, 14:112, 21 July 1994).
10. Among these organizations were the Sanatan Dharma Seva Samiti, the national committee of the Vishwa Hindu Parishad, the Advait Sanstha and the Nepal Arya Samaj.
11. *The Rising Nepal,* 6 June 1990.
12. Of the remaining 25 members, 10 are nominated by the king, the others are elected by representatives at the local level of the five development regions of the country.
13. For further statistical data see Poudyal, Ananta Raj, 1992, Nepal: Ethnicity in Democracy, in Lok Raj Baral (ed.), *South Asia: Democracy and the Road Ahead*, Kathmandu: Polsan 134–48.
14. The growing verbal militancy of the Shiv Nepal, which has close connections to its Hindu nationalist counterpart, is another alarming signal in this context.

Comments

Anne De Sales

I cannot but agree with most of Krämer's presentation of the janajati's case. It is a fact that the minorities (or ethnic groups) have little or no access to decision-making power, and that they are not represented in proportion with their population in the institutions where national politics is conducted. Krämer accruately describes a situation of flagrant inequality that has not improved since 1990, inspite of several declarations from the new government (or rather the various new governmental teams) concerning the multi-ethnic nation of Nepal.

The questions that I would like to raise here concerns our position as anthropologists in such a situation. What sort of questions should we try to address, and what sort of problematic can we develop? What is our role? We may consider Krämer's paper as a practical answer to such kind of theoretical questions. However, I think it is worth trying to make the debate more explicit.

Two possible reasons why Krämer reproduces the janajati leaders' discourse here are either to inform foreign academics who have failed to do their homework, or for their adhesion to this discourse. Leaving aside the first question, they are left with the matter of the anthropologists' adhesion to the cause of the people they write about. Krämer seems to advocate an engaged practice of anthropology.

Let us follow this line further. Ethnographers in the janajati yug, to take up the title of an important and controversial article by Marie Des Chene (1996), have to renew their old questions and goals. The author criticizes foreign anthropologists for being motivated by theoretical debates occurring in academic scenes far away (both in terms of geography and of concerns or interests) from the people whom they study. This is mostly true. The important point of the argument, as I read it, is that ethnical concern and methodological approach go together, like two sides of the same coin: unless the ethnographers are engaged in improving the condition of the people whom they study they will not understand them as they ought to be understood, because they will not be 'serious' (sic) enough, not committed enough and therefore unable to respect, or listen to the people's true motivations and interests. Beneath this argument lies the ultimate question of the legitimation of observation from outside—a question that has been hounding anthropology for some time now, and that you may want to answer here.

Besides this fundamental question that Krämer implicitly raises, I have a more specific question concerning the presentation of the janajati leaders' discourse. Taking this discourse seriously means, I think, reading it critically. And then it seems to me that much of what forms the basis of the janajati leaders' discourse has to be deconstructed.

Starting with the ethnic categories themselves: how do these categories come into existence? In an interesting and complex article Graham Clarke (1996) highlights the two concepts of blood (filiation, kinship) and territory as two paradigms for defining identity. He analyses the oscillation between these two poles where the identity of groups is formed. For example, people of the same kin gradually identify themselves with the territory which they share with people who are originally of another blood. They may then come to consider the people of the same territory as being of the same blood. This process in particular (there are other process involved in the formation of group identity) sheds an embarrassing light on the so called 'purity' of, say, the Gurung or the Magar 'race' (I read note 1 of Krämer's paper in this manner), a recurrent concept in janajati literature.

This is ironic, since it is a concept closely associated with the Hindu system, which the janajati vehemently reject. More generally, the janajati militants do not seem to reflect on the fact that they are using the concepts and symbols of their oppressors, the *sasak barga*, as the symbols of their claims. Literacy is another example. I refer to certain Magar historians who claim the discovery of an old Magar script that would have been supplanted by colonizing Devanagari. The research is far from convincing, but any attempt at questioning its validity is likely to be misunderstood as a prejudice against the Magars' capacity to have their own script.

These are signs of alienation. And this is a painful observation. In this respect the janajati are right: they are colonized. They are trapped in a distorted image of themselves that mirrors the Hindu high castes from whom they wish to distance themselves. This question would bring us closer to the title of this book, reflecting on the image of the self and of the other.

I would suggest that alienation may be more a feature of the janajati leaders' discourse than of ordinary villagers' representation of the situations. There are different levels of discourse in the janajati populations (as it appears in the book on identity edited by Gellner, Pfaff-Czarnecka and Whelpton). Militants are mostly urban and confronted by a complex sociological context. I am not sure that villagers, ordinary people, would subscribe to the same discourse.

As a matter of fact, my own experience in the western hills, in certain Magar villages, led me to think that people (in this particular case) did not bother much about defending their language, which they all spoke anyway, or about having a script. They did not worry about being 'pure' Magars either. They worried more about having good schools for their children, health posts, and some opportunities for making cash. In other words, they were little preoccupied with a definition of themselves, and much more with finding a way, their own way, to integrate themselves into a modern nation.

The need for self-definition comes downstream from the process of integration, after recurring failures, and suffering in achieving it. Then bitterness, anger or despair draw lines that were at first irrelevant.

Although I am well aware of the tremendous difficulties and injustices that janajatis have to deal with—injustices that justify political organizations and discourse set against them— it should be recalled that the representations that people have of themselves and of others are much more complex and subtle than may appear in the militant discourse that has been presented. Anthropologists have no lesson to offer; they just have to work towards understanding this complexity.

References

Clarke, G.E., 1996, 'Blood, Territory, and the History of National Identity in Himalayan States', in S. Torenson and H. Antlov (eds), *Asian Forms of Nation*, Copenhagen: NIAS/Curzon Press.

Des Chene, Marie, 1996, Ethnographers in the Janajati yug, *Studies in Nepal History and Society*, Vol. I, no. 1.

Insiders and Outsiders

Community and Identity in Kumaon, North India

JOANNE MOLLER

In the summer of 1994 the chief minister of the state of Uttar Pradesh (UP), Mulayam Singh Yadav, declared the governing coalition's plan to reserve 27 per cent of all government jobs and educational places in the state for the low castes, known in official parlance as the Other Backward Classes (OBCs), who form 37 per cent of the state's population. This, on top of the existing 22.5 per cent reservation for Scheduled Castes and Scheduled Tribes, who bring the total reservation provisions to 49.5% per cent. The political pragmatics of such an order by the governing coalition, made up of the Samajwadi and the Bahujan Samaj parties who represent the low castes and Dalits (Untouchables), were not hard to detect. This declaration, however, unleashed anti-reservation agitation in the hill area of Uttar Pradesh known as Uttarakhand, where OBCs constitute less than 2 per cent and high castes almost 80 per cent of the population, and led to bloody clashes between protesters and state authorities. The violent clashes with the state authorities peaked on 2 October 1994 when buses transporting between 5,000 to 8,000 Kumaonis and Garhwalis to an anti-reservation and pro-autonomy rally in New Delhi, were stopped by police near Muzaffarnagar, where they were tear-gased, *lathi*-charged and fired upon. Eight hill people were killed, seven women were raped, and several hundred other people were injured and illegally arrested.[1]

The reservation issue added fuel to the long-standing demand by hill people for secession from Lucknow and the UP state. The declaration of the state's reservation policy was perceived as yet another blow to their economic rights which threatened to exacerbate their existing economic backwardness. The anti-reservation activities and the call for separate statehood for Uttarakhand are both expressions and by-products of the hill people's long-standing resentment over successive governments' perfunctory treatment of the hill states and at the region's continued economic and political marginalization.

However, past anti-reservation protests and the present call for regional autonomy are not only about economics and politics, marginalization and disempowerment. They are also about the assertion and preservation of the hill people's sense of a separate identity. As such, these events can only be fully understood in terms of the hill peoples' constructions of self and other and their discourse of identity. The hill region's economic, political, and social history, as well as its current marginal and backward status, contribute to hill people's sense of self. However, just as important are the villagers' conceptual assumptions about 'insiders' and 'outsiders', hill and plains people, high and low castes. In addition to the economic and political threats it posed, the introduction of reservation in educational institutions and government jobs was seen not only as a ploy by the Chief Minister to flood the hills with his own followers from the plains, but as a threat of increased interference and domination by 'outsiders', in the form of both, plains people and the low castes. The anti-reservation activities and call for statehood are also about 'insiders' and 'outsiders' and the perceived dangers that 'outsiders' are thought to pose.

This essay focuses on the discourse of collective identity of high caste villagers of Kumaon. I argue that these villagers conceptually organize their social world on segmentary principles, which is articulated by the dominant opposition between 'insiders' and 'outsiders'. The conceptual opposition of 'inside' and 'outside' is replicated at various levels of society, and the social categories referred to as 'insiders' and 'outsiders' vary depending on the context and level of identification. The various levels of identity distinctions are tied together by the rhetoric of 'hunger'—in which 'outsiders' are seen to 'eat' at the expense of 'insiders'—and the ideology of autonomy—which emphasizes the separation and containment of social categories. The essay focuses on the elaboration of this discourse of identity at the levels of collective regional and caste identities, indicating what markers high caste Kumaoni villagers (as 'insiders') use to distinguish themselves from plains society and low caste people (as 'outsiders').

Recent political events in the region provide an effective context in which to examine the social ideology of collective identities in Kumaon. And, indeed, regional and caste identity distinctions are central to understanding the significance of these events to high caste Kumaoni villagers. I argue that, in addition to the pressing economic and political issues underlying their demonstrations and claims, is the desire to end centuries of domination by what hill people call 'outsiders'. The conceptual difference between high and low castes, and hill and plains people, I contend, mirrors the distinction hill people make between 'insiders' and 'outsiders', and that relations between these social sets are represented in terms of relations between 'insiders' and 'outsiders'. Thus, ideas about 'insiders' and 'outsiders', and the ideology of autonomy and the rhetoric of hunger which accompany them, are an important dimension to recent events in the region.

With regard to regional issues in particular, these concepts are especially important. They reveal how, from villagers' perspectives, local-level rural concerns and economic and political life are related to the wider state- and national-level structures ad contexts. I argue that members of this peripheral, marginalized area, conceptualize their relationship to the encompassing structures of the state and nation in terms of this segmentary model, and the underlying dichotomy between 'insiders' and 'outsiders' and rhetoric of hunger mediate Kumaon(i)'s relationships and integration into these larger entities.

The remainder of the essay briefly demonstrates how these conceptualizations, representations and attitudes are not confined to the macro levels of collective regional and caste identities, but are evident at other levels of high caste identity discrimination. Assumptions about 'insiders' and 'outsiders', the ideology of separation and the rhetoric of hunger are also pertinent to definitions of household and kinship communities and identities.

The regional focus of this study is the Himalayan region of Uttar Pradesh, known as Uttarakhand, the hill region bordering Nepal and Tibet. It is made up of two divisions, the old kingdoms of Garhwal and Kumaon, which together are composed of eight hill districts. The views presented here belong primarily to high caste residents of Silora village, Almora district, though similar views are held by high caste Kumaonis I spoke to on visits to Ranikhet, Almora and Nainital towns. Thus, henceforth, when I refer to hill people I am referring to Silora villagers in particular but also to high caste Kumaonis in general. Though much of what I say may be resonant to Garhwal, and some of the literature suggests this might be the case, I shall restrict my argument as applicable first and foremost to the Kumaon region.[2]

Kumaon Past and Present: political-economic history as the backdrop to recent campaigns

The anti-reservation pro-autonomy campaigns in Uttarakhand are inextricably linked to and based on very real political and economic grievances. In order to understand the impetus behind these protests we must look at these events and the issues they raise in the context of Kumaon's political and economic history, its history of incorporation into wider political entities, the nature of State–region relations over the past 200 years, and in light of the region's current backward and marginal status. The Kumaoni's present dissatisfactions, and their expression in recent events, are rooted in the region's unique history.

The call for separate statehood for Uttarakhand must be seen in light of the historically independent identity of the region. From the earliest times until the late eighteenth century Kumaon managed to maintain its economic, political and cultural identity. Thus, the ideal of regional autonomy and independence, which is part of the contemporary demands of the Uttarakhand movement, is not a new concept to hill people but is firmly established in Kumaon's early history.[3]

A main feature of Kumaon's history is that for several centuries from the Middle Ages until 1790, the region formed a central, autonomous and relatively isolated kingdom. As far as we know, the first rulers of Kumaon were the Katyuris, possibly a small Khasi tribe from Garhwal who moved to Almora district, Kumaon in the seventh century AD, although exactly when their reign began is not known. By the tenth century the centralized political authority of the Katyuri dynasty was in decline and Kumaon was ultimately broken up into several small kingdoms ruled by different tribes. During the Katyuri's decline, the Chands, a Rajput family from the North Indian plains entered Kumaon and set up a dynasty in Champawat around AD 953 and the seeds of the next centralized kingdom were sown. By the fifteenth century the Chands had expanded their territorial foothold throughout Kumaon and, by the sixteenth century they had secured firm control over all of Kumaon and had moved their capital from Champawat to Almora in central Kumaon. However, dynastic infighting and other struggles divided and weakened the Chand's position and in 1790 the Gurkhas marched on Kumaon, meeting little resistance.[4] The Gurkha occupation of Kumaon ended in 1815 when the British gained political authority over Kumaon.

Kumaon, therefore, had for centuries been characterized by geographical, political, and cultural isolation. The area had been sealed off to the north by the Greater Himalayas, and from the plains of North India by the marshy Terai and Siwalik hills to the south. Under the Chands, Kumaon was an autonomous political entity. With the arrival of the Gurkhas this changed, and with British rule Kumaon became a dependent political unit. Kumaon became a specific political division within a wider framework of India and the British empire. The British introduced a new centralized uniform system of administration. More importantly, this administration which directed Kumaon and its people, derived from a power base external to Kumaon.

In order for British administrative authority to work, a large and efficient communications network was needed. The hazardous Terai was cleared and brought under cultivation, many dangerous animals were hunted down, and roads and bridges were built, linking Kumaon to the plains of north India. Minerals and resources could now be extracted from the hills and transported to the plains and imports moved in the opposite direction. Employment opportunities were created for local people in forest management, public works, tea plantations and small metal industries. Hill stations emerged and tourism developed, bringing a continuous flow of plains people and culture. Kumaonis also began to descend into the plains in search of work. Kumaon had been irrevocably integrated into a larger politico-economic entity.

Although, Kumaon was gradually incorporated into a wider political economy, the region was, from the beginning, given a lowly place in this new order. During colonial rule, the British government developed great interest in the commercial potential of the Kumaon hill forests. They were earmarked to provide timber and fuel to the local administrative centres, and official interest in these forests increased when the profitability of resin production became evident. There was a progressive diminution of villagers' rights in the forests in Kumaon between 1815 and the early twentieth century. New legislation curtailed local's rights over the forests, and threatened the considerable autonomy and control they had once enjoyed. Simultaneously, the British introduced to Kumaon a system of forced labour, known as *coolie utar* or *begar*.[5] Combined, these governments policies constituted an unprecedented level of state intervention. At the same time, they challenged villager's notions of economic and social justice and morality (Guha 1985: 97–8). Locals keenly resented their loss of control over the forests, particularly as they could observe the government exploiting it for commercial gain. Protests against the early forest settlement reports erupted at the beginning of this century as peasants directly challenged the state authority. The end of British rule was marked by the near total antipathy between the state and the peasant population (Guha 1989: 137).

The recent history of relations between the hill districts and the state government based 500 kilometres away in the plains city of Lucknow, has also been marked by tension and conflict. Kumaon's history since Independence has been one of persistent exploitation of its forests and mineral wealth, and the neglect of its people. Post-independence governments have continued, if not increased, the exploitation of Himalayan forests to meet the needs of rapidly growing industrialization. Commercial forest operations have intensified to meet these demands. More roads have been built to transport this timber out of the hills to industries elsewhere while the hill economy and local population have been materially neglected. Indeed, improved communications has seen the arrival of tourists and concomitant ecological degradation. The eagerness of the state to extend commercial forestry and reap the benefits has entailed further restrictions on villagers' use of forests. Distress and anger over state policies culminated in the Chipko movement in the early 1970s. This represents the most sustained challenge to date against the advance of commercial forestry, environmental degradation, and economic neglect of the region by the government. In the 1980s and 1990s further resentment concerning regional backwardness has been targeted at other perceived government representatives: in particular construction contractors, part of the state government's so-called efforts to boost tourism in the area, and liquor contractors, both seen as outside attempts to despoil the area and as direct threats to the identity and culture of hill people in general.[6]

Today, Uttarakhand continues to be exploited and neglected. The region, which covers approximately one-sixth of the state of Uttar Pradesh and comprises less than five per cent (approximately six million) of the state's total population (140 million in 1991), has very little in common with the geography, economy, and social makeup of the plains of the Gangetic valley. The region's caste profile is very different from that of the rest of UP. Of the region's total population approximately 20 per cent is made up of Scheduled Castes and Tribes, over 70 per cent of the high castes, with OBCs totalling less than two per cent. This is compared to the state averages of 22, 21 and 37 per cent respectively. Furthermore, Uttarakhand is economically backward. The hill region's economy is predominantly agrarian with forestry, livestock farming, sheep-rearing, and horticulture constituting other important occupations. Most agriculture is carried out on small terraced fields, but the land is unproductive and irrigation covers less than 10 per cent of farming land. Dependence on agriculture, uneconomic cultivation of crops and environmental limits create food deficits. And, despite higher than state average literacy rates (60 per cent compared to 42 per cent), local job opportunities are meagre and unemployment rates high. Combined, these factors have resulted in a high degree of male out-migration, which effectively means the region subsists primarily on remittance by migrant workers. Development in this economically backward area has been lop-sided and there is little to show for the government's investment. The region lacks any industrial base to speak of, and has very little arable land. Its main source of revenue comes from its forests, pilgrimage and tourism, though the beneficiaries of these sectors forms an already well-endowed minority. The region has vast reserves of natural resources and provides a perennial source of water to the state of Uttar Pradesh. And, although forests are the most valuable natural asset of the region, huge areas have been cleared in the process of development and biotic deterioration. Moreover, Uttarakhand is politically marginal as hill people are poorly represented in the National Assembly and Parliament (4 Members of Parliament and 19 Members of Legislative Assembly for six million people and area of approximately 51.1 thousand square kilometres.[7]) With no one to effectively speak on their behalf and to represent their needs and interests, the hill people of Uttarakhand are all the more easily neglected and ignored.[8]

Since the beginning of the nineteenth century Kumaon has been ruled by 'foreign' powers, firstly by the British colonial powers, and then by post-Independence central and state governments. The region's more recent history has been one of conflicts and struggles against these predatory external powers, as hill people have attempted to preserve their environment and cultural heritage, as well as their place on the wider economic and political agenda. These factors have paved the way towards the call for statehood, which aims to bring about political and economic empowerment to the region, and to ensure hill people's right to manage their own affairs and the means with which to decide their own future.

The 27 per cent OBC reservation policy added insult to years of injury, representing the last in a sequence of acts meted out by the central and state governments which undermine hill people's integrality and reconfirm their economic and political marginality and domination by plains society. It was particularly resented, for, not only are there less than 2 per cent OBCs in the hill region, but the high caste majority are poor. Moreover, despite the region's lack of development, Kumaonis have always laid emphasis on education, which represents a passport to a better future. As members of an already backward economy, twice-born caste people already feel that they are unable to secure public posts. They regard themselves as being doubly disadvantaged, both as hill people and high caste people, and, with the threat of further reservations, fear their futures being snatched away from them for good.

A Sense of Self: Discourse of Collective Identity and 'Insiders' and 'Outsiders'

These anti-reservation and pro-autonomy campaigns are further related. They are also about the declaration and maintenance of a separate sense of self and can be understood in terms of high caste Kumaoni's construction and discourse of collective identity.

Kumaon's past sovereignty, physical and cultural isolation, the region's history of political and economic integration, domination and underdevelopment, and the harsh realities of life in the hills, are active foci of their collective self image today. Kumaon's history and the present position the region occupies in relation to the state and administrative centre, and within the wider framework of north Indian society, are central to Kumaoni negotiations of identity. The region's history of autonomy, which is presented as one characterized by magnificence and social justice, are celebrated in local stories and myths (see Leavitt 1992). In this history the Kumaon kingdom occupies a position of centrality, a far cry from the region's contemporary marginality, and the ideal of regional autonomy which this period of history enshrines. This remains an important value despite Kumaon's tense and conflict-ridden absorption into wider politico-economic structures. More recent socio-economic problems, cumulative economic marginalization and political obscurity, as well as large scale unemployment and disillusionment, all contribute to Kumaoni people's self-representations.

However, as central to high caste Kumaoni self-representations are their constructions of 'self' and 'other' in terms of the indigenously dominant concepts of 'insiders' and 'outsiders'.

High caste Silora villagers talk about their world in terms of a segmentary model articulated by a dominant opposition between *bhitar(ak)*, the 'insider(r), and byar(ak), the 'outside(r)'. This distinction between 'insiders' and 'outsiders' is not fixed, but is a process of negotiation and debate. Those persons, social categories and spaces which are identified with the 'inside' or the 'outside' alter depending on the context and level of identification. Thus, in some contexts the household is the 'inside' and is opposed to other households in the village, and in others these very households are united as agnates and co-villagers in opposition to affines. In this segmentary model the interests and enmities of the lower levels are subordinated at broader more inclusive levels.

On every level of identification and in any given context the 'inside' represents an ordered moral community and relations between 'insiders' are represented as compassionate, co-operative and altruistic. 'Insiders' claim moral excellence over 'outsiders' and in any given context 'outsiders' are, by definition, morally inferior. The 'inside', whether it is the household, the lineage, village or region, is the centre of the universe and their attitudes about and relations with those defined as 'outsiders' stem from this fact. 'Outsiders' stand beyond the moral order represented by the 'inside' and, as such, are dangerous. They are constructed as greedy, destructive and unworthy, are believed to be motivated by self-interest and personal gain, and are seen to make predatory claims on 'insiders'. People are suspicious of 'outsiders' and relations with them are presented as hostile, instrumental and pragmatic.

These different levels of discrimination between 'insiders' and 'outsiders' are inter-connected by the rhetoric of deprivation. Irrespective of the specific bases on which boundaries and distinctions between 'insiders' and 'outsiders' are drawn, 'outsiders', no matter how they are defined, are thought to 'eat' and get strong at the expense of 'insiders', and therefore represent a threat to the well-being of 'insiders'.

It comes as no surprise therefore, that accompanying this distinction between 'insiders' and 'outsiders' is the ideological stress on autonomy which emphasizes the separation and containment of social categories. Whereas 'outsiders' are attributed with base motives and identified as causing harm, 'insiders' are vulnerable and must be protected. Care must be taken not only to regulate what flows out across boundaries, but more importantly what flows in. Boundaries which divide the 'inside' from the 'outside' should be strengthened and the rhetoric of deprivation and characterization of relations with 'outsiders' as instrumental serve to reinforce the ideal model of closed and bounded social categories (Moller 1993).

High caste Kumaoni people refer to both plains people and non-twice born, low caste people as 'outsiders'. Recent anti-reservation and pro-autonomy movements represent, in part, efforts by hill people to curb and end centuries of what they perceive as the domination of their homeland and people by rapacious 'outsiders', and can be understood in terms of notions about 'insiders' and 'outsiders', by the accompanying ideology of autonomy and the rhetoric of hunger.

Representations of Self and Other: Representations of 'Insiders' and 'Outsiders'

Collective Regional Identity: Hill people versus plains people

When talking about themselves as distinct from the 'outside' world of the plains, Kumaonis make frequent reference to the distinction between *pahari* and *deshi.* For Kumaonis the term *deshi* means 'of the country' and *desh* refers to any area outside of Kumaon, save Garhwal, and in particular to the western Gangetic plains of North India. *Deshi* is opposed to *pahari*, that which is local, indigenous and 'of the mountains'. This *pahari–deshi* distinction covers many aspects of life including language, rituals, festivals, customs, standards of morality, ecology, and even types of cattle. It also informs people's own self-definition as well as their view and behaviour towards this particular category of 'outsiders', *Deshis.* Furthermore, although *pahari* has derogatory connotations for plains people, for a Kumaoni, to be a *pahari* is a matter of great pride. And, although Kumaon is by no means a homogenous and unified region, any internal differences pale into insignificance in opposition to plains people.[9]

High caste Kumaonis talk about *Deshis* (plains people) as 'outsiders' (*bhyarak*), whom they dislike and distrust. The 'inside', which in this case is hill society, is the centre of Kumaoni's moral universe, a fact that influences their attitudes about plains people and their representation of relations with these 'outsiders' as hostile and pragmatic.

Many authors have taken note of the suspicion and antipathy felt by Kumaonis towards the people of the plains. Traill wrote over 150 years ago: 'All mountaineers unite in an excessive distrust of the natives of the low country, whom they regard as a race of swindlers and extortioners' (1980:217–18). One hundred years later, in the 1930–1940s, Randhawa presents a similar picture. He describes Almora town as very politically conscoius and aware, and mentions the 'exuberant democratic tendencies' which exist there inspite of the factionalism which divides its population. He says, however, that when their interests come into conflict with those of the plains, 'the people of Almora develop a surprising sense of solidarity' (1970: 129). Randhawa explains this attitude as 'a relic of their former isolation' and predicts its disappearance in the future when hill men and plains people will understand each other more (1970: 129). Despite his prediction, the hostility and distrust persist. Finally, Kapur, in a more recent study, says that the Kumaoni villagers of Devagiri have a 'xenophobic attitude' towards plains Indians (1988: 18). According to my high caste informants, plains people are dishonest, cunning, arrogant, exploitative, unreliable, and cheats; they are also said to be black, which is not only a comment on their appearance, but also on their moral make-up. Pahari women berate plains women as shameless and immodest because of the short, brief tops (*choli*) they wear with their saris,[10] and any new 'bad' trend or habit is usually attributed to having come from the plains. Berreman's studies on Sirkanda and Garhwal (1962, 1972, 1983a, 1983b, 1985) suggest that the kinds of attitudes that Kumaonis hold about plains people are shared by Garhwali villagers too.

Just as *Deshis* are seen as wretched and repulsive, so too is the *desh* and *desh* society. The plains of North India are considered an undesirable place to live. Villagers say the *desh* is dirty, violent, dangerous, crowded and noisy, and that, unlike, the pure mountain springs and breezes, the water and air are polluted. In the plains Sikhs, Muslims and Hindus all live together, side by side in a mixed environment. From hill people's point of view, caste boundaries are not clearly marked or observed in the plains, and people there are thought to engage in mixed, cross-caste marriages and to eat with people of the lower castes.

One important factor which contributes to the image hill people have of the plains and plains society, is the former's equation of *desh* (plains) with *shahar* (city-town) and *pahar* (hills) with *gau* (village). In conversation people will interchange the one for the other contrasting *desh* to *gau*. In this thought process *pahar* is equivalent to village, and *desh* equivalent to town and city. Berreman touches upon this unwittingly when he implicitly equates the urban with the plains and the 'non-*pahari* world' (1972: 299, 305). He says, 'the city is an exciting but in many ways a mysterious and dangerous place for most Paharis' (1972: 308). In this quotation 'the city' could easily be replaced by 'the plains' and it would still ring true'.[11] The view that hill villagers have of the attractions and dangers of cities is similar to that of villagers elsewhere in India.[12] However, these *pahari* villager's equation of city with *desh* is a distinctive feature (and has ethnic overtones). The association of the plains with the urban suggests limited awareness of village life in the *desh* and indeed this is the case. This is not too difficult to imagine or believe. When Kumaonis go to the plains to find employment or visit kin they board a bus in the Kumaon-village area and go straight to the big cities in the *desh*. En route to Moradabad, Lucknow and Delhi all they see are large, fertile farms, tractors and well-stocked, busy town bazaars. They do not see the villages which lie beyond and away from the main roads. Once in Delhi or Lucknow, the eating habits, moral behaviour, styles and fashions observed there are defined as *deshi* customs. Seen through their eyes, the desh represents a very different environment to the *pahari* village they know.

When talking about their relations with this hostile category of 'outsiders' Kumaonis stress the pragmatic nature of their contact with this 'outside' world. Hill men claim they work in the plains out of economic necessity. They represent the plains as a source of employment and earnings, and portray people's attachment and involvement with the plains as purely instrumental in nature: villagers work there to earn a living, not to mix with plains people. These statements actually hide a large degree of ambivalence towards plains: whilst proclaiming dislike to plains people and society,

Kumaonis nevertheless yearn for the riches that life in the plains potentially offers. Nevertheless, and despite the fact that *desh* is regarded as a place of wealth and opportunities where life is easier and goods cheaper, most young unemployed men with whom I spoke declared unwillingness to go to the plains to work preferring to find a job in the hills. Various reasons were given for this: some simply said they did not like the *desh* or *deshi* people; and others complained about the cost of living in the plains, particularly in Delhi, where accommodation is expensive and cramped. Several men objected to the treatment they had received from employers and superiors there and some claimed to have resigned from their jobs because they were unwilling to tolerate such subordination and humiliation. Men repeatedly emphasized that they do not want to leave their homes but they are obliged to migrate to the plains to earn money to sustain their families in the hills. Moreover, Kumaonis who work in the plains or who have set up home there, are pitied by fellow villagers and are thought to be susceptible to the values and habits of the plains, and in danger of becoming less Kumaoni as a result. One elderly Brahman woman claimed:

> We are better off than those who live outside because they are all alone, like a *ghar-jawai* [in-married son-in-law]. Among one's own close kin one can fight and laugh. Among one's kin there is *shan* [love, affection]. Tourists can enjoy our wind and air for a few days. We 'eat' it all the time! Those people who have moved and set up home elsewhere only come back as tourists, staying for a day or two and then they go away.

This proclaimed aversion to living and working in the plains, and the representation of relations with the desh as purely utilitarian, express desire to live independently from the exploitation, domination and contamination of the outside world of the plains and confirms the ideal of containment. It is also based on a very real feeling of defiant self-reliance and pride in the face of unwarranted prejudice and discrimination. For, despite the magnificent setting of their homeland, plains people attribute hill people with a stereotyped stigmatized identity. The Himalayan area of Uttarakhand is the source of great holy rivers, the abode of the gods and saints, the site of the shrines of Badarinath and Kedarnath and a land replete with medicinal plants and herbs. It is the 'Holy Land of Hinduism' (Berreman 1985: 111), a place of great beauty and purity. However, the plains

Indians regard the hill people as rather less than pure and holy. To the average plains person hill people are backward, uneducated, and uncivilized simple country bumpkins (see Berreman 1962: 6, 1972: 322). Paharis are consistently thought to be morally inferior and practices which were common in the past but which are no longer so evident, such as bride-price marriages, widow remarriage and so on, continue to be referred to by plains people as proof of the hill persons' lower moral standards. Their form of Hinduism, and in particular that of the higher castes—who, like other castes in the region, eat meat, drink alcohol, sacrifice animals and rely heavily upon mediums and diviners (see Berreman 1970)—is deemed by plains people to be less orthodox and rigorous than the 'normal' Hinduism purportedly practised by the peoples of the western Gangetic plains.

Kumaonis bitterly resent and actively refute the stereotype of the hill person projected onto them by plains people. Though they feel economically neglected and constantly emphasize how 'hill people are poor people', they dispute the label that they are uncivilized or culturally backward. Instead they see themselves to be not only morally distinct, but morally superior to plains people, and believe they have preserved the moral and social values long since corrupted in the plains by modernity. In contrast to *Deshis*, *Paharis* ('insiders') are said to be honest, generous, compassionate, good natured and fair, and relations between Kumaonis ('insiders') are represented as friendly and harmonious. These representations are upheld by the allusion to the region as one large kin unit, and by the fact the Kumaonis will only marry other Kumaonis. By implication, Kumaon is associated with kinship, and not with strangers and anonymity. Villagers take great pride in their countryside and in their way of life and continually drew my attention to the purity of the water and air, reminding me how peaceful, safe and clean the hill region is. These qualities are believed to be unique to Uttarakhand and hill people consider themselves lucky to live in the region. Moreover, Kumaoni villagers implicitly assume that their hearts and souls, like the Himalayas themselves, are pure and good, and they see the *pahari* way of life as superior (Berreman 1972: 356).

As a community of 'insiders' Kumaon stands at the centre of the moral universe. This positioning of themselves at the moral centre, this claim to moral superiority over plains people, is central to

Kumaoni's definition and construction of plains as 'outsiders' and of themselves as 'insiders', and very significant component of Kumaoni's discourse of collective identity.

There are other traits, customs and social practices that Kumaoni villagers identify as distinctive to themselves, which they feel they share among themselves, and which mark them off from plains society. These distinctive markers are fundamental to the negotiation and formation of a Kumaoni identity and sense of self. It may be that the derogatory attitude of the plains people towards hill people informs hill men and women's own self-definition and that the features they identify as uniquely pahari are, to some extent, elaborated in direct opposition to the social values and practices of plains society. Kumaoni's define themselves as having unique linguistic, cultural and moral patterns which distinguish and separate them from plains society.

Language

Kumaonis regard their language as one of the most important indicators of their distinctiveness. They are proud of their language and say that it is 'sweet' (*mith*). Kumaoni is the language of the home, tea-stall and village shops. It is also the language used in the worship of regional divinities, particularly in the context of *jagars* (spirit possession seance). Hindi is the language of the *desh*, the north Indian plains. Hindi is also the language of the *desh*, the north Indian plains. It is also the language of authority and the government, and is the language of administration, business and education. Kumaonis use Hindi in formal contexts, as it constructs a distance between the speakers. When the Block Development officer visits he is spoken to in Hindi even if he is a Kumaoni man and *Pahari* teachers or government employees often alternate between Kumaoni and Hindi during the course of a conversation, as if unsure whether the context is, or should be, a formal or an informal one.

Hindi is associated with the plains, with *sarvis* (employment) and the official world in general: in short, Hindi is inextricably associated with *deshi* people. Those men who go to work in the plains are in contact with *deshis* and have to speak in Hindi for much of their working hours. Regardless of whether life in the plains is a comfortable experience, the popular assumption is that these men should leave that part of their identity behind them as soon as they enter the village again. Although Hindi may be seen by some as a status symbol, a marker of superiority, just as being able to speak English is for many people in India, for the majority of rural Kumaonis it is not a positive symbol. Speaking Hindi implies one has become less Kumaoni; that one has taken on the ways and attitudes of the plains. Plains men are thought to be arrogant and conceited, and it is feared that returned and visiting migrant men folk may also have adopted these attitudes, viewing their village relatives as backward and inferior. The owner of a sweet shop in Ranikhet bazaar made the following comment as he watched passengers disembark from a bus arriving from the plains:

People do not want to speak Kumaoni here; they return from the plains and speak Hindi. It isn't good. They should speak their mother tongue. It is as if they feel embarrassed to speak Kumaoni, as if they would be putting themselves down if they did. Men who speak Hindi in the village, especially in the tea-shops and with co-villagers, are criticized for thinking themselves bigger and better than everyone else, and of putting on airs of superiority. People will comment sarcastically: 'He has become a big man now!' (*u bar hai go*). In order to avoid this kind of sharp-edged teasing one should speak Kumaoni.

Rituals

Kumaonis hold *jagars* in the dead of night to deal mainly with misfortune and illness. Like Leavitt (1922: 20–21), I too found that Kumaonis consider these rituals to be peculiar to the mountains, and a distinctly *pahari* thing to do. *Jagars* involve regional gods; they are performed in the Kumaoni language; the legends and narrative songs sung by the bard to induce these gods to dance refer to events which took place in the Katyuri and Chand dynasties before 1795 when Kumaon ceased to be an independent kingdom (Gaborieau 1977: xl). Not only are the rituals seen as unique to the region, but so are the reasons for their performance, that is, the causes of human misfortune. Paharis think they are particularly affected by such agents. One man said:

In the plains people feed and educate their children and then say to them, 'you are on your own, make your living and lead your own life on your own feet.' But here in the hills, people feed and educate their children and then say to them 'now you give to us, you take of us.' If they don't then these ancestral curses (*banks*) multiply.

This man's contrast between plains and hills society on this point is spurious, and is a misconstruction of plains social life. Such notions of *seva* and inter-generational reciprocity and interdependence also exist in the plains (see Vatuk 1990) and ancestral curses are part of social life. The attribution of such distinctiveness extends to the calendars and annual ritual cycles (see Leavitt 1992).

Women and Work

Women villagers often volunteered comments of comparison between their situation and that of plains women. They are aware that they contribute much more than plains women do to the local agricultural economy. One woman said: 'Hill women do everything: they look after children, do the cooking and work in the fields. In the plains, women do house work and men work on the land'. Despite what any one woman may feel, and in other contexts many complained about how much work hill women have to do (see Moller 1993: 42–6), when contrasting their lives to that of plains women they represent their situation as the better of the two. In the plains women who work outside and in the fields are thought to come from households low in economic or social status. In the hills, however, this fact is celebrated as a positive aspect of Kumaoni woman's life. Village women take pride in their physical strength and consider their mobility as a kind of freedom not enjoyed by their sisters in the plains. Though women generally consider themselves to be suppressed (*daba*), they value the fact that they are not confined to the house all day. Going out to the fields or forest, for young daughters-in-law (*bwaris*) in particular, is a relief and (Moller 1993: 42–6). On one trip to the forest a young woman said: 'our way of life is better than that of the plains women. We go out; they just sit around in the house; they are not very strong in the body'. On another occasion a woman said proudly: 'Here women work, not as they do in the *desh* where they just sit around.'

Relations of Production

Another distinctive feature concerns the social relations and methods of production. People complain about the difficulties they face in ploughing and farming their terraced fields. The land is not profitable, it does not yield surplus produce of any significance, and labour costs are high. However, despite these complaints, people speak almost boastfully about the *pahari* people's way of farming. 'People do their work (*apan kam*) and there is no shame (*sharam*) in this.' This view derives from and confirms the strong ideological stress on egalitarianism in the village (see Moller 1993: Chapter five). Men speak with pride about their women and daughters who are good workers and literate too. The phenomena of large individualized land holdings, of landlords and the accompanying inequalities so characteristic of the plains system, do not exist in Silora or Kumaon in general. People express approval of the fact that the social relations of production are more fair and egalitarian than in the plains. As one man explained:

In the plains if people are rich they will not do the field work but will hire *naukars* (servants). Here in the hills, be they rich or poor, they do their own work; they are *barabar* (equal).[13]

This putative egalitarianism is presented by Paharis as a means of expressing their difference from plains society. This is, of course, a simplified image, but one which can become a rhetorical expression of Pahari virtue, and which can also feed back into their own sense of self. As Cohen remarks, a community's members 'may denigrate the disparities of wealth and power, or the competitiveness which they perceive elsewhere, to justify and give value to their espousal of equality' (1985: 35).

Poverty

And lastly, Kumaonis represent themselves as 'poor people'. Poverty is a key element in Kumaoni's discourse of a collective regional identity and is fundamentally linked to the region's political, economic and social marginality and with Kumaoni's self image as an oppressed people. This poverty and marginality is expressed in their description of themselves as 'thin' people (*pataw*). However, this thinness and poverty are not negatively valued. On the contrary, they are virtues. For, although most people try desperately to improve their economic standing and life-style, and although they may, in a way, envy the wealthy for their riches, being poor is given a positive value, and regarded as an essential part of what it is to be a Kumaoni hill person. Being 'thin' is equated with physical strength, being poor, ignored and marginal, and, more significantly, with moral superiority.

In direct contrast to this self-representation is Kumaoni's designation of plains people as 'fat' (*mot*). To be 'fat' is negatively valued.

Plains people are considered to be physically weak and therefore 'fat'. However, *Deshis* are 'fat' in another way. Kumaonis use the same word for 'fat' to refer to *Deshis* as rich (*mot*) people. Rich people are disliked by hill people because of the power, authority, and arrogance with which the wealthy are associated. In Kumaoni village society wealth does not give an individual authority over others in the community whereas in the plains it might. Plains people are said to show off their wealth and position, behaviour quite repugnant to hill people and their egalitarian ethos (see Moller 1993: Ch. 5). In addition, villagers express great contempt and suspicion towards people in positions of authority. Those in such positions in Kumaon are well-paid government officers who are usually also plains men. Government and state officials are seen as fraudulent and corrupt; they and their programmes are viewed with suspicion. The government and its agents are seen to 'get fat' at the expense of the local *pahari* population. 'Fatness', therefore, is a negative quality for quite different reasons: in one sense to be fat implies physical weakness, and in another, it refers to economic strength, power, authority, and arrogance. More importantly, it implies immorality. Whereas Kumaoni's are 'thin', poor, marginal, and moral, plains people are 'fat', wealthy, powerful, and immoral.[14]

This opposition between 'fat' and 'thin' people is part of Kumaoni's social ideology of identity in which 'outsiders' ('fat' people) 'eat' and get 'fat' at the expense of 'insiders' ('thin' people). The idiom of hunger and rhetoric of deprivation also bring to the fore the asymmetry which exists between the centre and periphery and reveal Kumaoni's perception of their relationship to the administrative centre and to the wider politico-economic entities by which they are, though reluctantly, encompassed. Hill people feel dominated by a set of outsiders who do not share their language, culture or concerns.

Silira villagers feel very strongly that these plains 'outsiders' and the government apparatus which plains society represent have, and continue to prosper, to the detriment of the local population, culture and environment. According to villagers the hill people and their way of life are dominated economically and politically by plains society, and they resent what they perceive to be a situation of 'internal colonization' of the hills by 'outsiders', such as plains men and the central and state governments. Berreman discusses this aspect of the *pahari* situation and asserts:

> . . . one might say that Uttarakhand has become a colony within the state and nation which administers it. It is an internal colony, a domestic colony, but a colony none-the-less, exploited by and for outsiders. (1985: 110)

People complain that their mountains are treated by outsiders as an unlimited and exploitable source of raw materials, while local *Paharis* receive little recompense. They say that the *pahari* people and land are being drained in favour of the plains: hill people feel economically disadvantaged, and complain that the government has not paid enough attention to developing the region for the local populace. The 'development' which has occurred has benefited the government and entrepreneurs. Projects emphasizing small-scale industries and skills were identified by locals as potential programmes which would bring employment and better living standards to the hill population. As one man said:

> People here feel cheated—they want their own state government and administration because money from here is put to use in the plains. Our money should be administered by our own local hill government to better our conditions. We want food prices to fall and jobs and employment to be available here.

Even though there are administrative and government posts in the districts of Nainital, Almora, and Pithoragarh, most of the high-grade posts are filled by well-educated high class plains men, the more menial lower scale officers are filled by local hill people. Locals feel unable to compete for high jobs and remain at the lower end of the social and economic ladder. Kumaoni people also feel politically marginalized and resent the fact that they have very little say in the running of Uttar Pradesh and of their hill region. They dislike being governed by Lucknow, where the administration of Kumaon is in the hands of non-Kumaoni, non-*pahari* civil servants.

Plains people are the 'outsiders' par excellence: standing beyond *Pahari* ecological, economic, moral and kinship systems, they drain the region of its resources and deny it of prosperity and strength. Relations between hill and plains people are represented as hostile and pragmatic, and claims for regional autonomy emphasize the virtues of regulated contact, containment, and separation. However, plains people are not the only 'outsiders'. From the perspective of high caste Kumaonis, *Deshis* are seen to share much in common with low caste people, who also represent a threat to the integrity of high castes identity and community.

Collective Caste Identity: High Caste versus Low Caste

Kumaonis responded so vociferously to the reservation policy not only because it was a blatant affront to their already meagre employment opportunities, but also because its implementation threatened to lead to an influx of low caste plains people into the hills to fill up the coveted government jobs and educational places. The policy represented increased domination by 'outsiders', not only in the form of plains people, but, and perhaps even worse, low caste people as well.

High caste Kumaoni's define low caste people as 'outsiders', and part of the anti-reservation protests in the past were aimed at preventing increased domination by 'outsiders', in the form of low caste people. High caste Kumaonis already resent the reservation policy for education, government jobs and promotions for the Scheduled Tribes and Scheduled Castes in the region, and see themselves as being ruled not only by plains men but by the lower castes. In Silora, villagers pointed out that their Chief Minister of the State was himself a plains man of low caste (OBC) descent, that the then Almora District Magistrate was a south Indian Harijan, and that the new block development officer was a Kumaoni Harijan (see Upadhyay 1990: 51).

High caste Kumaoni villagers talk about low caste people in the same way as they talk about plains people. Just as, at the level of regional identities, Kumaon represents a moral community of 'insiders' which is opposed to the plains, so too members of the twice born castes represent a moral community of 'insiders' in opposition to low caste categories. Low caste people are conceived of as 'outsiders' and are referred to as 'the outside caste' (*bhyar jat*). They are attributed with the dangers associated with all 'outsiders', and must be kept at a distance. Furthermore, the lower castes are thought to 'eat' and prosper at the expense of high caste people, a situation which the proposed reservation policy threatened to advance.

Caste is an important social division in Kumaon, but due to Kumaon's social history and unusual caste system, the distinction between the twice born and non-twice born castes is the most significant one. The range of castes found in Kumaon is very limited when compared to the vast range which exists in the plains of North India. In Kumaon only three *varna* categories are represented, each of which are internally divided. These are: the Brahmans, locally referred to as Baman or pandit; the Kshatriyas known as Thakurs or Rajputs; and the Untouchables, termed Harijan, Shilpakar or Dum.[15] The Vaishya (at 0.57 per cent of the population) and Shudra castes are not significantly represented, though some Dums have gained Shudra status (Fanger 1980; Sebrig 1972). In my fieldwork district of Almora, 76 per cent of the Hindu population consists of 'twice born' high castes, with Brahmans constituting approximately 24 per cent, Rajputs 50 per cent, and the low caste Shilpakars 21 per cent (India Census 1931).[16]

This strong binary division between high and low castes, and the identification of the low castes as 'outsiders' is, I suggest, rooted in Kumaon's social history. And, this social history shows that the division between the upper castes and the lower castes, referred to as Bith and Dum respectively, is not new, but has been a significant social distinction for a long time.

During Kumaon's pre-1790 history, when the region was an autonomous kingdom, both the Katyuri and Chand Kings sponsored and maintained orthodox Hinduism. They gave high administrative, religious, and military positions to Brahmans and Rajputs who, it is claimed, originated from the plains and (other parts of India) and who were not agriculturists. These high caste immigrants who held a monopoly on political and economic power, are referred to in the literature as Thul-jats. Though they were given land grants they did not cultivate their land, hiring others instead to perform such polluting work. These Thul-jats distinguished themselves from the majority indigenous population of Brahmans and Rajputs known collectively as Khasi or Khasiya.[17] These culturally homogenous small owner-cultivators were hired by the Thul-jats to perform agricultural and other duties as the latter's tenants.

It would seem that an important distinction, which cut across caste categories, existed between the immigrant settlers (Thul-jats) and the indigenes (Khasi) thus producing a unique ranking system with the Thul-jats ranked higher and considered ritually superior to Khasi Brahmans and Rajputs alike (Leavitt 1992: 31–2). At the same time however, these Thul-jat and Khasi high castes were collectively referred to as Bith and were united in their distinction from and opposition to, what they referred to as the 'outside caste': the Dums (Sanwal 1976: 61). The Dums occupied the lowest place in the social, economic, and ritual hierarchy. They were landless labourers, agricultural menials and artisans to the landlords and cultivators (i.e. Biths). Forbidden to own property they were totally dependent on their high-caste masters for everything (see Sanwal 1976: 71); they had to live in the lowest part of the village well away from high caste settlement areas, and they had their own water holes and cremation ground. In addition to agricultural and artisanal tasks, Dums were obliged to perform demeaning services such as carrying Bith wedding palanquins and burying their master's dead cattle (see Fanger 1980: 94–99 and Sanwal 1976 for more details).[18] Thus, according to historical sources, the initial division was between the indigenous Khasi and the Dums. With the arrival of the Katyuri and Chand dynasties, and the accompanying 'immigrants', the division, though apparently three-fold (i.e. Thul-jat, Khasi and Dum), was fundamentally between the Bith and the Dum.

Gurkha and British rule destroyed the political and economic foundations of Thul-jat dominance and the British rule brought an expanding economy, new opportunities, wealth and status mobility. A new land tenure system was introduced which handed property rights to the actual cultivator, thus irradiating servile tenancy relationships and enabling low castes to own land for the first time. Over time the Khasi merged with the Thul-jats and vice-versa. The number of Thul-jats has diminished and as a group has lost significance in the rural areas (Fanger 1980:49). British rule also brought opportunities to earn cash wages. Dums with specialized skills (e.g. carpenters and blacksmiths) could often earn a better wage than the non-skilled Khasi. This helped to mitigate the existing inequalities. However, only the artisan Dums had access to these opportunities, and associated improvements in wealth and status. The artisan Dums benefited from the British, the commercialization of the economy, and the new economic opportunities. A labour shortage ensued in the villages and high caste people had to give competitive rates to ensure they retained access to the artisan's skills and labour. These artisans or Shilpakars, received good wages from the British. At the beginning of this century many Dums joined the Arya Samaj movement which stimulated Dum social mobility.[19] Arya Samaj-trained Shilpakar priests led fellow Dums to change their life-style. Dums abandoned demeaning and defiling tasks such as transportation of their high caste master's dead cattle and ceased to eat buffalo meat. They adopted the sacred thread and observed Sanskritic life-cycle ceremonies officiated by their own Shilpakar priests, and refused to carry the palanquin and banners at high caste weddings and provide music for the latter's ceremonial occasions. However, in reality only the wealthier and educated artisans managed to attain total independence from the agricultural high castes. The majority of rural Dums still had a weak economic and political position and were not able to become independent of the Bith cultivators. Though slavery and serfdom had been abolished, Dums entered into quite rigid *jajmani*-like relations, locally called *khauki-gusai*, with the high caste villagers.

This basic social and ritual distinction between Bith and Dums, between the twice-born 'clean castes' and the impure 'outside' castes, has been absolutely fundamental throughout the region's history. And, despite the changes which have occurred in political and agricultural relations, and in particular the transformations which have taken place among the lower castes in the twentieth century, the binary opposition between the high caste Brahmans and Thakurs and the Untouchables continues to influence people's attitudes and behaviour. In contemporary rural Kumaon, the significant social and ritual barrier is between the twice-born and ritually clean castes and the Shilpakars.[20]

I shall now discuss inter-caste interaction, and Brahman and Thakur constructs of and ideas about their Harijan neighbours. The data presented was gathered in Silora which is made up of 75 per cent ploughing Brahmans, 20 per cent Thakurs, and about 5 per cent Harijans. Although Silora has very few Harijans, there are several almost all-Harijan neighbouring villages. It should be noted that my data are biased in so far as the opinions represented are only those of high caste people.

In Silora, Brahmans and Thakurs interact easily. Apart from a few stated food restrictions, they exchange invitations to each other's feasts and ceremonies, and enjoy a similar class status in terms of land ownership. Though high caste people are aware of the internal differences among the low castes they are irrelevant to them. Dums are *achhut* (defiling, impure) and are referred to as 'outsiders' (*bhyarak*). Though Thakurs may, at times, refer to Brahmans as 'outsiders' and vice versa in so much as they are not caste members, the most important opposition is between the 'inside' community of the clean castes and the 'outside' community of the impure low castes.

Harijans are conceived of as a different kind of being from the high castes. They have a different past and ancestry and different principles and rules (*niyams*). Furthermore, they are physically different. High caste people define Harijans, as they do plains people, as black, which signifies their inferior moral status. Not only are black people considered uncivilized, rude, ugly and dirty, they are also said to be dangerous, greedy and prone to giving the evil eye (see Moller 1993: 127–9). Like plains people, Harijans are thought to be immoral, dishonest, devious, liars, and cheats. Ghosts are spoken of as being black and Harijans are thought to be ghost and demon worshippers (see Moller 1993: Ch. 8): even though most have never entered a Harijan house, many high caste women believe that Harijans do not have shrines in their houses. This idea is confirmed in their minds by the fact that only Harijans act as *bhut-pujyaris*.

High caste villagers will not readily speak or behave in discriminatory ways towards Harijans in public, and seem very aware of the fact that Harijans are on guard and ready to bring the law on their side if they are discriminated against because of their caste (see Upadhyay 1990: 51). A Thakur woman, having told me that twice born women would not even take raw provisions (*kach rashan*) from Harijans quickly added, 'do not tell anyone; they'll put handcuffs on us and send us to jail!.' And a Brahman man reiterated this attitude when he told me not to use or publish the word 'Dum' in my work for if I did the Harijans would fight and take me to court because they are, he said 'ready to kick back'. Although these discriminatory and hostile attitudes are usually kept at bay in daily life they play an important part in the negotiation of high caste collective identity.

As 'outsiders' low caste people are perceived to have 'eaten' and prospered at the expense of the high castes. This rhetoric of deprivation is clearly illustrated by the bitterness expressed by Brahmans and Thakurs regarding reservation policies which have helped some low caste people gain employment and achieve economic success. The high castes see the low castes' growing independence, confidence, arrogance, and wealth as a threat. They also feel that it is they themselves who have had to pay and suffer for the Harijan's privileges and security.

High caste people comment bitterly about the Harijan's changed and changing position. Whereas in the past they were subservient and dependent, working for and serving the high castes, Harijans are now thought to enjoy independence and wealth, and to receive preferential treatment from the government.[21] They are helped in education and job opportunities and aid is given to build paths and other conveniences in their villages. Although the Harijans in Silora are quite poor many Harijans living near Silora have, according to high caste Silora villagers, visibly benefited from the government's policies and better economic conditions. In Saukhola, a neighbouring all-Harijan village, many of the houses are new and have televisions, comforts which high castes assume are direct results of preferential treatment. High caste people say of Saukhola residents: 'In the past they were house-builders, blacksmiths and tailors. Now they are *patawaris* (land records officer) and teachers.' Harijans receive education stipends from schools, colleges and the government, and government jobs are reserved for the low castes and promotion possibilities are good for them. One Brahman man in Silora said to me:

> The scheduled castes are now treated like gods. If a scheduled caste boy with a third class high school pass applies for a post and a Brahman boy with a first class applies, the scheduled caste boy will get it. Now there are many unemployed Brahmans.

Brahmans also express resentment at other perceived perks. I was told of Rs 11,300 government grants given to Harijans to purchase Jersey cows. Of this sum Harijans have only to repay Rs 5,000. Similar grants given to other castes total only Rs 6,000 and the grantees must repay Rs 3,000. I do not know if the details are correct, but they illustrate the widespread perception that there are inequalities and injustices, and that high caste villagers resent and deplore these. One man said with exasperation, 'everything, education benefits for children, job reservation for adults and now this cow facility for the uneducated and old people!'

The ideological stress at the caste level, from the high caste point of view, is on closure, containment and separation. Particular emphasis is given to the separateness and distinctiveness of the 'clean' Brahmans and Thakurs castes from the Shilpakars. Low caste people are seen to threaten and deprive twice-born people of their economic opportunities and to weaken their caste purity. As agents of disorder and harm Shilpakar people should be kept at bay. This is achieved mainly through limited interaction and exchange with them (see Moller 1993: 100–7).

The binary opposition of Harijans versus the upper castes has possibly worsened the recent events in UP since the early 1990s. Even if discrimination against Harijans is in some degrees less than it used to be, actual hostility between Harijans and non-Harijans may have increased. One young Brahman man explained: 'There is tension between Harijans and Brahmans, but that is the governments's fault due to the reservation for government jobs and such like. After all, are we any better off than Harijans?'

'Insiders' and 'Outsiders': Other Communities and Identities

We have seen that assumptions about 'insiders' and 'outsiders' and the ideology of separation and discourse of deprivation are central to constructions of caste and regional identities in rural Kumaon. However, these notions and models are also relevant at lower levels of identity distinction. Notions about 'insiders' and 'outsiders' permeate all aspects of social life. Not only are relations between castes and regions informed by and spoken about in terms of the 'insider'/'outsider' dichotomy, but so are relations between households and affines, and between humans and supernatural agents.

Non-household members are often referred to as 'outsiders', and this category includes lineal kin. Social relations within the village are presented as competitive and antagonistic, and a deep sense of distrust and hostility characterizes most forms of inter-household interaction (see Moller 1993: 108–43). Non-household members are perceived as malicious and are suspected of harbouring base motives. These 'outsiders' are covetous and inflict the evil eye which saps its victim's freshness and vitality, causes beauty and health to fade, and spoils milk and food stores by causing cow's udders and crops to 'dry up'. 'Outsiders' try to drain the house of its economic, moral and social strength: gossip, defamation and back-biting are thought to 'weaken' the social and economic fabric of the household with potentially disastrous effects. Non-household members are thought to 'eat' and get strong only at the expense of 'insiders' and relations with 'outsiders' are presented as instrumental.

In a society where being equal (barabar) is highly valued but personal gain is seen as the main motive for social interaction, the economic strength, honour and social boundaries of the house must be protected and maintained. Although there are no obvious 'antipenetration symbols' in Silora, such as the ferocious dogs and massive padlocks used by Sherpas (Ortner 1978: 40), or the high mud wall of the plains which protect the villager's family and possessions from a covetous outside world (Wiser and Wiser 1963), certain practices and attitudes serve to safeguard the house from claims on its resources. They also serve to reinforce the model of the closed, separate and bounded household unit. These include villagers' attitudes towards friendship and loans; the attention given to looking poor; and the value placed on the art of skilful deception. Household wealth is hoarded and concealed, lying and secrecy defend the house from community sanctions and from 'outsider's' greed, and leakages of information on household affairs to the outside world are avoided, though distorted facts are allowed out.

Though there is rivalry and suspicion between households, and though people complain about their kin and fellow villagers, in other contexts these households are united as village brothers and agnates in opposition to non-villagers and affines. Affines form another category of 'outsiders', who are attributed with negative mystical capacities which can have devastating consequences (see Moller 1993: 144–5, 172–4; Moller *in press*). On the broadest conceptual level, *bradar* (lineal kin, agnates, village brothers—agnatic kinship) and *poun* (non-agnatic consanguines and pure affines-affinal kinship) are fundamentally opposed: the basic opposition is between those who are agnates and co-villagers, that is 'insiders', and thus not marriageable persons, and those who are non-agnates and non co-villagers, that is 'outsiders'. Lineage and village exogamy and patrilocal residence mean that marriage must occur with 'outsiders'. As 'outsiders', affines are seen as potentially dangerous, wife-takers as well as wife-givers (see Moller *in press*). The wife-giver's spells (*jadu*) and the wife-takers's abuse (*gali*) can have harmful, if not fatal consequences. But it is perhaps the in-marrying daughter-in-law (*bwari*) who embodies the most threatening of all affinal powers. Not only does she represent a threat to the stability of the household, but she is also thought of as a messenger of misfortune. The *bwaris* said to convey and cast magic spells and evil spirits, and if any misfortune should occur in a house soon after her arrival, she may be held responsible. The in-marrying woman represents the affinal 'outsider' par excellence, and potentially the most dangerous as she must be let into the 'inside' communities of the household, lineage and village, and transformed into an 'insider'.

Finally, some supernatural agents are classified as 'insiders' and 'outsiders'. High caste Silora villagers talk about deities (*dyapts*), ancestors, ghosts of deceased kin (*bhuts*), and ancestral curses, (*hanks*) as *gharak* or *bhiterak* ('of the house' and 'of the insider'). In opposition to these divinities stand the evil ghosts and demons (*mashan, chal, bhut-pret*), which are referred to as *bhyarak*, 'of the outsider' (see Moller 1993: 205–32). 'Insider' spirits are members of 'the inside' community, be it the household or lineage, and uphold the moral order of these 'inside' communities. Attacks by 'insider' spirits follow breaches of the moral order and their afflictions are morally justified. In contrast, attacks by 'outsider' spirits do not follow breaches of the moral order. These ghosts hover on the edges of organized moral society, spoken about as 'the inside', and as such they are dangerous 'outsiders'. Depicted as black, dirty and ugly, these evil spirits lurk in impure places. Hungry, greedy and deceitful, they 'eat' their victims and inflict suffering as a means of extracting food from the living. In satisfying their own interests and desires, they weaken their victims by depriving them of health and vitality. Their attacks are not protective, but are motivated by pure selfish desire and craving. The pragmatic nature of interactions with 'outside' ghosts is stressed: these ghosts are given food and forced to leave. They are placated, not honoured, and once they have been expelled, no long-standing obligations to them remain: the relationship between humans and the 'outside' ghost is contractual and instrumental. The ideology of regulation and ideal of containment is relevant to the separation of 'outside' ghosts from the body of the individual victim, and from the social body of the household or kin group which also suffers from the spirit's affection. Whereas *puja* is performed after a sacrifice given to 'insider' spirits, serving to unite human actors and the spirits; the exorcisms and sacrifices performed for 'outside' ghosts serve to separate and distance human actors from the menacing spirits. As is the case on the levels of the household, caste and region, separation and detachment from 'outsiders' is the ideal, and considered the way to protect 'the inside'.

Concluding remarks

I have demonstrated that we can understand the recent anti-reservation and pro-autonomy in the hills of Uttar Pradesh both in terms of political-economy and indigenous concepts and discourses of identity. Together these analytical perspectives give us insight into the strength of feeling of high caste hill people about these policies and issues.

Since the events of autumn 1994 the people of Uttarakhand have vociferously pursued their demands and have come some way towards having them met. In August 1997 the Allahabad Supreme Court ruled that residents of the hill regions of Uttar Pradesh should be treated as socially and educationally backward classes (SEBC) of citizens, and are thus entitled to be considered for reserved places in all educational institutions and government services as long as the statutory scheme or reservation continues in the state. Although the state government is not bound to treat residents of Uttarakhand as SEBC citizens permanently, in May 1998 the UP government did decide to continue to extend reservation to hill people like other backward classes for the near future.

However, demands for the formation of a separate state have met with less success. Even though the region witnessed two years of continued agitation for a separate hill state, and the UP assembly has recommended its creation to the centre three times (1992, 1994, 1997), and two prime ministers have promised to establish a hill state on separate occasions, it has not yet materialized. Over recent years almost all political parties seem to have reconciled themselves to the demand for a separate state, and most have used the issues to woo hill voters in their election campaigns. Even senior politicians at election rallies in the region have promised a separate hill state if their party came to power at the centre. The BJP in 1998 promised that, if it were elected to the centre, it would set up the new state within 90 days of coming to power. However, after their victory in March this year, the new government announced its National Agenda, which undertakes to create three new states: Uttaranchal (the new government name replacing the previously suggested name of Uttarakhand), Vananchal, and Chattisgarh. Uttaranchal would cover the same territory as Uttarakhand, the only change being in the proposed name. In changing the state-to be's name from Uttarakhand to Uttaranchal, however, and in linking the setting up of Uttaranchal with that of two other states, the government could be seen to be diluting its commitment to the hill people.[22]

It has yet to be seen whether a new hill state of Uttaranchal will be formed. But, if it is, and if SEBC reservation rights continue to be extended to high caste hill people, how will hill people's discourses of collective caste and regional identities change in response? How will hill people conceptualize their relationship to the new state and wider nation beyond? Who will become the new 'outsiders', the new oppressors, once the plains man is cast off and high caste *Paharis* reap the benefits of reservation? Will we find new, more localized divisions taking on increased significance, such as those between different classes, or between the rural and the urban populations within the region? As graffiti scrawled in red point on the wall of a school in Uttarkashi district declared: 'Until yesterday, it was the outsider who we blamed for ravaging the forests, sucking our blood and thwarting our ambitions. Tomorrow, it will be one of us. . .' (India Today, 15/10/96: 51).

Notes

1. For details of the agitation and events which occurred in the summer and autumn of 1994 and developments since then see *India Today*, (15/9/94: 54–5, 30/9/94: 30–5, 31/10/94: 35, 30/6/95: 30–3, 31/10/95: 44–5, 15/10/96: 50–3) and Uttarakhand Homepage at http://www.geocities.com/RainForest/vines/7039.
2. The data in this paper were gathered during 15 months of doctoral fieldword conducted in Almora district between 1989 and 1991 and a field visit between December 1993 and January 1994. Doctoral studies at the London School of Economics and Political Sciences, including field research in Kumaon, were generously funded by an Economic and Social Research Council Competition Award (1988–92). Silora is a pseudonym.
3. Sources on Kumaon's history include Atkinson (1973, 1974), Sanwal (1976), Mittal (1986, 1990), Guha (1985, 1989).
4. The Gurkhas conquered Garhwal in 1804.
5. For more information on this system of coolie *utar* see references in Guha (1985, 1989).
6. Almora district was declared a dry zone in June 1984. According to Pathak (1985) the history of alcohol dates from the British period. He says that liquor became more available and its consumption increased with the advent of the army and other government departments and the establishment of military cantonments and hill stations (1985: 1360–1). Prior to that, liquor consumption was limited to the Bhotiya traders and Terai populations. Traill, soon after the commencement of British rule in Kumaon, comments upon the virtual absence of alcohol consumption in settled areas, stating that it was an activity confined to the lower classes, the Dums (1980: 213–214). Alcohol was, for the British, and is for the present day governments, a valuable source of revenue. Pathak considers alcoholism to be a 'means by which state commercialisation has sapped the vitality of hill soceity' (1985: 1360) and contributed to its social and cultural disintegration.
7. For example, Himachal Pradesh, with an area of approximately 55.7 thousand sq. km. and a population of 5 million, has 5 MPs and 68 MLAs; and Manipur, with 22.5 thousand sq. km. and a population of under two million, has 1 MP and 60 MLAs (*India Today* 30/9/94: 35).
8. For more on the environmental and economic profile of the region see Akhtar (1980), Valdiya (1988), Vidyarthi and Jha (1986), Swarup (1991), Singh (1983).
9. The representations of plains people society described here are those of high caste Kumaoni villagers.
10. Pahari women wear long-sleeve tops which also cover the woman's middle, allowing almost no flesh to be seen.

11. When considering the history of Kumaon, Leavitt says that Sanskritic Hinduism, supposedly brought to the hills from the plains, is found mainly in the towns. The plains settlers stayed in urban areas and have maintained contact with developments in the plains and practise a highly Sanskritized Hinduism. The countryside, on the other hand, has generally been inhabited by the indigenous hill people who worship local gods and have a less Sanskritized Hinduism. Leavitt states that 'Kumaonis still tend to equate the rural with the specifically regional and the urban with pan-Hindu civilisation' (1992: 24). Here again, though in the context of religious practices, the rural–*pahari* urban-*deshi* dominant society distinction is being made.
12. Wiser and Wiser report that plains villagers see those in the bazaars and towns as people waiting to cheat them of their precious money (1963: 124).
13. While the division of agricultural labour may, in men's opinion, contrast favourably (as more egalitarian and fair) with that in the plains, men do relatively little farm work and the main inequalities lie not among men or women or between castes, but between men and women.
14. Berreman alludes to this rich/poor–plains/hills opposition. Sirkanda villagers see city life as 'easy, entertaining, sinful, and expensive. For well-to-do plains people it is fine, but it is not suitable for poor paharis' (1972: 305).
15. Dum is a derogatory word, and has officially been replaced by Harijan or Shilpakar in daily public life.However, high caste villagers continue to use Dum to refer to the low caste.
16. The 1931 Indian census was the last to report data concerning caste in the region. It would seem that these figures have remained relatively constant, as the most recent district census of 1981 reports approximately 21 per cent of the population belonging to Scheduled Castes (Dums–Shilpakars).
17. Like Dum, Khasi and Khasiya are derogatory terms and are no longer used. People are now referred to as Brahmans or Thakurs.
18. The Dums do not correspond entirely or exactly to the Untouchables of the plains. This category includes artisans who practise trades and skills which in other parts of India are associated with Shudras. Most of the occupational groups found among plains Shudras and Untouchables are included in the category of Dum (see Berreman 1972: 201). A few, such as washermen and barbers, however, are not represented in Kumaon.
19. For details regarding the Arya Samaj movement and practices in Kumaon see Sanwal (1976: 75–6); Fanger (1980: 150–61); Sebring (1972). Sebring says that the Arya Samaj came to Kumaon in the 1930s. Many Dums then took on the name of Arya.
20. According to Upadhyay (1990: 50) Kumaon society can be divided into two categories, the Harijans and the non-Harijans.

21. Upadhyay explains that 'high caste people abhor the idea of low caste Harijans coming close to them, they are opposed to the idea of Harijan upliftment and disfavour the casteless society approach of the Government and social reformers'. (1990: 50). For more information on the kinds of government programmes and grants to assist Harijans in Kumaon, see Upadhyay (ibid. 199–249).
22. The state of Uttaranchal came into being on 9 November 2000.

References

Akhtar, R., 1980, *Environment, Agriculture and Nutrition in Kumaon Region*, Delhi: Marwah Publications.

Atkinson, E.T., 1973, *The Himalayan Gazetteer*, Delhi: Cosmo.

———, 1974, *Kumaon Hills: Its History, Geography and Anthropology with Reference to Garhwal and Nepal*, Delhi: Cosmo.

Berreman, G.D., 1962, *Behind Many Masks: Ethnography and Impression Management in a Himalayan Village*, Monograph 4, Ithaca, N.Y.: Society for Applied Anthropology.

———, 1970, 'Pahari Culture: Diversity and Change in the Lower Himalayas', in K. Ishwaran (ed.), *Change and Continuity in India's Villages*, New York: Columbia University Press.

———, 1972, *Hindus of the Himalayas: Ethnography and Change*, Berkeley: University of California Press.

———, 1983a, 'Identity Definition, Assertion and Politicization in the Central Himalayas', in A. Jacobson-Widding (ed.), *Identity: Personal and Socio-Cultural*, Uppsala: Almqvist and Wilksell.

———, 1983b, 'The U.P. Himalaya: Culture, Cultures, and Regionalism,' in O.P. Singh (ed.), *Himalaya: Nature, Man and Culture*. New Delhi: Rajesh Publications.

———, 1985, 'Internal colonialism and Fourth-world Movements in the Indian Himalayas', in J. Brosted (ed.), *Native Power: the Quest for Autonomy and Nationhood of Indigenous Peoples*, Oslo: Universitettsfirlaget.

Cohen, A.P., 1985, *The Symbolic Construction of Community*, Ellis Harwood Limited and Tavistock Publications.

Fanger, A.C., 1980, 'Diachronic and Synchronic Perspectives on Kumaoni Society and Culture', Ph.D. Thesis, Syracuse University.

Gaborieau, M., 1977, Introduction, in E.S. Oakley and T.D. Gairola (eds), *Himalayan Folklore: Kumaon and West Nepal*, Kathmandu: Ratna Pustak Bhandar.

Guha, Ramachandra, 1985, 'Forestry and Social Protest in British Kumaun, *c.* 1893–1921', in Ranajit Guha (ed.), *Subaltern Studies IV. Writings on South Asian History and Society*, Delhi: Oxford University Press.

———, 1989, *The Unquiet Woods: Ecological Change and Peasant Resistance in the Himalaya*, Delhi: Oxford University Press.

Kapur, T., 1988, *Religion and Ritual in Rural North India: A Case Study in Kumaon*, New Delhi: Abhinav.

Leavitt, J., 1992, 'Cultural Holism in the Anthropology of South Asia: The Challenge of Regional Traditions', *Contributions to Indian Sociology*. (N.S.) 26, 3–49.

Mittal, A.K., 1986, *British Administration in Kumaon Himalaya*, Delhi: Mittal Publications.

Mittal, A.K., 1990, 'Some Aspects of Economic History of Kumaon under the British rule', in M.P. Joshi, A.C. Fanger, C.W. Brown (eds), *Himalaya: Past and Present*, Almora: Shree Almora Book Depot.

Moller, J., 1993, 'Inside and Outside: Conceptual Continuities from Household to Region in Kumaon, North India'. Ph.D. Thesis, University of London.

————, *In press*, 'Symmetry and consanguinity in the Kinship System of Kumaon, North India', in M.P. Joshi, A.C. Fanger and C.W. Brown, (eds), *Himalaya: Past and Present Vol. IV*, Almora: Almora Book Depot.

Ortner, S.B., 1978, *Sherpas Through Their Rituals*, Cambridge: Cambridge University Press.

Pathak, S., 1985, 'Intoxication as a Social Evil: Anti-alcohol Movement in Uttarakhand, *Economic and Political Weekly*. 20, 1360–5.

Randhawa, M.S., 1970, *The Kumaon Himalayas*, New Delhi: Oxford and IBH.

Sanwal, R.D., 1976, *Social Stratification in Rural Kumaon*, Delhi: Oxford University Press.

Sebring, J.M., 1972, The Formation of New Castes: A Probable Case from North India', *American Anthropologist*. 74, 587–600.

Singh, O.P., 1983, 'The U.P. Himalaya: An Overview', in *The Himalaya: Nature, Man and Culture*, New Delhi: Rajesh Publications.

Swarup, R., 1991, *Agricultural Economy of Himalayan Region: with Special Reference to Kumaon*, Nainital: Gyanodaya Prakashan.

Traill, G.W., 1980 [1828], 'Statistical Sketch of Kumaon', *Asiatic Researches*. 16, 137–234.

Upadhyay, H.C., 1990, *Harijans of the Himalaya: with Special Reference to the Harijans of Kumaun Hills*, Nainital: Gyanodaya Prakashan.

Valdiya, K.S., 1988, *Kumaun Land and People*, Nainital: Gyandodaya Prakashan.

Vatuk, S., 1990, 'To be a Burden on Others: Dependency Anxiety among the Elderly in India, in O.M. Lynch (ed.), *Divine Passions: the Social Construction of Emotion in India*, Berkeley: University of California Press.

Vidyarthi, L.P., and Jha, M., 1986, *Ecology, Economy and Religion of Himalayas*, Delhi: Orient Publications.

Wiser, W.H. and Wiser, C.V., 1963, *Behind Mud Walls 1930–1960*, Berkeley and Los Angeles: University of California Press.

Comments

ANTJE LINKENBACH

In her very detailed and interesting paper Joanne Moller (JM) refers to an important political issue: the anti-reservation protest and the struggle for regional autonomy in the UP Himalayas (Garhwal and Kumaon), in which large parts of the local population have been actively involved since the middle of 1994. JM does not concentrate on the autonomy movement as such, she rather makes an attempt to uncover some of the basic motivations and feelings of the hill people which apparently have provoked their struggle. Arguing that the recent political events 'can only be fully understood in terms of hill peoples' constructions of self and other' she focuses on their discourse of identity.

JM identifies a basic binary concept along which the hill people construct their social world: the opposition between 'inside' and 'outside', 'insiders' and 'outsiders'. This conceptual opposition, according to JM, is replicated at different levels of society. Which persons, social categories and spaces are being identified as 'inside' or 'outside' depends on context and perspective. No matter which level of identification or which context is taken, 'inside' always represents the moral community, whereas 'outsiders' are seen as morally inferior, dishonest, greedy, shameless. The relation between 'insiders' and 'outsiders' is expressed in a rhetoric of hunger (the 'outsider' eats at the expenses of the 'insider') and also may be linked with an ideology of autonomy. In the context of her paper she only speaks about cases in which the 'insider'–'outsider' dichotomy is used to characterize the high caste Kumaoni construction of the relationship between the people from the hills (*pahari*) and the people from the plains (deshis) as well as their construction of the relation between high and low caste Kumaonis. The construction seems to JM to constitute the current political struggle.

The following reflections on JM's paper are based on my own field experiences in several districts of Garhwal and Kumaon, where I have worked on forest issues and social movements, including the autonomy movement, since 1993. To *limit* the construction of Kumaoni identity and Kumaoni social world to a single pattern, to the binary concept of 'inside' and 'outside'—mostly synonymous with the structural opposition of good and bad, superior and inferior—seems to me problematic. Although there definitely are cases in which such a way of thinking comes to the fore and under certain circumstances or among certain groups may even be dominant, I would propose a stronger sensibility for other ways of perception and other concepts which may also contribute to the construction of self and other in the UP hills. I want to elaborate my argument by mentioning three aspects.

The Research Sample: Demand for Greater Differentiation

Joanne Moller underlines that during her field research she had concentrated on high caste Kumaonis in Silora, a village near Almora. Additionally she had visited and worked with upper caste groups in the cities of Ranikhet, Almora, and Nainital. She is very much aware of the fact that her information is drawn, from specific status groups in a specific region, even though she uses the general term 'hill people' and suggests that her results may be valid for Garhwal as well. I think it would be more illuminating to try to work out differences in peoples' perception than to postulate similarities. (a) One should differentiate *between different high caste groups*. From my own experience it is obvious that Brahmins and Rajputs (Thakurs) in certain respects profess different views. In Garhwal it is especially the Rajputs who follow a discourse of autonomy and vehemently express their strong territorial claim; they complain that traditional rights have been denied to them by the state and its institutions. (b) One should differentiate *between age groups and between the sexes.* (c) The degree of *exposure to modern, translocal discourses* (through modern *education*, media, etc.) should be taken into consideration as well as peoples' *involvement in existing NGO work or in previous social movements* (Chipko movement, anti-alcohol movements). The last aspect seems to me of crucial significance in the context of identity formation and for the way people relate to the autonomy struggle and the future state. As I could observe, educated and socially active individuals (men as well as women) tend to develop a political identity as 'Uttarakhandis', i.e., as citizens of a future federal state, as part of a 'public' (*Öffentlichkeit*) which holds itself responsible for, and tries to participate in, the process of state building. (d) Especially in the context of the autonomy struggle, which is labelled by some extern observers as 'Brahmin movement' or 'upper caste movement' one should concentrate on the perspective of the Harijans as interesting to ask how for the Harijans see themselves as part of the hill community and how the plains people are perceived by them.

I also would hesitate to apply the findings of JM's research in Kumaon to Garhwal without further examination. At least one should differentiate between the region of the former princely state of Tehri Garhwal and the area east of the Alaknanda which belonged to the Kumaon division. Exploitation (forest, *begar*) was de facto done by 'outsiders' (the colonial power), whereas the people of Tehri Garhwal suffered at the hands of their local *raja*. The forms of resistance also differed (see Guha, *The Unquiet Woods*, 1989). If history and historical memory are claimed to be markers of identity, then different histories *may* imply differences in identity construction.

The Relations Between Hills and Plains People: Longstanding Processes of Interaction

According to JM's argument the relations between hill and plains people are merely instrumental —*Paharis* go to the plains to earn money—or are characterized by tension and conflict—*Paharis* react to the exploitation they have to suffer at the hands of the *deshis*. She also states that in historical as well as recent times contact between hill and plains people was established by the 'outsiders', i.e. by the colonial power and the national development policy. That means the integration process was imposed on the Kumaonis. This perspective suggests that the 'traditional' society was a 'closed' society and ignores processes of interaction. In my main research region (district Uttarkashi) people narrate of their long tradition of trade with Delhi. One of their main local gods was 'imported' from Delhi. Since a long time able-bodied men from Garhwal and Kumaon have been going to the military. Kumaonis took part in the national movement. Ideas of modernization, especially education, entered the hills and were eagerly adopted. The introduction to a book on the history of Kumaon (written by Badri Dutt Pande in 1933, transl. and repr. 1993) reflects the general tension between both the claim for regional identity and for national integration inherent in the nationalist project. Since the early sixties Gandhian activists have started welfare and development programmes in the UP hills and have helped to intensify exchange and interaction between plains and hill people.

Another interesting aspect would have been to find out how the plains people (the 'outsiders') perceive or construct the hill people. In JM's argument it seems that their perception is simply a reversal of the view of the hill people: for the plains people the *Paharis* are economically, morally and socially inferior. Even though that is true to a certain extent, in conversation and text another perspective shows up as well. Plains people often express admiration for the hills and for the hill people. Uttarakhand is seen as the cradle of Indian religious civilization; nature's beauty, purity and sanctity is often depicted in an emotional way. The hill villagers are characterized as a simple but comparatively well-off people, self-sufficient, honest, and peaceful. Especially honesty is still attributed to them and is highly valued. *Paharis* are preferred as servants, drivers and hotel personnel in the cities of the plains.

Representation of Self and Others: Ambivalences and Tension as Constitutive Elements

Instead of restricting the identity discourse of hill people, their representation of self and others, to a one-dimensional model, I would suggest we accept *ambivalences, tensions* and even *contradictions* in perception and thought. Just to give a few examples:

It seems to be true that many high caste villagers (men and women) appreciate their way of life and value their customs. But at the same time people tend to give up certain customs like bride-price marriage, polyandry and polygyny (still to be found in parts of western Garhwal). They call themselves 'backward' (*piche*, often also using the English term). They want to have their share of modern facilities and try to adapt to the mainstream to a certain extent.

JM underlines that to be poor is a positive self-description of the Kumaonis. But as I know from Garhwal, poverty is not necessarily positively valued,it is a rhetorical device to describe the marginalization and neglect that villagers experience from the state or the administration. Villagers are 'poor' not in the sense of lacking consumer goods or food, but in the sense that proper education, health care, participation, and 'development' is denied to them. 'Poor' is used in a similar way as 'backward'.

Migration to the cities of the plains may stem from economic needs (it may be 'instrumental') and the migrant may miss the experience of community, the security and brotherhood of the village. But at the same time it is highly prestigious to get a good job in the plains (or in the army) and to send sufficient money to the family in the village, to show off some consumer goods (like TV, cameras, etc).

JM says that women are proud of their freedom and mobility they enjoy in the village context. But some of them also see the limitations. They complain that lack of education and the 'traditional' gender roles do not allow them to transcend the village context, to move self-confidently in the outer world.

The lack of education is seen as the basic stigma of hill people and the greatest advancement of plains people. Nowadays upper and lower caste villagers try to secure education for their male as well as female offspring. They explain that only education opens up life opportunities and gives new options in and outside the world of the village. JM states that one of the basic elements of Kumaoni representation of self and others is the conceptual opposition of honesty and dishonesty. But exactly this concept seems to lose persuasiveness for the hill people. When I recently conducted interviews in villages of Garhwal and Kumaon I came across three different opinions: Many respondents still emphasized that hill people are honest, that crime and fraud is non-existent in the hill regions. But others stated that one cannot simply categorize *Paharis* as good and *Deshis* as bad, everywhere honest as well as dishonest people could be found. And a third category of respondents, some high caste Kumaonis from a village near Jageshwar, reported that since several years dishonesty and crime has spread in the hills as well. They accuse especially the younger generation and the migrants of having 'learned' bad habits from the plains people.

To sum up, in my opinion, the attempt to explain the search for an autonomous state Uttarakhand with ethnicistic arguments seems disputable. *Paharis* do not show a one-dimensional identity and their models of representation do not follow a single interpretative line. I think *Paharis*—if we use this general term—display both feelings of identification with and distanciation from the region and their ways of life. Additionally, any explanation of the motivational backgrounds of the struggle for autonomy has to take into consideration the recent history of the region which to a high extent was characterized by social movements and grassroot activism. Many people in Garhwal and Kumaon have developed a strong *political consciousness* and a feeling of *responsibility* for their region and themselves. *Paharis*—and here I agree with JM—recognize themselves as being dispossessed of their ability to decide about their own future (their region, their environment) and they want to be integrated into the nation on an equal footing, they want to take their future into their own hands.

References

Guha, Ramachandra, 1994/1989, *The Unquiet Woods: Ecological Change and Peasant Resistance in the Himalaya*, Delhi: Oxford University Press.

Pande, Badri Dutt, 1993, *History of Kumaon, 2 vols*, Almora: Shree Almora Book Depot.

The Art of Representation

Domesticating Ladakhi 'Identity'

MARTIJN VAN BEEK

On a rainy afternoon in September 1995 four horsemen stormed onto the pologround of Leh, headquarters of the district of the same name and capital of the former kingdom of Ladakh[1]. Thupstan Chhewang, Chief Executive Councillor, tied ceremonial scarves (*kha btagsl*) to the staffs adorned with prayer flags (*dar lcog*) presented by the horsemen. Turning their horses, the men rode off towards Namgyal Tsemo overlooking the city, where the flags would 'flutter spreading the message of truth, peace and prosperity'.[2] Freshly elected members of the Ladakh Autonomous Hill Development Council individually approached a small podium and were sworn into office in the presence of the governor of the state of Jammu and Kashmir. After short speeches by the Chief Executive Councillor and the Governor, troupes of dancers dressed in the different 'traditional' dresses of the officially recognized 'tribes' of Ladakh performed to entertain the large crowd of onlookers. In spite of the cold drizzle, the general mood was one of celebration and unity, as a decades long struggle had finally come to an end.

As the Governor, General K.V. Krishna Rao (retired), noted in his address to the first official meeting of the Hill Council, 'Ladakh has its unique culture and traditions.[3] The Indian government based its granting of a significant measure of regional autonomy to Ladakh on its 'distinct regional' identity.[4] Indeed, memoranda, posters, and slogans produced by Ladakh's political leaders since the 1930s had emphasized the need to preserve and protect Ladakh's 'unique identity', its plight increasingly attributed to discrimination suffered because of this difference from the rest of the State of Jammu and Kashmir and the nation as a whole. At the occasion of the swearing-in ceremony, then, this identity was marked, recognized, and celebrated.

Questions of Identification

In a recent article, William Roseberry suggests that we should understand ethnicity and other forms of association as 'language of community and contention' (1996: 71). Drawing on insights from poststructuralist and neo-Gramscian perspectives, he situates the production of 'a common material and meaningful framework for living through, talking about and acting upon social orders characterized by domination' (Roseberry 1996: 80) in a context of state projects and hegemonic processes. A similar emphasis on discursive frames and language is also present in the analysis of the social production of indifference and the poetics of nationhood offered by Michael Herzfeld (1992; 1996). Herzfeld suggests that we should understand nationhood as an elaborate metaphor, and the entirety of social interaction as rhetoric (Herzfeld 1996: 141). Following Anderson (1991), Herzfeld understands this rhetoric also to be expressed in images, and to involve processes of remembering and forgetting that make it possible for unity to be imagined. Roseberry and Herzfeld like so many others, emphasize the fictive character of the common ground that is imagined and constructed in these processes, while simultaneously emphasizing the materiality, the reality of the images, and the force of the emotions they can and often do elicit.

Although essentialist and primordialist approaches to the problem of identity continue to have some currency, particularly in political science, it would appear that the 'constructivist' understanding has emerged as the dominant one in anthropology. However, in his 'Report to the Academy', Taussig complains that social construction is taken too lightly, and that the 'literary turn in the social sciences and history has yielded naught else but more meta-commentary in place of poiesis, of making anew' (Taussig1993: xvii). I agree. Only too often, the 'invention of tradition', social constructionist approach produces elaborate historical analyses of how a certain 'identity' is created, maintained, or transformed without ever questioning the very concept, the meaning of 'identity'. Having accepted the constructedness of specific identities, the concept of 'identity' itself remaining reified, often serving as a new 'codeword' for concepts such as 'tradition' or 'culture' that are now viewed with suspicion (Handler 1996: 27). Too often, all we are offered is yet another discussion of elite manipulations in resource competition between groups who apparently have miraculously emerged out of nowhere (but have always existed).

The contemporary world, organized through the states system, is characterized by what Billig (1995: 73) calls a 'universal code of particularity' that constitutes national identity as a 'form life', a code that assumes an 'identity of identities'. The prevalence of the politics of identity and identity discourse testifies above all to the hegemony of modern ideas and institutions (Handler 1996: 38). It obscures the constitution of imagined identities in the first place as well as the conditions and processes that produce demands for representation, resource access and allocation. In short, the universal code of particularities, of identities, constitutes a fetishism of identities.[5] But how, then, should we understand the simultaneous reality and fictitiousness of 'identity'? In this essay, I will examine aspects of the production of Ladakhi 'identity' *not* to show how its 'it'-ness came to be, but to indicate some of the conditions for the possibility of its representation. These conditions include its compliance with the hegemonic discourse of identity, that forms the heart of the nation-state project, as well as that of science.

Here I will discuss how in the contestation between academics, state and local actors, over the 'true' characteristics of Ladakhi 'identity'— which must serve as the basis for the distribution of resources (political, economic, cultural) that in turn constitutes the *raison d'être* and basis of legitimacy of the developmentalist, democratic Indian state—representations of domesticated Ladakhi 'identity' are produced.[6] These representations, appearing as 'identities', are premised on abstraction, literalization and textualization, which demand an active/unconscious forgetting of their relative arbitrariness. Each identity, moreover, is represented as *the* authentic and real Ladakhi identity. These 'identities', like all 'identities', are neither real, nor really made-up, but somewhere in between, as Taussig (1993) suggests. If we want to understand the emergence, contents, and meanings of such concepts of Ladakhi 'identity' in political discourse, we must turn to an investigation of the culture of the state and its conception of identity, rather than the imputed links with practices of identification in Ladakh.[7] As Herzfeld (1992: 108) notes, 'cultural identity is the material of national rhetoric, social variation that of everyday experience'. What is at stake in these processes, then, is not 'identity', but representations, and the stability of the 'identities' is only apparent, a dissimulation dependent on a public secret possible through the complicity of representers and represented alike.

An Identity of One's Own

The granting of autonomy to Ladakh was warmly welcomed by the press and by politicians from the main political parties at the Centre. Already in the 1930s political leaders from Ladakh had been demanding special administrative arrangements, resources, and policies in recognition of the 'distinct identity' of the region (van Beek 1996; 1998a). At last everyone agreed, it seems, that the recognition of Ladakhis' demands was timely, necessary, and just. But what culture and identity should we consider in the case of Ladakh? 'Ladakhi', 'Indian', 'Tibetan Buddhist', 'Muslim/Balti'? The choice of any, all, or none can be considered and supported, and the list could be extended considerably by adding dimensions such as gender, age, kinship, location, occupation, class, sect, and 'clan'. To create a discourse about 'the Ladakhi', to paraphrase Taussig, 'is in fact to create and solidify what really needs analysis—namely that identity' (Taussig 1993: 137).

If there is any single characteristic of 'Ladakhi identity' or of 'Ladakhi culture', it is that it is irreducible. Ladakhiness does not exist as a stable or uniform set of characteristics, forms, idioms, or practice, and neither do any of the other 'identities'. Even the leaders of Ladakh's autonomy movement, which was firmly grounded in a communal strategy, offer different characterizations of Ladakhiness, if they can offer one at all. Yet, when one asks a person '*Nyerang Ladagspa inog?*' (Are you (a) Ladakhi?), there will generally be an unequivocal answer, offered unhesitatingly.

There is an interesting paradox here: the ambiguity of local practices of identification makes it possible for people to imagine their shared identity ('Ladakhi') in an unproblematic, even unreflected fashion. It is precisely the lack of narrowly defined characteristics and criteria of proper Ladakhiness that makes Ladakhiness possible in social practice: 'it' can exist, because it remains undefined, unmarked, uncircumscribed in any rigid sense, allowed to exist somewhere in between the real and the really madeup. Academic and official categorizations, by contrast, seek to identify and organize the characteristics of Ladakhiness once and for all. Science and bureaucracy insist on unambiguous order. This will to order leads to ambiguity, because such order cannot be found in the social practices of identification in Ladakh.[8] At the same time, their (scientists' and bureaucrats') frames of classification are normative to the extent that benefits, rights, and resources are allocated to those who fit the frame and the grammar of identification that organizes it. The justifications of demands offered by Ladakhi political activists in terms of Ladakhi 'identity' are therefore to be understood in the context of the normative frame of identification offered by the state.[9]

The tension between these different kinds of realities, which simultaneously share the same reality, needed to be domesticated in two senses. First, the multiplicity of 'identities' in Ladakh needed to be ordered, classified unambiguously. Scientists and bureaucrats set out to 'capture' the population once and for all according to their true identities. Several different 'essences' were suggested, none of which, however, could accommodate the diversity of local practices, so in 1989 the population was officially classified into eight tribes. Secondly, this illustrates how Ladakhi identity/-ies were domesticated through their 'Indianization' in accordance with colonial and post-colonial views of Indian society and polity.[10] This Indianization also produced representations with an essential and irreducible division of Muslims and Buddhists, with the latter deemed the more authentic Ladakhis. The fictitiousness of the official and officially non-religious tribal classification stands revealed in the Muslim-Buddhist-Christian antagonism of contemporary Ladakhi political discourse, although this communal antagonism similarly fails to capture the 'essential' fault lines of social identification in Ladakh.[11]

The tension between these different kinds of official/unofficial classifications is irresolvable. The granting of regional autonomy, officially in recognition of a unique Ladakhi 'identity', in fact required the shared imagining of a Ladakhiness that is not present in any official classifications of the population, nor in the communally charged rhetoric of the agitation for regional autonomy, but rather in that 'traditional', more fluid practice of identification. It is this 'identity', officially and politically impossible, which is celebrated and recognized in the granting of autonomy.

Ladakhi Identifications and the Culture of the Indian State

Although there are anthropological monographs on *The Ladakhi* (Mann 1986) and *Les Ladakhi du Cachemire* (Kaplanian 1981), one will generally look in vain for a category 'Ladakhi' in semi-official and official descriptions of the population of India (e.g. Singh 1994). Tourism promotion material, travel guides, and popular press articles on the region will celebrate Ladakh as a Buddhist region: Ladakhis are Buddhist. At the same time, close to fifty per cent of the population of Ladakh are Muslims, predominantly Shias. And the official list of Scheduled Tribes of Jammu and Kashmir identifies almost 90 per cent of the population of Ladakh as members of one of eight 'Scheduled Tribes', none of which is called Ladakhi.[12] Inspite of this official non-existence of Ladakhis, it is precisely such a common Ladakhi identity that is referred to in justifying local autonomy and in demands made by Ladakhi political leaders and activists.

People in Ladakh, like people everywhere, identify with different social groups and shift 'identities' frequently and often unreflectedly depending on their own and others' readings and expectations of their situation. They are, unsurprisingly, embedded in a series of often overlapping and/ or cross-cutting webs of belonging, which may be based on age, gender, kinship, occupation, or other dimensions of social life. Buddhism, for example, can serve as a shared reference for nearly half the population, but generally more important for daily religious practice are the sub-sect and monastic affiliation of the household, or the personal links with specific teachers and deities who may belong to different traditions.[13] Households, in many respects the most important social units in Ladakh, are commonly connected by different labour sharing arrangements, 'clan' affiliations and religious obligations, but these networks are not commonly congruent.[14] Regional antagonisms, traditional hierarchies, new money and political affiliations all conspire against singular identifications across Ladakh, although especially when travelling outside the region or interacting with outsiders people do identify and are indeed identified as Ladakhi.[15]

Development is the primary goal and basis of legitimacy of the post-colonial Indian state. The explicit mention of development, social justice and equity in the constitution of the republic as well as in the everyday rhetoric of politicians, media and the general public, illustrate the centrality of state intervention for the betterment of livelihoods of its citizenship.[16] This promise also means that government can be held accountable for its performance, or lack thereof, in these fields. Developmentalist government also serves to legitimize the collection and ordering of vast amounts of information on the population, and the construction of a complex series of institutions, officials, and practices of government to classify, allocate and manage 'society'. Such governmentality (Foucault 1991) cannot tolerate ambiguity, and hence the fluidity of identification that may exist in social practice needs to domesticated: they must be made singular and Indian. For the state, clear, unambiguous classification of Ladakh's population and the region as a whole are necessary in order to administer and develop the area. For Ladakh's political leaders, a distinct, unambiguously defined, singular Ladakhi 'identity' would serve to strengthen and justify the demands for autonomy, positive discrimination, and other benefits.

Searching Ladakhi 'Identity': Race, Tribe, Religion

The representations of Ladakhi identity, whether official, bureaucratic, elite, or popular, relied on the expert visions and images presented in the work of earlier administrators and scientists. Principal among these were the earliest encyclopaedic accounts of the region offered by British bureaucrats and scientists, whose formulations continue to be discernible in today's scholarly and official accounts. Especially the descriptions of Ladakh's population in Frederic Drew's *Jammu and Kashmir Territories* (Drew 1976 originally 1875), Cunningham's *Ladak* (1973), and Francke's *History of Western Tibet* (1978) have had a strong influence on perceptions and representations of the people of the region. Consistency was conspicuously absent, and concepts such as 'race', 'tribe' and 'community' were used rather indiscriminately. A.S. Singh (1912) for example, reports that this information is based on 'a gathering fully representing the *tribes* concerned', but proceeds with a discussion of the *races* of Ladakh, reflecting the influence of Drew, which is clearly visible in his list.

Such attempts at unambiguous classification were always plagued with difficulty, given the ambiguous social reality they were supposed to tame. As census operations in the State became more 'scientific', the problem was revealed in quite hilarious ways. The 1921 census, which allowed self-identification, produced almost 6000 castes and 28000 sub-caste names, and subsequently the list of possible choices was progressively limited until the recording of race/caste/class/community was discontinued in the spirit of national equality in 1947 (van Beek 1997a). In official texts on Ladakh other than the census, such as gazetteers, and semi-official publications such as Mann's *The Ladakhi*, such classifications of Ladakh's population into 'tribal' and other 'communities' continued to be proposed. Finally, confusion was officially ended through the recognition of the eight Scheduled Tribes of Ladakh, whose prior existence in any anthropologically meaningful sense would be unlikely to withstand scrutiny (van Beek 1997a). Nevertheless, the official Schedule Tribe (ST) certificate, which states the tribal identity of the holder, fixed people's identities at least on paper. But why not simply 'Ladakhis'?

In several of the most important classical sources, it is evident that behind the diversity of classifications, religion is deployed as the effective organizer.[17] Frequently the term Ladakhis is reserved for Buddhists, while Balti and Beda are treated as exclusively Muslim. Although in a somewhat modified from, this is common practice even today, as Mann's *The Ladakhi* shows. Mann distinguishes a larger number of 'ethnic groups', as he calls them, but maintains that Ladakhis are properly Buddhist (Mann 1986: 12)[18]. This preoccupation with religion as constituting the fundamental, irreducible principle of classification derives from British imaginings of India, rather than social practice in Ladakh. Religion, in British imagination and political practice was the irreducible essence of community identity, as the term communalism signifies.[19] Hence a single community (Ladakhis) adhering to two distinct religions was inconceivable. Ladakhis, therefore, had to be Buddhists, and Muslims had to be something else.

To ignore, downplay, or dismiss the Islamic element as 'foreign' was also in line with scholarly preoccupations with Ladakh as a surrogate for Tibet. Often referred to as western or Little Tibet, Ladakh was widely regarded and continues to be seen by many, as a sufficient substitute for the study of traditional Tibetan culture and religion as long as Tibet remained off-limits for Europeans.[20] Scholarly publications, also recent ones, generally reflect this 'Tibetocentricity' and rarely give adequate attention to Islam and its contribution to what people in Ladakh themselves commonly regard as a hybrid culture.[21]

Indian Fragments

When the Praja Sabha, Kashmir's legislative assembly, was created in 1934, religious community became the basis of representation.[22] In accordance with this communal logic, Ladakhi political activists, aided and informed by neo-Buddhist Kashmiri Pandits and other outsiders, quickly learned to formulate their demands in terms of religious community.[23] Regardless of whether unambiguous communities on the basis of religion existed on the ground in Ladakh, religious identity became a central theme in political strategies of Ladakhis, especially—and violently—during the agitation of 1989–92.[24] This campaign, which aimed to 'Free Ladakh from Kashmir' was led by the Ladakh Buddhist Association (LBA) and involved a three-year social boycott of Muslims, banning all types of interaction between the 'communities'.[25]

The communal agitation entailed a strong emphasis on Buddhism as Ladakh's sole authentic 'identity' and culture. Efforts were made to mark Buddhist and Muslim spaces, structures, speech and bodies unambiguously. Buddhist youths, who formed the vigilante groups who enforced the boycott on the public, adopted the earring once worn by Buddhist nobles; signs in the Tibetan script, previously practically absent from Leh's public spaces, were put up to identify shops not owned by Muslims; and on religious holidays, loudspeakers on the main temple in Leh rang with the tape-recorded recitations of monks.[26]

Many observers, including academics, were quick to read the Buddhist agitation as the spontaneous uprising of the Ladakhis against the discriminatory policies of the Muslim dominated state government. The history and actual practices of the agitation resist such easy domestication. The demand for autonomy had been raised repeatedly over the past sixty years and generally *not* in religious partisan ways, but through all Ladakh idioms. Also, the Buddhist 'community' is deeply divided along class, religional, political ideological, and sectarian lines. Similarly, it is impossible to identify a homogenous Muslim community in the complex social and political realities on the ground. Moreover, the mobilization of Buddhists and Muslims in the course of the agitation was a difficult and long process, and never could be maintained except for short period and through the use of incentives including threats and actual physical punishment.[27] The unity of Ladakh's Buddhists, then, existed mostly as a representation, a claim and performance, and the 'identity' it supposedly reflected and constituted was of that elusive character in between the real and the really made-up.

The imposition and adoption of communal frames of identification and representation by politicians, bureaucrats, academics, and activists in Ladakh signals the second aspect of the domestication of Ladakhi identity. Communalism gave birth to partition, and hence was an indissoluble part of the 'identity' of the Indian state, even if India explicitly defines itself as a secular state. Rightly or not, the common perception of many people in India, and certainly of many Buddhists in Ladakh, is that the system is in fact communal and the politics must be carried on through communal idioms. Especially in the wake of the destruction of the Babri Masjid in Ayodhya and the rise of the Hindu nationalists, Muslims are easily marked as foreign and the other. Political leaders of Ladakh, part of a Muslim majority state that has been the scene of severe secessionist violence for the past eight years, have chosen to join India and will stay with it. Buddhism, as an 'indigenous' religion—a mere sect of Hinduism according to some—is easily seen as an appropriate, proper identity for Ladakh as part of India.

During the 1989 agitation, the LBA sought and found support from the Hindu nationalist BJP and VHP. More recently, a Ladakhi unit of the BJP has been established.[28] On 25–26 August 1998, a two-day 'cultural event', Sindhu Darshan Abhiyan, organized by the RSS, was to be held at Leh, celebrating the Indus river as a symbol of national integration. The presence of the Home Minister, L.K. Advani, Defence Minister George Fernandes, and CM Farooq Abdullah along with other dignitaries served to underline the importance of the event. The programme included the 'unfurling of the national flag and felicitation of the highest ranking military officer in Ladakh'. *Indian Express* further quoted one of the organizers of the event explaining the purpose of the event by writing that 'Ladakhis often feel a sense of isolation because very few people visit the area. Sindhu, stands for communal harmony and peaceful coexistence'.[29] Thus, Ladakh was further tied into the symbolic space of Hindutva, and placed on the map of *national Hindu pilgrimages*.

Conclusion

I have sought to illustrate briefly the complicity of different (kinds of) actors in the production of a web of silences and articulations, of challenges and concessions, of invitations and exclusions, to illustrate the processes of domestication of Ladakhi identity that preceded the installation of a Ladakh Autonomous Hill Development Council on 9 September 1995. Marked by great fanfare and tumult, that fleeting moment of stillness, standing out from the everyday chaos of contested claims,demands, identifications and representations, derived its significance for the duly elected representatives of the 'brave people of Ladakh' simultaneously from its singularity *and* its familiarity as part of the series of secular rituals of liberation and independence.[30] Governor Krishna Rao, addressing the first meeting of the Ladakh Autonomous Hill Development Council, acknowledged the existence of Islam, and explicity stated that 'Our country is a tapestry of different cultures, customs and traditions. . . . This land [Ladakh] has been blessed by the confluence of two of the greatest religions of the world. May this glorious intermingling of cultures be strengthened'.[31] This is the formal discourse of 'unity in diversity' which is so difficult to accommodate in a system of bureaucratic management and political practice that relies on singular, straightforward categories. For the representatives of the Indian nation-state, then, the ceremony reaffirmed the nation's viability and practical pluralism. Ladakh and the people of Ladakh were now, finally, domesticated as reassuringly familiar *Indian* fragments of the nation. Events such as the Sindhu Darshan Abhiyan, as also the increasing use of Ladakhi themes in advertising on national television, serve to strengthen and affirm its normality as an *Indian* region.

Communalism is publicly deplored and generally regarded as the source of all evil and a most serious threat to the survival of the nation. Ladakh's Buddhist 'identity', therefore, could not be officially recognized, and certainly could not be made the basis for political representation and empowerment. Yet, in the contestation over the allocation of political, economic, and other resources, state actors, academics, and local activists in Ladakh represent their demands and justification in terms of the hegemonic discourse of the Indian state. Since difference—cultural, economic, climatic—warrants special attention, measures, and privileges, the art of representation consists in finding a way of balancing the irreducible complexity and multiplicity, the tensions and contradictions of local identifications, and practices of belonging, with the expectations and demands for an unambiguous singular collective identity of the state and the academics and other experts it relies on. The stability or persistence of certain kinds of 'identities'—for example 'religious identity' through the erasure of Muslims from many academic, official, and popular understandings of Ladakhi identity—is evanescent in that it is premised on an acceptance of a representation of Ladakhiness that is convincing not by virtue of its 'reality' or 'deep' rootedness' in Ladakhi culture, but by its correspondence with the excepted (cultural) forms of singular identities that are characteristic of the hegemonic discourse of identity and difference in its Indian form.[32]

The composition and structure of the Hill Council reflects the simultaneous and contradictory operation of several principles of social and official identification. For example, people are elected to represent different constituencies, which are geographically defined. In drawing the boundaries of constituencies, religious, political ideological, and economic considerations have all played a role, to prevent domination by the urban centres and to ensure representation of at least some Muslims.[33] In addition, the governor appoints four members to represent 'principal minorities', i.e. Muslims, women, and a representative for 'backward classes'. The attempt at accommodating these different kinds of 'identities' illustrates the impossibility of complete domestication, of matching bureaucratic and scientific rigour with (other) everyday social realities.

Ladakh's 'unique identity', celebrated on the pologround and referred to time and again in academic, bureaucratic, and political texts, is not an 'identity' in any formal sense. It does not constitute a homogenous, singular, unambiguously defined and bounded entity. As the rapid fragmentation of the precarious unity displayed at the first meeting of the Hill Council illustrates, there is little unity to be found beyond the metaphors. Ladakh 'identity' was not, is not, and cannot be just or really Buddhist; neither is it just or really a series of tribal communities. Its ambiguity, multiplicity, and fluidity is irreducible. At the same time the represented identities of Ladakh are a necessary 'fiction', since only through the imagining of such order, its 'proper' identification and representation, can the state recognize Ladakhi existence, manage and perhaps empower local actors.

Notes

1. In accordance with the instructions of the editors of this volume, this is an only lightly edited version of a draft read at the workshop, and consequently should be considered as a working paper. It draws on ongoing research conducted in Ladakh since 1985. Research was supported in 1994–95 by a Peace Scholar Award from the United States Institute of Peace. Additional funding was generously provided by the Peace Studies Program, International Political Economy Program, and South Asia Program, all at Cornell University. Opinions expressed in this paper are mine and do not reflect those of funders.

2. Address by General K.V. Krishna Rao, PVSM (Retd.), His Excellency the Governor of Jammu and Kashmir State of Ladakh Autonomous Hill Development Council, Leh, on 3 September 1995', paragraph 8.
3. The Ladakh Autonomous Hill Development Council Act 1995: The Gazette of India, New Delhi, pp. 1–18. The quote is from the 'Reasons for Enactment' accompanying the Act.
4. *Locus Classicus* for the invention of tradition debate is Hobsbawm and Ranger (1983).
5. This draws on Taussig (1980:30–1), elaborating the classic formulation by Marx in volume one of *Capital* on the fetishism of commodities. For a more elaborate discussion of the theoretical argument put forward here, see my dissertation (van Beek 1996) and van Beek (2000).
6. The 'state' is here not understood as a monolithic, disembodied entity, but as a peopled, and hence relatively unstable, contradictory, and incomplete process. My understanding of the state is informed especially by the work of Jessop (1990) and the writings of Herzfeld (1987; 1992; 1996).
7. Ashis Nandy (1990) calls this an 'imperialism of categories'.
8. As Derek Gregory (1994) notes, 'The will to order is a lack of experience'. p. 69.
9. This is not to suggest that scientists and bureaucrats unilaterally construct representations of Ladakhi identity/-ies out of thin air. They also draw on local practices, and local actors are implicated in the same process of production of representation of singular identities. It should also be noted that there is no simple, determining influence on local everyday practices of identification.
10. See Inden (1990); Pandey (1990); Appadurai (1993).
11. Necessarily, the term 'Ladakhi' is used here without offering an unambiguous definition of the concept, but may be understood in a loose cultural-geographical sense. The use of the term here reflects local practice, whose 'unscientific' ambiguity is essential.
12. They are: Bhalti, Beda, Bot/Boto, Balti, Brokpa/Drokpa/ Dard/Shin, Changpa, Garra, Mon, and Purigpa. See van Beek (1997b) for a detailed discussion.
13. Muslims similarly identify with different religious traditions, such as Sunni, Shia, and Nurbakshia, and among Shias people follow different Aghas. There is no Muslim community in any simple sense, more than there is a Buddhist 'community' in Ladakh. Yet, in both traditions the principle of such a community is recognized and emphasized. This illustrates that the tension between lived practice and official discourse is not merely a modern one.
14. On levels of integrations into different forms of 'community' in Ladakh see Srinivas (1997; 1998). For discussions of the household and

cooperation, see also Dollfus (1989), Gutschow (1998, especially ch. 2) and Phylactou (1989).

15. The recognition and importance of regional provenance is illustrated by the fact that the large monastic university Tashilhunpo in Shigatse had a separate 'residence' for monks from Ladakh.
16. See Akhil Gupta's excellent discussion of 'postcolonial developments' (Gupta 1998) for a thorough analysis of the developmentalism of the Indian state.
17. See e.g. Drew (Drew 1976/1875), Singh's 'Code of Tribal Custom', Ramsay's *Practical Dictionary* (1890), census reports, and the Gazetteer of 1890 (1974).
18. In a more recent paper, Mann continues this practice. Here he categorically states: 'In Ladakh, Ladakhis are the dominant group. They are all Buddhist' (1993).
19. On the British perception of religious community in India, see Pandey (1990) and Inden (1990).
20. This unambiguous equation of Ladakh with (Buddhist) Tibet became in fact more common in the twentieth century, illustrated for example by the fact that earlier the term 'Little Tibet' was more commonly applied to Baltistan, inspite of the obvious predominance of Islam in that region.
21. See Aggarwal (1994: 1997) for a discussion of this issue. More recently, anthropologists and sociologists working in Ladakh have begun to pay more attention to Islam. Examples include the work of Dollfus (1995), Grist (1993; 1995), and Srinivas (1995; 1997). See also (Henry 1997) and van Beek (1998b).
22. See e.g. Lamb (1993: 92) for a discussion of these events.
23. For a detailed discussion of the role of neo-Buddhists,see Bertelsen (1997).
24. See also Bray (1991). Srinivas (1991; 1993) offers first-hand and insightful reporting.
25. See van Beek (1996) for a more comprehensive discussion of this process. Srinivas (1998) suggests that the boycott lasted only for two years, but this mistakes the *promise* made by LBA leadership in 1991 to end the boycott for the actual end. The boycott was only lifted at the end of 1992 as part of agreement between Buddhist and Muslim leaders. From then on, a 'Coordination Committee' including a representative of the small Christian community, negotiated with Central and State authorities towards the autonomous council solution.
26. In 1995 this practice escalated into a competition between the muezzin of the Leh Sunni mosque and the tape monks of the Chokhang, just across the street from one another. Whenever the Muslims were called to prayer, the sound of the monks rang out as well. As a Buddhist activist joked, 'Now Buddhists are also called to prayer five times a day'.

This still continued in the spring of 1998, despite much popular resentment.

27. I have argued these points extensively in my dissertation (1996). Some of the main points are summarized in van Beek and Bertelsen (1995; 1997).
28. The BJP fielded a local candidate, Spalzis Angmo, for the Lok Sabha elections of June 1998. Her success in garnering more than 8000 votes contributed to the stunning defeat of P. Namgyal (Congress I) by the Kashmir National Conference candidate, Aga Syed Hussain from Kargil.
29. Quotes from *The Indian Express*, 22 August 1998.
30. On seriality and its importance for imagining communities, see Anderson (1991), especially chapter 10, and his recent elaboration (1998).
31. Earlier, he only refers to Buddhism as Ladakh's 'unique cultural heritage' and even quotes the Buddha.
32. This 'imperialism of categories' (Nandy 1990: 69) constitutes the essence of colonization, as Comaroff and Comaroff suggest (1991: 19). This colonization is an expression of 'governmentality', rather than of colonialism per se (Foucault 1991). I disagree with the Comaroffs, however, when they argue that this kind of process turns the colonized others into 'pliant objects and silenced subjects of our scripts and scenarios'. Rather, the colonized other are themselves actively involved in the process of 'conceptualizing, inscribing and interacting'.
33. This was emphasized in 1995 by several of the people involved in the process of implementing the Hill Council Act on the ground in Leh.

References

________, 1974, *Gazetteer of Kashmir and Ladakh,* Delhi: Vikas Publications.

Aggarwal Ravina, 1994, 'From Mixed Strains of Barley Grain: Person and Place in a Ladakhi Village, Ph.D. dissertation. Indiana University.

________, 1997, 'From Utopia to Heterotopia: Towards an Anthropology of Ladakh', *in Recent Research on Ladakh* 6, Proceedings of the Sixth International Colloquia on Ladakh. Leh, 1993, H. Osmaston and Nawang Tsering (eds) pp. 21–28. Bristol: Bristol University.

Anderson, Benedict R.O'G., 1991, *Imagined Communities: Reflections on the Origin and Spread of Nationalism,* London: Verso.

________, 1998, 'Nationalism, Identity, and the Logic of Seriality', *in The Spectre of Comparisons: Nationalism Southeast Asia and the World*, pp. 29–45. London: Verso.

Appadurai, Arjun, 1993, 'Number in the Colonial Imagination' in Carol Breckenridge and Peter van der Veer (eds), *Orientalism and the Postcolonial Predicament*, Philadelphia: University of Pennsylvania Press.

van Beek, Martijn, 1996, 'Identity Fetishism and the Art of Representation: the Long Struggle for Regional Autonomy in Ladakh', Ph.D. dissertation, Cornell University.

———, 1997a, Contested Classifications of People in Ladakh: An Analysis of the Census of Kashmir, 1873–1941, in H. Krasser, M.T. Much, E. Steinkellner, and H. Tauscher (eds) *Tibetan Studies*, Proceedings of the Seventh Seminar of the International Association for Tibetan Studies, Graz 1995. Vol. 1, pp. 35–49. Beiträge zur Kultur-und Geistesgeschichte Asiens, Nr. 21. Graz.

———, 1997b, 'The Importance of Being Tribal, or: the Impossibility of Being Ladakhis', in T. Dodin and H. Räther (eds) *Recent Research on Ladakh 7,* Proceedings of the Seventh Colloquium of the International Association for Ladakh Studies held at Bonn/St. Augustin, 12–15 June 1995, pp. 21–41. UKAS: Ulmer Kulturanthropologische Schriften, Band 9. Ulm: Universität Ulm.

———, 1998a, 'True Patriots: Justifying Autonomy for Ladakh', *Himalayan Research Bulletin* 18(1): 35–45.

———, 1998b, World Apart: Autobiographies of Two Ladakhi Caravaneers Compared', *Focaal* 32:51–69.

———, 2000, Dissimulation: Representing Ladakhi 'Identity', in H. Driessen and T. Otto (eds) *Perplexities of Identification: Anthropological Studies in Cultural Differentiation and the Use of Resources,* Aarhus: Aarhus University Press: pp. 161–84.

van Beek, Martijn, and Kristoffer Brix Bertelsen, 1995, 'Ladakh: "Independence" Is Not Enough', in *Himal.* Vol. 8, pp. 7–15.

———, 1997, No Present without Past: The 1989 Agitation in Ladakh, in T. Dodin and H. Räther (eds) *Recent Research on Ladakh 7,* Proceedings of the Seventh Colloquium of the International Association for Ladakh Studies held at Bonn/St. Augustin, 12–15 June 1995, pp. 43–65. UKAS: Ulmer Kulturanthropologische Schriften, Band 9, Ulm: Universität Ulm.

Bertelsen, Kristoffer Brix, 1997, 'Protestant Buddhism and Social Identification in Ladakh', *Archives de Sciences sociales des Religions* 99 (Juillet-Septembre): 129–51.

Billig, Michael, 1995, *Banal Nationalism*. London: Sage Publications.

Bray, John, 1991, 'Ladakhi History and Indian Nationhood', *South Asia Research* 11(2): 115–33.

Comaroff, John, and Jean Comaroff, 1991, *Of Revelation and Revolution: Christianity, Colonialism, and Consciousness in South Africa,* Chicago: Chicago University Press.

Cunningham, Alexander, 1973, *Ladak, Physical, Statistical and Historical,* Delhi: Sagar Publications.

Dollfus, Pascale, 1989, *Lieu de Neige et de Genévriers: Organisation Sociale*

et Religieuse des Communautés Bouddhistes du Ladakh, Paris: Centre National de la Recherche Scientifique.
Dollfus, Pascale, 1995, 'The History of Muslims in Central Ladakh', *The Tibet Journal* 20 (3): 35–58.
Drew, Frederic, 1976 [1875], *The Jummoo and Kashmir Territories,* New Delhi: Cosmo Publications.
Foucault, Michel, 1991, 'Governmentality', in G. Burchell, C. Gordon, and P. Miller (eds) *The Foucault Effect: Studies in Governmentality,* pp. 87–104, London: Harvester Wheatsheaf.
Francke, August Hermann, 1978, *Ladakh the Mysterious,* New Delhi: Cosmo Publications.
Government of India, 1995, 'The Ladakh Autonomous Hill Development Council Act 1995', in *The Gazette of India,* New Delhi, 9 May 195, 1–18.
Gregory, Derek, 1994, *Geographical Imaginations,* Oxford: Basil Blackwell.
Grist, Nicola, 1993, 'Muslim Kinship and Marriage in Ladakh', in C. Ramble and M. Brauen (eds) *Anthropology of Tibet and the Himalaya,* pp. 80–92. Zürich: Ethnological Museum of the University of Zürich.
________, 1995, Muslims in Western Ladak, in *The Tibet Journal* 20 (3): 59–70.
Gupta, Akhil, 1998, *Postcolonial Developments,* Durham, NC: Duke University Press.
Gutschow, Kim Irmgard, 1998, 'An Economy of Merit: Women and Buddhist Monasticism in Zangskar, Northwest India', Ph.D. dissertation, Department of Anthropology, Harvard University, Cambridge, MA.
Handler, Richard, 1996, 'Is 'Identity' a Useful Cross-Cultural Concept?', in J.R. Gillis, (ed) *Commemorations: The Politics of National Identity,* pp. 27–40. Princeton, NJ: Princeton University Press.
Henry, Gray, 1997, *Islam in Tibet and the Illustrated Narrative Tibetan Caravans,* pp. 311. Louisville, KY: Fons Vitae.
Herzfeld, Michael, 1987, *Anthropology Through the Looking Glass,* Cambridge: Cambridge University Press.
________, 1992, *The Social Production of Indifference: Exploring the Symbolic Roots of Western Bureaucracy,* Chicago: University of Chicago Press.
________, 1996, *Cultural Intimacy: Social Poetics in the Nation-state,* London: Routledge.
Hobsbawn, Eric J., and Terence Ranger, 1983, *The Invention of Tradition,* Cambridge: Cambridge University Press.
Inden, Ronald, 1990, *Imagining India,* Cambridge MA and Oxford: Basil Blackwell.
Jessop, Bob, 1993, *Kashmir: A Disputed Legacy 1846–1990,* Lahore: Oxford University Press.
Kaplanian, Patrick, 1981, *Les Ladakhi du Cachemire,* Paris: Hachette.

Mann, R.S.,, 1986, 'The Ladakhis: A Cultural Ecological Perspective', in L. P. Vidyathi and M. Jha (eds) *Ecology, Economy and Religion of the Himalayas*, pp. 3–16. Delhi: Orient Publications.

________, 1993, 'Some Theoretical Concerns of Ethnicity in the Ladakhi Situation', in K.S. Singh (ed.) *Ethnicity, Caste and People, Proceedings of Indo-Soviet Seminars*, New Delhi, 1993, pp. 121–31.

Nandy, Ashis, 1990, 'The Politics of Secularism and the Recovery of Religious Tolerance', in Veena Das (ed) *Communities, Riots and Survivors in South Asia*, pp. 69–93, Delhi: Oxford University Press.

Pandey, Gyanendra, 1990, *The Colonial Construction of Communalism in Colonial North India*, Delhi: Oxford University Press.

Phylactou, Maria, 1989, 'Household Organisation and Marriage in Ladakh, Indian Himalaya', Ph.D. dissertation, University of London.

Ramsay, H., 1890, *Western Tibet: A Practical Dictionary of the Language and Customs of the Districts Included in the Ladakh Wazarat*, Lahore: W. Ball.

Roseberry, William, 1996, Hegemony, Power, and Languages of Contention, in E.N. Wilmsen and P. McAllister (eds) *The Politics of Difference: Ethnic Premises in a World of Power*, pp. 71–84, Chicago and London: University of Chicago Press.

Singh, K.S., 1994, *People of India: The Scheduled Tribes*, Delhi: OUP.

Singh, Thakar, 1912, *Code of Tribal Custom in the Ladakh Tahsil, Jammu and Kashmir State*, Allahabad: The Pioneer Press.

Srinivas, Smriti, 1991, 'The Lost Horizon: Trouble in a Strategic Spot', in *Frontline*, pp. 81–7.

________, 1993, 'Hope on the Horizon', in *Frontline*, pp. 52–5.

________, 1995, Conjunction, Parallelism and Cross-Cutting Ties Among the Muslims of Ladakh, in *The Tibet Journal* 20 (3): 71–95.

________, 1997, 'The Household, Integration and Exchange: Buddhists and Muslims in the Nubra Valley', in H. Osmaston and Nawang Tsering, (eds) *Recent Research on Ladakh 6*, Proceedings of the Sixth International Colloquium on Ladakh, Leh 1993, pp. 251–80, Bristol: Bristol University.

________, 1998, *The Mouths of People, the Voice of God: Buddhists and Muslims in a Frontier Community of Ladakh*, Delhi: Oxford University Press.

Taussig, Michael, 1980, *The Devil and Commodity Fetishism in Latin America*, Chicago: Chicago University Press.

________, 1993, *Mimesis and Alterity: A Particular History of the Senses*, London: Routledge.

Comments

PASCALE DOLLFUS

In his paper, van Beek has chosen to examine, 'the production of Ladakhi "identity" and the conditions for the possibility of its representation'. He clearly points out that there is not a single Ladakhi identity, but a multiplicity of identities and differences. And, that each identity, moreover, is represented as *the* authentic Ladakhi identity. On that point he agrees with Martin Sökefeld when he says that identity does not exist in the singular, but only in the plural, as *identities*.

As the author further emphasizes, '"Ladakhiness" does not exist as a stable or uniform set of characteristics, forms, idioms or practices'. It is a fluid and unbounded entity varying according to a given context. Or, in other words, Ladakhi identity does not refer to an objective well-defined ethnic group. It exists primarily as a concept. I agree. Ethnonyms, common myths, which prevail among the Nepalese ethnic groups, are almost absent in Ladakh. The term Ladakhi or Ladakh-pa only means people of Ladakh, 'a dwelling amidst high mountain passes'. Its borders are not even clear for the local 'nationalists'. As Bray[1] pointed out, there is no unifying sense of Ladakhi 'national identity'. 'Ladakh farmers may have identified with their village, their valley or perhaps their monastery but not with the region as a whole'.

People in Ladakh, like people in the Gilgit area[2] and elsewhere, shift identities frequently within the dimensions of religion, locality, language, kinship or political affiliation. For example, during the 1989 agitation 'to free Ladakh from Kashmir's rule', led by the Ladakhi Buddhist Association against the Muslims, Buddhist activists simply denied their 'Ladakhiness' to the Sunni Muslims of Leh, the political, administrative and economic centre of Ladakh. They stigmatized them as *phyi pa,* 'foreigners' or 'outsiders' in contrast with *nang pa* 'insiders', designating usually those who follow the

Dharma. In broad terms, Ladakhi Buddhists like to think of themselves as the only *real* Ladakhis, the only *rightful* inhabitants of Ladakh. Within this framework, to be both Muslim (or Christian) and Ladakhi was no longer possible.

I would not here dispute the possibility of western influence in the conflict between Buddhists and Muslims along communal lines, from the first missionaries, through British agents, down to modern writers of travel guides, as in the statement 'In Ladakh, Ladakhis are the dominant group. They are all Buddhists'. At the same time, I would not deny that, until recently, much of the studies and analyses of Ladakhi society and culture has been done from a Tibetan or Buddhist frame.

I only want to examine the way people show themselves in everyday discourse, strategies, and practices.[3] In this specific case, in order to express their difference, the Ladakh Buddhist Association (LBA) activists, followed by a large part of Buddhist population, started to employ visible signs. They put a Buddhist flag (but not a Ladakhi flag) on the roof of their houses among prayer flags. They gave up jackets and pants for the traditional Ladakhi *gonchas.* The young wore the earrings once worn by Buddhist noblemen. In the streets, the Tibetan script suddenly appeared on the signs of shops, not owned by Muslims (but possibly by Hindus or Sikhs). Even this summer, six years after the end of the three year social boycott imposed on the whole Muslim community, the LBA still refused access to the Dalai-Lama's teachings to anyone who was not dressed in the local 'traditional' garments. Ironically, for the young women and girls at least, it took the form of the Tibetan-style sleeveless robe. Besides the appearance or flags, stickers and badges in the Buddhist colours or garments, there is evidence of a revival of orthodox Buddhist practices and religious sentiment (or at least its outward expression). Although apotropaïc practices are beginning to disappear, such as those consisting of protecting a newly constructed house from the evil eye and demonic attacks by painting protective designs, and the adjunction of protective elements (wooden penis for instance). Other practices reappear, particularly among the youth, such as the circumambulation of the holy sites and completely prostrating the body; the collective recitation of canonical texts; or fasting during the first Tibetan month. But, paradoxically the LBA leaders knew perfectly well that the practice of Tibetan Buddhism cannot separate them from their neighbours. Moreover, they refused to be associated with the Tibetan refugees living in Ladakh Leh district. Finally the use of social and economic boycotts is hard to reconcile with the teachings of Gautama Buddha.

Muslim leaders responded to the denial of their Ladakhiness with a booklet written in English.[4] In this booklet, they referred to history books written by European scholars to confirm their Ladakhi identity, being in Ladakh at least since the sixteenth century. But, to my knowledge, they did not use any visible signs to process their 'Ladakhiness'. In fact, in the case of Muslims, to express their own local traditions without contradicting orthodox Islamic practice or, on the other hand, being viewed as allies of their co-religionists in Kashmir and Pakistan, is a hazardous challenge. It would have been useful to know more about Muslims' own representation of themselves and their representation of the Buddhists—as far as we can speak about a Buddhist or a Muslim community.

The fact is that dislike goes back a long time in the Sunni–Shia history. As late Akbar Ladakhi, the former president of the Ladakh Muslim Association (LMA) used to say: 'When there is a Buddhist–Muslim conflict the two groups come together. Otherwise they also fight!' A view shared, on the other hand, by Shia residents interviewed by Pinault[5] who thus explained, 'The Sunnis want to make a statement to the Buddhists: "*ham musulman log sab eik hein*" "we Muslim, folk are all one". But that's not the way things really are. The Sunnis don't really like us'. They asserted that Sunnis used to make fun of their Muharram self-mortification practices and throw stones at the procession commemorating the battlefield death of the Imam Husain, the Prophet Muhammad's grandson.

With the end of the boycott directed by the LBA against the Muslims and the granting to this district the Ladakh Autonomous Hill Council, a status which gave it greater independence from the state of Jammu and Kashmir (J and K), the political context has changed. In this new context, which criteria have the people of Ladakh (and not only its elite) chosen to highlight to show their shared (Ladakhi) identity? Which distinctive markers do they use to separate themselves from others? And how are others defined? How is this distinctiveness, this uniqueness, stressed in the discourse of both the political leaders of Ladakh and the Governor of the state of J and K recognized by the others?

van Beek has shown here, 'Ladakhis do not exist' or to paraphrase Adams they are only virtual Ladakhis. According to his analysis, Ladakhi identity is a necessary fiction,which is constructed from time to time to serve concrete actions, not only political ones. In other respects, throughout his paper, there is a parallel between Ladakhi identity and Ladakhi culture. Does this mean that the Ladakhi culture is also a fiction, even with material presence? It would be worthwhile to elaborate on this and on 'identity fetishism'. It would also be useful to understand, from van Beek's point of view, what we should look for if we want to understand how the Ladakhis—or the Ladakh-pa as they call themselves—traditionally see themselves and how they view their place in the order of things and vis-à-vis other groups.

However, as the author stated, Ladakh's political leaders based their claim for a special status arguing that the Indian government based its granting of the 'Ladakh Autonomous Hill Council on its distinct regional identity'. Every year, since the creation of the Leh Cultural Academy in 1969, native scholars have published several volumes of folksongs, folktales, local history and customs to preserve what they themselves called Ladakhi culture.[6] But, those publications do not have a wide audience. In fact, for various reasons (spelling difficulties, lack of clear guidelines in schools, usefulness in Indian administration and daily practices, etc.) a large proportion of Ladakhis—both Buddhist and Muslims—can read or write Urdu or English, but are illiterate in their own language.

Do the people of Ladakh consider themselves as a single group? How do they view themselves? In the absence of a common religion, a regional mythical hero or a clearly bounded territory, which criterion has the local population—or at least its elite—chosen to highlight? In theory, one basis of such a shared identity might be the language. However, in practice this is not a simple. There are wide local differences in dialect: between for instance the language spoken in the high plateaux of eastern Ladakh, the language spoken in Leh area, and the language spoken in the far-western valley located at the India-Pakistan Line of Control.

Notes

1. J. Bray, 'Ladakhi History and Indian Nationahood', *South Asia Research*, vol. 11, no. 2, November 1991, pp. 115–33.
2. See Sökefeld in this volume.
3. For other examples from Bhutan, Sikkim, and Tibet, see C. Ramble, 1997, 'Tibetan Pride of Place: On why Nepal's Bhotiyas are not an Ethnic group', in D.N. Gellner, J. Pfaff-Czarnecka, and J. Whelpton (eds), *Nationalism and Ethnicity in a Hindu Kingdom*, Amsterdam: Harwood Academic Publishers, pp. 379–414.
4. *History repeated in Ladakh—The Muslim Viewpoint of the Ladakh Agitation of 1989,* Muslims of Leh and Kargil District.
5. D. Pinault, 'The Day of the Lion: Lamentation Rituals and Shia Identity in Ladakh', *Ladakh Studies* no. 12, Autumn 1999.
6. 1982 saw the inauguration of *Ladakhi Sheeraza (Shees rab zom)*, a Ladakhi language quarterly.

Selves and Others

Representing Multiplicities of Difference in Gilgit and Northern Areas of Pakistan

MARTIN SÖKEFELD

A New Approach to the Study of Identities

The conceptualization of identity and ethnicity has undergone a major change during the last few decades. In the human sciences, identity has two differing meanings, the first mainly pertaining to psychology and the other to the social and cultural sciences. In the conventional psychological sense, identity refers primarily to self-identity, that is identity of the individual self with itself (Erikson 1980). In anthropology, in contrast, identity, used mostly in the compound concept of 'ethnic identity', points to the identity of an individual with other individuals, that is, to the identity of a group. Whereas the first concept affirms individuality, the peculiarity of the human individual, the second tendentially negates it by stressing those characteristics which an individual supposedly shares with others. At least in anthropological discourse, both meanings of identity are almost completely unrelated. Very rarely does a text about ethnic identity (or, for that matter, religious identity or some other identity of that kind) refers also to self-identity. But the change in the concept of identity which I want to discuss here produced a certain (re-) alignment of both meanings.

This change may be indicated by the current employment of three related terms: multiplicity, difference, and intersectionality. Multiplicity indicates that identity does not exist in the singular but only as identities—formed through a plurality of relationships of belonging and otherness. This insight is not entirely new. Already over a hundred years ago, the American psychologist William James wrote that the person 'has as many social selves as there are individuals who recognize him' (James 1890: 294). The postmodern questioning of the unified and universal 'western' subject, inherited from Descartes, gave new currency to this insight. It stems from the view that identity or self are no original essences of the human being but rather projects and constructions that are, more or less self-consciously, continued and reworked during the whole life span of the individual in a great number of different contexts and in juxtaposition to a multiplicity of others.

The concept of difference has in a certain sense almost replaced the concept of identity in contemporary discourse (Felski 1997). Difference emphasizes that identity only exists as different identity, distinguishing somebody from somebody else, respectively one group or category from another. It points to the fact that identity is developed in contrast to and contradiction with others. Whereas *identity* stresses the aspect of being identical with others or with the self, *difference* emphasizes the contrast which is the necessary premise for establishing this being identical. Both, of course, cannot be separated and are two sides of the same coin. But, difference, combined with multiplicity, also challenges identity. If difference characterizes the relation between a self and a multiplicity of others, then the self itself is not identical (a singular unity) but a differing multiplicity, depending on against which specific other it momentarily establishes its being different.[1]

Intersectionality, finally, points to the fact that the different identities (or, the various differences) which characterize an individual are not unrelated among themselves. On the contrary, the different identities embraced by a person may heavily influence each other, not necessarily in the sense that they all are somehow mutually trimmed in order to enable a consistent personality or 'overall identity', but rather in the sense that they entail conflict and antagonism, that is, they breed inconsistency and ambivalence. The aspect of intersectionality of identities is frequently related to Jacques Derrida's concept of *différance* (Derrida 1982) which points out that the meaning of signs in an ongoing chain of signification can never be finally fixed but that meaning is always affected or changed by the context or 'environment' or other related signs and meanings—and changes them too. Differences/identities then are signs in such interrelated, or, better, interrelating environments of meanings.

Together, these three aspects of a new conceptualization of identity enable the psychological (individual-oriented) concept of identity and the social or cultural (group-oriented) concept to fuse to an unprecedented extent. Rather than negating individuality, social identities contribute to the peculiarity of the individual because each single human being is characterized by a specific combination (multiplicity) of identities (differences) that relate to each other in specific and shifting ways (intersectionality).

This conceptualization of identity/identities developed from debates in feminism and immigrant identities in the west. Identities deemed unproblematic before turned out to be disputable: Feminists had to discover that there was no female identity shared by all women, but only identities of women subject to other differences too. Women do not share experiences simply because they belong to that category. Their experiences are marked differently by other identities like belonging to a certain class, 'race', and nation. What had been supposed to be a common identity of women earlier was unmasked as a specific perspective of some women occupying positions of dominance that allowed them to disseminate their view as the general one (Crosby 1992; Felski 1997). Indeed, the general category 'woman' became highly questionable. Similarly, identities of immigrants in the diasporas in the west were deconstructed into whole ranges of differing subject positions that made general categories debatable (Brah 1996, Rattansi 1994).

In the light of this critique of identity, anthropological studies of ethnicity have to be questioned for their often simplifying stance as they mostly foreground *one* identity (the one which is dubbed 'ethnic') at the expense of others. Sometimes a number of identities is considered which is represented as fitting into an overall system or taxonomy, that is, they are constructed according to a particular and singular type which effectively eclipses intersectionality.

Identities that can be sorted into a taxonomy are ordered, they do not contradict one another or produce friction among themselves—that is, they seem not to be subject to *differance*.

In this paper I want to discuss the multiplicity of identities in the town Gilgit in the Northern Areas of Pakistan. My representation of this multiplicity will be oriented at the understanding of identity outlined in this introduction. Thereby I want to show that this approach is not only apt for the analysis of multiple identities in the west but also for more 'conventional' locations of anthropological research.

A Multiplicity of Difference in Gilgit

Gilgit, a town of approximately 50,000 inhabitants, is the political administrative, and economic centre of the Northern Areas of Pakistan. Since the inception of the Kashmir dispute, these Northern Areas that until the 1970s were called Gilgit-Baltistan are controlled by Pakistan, but they do not *de jure* from a part of Pakistan. The centrality of the town is due to its strategic position at the intersection of valleys in the high mountainous area. Having been alternately a centre of power and a target of attack the population of the place suffered more than one upheaval and faced near extinction as well as waves of immigration from different directions. Consequently, the present population of Gilgit is characterized by a high degree of difference.

While studying discourses and processes of identity in Gilgit, I analysed mainly five 'dimensions of difference'. These are: religion, *qōm*,[2] clan, locality, and language. Along each dimension a number of identities can be distinguished. Within the dimension of religion, for instance, there are Shiites, Sunnis and Ismails. Within the dimension of *qōm*, groups, and identities like Ṣīn, Yeshkun, Paṭhān, and Kashmīrī can be distinguished. Locality distinguishes Gilgitwālē, Hunzawālē, Paṭhān and many others. My postulation of these five dimensions of difference is of course a heuristic simplification. Most of these dimensions encompass a *disorder* of differences rather than ordered systems. Only in two dimensions, religion and language, the number of encompassed differences is finite. There are three relevant religious groups in Gilgit and fifteen different mother tongues are spoken. The other three dimensions are rather indefinite because the encompassed differences are very numerous, because new differences can always be constructed and because the encompassed differences can themselves be organized into (rather disordered) systems. Locality may distinguish people belonging to different neighbourhoods in Gilgit (*het* or *mohallē*), but also people belonging to different valleys (e.g. Hunza, Nagar, Gilgit), subregions of valleys (e.g. Shinaki, Hunza, Gujal) or countries and nations (e.g. Pakistani and non-Pakistani). Identity derived from locality may also be structured by a simple dichotomy (e.g. people of Gilgit versus people from outside). Finally, not all dimensions are mutually exclusive. When I mentioned Paṭhān as an identity that can be subsumed under locality as well as under *qōm* it may already have raised questions. Similarly Hunzawālē can be understood as an identity derived from a certain place or area as well as a *qōm*.[3]

Elsewhere I have analysed the multiplicity of identities in Gilgit as a system of practical logic that is employed to distinguish between kinds of persons according to always specific (and practical) necessities and circumstances and for particular purposes (Sökefeld 1997a). A major characteristic of this system is its inherent ambivalence. Such a discovered system cannot be turned into a taxonomically ordered system without changing its character completely, that is most importantly, without replacing its underlying practical logic of agents by a theoretical logic of observers.

So far I have described the multiplicity of identities that can be found in the town of Gilgit on the level of groups and congregations of people. But of course, multiplicity also characterizes the identities of each individual. Every person draws identities from each of the mentioned dimensions of difference—and from others like gender, age or class. An individual in Gilgit may be, for example, at the same time Gilgitwālā from the village of Barmas, Shiite, Ṣīn, belonging to the Ṣalē-lineage, and speaking Shina. A second person may share some of these identities, being from the same village, but may be a Sunni, Yeshkun, belonging to the same lineage Ṣalē and also speaking Shina. Another man may have a completely different set of identities, i.e. being immigrant from Hunza, belonging to the *qōm* Dhiramiting, to the Ismailia and speaking

Burushaski. From these examples it follows that the question whether two persons share an identity or are different cannot be easily answered. Most frequently, persons share only *some* identity but differ in some others. They can be '*both* the same *and* different' (Hall 1990: 227, original italics). Each identity/difference places the individual into a specific discursive space. That is, his or her total repertory of identities entails his or her participation in a number of discursive spaces that may effectively be related by contradiction. Consider two persons, the first being Shiite and Yeshkun, the second Sunni and Yeskun. According to their religious identity, they are antagonists because Shiites and Sunnis are by now divided by an almost thirty-years-old history of violent 'sectarian tensions'. On the other hand, by their *qōm* identity, both belong to the same group Yeshkun, and it is generally maintained that a high degree of solidarity should be practised within the *qōm*. From both these shared and antagonistic identities considerable ambivalence arises for social actors (Sökefeld 1997b). Intersectionality of identities here entails that in certain contexts actors may play down religious antagonism in order to maintain *qōm* solidarity, or the other way round. The meaning of either of the identities for the person who embraces them is not fixed but a matter of momentary positioning within the total environment of identities/differences.

If we frame relations of identities by way of the dichotomy self versus other, it follows that it is not always clear whether another person is construed as self or as other. There is, then, only multiplicity of selves, also *within* the individual, to be distinguished from a multiplicity of others. Instead of a dichotomy self versus other, we should speak of multiple dichotomies of selves and others that are not fixed but that only structure momentary relations with particular persons in a specific environment of differences.

This does not mean that all differently constructed dichotomies of self versus other share the same degree of relevance within the society of Gilgit. Some are certainly more important than others. In what follows I would like to discuss the difference between Shiite-Sunni which assumed great importance in the first half of the 1990s. After that I will show that despite this salience the religious difference is still subject to multiplicity and intersectionality, and I will explore some examples of how the religious difference is exchanged for other differences.

Shiites and Sunnis in Gilgit: The Development of Antagonism

The antagonism between Shiites and Sunnis is nearly as old as is Islam. Still, in Gilgit this difference is said not to have had much significance before the beginning of the 1970s. Accounts of conflictual events before 1970 can be heard, but it is generally accepted that it is only since that the difference acquired a salience that effectively divided the population of Gilgit town into two antagonistic parts.[4] The origins of the dispute in the 1970s are not very clear, but it seems that some *ulemā* (scholars) of both sects started at that time to raise the question whether the members of the other groups are really Muslims or not.

In particularly, the special ritual practices of the Shia became a bone of contention between both groups. Most important was the mourning procession on *ashūra* (the tenth day of *muharram*) in which Shiites lament the martyrdom of the Imam Hussein and his companions in the battle of Kerbela. In Gilgit, the *julūs* (procession) of *ashūra* ended always at a place in the centre of the town in front of the Sunni main mosque where speeches were delivered to the participants. In the 1960s many Sunnis also joined the procession or assisted the Shiites who practised flagellation (*zanjīrī mātam*) by handing them water and pieces of cloth with which the Shiites wiped off their blood. On the grounds that the blood stained clothes thrown always defiled the mosque, Sunni leaders demanded in 1972 that the assembly at the end of the *julūs* be shifted to another place but the Shiites refused to comply with that demand. Three years later, in 1975, the Shiite assembly was shot at from the Sunni mosque. Because of this incident the Sunni *qāzī* was arrested. His detention caused great unrest in the Sunni areas of the Indus valley and its side-valleys like Gor, Darel and Tangir. Sunnis from these regions threatened to attack Gilgit. The next year the administration demanded that the assembly take place at another location. Again the Shiites refused to give up what they considered their habitual right. Consequently, the *julūs* was prohibited in the next two years and only after that the Shiites conceded to move their assembly to another place. But the dispute was not solved because now the Sunnis demanded an entirely different course of the procession. A solution that satisfied both parties could not be found and even now *muharram* is a time of potential sectarian tension in Gilgit.

The dispute forced the people in Gilgit increasingly to identify themselves either as Sunnis or as Shiites. Earlier one did not know exactly to which sect one belonged and Shiites and Sunnis frequently prayed together in the same mosque. What reportedly had been only a nominal difference became important in many realms of social life because it had become a matter of conflict. Since the beginning of the 1970s there have been no marriages between Shiities and Sunnis, in contrast with earlier times when intermarriage was not infrequent. In the 1980s the difference entered politics and in the elections of local bodies the appeal to shared religious denomination became the most important strategy for securing votes. In 1988 the tensions culminated in a massacre when Sunni warriors from Kohistan and the Sunni-majority regions of the Northern Areas attacked Shiite villages in the vicinity of Gilgit, destroying houses, fields, and trees and killing many people (Sökefeld 1997a: 205ff.). From 1988 until 1993 many more people fell victims to armed tensions.

In the 1980s, another Shiite practice was challenged by the Sunni *ulemā*. On festive occasions like the birthday of Imam Ali, Shiites used to light bonfires on mountain slopes surrounding Gilgit. Using fire they wrote words like 'Allah', 'Mohammad' or 'Ali' on the slopes. Again some Sunni *ulemā* considered this an 'un-Islamic' practice because it defiled the names of God and the Prophet (after all, cloth soaked with kerosene were used to produce the fire-writing) and demanded that it be stopped especially on the slopes above Sunni mosques and *madrasē* (religious schools). In February 1990, two young men who had lit such fires were shot to death from a Sunni *madrasa*.

In 1991 a bomb was found buried in the Sunni *īdgah* and Shiites were accused of having planned the blasting of the whole Sunni congregation during *īd*-prayer. Shiites, in return, alleged that they were victims of a conspiracy that aimed at accusing them of fostering tensions. Several persons were killed later that year and the army started to patrol the bazaar area in Gilgit. In May 1992 the assassination of a Sunni youth leader provoked the killing of at least ten more person in revenge and counter-revenge. Curfew was imposed on Gilgit, but this measure could not prevent other similar events from recurring only six weeks later.

Society in Gilgit became effectively polarized by the Shiite-Sunni dichotomy. Families living in neighbourhoods where the opposite sect formed the majority moved to majority areas of their own groups. Economic cooperation across religious boundaries declined and even commerciality between Shiites and Sunnis almost ended—especially when it came to having meals containing meat.[15] The Shiite-Sunni dichotomy became effectively a premise that structured the perception of the social space.

According to Kuper (1977), polarization of identities implies also a deplurization of identities. That is, the identities that have become polarized supersede almost all non-polarized identities. This happened in Gilgit too. Religious identity became the most important identity in many contexts, and most persons mentioned their religious affiliation when they were asked their most important identity. Still, this does not mean that multiplicity and intersectionality were eliminated. Instead, it could be observed that in certain contexts people explicitly attempted to foreground other identities at the expense of religious difference. I would like to present three cases of attempts at replacement of differences that occurred in the beginning of 1993. In two of them, religious difference was traded for other identities (*qōm* and nationality), whereas in the third case religious difference was given relevance in the context of a struggle over land rights although this is originally simply a matter of locality.

Qōm versus Religion

In the summer of 1992 two periods of acute tensions had occurred within six weeks. Almost twenty people were killed. The first period started when a leader of a Sunni youth organization was murdered and the second began with the assassination of a local politician who happened to be Shiite and Yeshkun. The administration tried to control the incidents by imposing curfew which in each case lasted more than a week. Also after the shooting had ended and curfew had been lifted, people in Gilgit continued to be very anxious. After dusk, the bazaar area where tensions mostly took place could be deserted. People generally avoided entering the bazaar and restricted their movements to the majority areas of their own sect. Even months after the last assassination public employees did not appear in their offices for work if those happened to be situated in a majority area of the opposite sect. The threat and fear of further tensions was so strong that people felt very uneasy. In a certain way this fear of new tensions, although strongly lamented, aggravated the situation, because most people accorded the responsibility for it to those of the other sect. The rift among relatives of members of a *qōm* belonging to different sects became very strong. For example, a Sunni who had been on *hāj* at the time of the tensions in summer complained that he was not even welcomed and greeted by his Shiite relatives on the event of his return. Almost every incident in the town was at first interpreted within the framework of the conflict between Shiites and Sunnis. Polarizations, then, remained on a climax even after acute tensions had stopped.

But in winter 1992-93 a discourse emerged among Yeshkun in Gilgit that tried to foreground *qōm* as difference instead of the religious distinction. I learnt that several Yeshkun were busily organizing an assembly of Yeshkun *motobarān* (respected elders) in Gilgit irrespective of religious affiliation or locality. At the same time, younger Yeshkun, students and recent graduates, talked about the necessity of holding a similar meeting among themselves. There was an urgent sense that the tensions ultimately endangered the 'identity' of Yeshkun. What I label 'identity' here was represented mainly as both a practice and sentiment of solidarity, belonging and unity among Yeshkun facing other *qōm*, especially Ṣīn.[6] The necessity of an assembly of Yeshkun and the threat for the identity of the Yeshkun posed by religious antagonism was explained in two inconsistent ways. The first explanation simply considered the forging of unity among Yeshkun irrespective of their religious affiliation as an important step towards the overcoming of sectarian conflict in general. I was given to understand that if Yeshkun solved the religious antagonism among themselves and Ṣīn did the same, the conflict would almost be finished for want of antagonists. Further, because there were both Sunni and Shiite Yeshkun they could tell persons of both sects belonging to the other *qōm* to stop sectarianism. Here, the purpose was to solve the religious conflict, and the first step was to overcome the religious difference within 'the own group'. The second reasoning was very different. It subordinated the religious difference completely to the difference of *qōm* and declared the sectarian tensions to be a conspiracy of the Ṣīn against Yeshkun. The evidence for this, I was told, was that mostly Yeshkun, both Shiites and Sunnis, had been the victims of violent incidents. It was alleged that Ṣīn, the numerically much inferior *qōm*, had successfully broken the strength of Yeshkun by disseminating sectarian strife. Some Yeshkun who did not accept this thesis at least conceded that the murder of the Shiite Yeshkun politician that had started the second wave of tensions in summer 1992 had been a Ṣīn-Yeshkun issue rather than a Shiite-Sunni matter because this man had distinguished himself as an important leader of Yeshkun and because his alleged murderer was a Ṣīn.

Although not consistent in their diagnosis, both perspectives argued for the necessity of promoting unity among Yeshkun and considered the call for a *qōm*-assembly, a promising state in that direction. And both opinions converged in the assessment that Ṣīn possessed a much greater internal unity than Yeshkun. Many Yeshkun told me that for the Yeshkun religion had become much more important than *qōm* contrary to Ṣīn for whom *qōm* took precedence and who, for instance, in local body elections gave their support only to other Ṣīn, irrespective of whether they were Sunnis or Shiites.[7]

I learnt that similar meetings (both of young and of elder men) had taken place earlier although it was not very clear who actually had taken part and what had been the result of these meetings. Some persons who according to others had taken part in such meetings denied their participation when I inquired about it. All these meetings had been quite clandestine because the Yeshkun did not want to arouse a feeling of threat among Ṣīn. Further, it seemed that most persons involved were not very eager to talk about such meetings because they obviously contradicted the value of equality and brotherhood among all Muslims, irrespective of descent and similar distinctions. There was no formal organization of Yeshkun but rather a loose network of men of different places in and around Gilgit, all of them Shina-speakers, who were considered as important leaders of the *qōm* and who had to take part in such an assembly in order to give it the required vigour.

Some Yeshkun not only talked about a meeting but were busily engaged in visiting other influential Yeshkun in order to convince them of its necessity. Some of this canvassing activity really surprised me because it involved very close interaction across the religious divide inspite of the still current strife. For example, a Sunni *lambardār* of one of the southern valleys of the Northern Areas, the population which consists entirely of Sunnis, stayed for more than a week in the house of a Shiite Yeshkun in a Shiite neighbourhood that had always been a Shiite hotbed of sectarian involvement.[8] From this base he met other Yeshkun in the town in order to win over support for the meeting. While he was present, his host discussed very frankly the sectarian issue with me, although such discussions in the presence of members of the opposite sect were generally avoided otherwise they always led to very emotional exchanges and mutual accusations. The host was a strong advocate of the Ṣīn-conspiracy theory of sectarianism and he articulated the issue within the framework of *qōm* in a way that his guest did not feel offended.

Still, to organize an assembly was no easy matter. I had to leave Gilgit in March 1993 and until then a meeting of Yeshkun had not taken place. First, another period of tensions had seemed imminent[9] and then the beginning of *ramadān* intervened. I do not know whether such an assembly had materialized since. Inspite of the fact that here the difference of religion seems to have won over the difference of *qōm* it becomes clear that both differences and the related issues have to be considered as mutual contexts. No matter whether a *qōm*-assembly of Yeshkun finally took place or not, the issue became important for many Yeshkun precisely because of the high degree of religious antagonism. Both differences were related to each other by actors in many contexts. For example, one of the *motobarān* who was committed to organizing the Yeshkun assembly was at the same time looking for a suitable match for one of his sons. His wife also visited a (Shiite) Ṣīn-family in order to ask whether they were ready to give their daughter to her son for marriage. The mother of the girl answered: 'I would rather change my religion than give my daughter to a Yeshkun!'[10] Here too then, *qōm* was verbally accorded primacy.

The intersectionality of the differences that *qōm* and religion entails signal a contradiction of ideologies and values. From the point of view of Islam, *qōm* had no positive significance. Islam teaches that all Muslims are brothers (and sisters) irrespective of ethnicity or any other intervening identity. Some persons in Gilgit therefore explicitly drew the conclusion that in the face of the superior value of religion their belonging to a *qōm* or kinship group was nothing and that their affiliation to a religious community was all that counted. But most persons whom I met admitted the contradiction of values between *qōm* and religion without being able to generally opt for or against one of them. The host of the Sunni *lambardār* who toured Gilgit in order to win support for a *qōm* assembly put this in the following terms: 'Shia or Sunni, this is nonsense. In the Quran there are neither Shiites nor Sunnis. And in the last instance also Ṣīn-Yeshkun is nonsense. After all, we are all the children of Adam and Eve.' As we know, this theoretical insight did not prevent him from attempting to enhance the importance of *qōm* in the society of Gilgit.

Religion versus Nation[11]

The second challenge to religious difference emerged from the oppositional politics against the special political status of the Northern Areas which resulted from its involvement in the Kashmir dispute and has therefore a long pre-history. Since the winter of 1947, the Northern Areas are under the control of Pakistan. After an uprising of the local military against the rule of the maharaja of Kashmir, local leaders had favoured joining Pakistan (Sökefeld 1997c). But the Northern Areas continued to be regarded as 'disputed territory' because the conflict between India and Pakistan about Kashmir was and is still pending. Due to this the region is not a regular part of Pakistan and its inhabitants lack a number of constitutional and political rights that Pakistanis enjoy. This political status of the Northern Areas generally caused much resentment among the people, who, to put it briefly complain that they had opted for Pakistan in 1947 but that Pakistan has not accepted their decision since.

In local political discourse the Shiite-Sunni-conflict is frequently related to this political issue. In 1971 there was a major insurgency in Gilgit against the Pakistani administration including a general strike and a storming of the police station and the prison.[12] As it happened, the militant religious dispute started only *after* this upheaval. It is therefore alleged that sectarianism was fanned by the government as a divide-and-rule strategy against political mobilization. Indeed, in the subsequent years Gilgitwālē were more preoccupied with the sectarian conflict than with the struggle for political change, but voices that demanded 'political rights' for the Northern Areas never died out.

Since the second half of the 1980s Gilgit witnessed a new kind of opposition against the political status of the area. This opposition was increasingly framed in *nationalist* terms. Political groups postulated a nation of the Northern Areas that was different from Pakistan. This difference was represented as constituted by history, culture and the unique linguistic and geographical conditions of the Northern Areas (Sökefeld 1997a: 296ff.). Nationalism was a two-edged strategy as it emphasized not only the difference between the Northern Areas and Pakistan, denying the right of Pakistan to determine the fate of the area, but affirmed also the 'natural' unity of the people of the Northern Areas as a nation. To promote this unity which had been endangered by the disruptive strategy of Pakistan became an objective of prime importance. The greatest threat to national unity was, of course, sectarianism.

In the beginning of the 1990s, the political opposition was clearly marked by the sectarian divide. Two political projects could be discerned. The first demanded the separation of the political fate of the Northern Areas from the Kashmir dispute, questioning that the former Gilgit Agency had ever been a part of Jammu and Kashmir state in any meaningful sense, and favoured the regular inclusion of the Northern Areas as a fifth province into the state of Pakistan. The other project affirmed the region's historical and cultural relation with Kashmir and demanded the merger of the Northern Areas with what is called Azad Kashmir and, in the long run, with the whole of Jammu and Kashmir.[13] Whereas the activists endorsing the first project were mostly Shiites and Ismailis, although there were also some Sunni supporters, the second project was favoured exclusively by Sunnis, most of them Kashmiri,[14] but also Sunni Ṣīn and Yeshkun. The sectarian rationale behind the two projects is obvious: Shiites and Ismailis feared belonging to an insignificant minority in a predominately Sunni state of Jammu and Kashmir whereas, Sunnis feared remaining a minority within a province of the Northern Areas in Pakistan.

The nationalist vision of the Northern Areas evolved from the provincial project endorsed mostly by Shiites and Ismailis and rejected by those Sunnis who favoured the merger with Kashmir instead. But the nationalists, belonging mostly to the small local parties Karakorum National Movement (KNM) and Balawaristan National Front (BNF), envisaged their project in a way that endeavoured to accommodate Sunnis too. No matter whether the aim was a province within Pakistan or a totally separate political entity (on this matter the nationalists in the beginning considered various options), they delimited the projected homelands and territory of the nation of the Northern Areas in a way that would guarantee almost numerical equality of Sunnis and Shiites within its population.[15]

The BNF organized a conference on the political status of the Northern Areas on 9 April 1993 and in which most local parties as well as local sections of Pakistani political parties like PPP (Pakistan People's Party) and PML (Pakistan Muslim League) participated. The speeches delivered on this occasion were characterized by a spirit of cooperation inspite of differential political aims. The conference was remarkable for the fact that it brought together some local politicians who were at the same time important leaders of both Shiite and Sunni communities. The participants expressed the view that internal political differences had to be postponed in order to achieve a change in the political status of the Northern Areas, and they argued for unity in opposition to the oppressive grip of the Pakistani bureaucracy.[16] The charge that Pakistan promoted sectarianism in the Northern Areas was made again and the speakers called for 'sectarian harmony'. As a result of the conference, the 'United Front of the Northern Areas' was founded as a body in which many different political organizations worked for the common cause. This committee organized many demonstrations, press conferences, and other political events during the following years, some of which the police tried to prevent and repress by force. Although violent sectarian tensions in which more than twenty persons were killed swept Gilgit again in August 1993, the United Front of the Northern Areas did not break up but continued its activities.

Here I am not interested in the political success or failure of oppositional political groups in Gilgit but in their reframing of the religious issue by constructing a nation. The nationalist groups interpreted sectarianism as an instrument of power employed by the Pakistani government in order to safeguard control of the Northern Areas. The alleged divide-and-rule strategy is countered by a new politics of representation that depicts the people of the Northern Areas as a nation fundamentally united and naturally different from Pakistan.

The attempt to replace the difference of religion by a difference of nations occurred in a complex web of overlapping discourses. There was no clear and unequivocal demarcation between 'political' discourses in Gilgit. Shiite functionaries in particular drew a number of connections between both issues, not only by the allegations that sectarianism had to be understood as a disruptive governmental strategy against political commitment and change in the area but also because they sometimes represented the political discrimination of the Northern Areas as a discrimination mainly of Shiites. The issue was further complicated by the unstable political situation in Pakistan with frequent change of governments and policies during the last decade. As a thumb rule it can be said that any national party (the most important being PPP and PML) exhibited a more sympathetic position towards the Northern Areas as long as it remained in opposition, but receded from reform schemes as soon as it took over government. Members and functionaries of local branches of these national parties even participated in political activities against Pakistan in the Northern Areas.

Certainly, religious discourse and religious antagonism did not become completely replaced by nationalist discourse and national unity. But Pakistan indeed emerged during the 1990s much more clearly as 'the other' of the Northern Areas than ever before.

Locality versus religion

My last case refers to a reverse change of differences: here there is no attempt to supersede the religious divide by some other difference, but religious difference becomes significant in a conflict about village common lands that arose originally in the framework of locality. This conflict occurred in Manot (a pseudonym), one of the more peripheral *mohallē* of Gilgit. The issue is very complicated because of legal uncertainty and a great number of intertwined perspectives so that it can be presented here only in an abridged form.[17]

Agriculture in Gilgit depends on irrigation and irrigated land (*ābādi zamiñ* is distinguished from unirrigated land. In the past, unirrigated land was mostly the common land of the village (*khālisa-e deh*). Those who were recognized as original inhabitants of the village (*muṭhulfau*) were entitled to use this common land, for instance for grazing, and they could also take certain portions of this land into 'individual' possession. By this, *khālisa* was turned into *nautōṛ* ('newly broken' land). Formerly, the usefulness of *khālisa* was rather restricted and therefore small portions were appropriated as *nautōṛ* in most of the cases only if the irrigation system was extended so that more land could be irrigated. But since some decades, land in Gilgit is in much more demand for construction purposes than for cultivation and prices of land therefore have risen sharply. Accordingly, also unirrigated *khālisa* that can be turned into *nautōr* has become very valuable. A prescribed procedure has to be followed in order to make pieces of *khālisa* into *nautōṛ*. Only *muṭhulfau* are entitled for allotment, applications have to be made public and they have to be approved by both the settlement office and the village headman *(lambardār)*.

For a number of reasons land in Manot is much sought after by immigrants and the correct procedure for allotment of land has not always been followed. Compared to the irrigated land, unirrigated *khālisa* in Manot was relatively large. After the freedom struggle, *khālisa* was allotted to non-*muṭhulfau* veterans of the freedom struggle as inām (remuneration). Because *khālisa* was fairly abundant and its usefulness still quite restricted, there were hardly local complaints against this practice. This changed when during the 1970s and 80s such effectively illegal allotment continued and the remaining *khālisa* became smaller and smaller.

In the beginning of the twentieth century, only five families were registered as *muṭhulfau* in the settlement records of Manot. All of these were Shiites and Yeshkun. At the time of the next settlement, a few more families were registered, among them an immigrant family from Chilas that was Sunni and was accorded all rights of *muṭhulfau*. It had been given some land in Manot by the other families. One of the original *muṭhulfau* families also converted to the Sunna. Today, *muṭhulfau* are only a small minority in Manot. Most of the inhabitants are immigrants from Nager, all of them Shiites, and Hunza, who are both Shiites and Ismailis.

Over the generations, the Sunni family from Chilas became relatively rich and powerful. Contrary to the original Shiite *muṭhulfau*, they are well educated. Today, the villages have a dual structure of authority. Although the *lambardār* is now devoid of most official functions, he continues to be a person of high respect in most places. His 'office' is passed hereditarily from father to son. On the other hand, since the beginning of the 1970s there are the elected '*members*' who represent the village in the municipal committee and who became responsible, among other things, for the infrastructural development of the *mohallē*. They deal with the administration and have considerable influence that is difficult to assess from the outside. In some parts of Gilgit, the *lambardārs* have also become *members*. Not so in Manot. Here the *lambardār* family was uneducated and promised little in the negotiations with modern administration. Therefore, *members* always belonged to influential immigrant families. In 1993, the office of *member* had gone since two electoral periods to the family from Chilas.[18]

The *muṭhulfau* had become more and more incensed because of the practice of allegedly illegal allotment. They alleged that both people from outside that were not entitled at all got *nautōṛ* had got much more land than they were entitled to. In the beginning of 1993, the *muṭhulfau* of Manot, except the Sunni *muṭhulfau*/immigrants,[19] occupied an area of *nautōṛ* that in their view, had been allotted illegally to persons not entitled to it. They tore down the walls surrounding a few of the plots, planted some trees there and demanded that the land be reallotted among the villages of Manot.

But the settlement office confirmed the legality of the previous allotment and prohibited the irrigation of the newly planted trees which were consequentially about to die from drought.

At the same time, the *muṭhulfau* of Manot lacked the means to defend their rights legally. To see through a juridical process on the matter of *nautōṛ* they required much more resources for advocates and bribes than they could afford. Formerly, they had been represented both in the judiciary and in the administration by members of the Chilas family, but now they accused them of having collaborated in and gained from illegal allotment. Therefore, they sought other alliances. Earlier, they had combined with the inhabitants of the neighbouring village Haban (a pseudonym) which, situated a little further down on the slope, shared the water channel with Manot. The *muṭhulfau* of Manot describe those of Haban (they are also mostly Shiites) as much more shrewd and skilled in the business of modern local politics. In a similar case which had occurred in the beginning of the 1980s, the *muṭhulfau* of Manot were also supported by people from Hunza and Nager in the village that participated in the occupation of land. It turned out, that all those supporters who originally were not entitled to *nautōṛ* in Manot were Shiites like the overwhelming majority of the *muṭhulfau* in Manot. They too had been promised a share of *nautōṛ* in case of success whereas the Sunni *muṭhulfau* were excluded. Also people of Haban, who offered their assistance again, were to receive nothing now because, as I was told, 'there was too little land left.'

There was no open, public discourse among the Shiites about the fact that Sunnis were excluded from the issue. Rather, the persons involved preferred not to mention this aspect. Still, the Sunni *muṭhulfau* accused Shiite *muṭhulfau* of turning the conflict for *nautōṛ* into a sectarian affair. But the Shiites denied that the Sunnis were excluded due to a sectarian rationale and explained that they were excluded now because they were originally people from outside, that is, non-*muṭhulfau*, and because they had taken advantage of the 'real' *muṭhulfau* for too long.

Here, the religious difference became a base for the recruitment of support. According to their self-assessment, the Shiite *muṭhulfau* of Manot were not resourceful enough to defend what they considered their right. They had to win others to support their cause, to contribute funds for the plantation action and for the subsequent legal procedure. These others were of course not ready to offer assistance without return and had to be baited with the promise of a share *khālisa*. By this promise of land people not entitled to it, the Shiite *muṭhulfau* lost part of their legitimacy and became vulnerable to the accusation of sectarian action. A power strategy of the Shiite *muṭhulfau*, then, was interpreted as sectarianism by the Sunnis of Manot. The events in Manot can be related to the above mentioned polarization of society due to the Shiite–Sunni conflict. The context of religious antagonism bore upon the conflict about *nautōṛ* in that it made the religious differentiation readily available as a base for recruiting support in an originally unrelated issue and in that it made this action easily recognizable as 'sectarianism' by the opponents in the village conflict.

Difference, Multiplicity, Intersectionality

All the three cases presented here dealt with the redefinition of dichotomies of 'self versus other' showing that a choice of others its available in Gilgit for specifically and contrastingly crafting selves. Older approaches to identity which, for example, singled out ethnicity as the 'most basic identity' that structures social action (Barth 1969) are challenged by this setting. 'Basic' is indeed the whole environment of differences that provides meaningful contexts for a range of different and, at times, contradicting ways of action. The reframing of relations of identity through the opposition 'self versus other' takes this critique up by desisting from ascribing any specific content to the opposition. But this purely formal, structural dichotomy 'self versus other' presuming simple binary relations, still predicates a singularity of identity—a category that is refuted by the condition of multiplicity of identities in Gilgit. The presentation of my three cases makes obvious that identities which no doubt are often supposed by actors to be structured by a singular and basic relation (opposition) between self and other are strongly challenged by other constructions of that relation which deny the first to be singular and fundamental—attributing these conditions to some other difference. What can be observed from the outside is then a multiplicity of relations between selves and others that in many cases assume singularity but that anyway have to take this multiplicity and the challenge it poses to the respectively foregrounded difference into account. Difference, combined with multiplicity and intersectionality challenges and destabilizes identity. Movements of identity politics take efforts to stabilize a particular identity at the expense of another one. The differently defined selves and others contradict and threaten each other with erasure. Brah writes accordingly:

> Collective identity is the process of signification whereby commonalities of experience around a specific axis of differentiation, say class, caste, or religion, are invested with particular meanings. In this sense a given collective identity partially erases but also carries traces of other identities. That is to say that a heightened awareness of one *construction* of identity in a given moment always entails a partial erasure of *memory or subjective sense* of internal heterogeneity of a group (Brah 1996: 124).

Even if one difference is taken to erase another one, traces of the difference-to-erase remain. The foregrounding of *qōm*-identity (being Yeshkun) rather than religious affiliation always remained of the sectarian divide because it arose precisely in the context of the threat that sectarianism posed to *qōm*. Similarly, the nationalist discourse continually referred to the problem of sectarianism, never stopping to attribute it to the nefarious action of the government of Pakistan (that is, to the other in nationalist discourse). By trying to negate the difference of religion through the introduction of the difference of nation, sectarianism was effectively retained *within* that discourse, but its significance was changed from being an essential and violent actuality to being the product of an adverse other.

The nationalism of the Northern Areas can be read as a re-identification and reconstruction of an identity/difference that was to be eclipsed by Pakistani politics. The alleged production of Shiite–Sunni tensions was interpreted as an element of this politics or erasure, but it was not the only one. Equally important was that the Northern Areas were deprived of their political agency. The de facto inclusion of the Northern Areas into Pakistan implicated its incapacitation in the political arena and the Northern Areas were literally replaced by Pakistan as agent in the field of politics.[20]

In the political struggle between the Northern Areas and Pakistan the intersectionality of identities/differences, becomes obvious. From the Pakistani perspective, the Northern Areas were 'the other' that was to be accommodated and to come to rest within a shared national identity of Pakistan. But this accommodation could not be put through due to the involvement of the Northern Areas in another arena of dispute—the Kashmir conflict. Difference then is exemplified by the Northern Areas' uneasy and unresolved positions as both part/not part of Pakistan. At the level of political rights of the individual, this condition is expressed in the inconvenient position of having been subject to martial law since 1977 like Pakistan (although unlike 'Azad Kashmir') but being denied democratization when the rest of the country was liberated from dictatorship in 1988.

In the nationalist view, the identity of the Northern Areas was threatened both from within by sectarianism and from the outside by the disempowering politics of Pakistan. The threat of sectarianism from within was certainly more dangerous because it shifted the struggle to another site and effectively denied nationality as a fundamental identity by postulating religious affiliation as more basic. The attribution of this apparent threat from within to the enemy from outside by declaring Pakistan responsible for sectarianism was an ingenious sleight of hand which turned the threat to nationality into its affirmation. For what had seemed to be fragmenting the 'national' self of the Northern Areas and there by to question its actuality turned out to be a disruptive strategy of an other (Pakistan) that was actually aimed at this nation (affirming it thereby) and that found no other way to counter the demands put forward by this national self.

In the case of Manot, finally, an important aspect of the conflict was the question of which difference was to be applied in order to specify the meaning of the antagonism. Was it matter of Shiites versus Sunnis or Sunnis of *muṭhulfau* versus immigrants? The content of the dichotomy of self versus other, accordingly, was decisive for the legitimacy of the contested claims.

The multiplicity of identities/differences in Gilgit obviously is one of diverse elements that are either situated on a common, equal level or that are inserted into uncontested hierarchial relations of inclusion and exclusion. Instead, these identities/differences are related by continuous struggle, each one entailing a vision that questions the legitimacy of other differences, or reduces them to a subordinate position. Homi Bhaba (1994) distinguishes *diversity and difference* as relations between (in his case cultural) identities. The first is unproblematic, subject to clear boundaries derives from a taken for granted universal frame. But the second is characterized by mutual questioning and challenge, i.e. intersectionality. The multiplicity of identities in Gilgit then clearly falls into Bhabha's category of difference. There is no solution to the contradiction of identities acceptable by all and for all time. Neither can nationality be generally subordinated to religious affiliation, nor the other way round. Persons, deriving identities from both conflicting differences have to live with that conflict, maybe by almost 'compartmentalizing' their life and attributing primary importance to either of the differences in shifting contexts. Also a straight nationalist values his religious affiliation more than the presumed nationality when it comes to marriage. The possibility of compartmentalizing means that the discourses of different identities intersect only at certain, crucial sites.

Whereas social identity can be constructed discursively in less ambivalent ways, arguing for instance unequivocally for the primacy of the nation, personal identity has to be conceived of as a complex chain of identities in which each one necessarily supplements (and partly erases) the previous identity. We could conceptualize personal identity as a sequence of appendices that explain, specify, reframe, limit, question, and restrict each other. Personal identity is subject to the condition described by Derrida's concept of *différance* in that its final and total meaning is always deferred by the intervention of other differences and their social and political predicament.

This was expressed by Mohammad Ali, a student active in oppositional politics and in forging *qōm* identity among young Yeshkun who tried to explain to me what he *was* in the following terms:

> At first I am Pakistani. Then I am Gilgitwālā because I have been born in this area. And I am Yeshkun, this is very important for this is my blood. But the most important of all is religion because one has to think about what comes after death. Therefore I am at first Shiite.

We note that almost everything comes first although this results in an apparently unfeasible, contradictory totality. I recorded his statement at a time when nationalism in Gilgit had only started to develop and when most oppositional activists still opted for the regular inclusion of the Northern Areas into Pakistani as a fifth province. In the subsequent years Mohammad Ali's political stance may well have changed to a more nationalist position resulting in that his being Gilgitwālā effectively replaced and erased his being Pakistani.

Conclusion: Representing Multiplicities of Identities

Although it was probably intended that contributors discuss the manner in which the self and other are represented by Himalayan actors themselves, I took the liberty, by focussing on the conceptual issue, to foreground the question of how these selves and others can be represented within the framework of cultural sciences and, more specifically, anthropology. Both topics cannot be separated but have to be combined in an overall framework because the way how we conceptualize and represent identities and differences form our understanding of how the 'others' we study represent selves and others among themselves. In this conclusion I would like to outline tentatively some consequences of the present approach.

1. Although Gilgit, where I studied the multiplicity of differences referred to here, is of course a place with particular historical and political conditions that generated a social configuration with a high degree of multiplicity, I am not of the opinion that this is an extraordinary condition and that other places are necessarily less (or even not) characterized by multiplicity. In the Northern Areas of Pakistan, I do not know a single village that does not display such a multiplicity of intersecting differences, derived from descent, migration, habitat, language, religious affiliation or other determinants and I suppose that the same holds true for other regions of the Himalaya. If we extend the discussion to other sources of difference, like gender, age or class, it becomes clear, that multiplicity of differences is nothing special but rather a general human condition. Anthropological studies of identity, ethnicity or, in general, oppositions of self versus other accordingly should analyse the intersectionality *between* multiple identities/differences rather than

single out a particular difference at the expense of others. They have to explore and acknowledge a plurality of perspectives in analogy to what Nigel Rapport calls 'epistemic diversity'.

> Any attempt to force social life into one or other perspective ends in tautology and serves only to destroy the 'reality' under study. To adopt an eclecticism of narrational style, however, is to free one's account from an obsessional Aristotelian combat between battling singularities. And only in such eclecticism—locating human behaviour in more than one frame of reference at once; locating such (often mutually exclusive) frames of reference in conversation with one another—can one escape the notion that, ultimately, epistemic diversity can and should be 'resolved' in terms of a finite limit of possibility (society; structure) or an ultimately determining and integrating code (God; grammar). (Rapport 1997: 183f)

2. The emphasis on intersectionality changes also the conceptualization of single identities. If we take into account that different differences relate to each other or, more precisely, are related to each other by the actors that embody them, it becomes almost impossible to conceptualize identities/differences as essentialities. If, like in my examples of Gilgit, nation and *qōm* are employed to challenge the religious difference, or religious affiliation is used to increase power in a conflict originally defined by locality, it becomes clear that identities may be employed consciously as *strategies* to achieve certain ends, that is, they are part of power games, where inequalities in the availability of power are attempted to be levelled out or even to be inverted by a reframing of differences. Essentialism then has to be understood as a strategy itself. The nation or the *qōm* are indeed represented as almost timeless essences that possess nearly fathomless historical depth and that are irrevocably anchored in the core and bottom of each human being. There is even something like competition for the greatest 'essentiality' between intersecting differences like religion and *qōm*. While essentialism has to be rejected as an approach in anthropological discourse, it nevertheless remains a powerful topos in the discourses of difference we study.

3. Being attentive to the intersectionality of multiple differences directs attention to an aspect of human life that largely remains a blind spot in much of anthropology: individuality, the unique conditions of each human self (Cohen 1992, 1994). For, following the

approach to identities outlined here, it is obvious that it is not sufficient to simply sort individual human beings for analytical purposes into a grid of groups or identities. Rather than self-evident, the constitution of groups and categories becomes a problem. Every human being occupies a specific and unique subject position within the multiplicity of intersecting differences. Further, not all individuals invest to the same degree in particular identities (Rattansi 1995). This element of choice is most obvious in the question of national identity because not everybody in Gilgit subscribes to a common nationality of the country. But a similar difference of 'investment' into difference also applies *qōm* (not for all Yeshkun is a meeting of Yeshkun a crucial issue) and religion (non everybody is ready to kill members of the other sect or to die for one's own sect). Accordingly, human beings have to be represented as agents who more or less self-consciously and creatively act with the differences at hand within the constraints of historical and political setting.[21]

4. The deconstruction of the dichotomy self/other into a multiplicity of selves and others also has consequences for the great 'meta-dichotomy' that provides the fundament of the anthropological approach: the dichotomy of the anthropologist as self versus his/her objects of study as other—a dichotomy which is still sometimes represented as parallel to the (not less questionable) dichotomy of west versus non-west. Critical works, most importantly Fabian (1983), have shown that this dichotomy too is not an essential given but outcome of a process of other*ing* (and, conversely, self*ing*) which is actively if often unwittingly put into motion by the anthropological approach. Being attentive to the multiplicity and intersectionality of differences then demands the dissolution of this unequivocal and unequal dichotomy into a plurality of relations between the anthropologist (as a subject) and the *subjects* he or she studies that can signify both difference and identity. This perspective is put into practice, of course, by female (and feminist) anthropologists who have access to areas of life that due to the difference of gender are mostly closed to male researchers. It requires us not only to look out for differences but also for continuities between their lives and our own—continuities that after all—as Tim Ingold (1993) reminds us—are necessary precondition for the feasibility of the anthropological project.

Notes

1. 'Self' is of course a concept with many meanings. In the present context of multiple oppositions of selves and others it refers more to what I otherwise call 'identity' and not to the 'person' or the 'individual' embracing identities. Relations between both levels or aspects are discussed in Sökefeld (forthcoming).
2. *Qōm* is a very ambiguous term with a number of significances. Here, I use the term for those groups that in the older literature of the area had been referred to as 'castes' or 'tribes' (e.g. in Biddulph 1971). It is generally maintained that the members of such groups are related by kinship but not necessarily by common descent. Sometimes, these groups are also called 'ethnic groups' but because I see no advantage in replacing one ambiguous term by another one I stick to the local term (Sökefeld, in press a). '*Qōm*' is originally Arabic. Its correct plural form is '*acwām*', but this form is rarely employed in local discourse. Therefore I too use *qōm* for both.
3. See Sökefeld 1997a: 38ff. for a more complete exploration of such categories and their pitfalls.
4. The Ismailis form a third religious group of the population of Gilgit town but because they do not take part in the antagonism they are not considered here.
5. Muslims are only allowed to eat meat from animals butchered by Muslims. When people in Gilgit refused to consume meat that was provided by butchers of the other sect, their refusal amounted to the tacit conclusion that the others were *kuffār* (non-Muslims).
6. As a *qōm*, Yeshkun define themselves first of all in opposition to Ṣīn. Ṣīn and Yeshkun are considered the two important autochthonous *qōm* of Gilgit. The relationship between both groups is not devoid of ambiguities and vacillates between strong rivalry and only casual delimitation (Sökefeld 1994). In the discourse considered here, the relation between the *qōm* was envisaged as antagonism.
7. Some Ṣīn told me this about Yeshkun with almost the same words.
8. In the religious topography of Gilgit, some quarters and neighbourhoods are much more prone to involvement in sectarian clashes than others. The part of the town to which I refer here had invariably been involved. It is situated just opposite a pure Sunni area. Both *mohallē* are clearly separated by fields across which shootings occurred frequently during periods of acute tension.
9. A Sunni *mullah* had been killed and that murder was instantly interpreted as a sectarian incident by Sunnis who openly accused Shias of the crime. Shias, in return, accused Sunnis of fanning sectarianism by making the Shias indiscriminately responsible for all such incidents without any

justification. An outbreak of clashes could be prevented by the strong presence of police and military, but even after it had become clear that the man had been killed by his own son-in-law because of some family issue, the atmosphere in Gilgit remained strained.

10. This terse reply does not mean that there are no marriages between Ṣīn and Yeshkun although both groups are mostly described as endogamous in the literature. Decisions about marriages between both *qōm* are quite individual matters, although it is true that such intermarriages are generally regarded much more critically by Ṣīn than by Yeshkun.
11. Although both quasi-kinship groups like Ṣīn and Yeshkun and politically constructed nations like Pakistan or Germany are locally referred to as *qōm*, I will use here the English term for the political nation in order to prevent confusion.
12. See Sökefeld 1997a: 284ff.
13. The so called Azad Kashmir ('Free Kashmir') was created in 1947 by an uprising of Kashmiri Muslims who were not ready to accept declaration of accession of Jammu and Kashmir state to the Indian Union with the perceived support and help of Pakistan. 'Azad Kashmir' is only a puppet of the government of Pakistan.
14. These Kashmiri of Gilgit are the descendants of migrants from Kashmir who settled in the area probably in the 18th century as artisans and peasants. Today they form a very large segment of the town's population and occupy one of its most central *mohallē*, Kashrot. They are all Shina-speakers and have to be distinguished from latter migrants from Kashmir who came as merchants only after Gilgit was conquered by troops from Jammu and Kashmir.
15. For example, a section of the district Kohistan which is inhabited by only Sunnis and which now forms part of the North West Frontier Province was to be included into the territory of the Northern Areas, in order to increase the numerical strength of Sunnis in the area.
16. *Khabrēṇ* (Urdu Daily), 13 April 1993.
17. For a more detailed analysis see Sökefeld 1998.
18. To still call this family 'immigrants' is of course debatable and points already to the change of perspective that is decisive in the conflict.
19. That is, both the descendants of the immigrants from Chilas that had been registered as *muṭhulfau* and the family of 'original' *muṭhulfau* that had converted to the Sunna.
20. This replacement is represented in the nationalist discourse as a new colonialism, see Sökefeld, in press b.
21. I explored this issue in Sökefeld, forthcoming.

References

Barth, Fredrik, 1969, 'Introduction', in Fredrik Barth (ed.), *Ethnic Groups and Boundaries*, Boston: Little, Brown and Company: 9–39.

Bhabha, Homi K., 1994, 'The Commitment to Theory', in *The Location of Culture*, London: Routledge: 19–39.

Biddulph, John, 1971 [1880]), *Tribes of the Hindoo Koosh*. Graz: Akademische Druck-und Verlagsanstalt.

Brah, Actar., 1996, *Cartographies of Diaspora: Contexting Identities*, London: Routledge.

Cohen, Anthony P., 1994, 'The Future of the Self: Anthropology and the City', in A.P. Cohen, K. Fukui (eds.), *Humanising the City? Social Contexts of Urban Life at the Trun of the Millennium*, Edinburgh: Edinburgh University Press. 201–21.

Cohen, Anthony P, 1994, *Self Consciousness: An Alternative Anthropology of Identity*, London: Routledge.

Crosby, Christina, 1992, 'Dealing with Differences', in J. Butler, Joan W. Scott (eds), *Feminists Theorize the Political*, New York: Routledge. 130–43.

Derrida, Jacques, 1982, *Margins of Philosophy*. Chicago, University of Chicago Press.

Erikson, Erik, 1980, *Identity and Life-Cycle*, New York: Norton and Company.

Fabian, Johannes, 1983, *Time and the Other. How Anthropology Makes its Object*. New York: Columbia University Press.

Felski, Rita, 1997, The Doxa of Difference, *Signs*, 23:1–12.

Hall, Stuart, 1990, Cultural Identity and Diaspora, in Rutherford, Jonathan (ed.), *Identity: Community, Culture, Difference*. London: Lawrence and Wishart. 222–37.

Ingold, Tim, 1993, The Art of Translation in a Continuous World, in Palsson, Gisli (ed.), *Beyond Boundaries: Understanding, Translation and Anthropological Discourse*, Oxford: Berg. 210–30.

James, W, 1890, *Principles of Sociology*, New York: Holt.

Kaper, Leo, 1977, *The Pity of it All: Polarization of Racial and Ethnic Relations*, London: Duckworth.

Rapport, Nigel, 1977, Edifying Anthropology: Culture as Conversation; Representation as Conversation, in Alison James, Jenny Hockey, Andrew Dawson (eds.), *After Writing Culture*. London: Routledge. 177–93.

Rattansi, Ali, 1994, '"Western" Racisms, Ethnicities and Identities in a "Postmodern" Frame, in Rattansi, Ali and Sally Westwood (eds.), *Racism, Modernity and Identity: On the Western Front*, Cambridge: Polity Press. 15–86.

________, 1995, Just Framing: Ethnicities and Racism in a 'Post Modern' Framework, in Nicholson, Linda, Steven Seidman (eds.), *Social*

Postmodernism: Beyond Identity Politics, Cambridge: Cambridge University Press. 250–86.

Sökefeld, Martin, 1994, Ṣin und Yeškun in Gilgit: Die Abgrenzung zwischen zwei Identitätsgruppen und das Problem ethnographischen Schreibens, in *Petermanns Geographische Mitteilungen*, Bd. 138. Gotha 357–69.

________, 1997a, 'Ein Labyrinth von Identitäten in Nordpakistan: Zwischen Landbesitz, Religion und Kashmir-Konflikt' in Nordpakistan, Köln: Köppe.

________, 1997b, Discourse and Action: Unequivocalness and Ambivalence in Identifications, in: I. Strellrecht, and M. Winniger (eds.), *Perspectives on History and Change in the Karakorum, Hindukush, and Himalaya*, Köln: Köppe. 101–17.

________, 1997c, *Jang Azadi*: Perspective on a Major Theme in Northern Areas' History, in I. Stellrecht, I. (ed.), *The Past in the Present: Horizons of Remembering in the Pakistan Himalaya,* Köln: Köppe. 61–82.

________; 1998, '"The People Who Really Belong to Gilgit": Perspectives on Identity and Conflict in Theory and Ethnography', in I. Stellrecht, and H.G. Bohle (eds.), *Transformations of Social and Economic Relationships in Northern Pakistan*, Köln: Köppe. 94–224.

________, 1998, 'On the Concept "Ethnic Groups"', in I. Stellrecht (ed.), *Karakorum-Hindukush-Himalaya: Dynamics of Change,* Köln: Köppe. 383–403.

________, (*In press* b), From Colonialism to Post-Colonial Colonialism: Changing Models of Dominance in the Northern Areas of Pakistan, in Macdonald, Ken and David Butz (eds), *Colonialism in the Western Himalaya*, Toronto.

________, 1999, 'Debating Self, Identity and Culture in Anthropology', in *Current Anthropology*, 40:417–47.

Comments

MARC GABORIEAU

Sökefeld deals with identities in Gilgit, in the Northern Areas of Pakistan, a question which is difficult for two reasons. First the region is ethnically very complex, no less than fifteen mother tongues being spoken. Second, the fact that the population is Muslim introduces further complications: we find here sectarian differences specific of Islam; but on the other hand, Islamic ideology, which stresses unity and equality, tends to hide or to relegate to the background cleavages and hierarchies, making the work of the social anthropologist more difficult than, for instance, in Hindu context where differences are openly emphasized.

The author shows an intimate knowledge of an area which had been neglected up to now by ethnological research.

He devised a sophisticated methodology which is suitable to account for the complexity of his material. The challenge was to find a theoretical framework which would accommodate the five distinct dimensions of difference: sectarian affiliation (Sunni, Shia, Ismaili), *qōm* (i.e. roughly speaking 'ethnic groups': Ṣīn Yashkun, Pathan, Kashmiri. . .), clan, locality, and language. Secondly this framework had also to take 'intersectionality' into account: according to the difference one choose to emphasize, different overlapping sets of people are concerned, so that the summation of the differences can in no way lead to the constitution of distinct corporate groups. This leaves to individuals, or groups of individuals, a great range of choice as to which difference to emphasize in any given circumstances, and by way of consequence as to which of the many possible shifting alliance is to be made.

This sophisticated theoretical framework is expressed in a postmodernist terminology which may sometimes be puzzling to older people who stick to terminologies or theories which may appear today old-fashioned, and prefer for instance to speak, as I do, of the summation of 'elements of status', rather than of differences; and who may be afraid of the neologism *différance* borrowed from Derrida. But we will not quarrel about terminology: the concepts used by Sökefeld are very adequate to analyse with precision the way identities intersect and vary over time as a result of the shifting strategies of the people concerned.

The analysis presented here is not merely formal. The concepts which are used here prove operative in accounting for substantive historical and political problems like the growing Sunni/Shia divide which has become nowadays a major problem all over Pakistan. On some points Sökefeld's analysis proves truly innovative: it is traditionally said that in Islam, the call to holy war or *jihād* overcomes all social, political and religious differences and is a great factor of unity. Here in the Northern areas of Pakistan, the call to carve a nation separate from Pakistan has the same effect of superseding all differences. I would say—this is not Sökefeld's contention , but mine—that nationalism in modern times is invested with the same conceptual and emotional content as religion was in medieval times.

Concluding Remarks

STEVE BROWN

Changing aspects of State, dwelling patterns and developing modes of economic production provide a complex contemporary context in which the uses of cultural nationalism in Nepal—the formation of different and competing ethnic groups—can be clearly observed. We should not however lose sight of the wider political and historical contexts which enable us to explain some of the changing features of Nepalese society, or our changing interpretations. That questions of identity or status are explict now does not mean that they were not important, even if they were implicit—a debatable point—in a so-called pre-modern period. Identities, indeed, are always multiple, consisting of conflicting elements, and this is true even of times before the invention of terms currently in fashion. Part of the question for the social scientist is thus to decide and explain which particular polarization the actors place above other differences in their search for a source of legitimization. The essay chapters in this book indicate a wide range of possible answers, and point to the multiplicity of selves and others, and the contradictory shifting identities that can be held by the same individuals or groups as they compete for access to resources. Local, regional, national, pan-national referential frames are juxtaposed and cut into each other.

Identities in contemporary countries and regions of the Himalayan range are often difficult to discern, leaving aside questions of approach, due to ethnic complexity and a multiplicity of influences, be they Islam (Sökefeld), questions of authenticity or authority (Van Beek), geographical location (Moller), community appurtenance (Pfaff-Czarnecka), or the historical depth to which written texts, cultural practices, or archaeological sources permit us to delve. To complicate matters, concepts such as 'caste' or 'ethnic group' are permeable and changeable through time and across different spaces. The emphasis of the papers in this volume on constructions, or rather reconstructions, should warm us against considering named categories as given, natural or essential: they are rather fluid, permeable, socially constructed; convenient pegs to hang our temporally and spatially specific interpretations on. This is of vital importance in Nepal, where it has been argued that we are witnessing a disintegrating society, where, as Horch argued, nationalisms or ethnic allegiances become a substitute for factors of integration, the nation (on an enlarged or reduced scale) appearing as the ultimate guarantee. What is clear is that some communities, or parts thereof, and their associated researchers, are driven by primordialist, essentialist motivations. To this researchers can oppose alternative approaches, following perhaps an impulse to situate the cultural national movements as 'objectively' as possible in their history, a resolutely comparativist interdisciplinary approach, or a post-modernist critique. That this divide is often along national (western European) lines merely highlights our own subjectivities.

The level of consciousness is of course uneven among the differing groups and regions and plays a varying role as part of the strategies of management adopted. But the point is that these choices are not transparent, objective or uncontested, as Barth noted: individuals and groups propose and negotiate particular cultural understandings. To the question of how to read the various and varying discourses ciritcally—of how to solve the problem of legitimacy—the principles of comparison stand out. Comparison through time (which implies a dynamic, dialectic vision of history, incorporating multiple temporalties), through space, and across disciplines (the exchange of objections between disciplinary fields over the same subject/object of study.) There is a danger in basing judgements about identity merely or principally on conflict, despite the evidently conflictual nature of contemporary Nepalese societies. We must therefore be careful to relativise the representativity of the opinions studied, and to consider the real impact of cultural groups on the way people live. The extent to which we engage, as social scientists, in re-constructing and/ or revising history, in filling up ascriptions with cultural categories, in applying specific methodologies to particular or geographic areas, is one that each of us must attend to.

References

Horch, M., 1968, *Dic Vorkämpfer der nationalen Bewegurg bei der Kleinen Völkenin Europas,* Progue.

Barth, F. (ed.), 1969, *Ethnic Groups and Boundaries: The Social Organization of Cultural Difference,* Boston: Little Brown.